Theories of Education in Early America 1655–1819

The American Heritage Series

The American Heritage Series

UNDER THE GENERAL EDITORSHIP OF

Leonard W. Levy and Alfred F. Young

Theories of Education in Early America

1655–1819

Edited by

Wilson Smith

THE BOBBS-MERRILL COMPANY, INC.
Publishers   Indianapolis and New York

To the Memory of Richard Hofstadter

Foreword

Replying in 1671 to a query put to him by the Lords Commissioners of Foreign Plantations, Governor Berkeley of Virginia answered, "I thank God, there are no free schools nor printing, and I hope we shall not have these [for a] hundred years; for learning has brought disobedience, and heresy, and sects into the world. . . ." Berkeley did not understand, as did the Puritans in New England, that free schools were instrumentalities of social control and that learning, though dangerous indeed, could perpetuate fundamental cultural values.

Education, in the broad sense that Wilson Smith uses it in this volume, is an effort by various institutions, family and church among them, to transmit skills, knowledge, attitudes, and the process of socialization itself; education is very much a part of and similar to what anthropologists call acculturation. Every baby, they say, is born with the beard of its culture. Education reflects and helps shape that beard. Thus education is far more than a history of schools, even more than a history of ideas, aims, and practices of educators.

This is probably the only documentary history of education in our formative period that does not reprint "Ye Old Deluder Satan" law enacted in 1647 by Massachusetts to require that all children be taught to read and write. In Virginia, incidentally, a law of the same vintage, which was passed to "avoid sloth" in young children rather than to delude Satan, required that children be bound to "tradesmen or husbandmen" to be taught a calling. Wilson Smith's concern is not merely with the history of formal instruction in language skills or jobs. His concern, rather, is with education as part of the whole history of American civilization. As such this documentary is a splendid accompaniment to the new educational history so superbly epitomized by Lawrence A. Cremin's monumental *American Education: the Colonial Experience* (1970).

By placing educational history within the stream of cultural history, Smith has selected his sources from ministers, statesmen, lawyers, philosophers, historians, scientists, moralists, planters, and journalists, as well as schoolmasters. The result is a collection of significant documents that are readable, richly diverse, and comprehensive in scope. Some are representative, others original, and all as multifaceted as the pluralistic people whose destiny was molded by the ideologies and experiences reflected by the various authors. Smith's penetrating editorial comments augment the value of their writings.

This book is one of a series created to provide the essential primary sources of the American experience, especially of American thought. The American Heritage Series constitutes a documentary library of United States history, filling a need long felt among scholars, students, libraries, and general readers for authoritative collections of original materials. Some volumes illuminate the thought of significant individuals, such as James Madison or John Marshall; some deal with movements, such as the Antifederalist or the Populist; others are organized around special themes, such as Puritan political thought or American Catholic thought on social questions. Many volumes take up the large number of subjects traditionally studied in American history for which surprisingly there are no documentary anthologies; others pioneer in introducing new subjects of increasing importance to scholars and to the contemporary world. The series aspires to maintain the high standards demanded of contemporary editing, providing authentic texts, intelligently and unobtrusively edited. It also has the distinction of presenting pieces of substantial length which give the full character and flavor of the original. The American Heritage Series is, we believe, the most comprehensive and authoritative of its kind.

Leonard W. Levy
Alfred F. Young

Contents

ix

Introduction

The noun *education* was fairly new to our language when the North American colonies began. *The Oxford English Dictionary* says that it came into the language only in the preceding century, when, in 1531, education meant the process or manner of bringing up young persons. Then the word also meant systematic instruction, but this meaning evidently was not generally used until the early seventeenth century. For Shakespeare, in 1588, the verb *to educate* meant to provide schooling; but its broader definition, one with which some of these readings are concerned, came into use by 1618. Twelve years after the settlement of Jamestown, the verb *to educate* was beginning to mean the bringing up of young people from childhood so as to form their habits, manners, and mental and physical aptitudes. In other words, the concept of a person's education as a social process, distinguished from the specific tasks of formal schooling, was no less a seventeenth-century idea than it is a twentieth-century concern.

The word *education* defied semantic exactitude among colonists. Here was its advantage. Then, as now, everyone sensed what the word meant. Education was concerned with most of the important happenings of life in a new land. It meant much more than proper training to read the Scriptures; it meant a lot more than formal instruction from tutors, masters, or dame school teachers. Education involved the plan and the picture of life that new Americans had for understanding and raising their place in society, for smoothing family relationships, for establishing lines of loyalty, obedience, and respect within families and within communities. It concerned personal and public morality, the relationships between masters and servants and between settlers and Indians. Education dealt with the specific aims of vocational training as it dealt with the broad sanctions and goals of civic authority and control. It increasingly had to do with the raising of institutions for the preservation and transmission of knowledge, such as printing establishments newspapers, libraries, or colleges. In all of this, education was as much concerned with practical everyday problems of survival and advancement in a new society as it was with the development, improvement, and refinement of man's reasoning powers.

This point of view that sees education as bearing upon virtually the entire cultural experience of successive generations has become a fashionable outlook among historians. There is sound historical basis for it. For example, one of the most indomitable Puritans of them all, Cotton Mather, preached and published four sermons between 1696 and 1708, two of which are reprinted in this volume, that voiced practical educational policies as well as far-ranging theory. They are especially intriguing as examples of Puritan concern for what we today call the "social process" of education because they come from a man whose discourses, even in this later, "liberal" part of his life, once were used by teachers to illustrate the exclusive salvation-mindedness or next-worldiness of Puritan divines instructing the young. That teachers of history once read the sermons this way is partly understandable for a reason that still has merit. These sermons carry the authoritative logic of a legal brief prepared to defend a theological point of view (what else could one expect from a Mather?) rather than a description of social fact. Historians of ideas are thus still drawn to them as primary statements of faith, if not of authority. But American intellectual history has come some distance in the decades since Vernon Parrington wrote about it. Most intellectual historians try to recognize that the formal expression of an idea is also a social fact to be fitted in with the circumstances surrounding the speaker and his audience.

Mather's first purpose in these sermons was of course to fix his listeners' minds upon the elusive goal of salvation. We misread him if we do not first see that, for him, a child's heart becomes a "dungeon of wickedness" if it is not purified by knowledge of the Holy Scriptures. But, while exploring the practical problems of preparing one's soul for possible (never certain) salvation, Mather was telling his people much about the everyday utility and the community aims of education. In his *A Good Master Well Served* (Boston, 1696) Mather explained in fifty-five pages the master-servant and master-apprentice relationship. All the responsibilities and duties between them were delineated with infinite care and Biblical justifications. He was promulgating an educational code for the most important instructional device and social conditioner within the colonies, training for a trade or vocation. In his *A Family Well-Ordered* (Boston, 1699) Mather went to what was for him the root of the matter of education. In families, he said, we find the "*Nurseries* of all Societies." "*Well-ordered families* naturally produce a *Good Order* in other *Societies*. When *Families* are under an *Ill Discipline,* all other *Societies* being therefore *Ill Disciplined,* will feel that Error in the *First* Concoction."

In the third of these sermons, *Cares About the Nurseries* (Boston, 1702), *Selection 2,* Mather proffered secular educational advice within the context of an admonition to parents to catechize their children regularly. Here he especially emphasized the usefulness of knowledge. Teach your children well "in a profitable calling," he told parents, and make your sons "beneficial to human society." When he spoke of the "mischief of ignorance," he meant not only impiety but also the social uselessness of the uneducated man. What usually has been cited from this sermon is Mather's concept of education as indoctrination of children in codes of social behavior derived from Scriptural authority. The fourth educational tract by Mather in this period is of course his famous eulogy of Ezekiel Cheever, *Corderius Americanus* (Boston, 1708), *Selection 3.*

The great teacher who brought so many Puritan sons to be men was no less great to Mather for having sent them forth to serve in "all Good Employments" as well as in "the Tabernacle."

To dwell upon Mather here is not to suggest that his was the most illuminating or perceptive educational mind among all these authors. Yet he possessed a breadth of educational view often unsuspected of him by moderns; his concerns were practical, mundane, and secular, though always pointed toward Puritan purpose, as well as they were intellectual, aesthetic, or sacred. In these respects his sermons are representative of the comprehensiveness that characterizes significant educational theory.

Most of the authors included here brought this quality to their educational thought through a lifetime of writing or perhaps in a single penetrating essay. For most of them, educational idea and educational interest—that is, theory and the circumstances of instruction—were inseparable parts of the overall social yet personal problem of learning. Among Puritan writers as among their successors, learning seldom was separated from worldly affairs. Knowledge was thought of in terms of its possible application. Good colonists knew how to acquire and to use proper knowledge—"proper" meaning sacred in the seventeenth-century, and moral or prudential in the eighteenth century. The utility of knowledge was to furnish them with the personal equipment to face what life offered. Seventeenth-century men did not think that education could guarantee the results of life, in this world or the next, even for the best equipped either in the sense of the most pious or in the sense of the best informed. The uncertainties of chance or of fate in a new land where man could do so little to govern nature were a sign of man's helplessness before the ways of God just as later they were a challenge to be overcome by enlightened empiricists of the Jeffersonian world. The shaping and disciplining of experience, which for the Puritan was education, could, however, help man toward the "right" choices—or in eighteenth-century terms it could improve one's chances—for obtaining what one was granted by God in his infinite mercy or what one was allowed by society or what one expected from labor upon the sea or the land.

With this view, education in early America became an ideology that was a kind of social cement. Education held society together as an active idea of common opportunities for everyone except slaves. It formed a common bond by bringing people to recognize the norms and sanctions of acceptable behavior through educational agencies such as the family, the church, the apprenticeship system, or civic enterprises like political participation, military musters, or jury duty. To read the cultural history of the colonial period this way is, of course, nothing new. It is only to recognize what colonial writers themselves understood. From William Bradford's memories of Plymouth Plantation down to Benjamin Franklin's *Autobiography* inquiring men were aware of the educational effects of social institutions.

Since the early years of the professional study of American history gifted historians have pursued this theme. They have included Edward Eggleston at the turn into this century, and after him Samuel Eliot Morison, Edmund S. Morgan, and Louis B. Wright.* Two books marking the 1960s sent this theme of social inquiry directly to the heart of educational history. They were Bernard Bailyn's *Education in the Forming of American Society* (1960) and Lawrence A. Cremin's *American Education, the Colonial Experience, 1607–1783* (1970). Bailyn's monograph, depicting education as the "entire process by which a culture transmits itself across the generations," revealed wide-ranging possibilities for scholarly inquiry. Cremin's volume brought some of these possibilities to reality by advancing the comprehensive study of our educational past.

Sometimes these studies and others like them are considered a part of social history. This is a field which at present is enjoying new life largely because historians have begun to apply to it some of the techniques of the newer social sciences. Quantitative and demographic studies are increasingly reward-

---

* Books by these and other authors mentioned in this Introduction are fully cited in the Select Bibliography.

ing here. They are beginning to reveal, for example, heretofore obscure patterns of group life in colonial towns. Studies like those by John Demos, Philip J. Greven, Kenneth A. Lockridge, and Sumner C. Powell have contributed to our understanding of cultural inheritance in early America.

The new educational history, however, seems to be potentially most rewarding when placed in the broad area of cultural history. Here it is free to stand independently yet hospitably as a meeting ground for the social sciences and the humanities. Here it is most expressive of the interplay between ideas and social phenomena. Ideally, of course, free scholarly work spurns labels. Surely comprehensive educational history impinges upon so many themes that we pointlessly lock it up within one conceptual box. Yet, if in our age of academic specialization and university compartmentalization of subject matter, titles and labels for academic fields are confining institutional necessities, they are still at times handy shorthand devices for communicating intellectual purposes. Cultural history seen as the most perceptive kind of general history is then the least restrictive frame of reference for the new themes and new questions out of our educational past.

The purpose of these discursive comments is simply to urge the reader to see the selections in this volume as specimens of cultural history. To do so is to escape the question educational historians usually do well to avoid: Are these readings in intellectual or in social history? They are both and they are neither. John Clarke's scheme for secondary instruction and Thomas Jefferson's plans for schooling in Virginia surely reflect the social climate and the institutional atmosphere of eighteenth-century England and Virginia as well as they follow the Lockian vision of the human mind and the ideals of the British Enlightenment. Yet we can read into them more than their authors perhaps intended to say about unwritten standards of conduct, patterns of community behavior, or life expectations for educated people. When we put these far-reaching historical concerns together with the claims for religious education advanced by Cotton Mather, Isaac Watts, and Benjamin Rush, with the zealous dedication of David Ramsay and Noah Web-

ster to a new nationalism, with the determination of William
Livingston and William Smith, Jr. for intellectual freedom, or
with the newer commitment of DeWitt Clinton and Archibald
De Bow Murphey to organized schooling under city and state
auspices—then we see how broad in human concern yet perti-
nent to specific issues is the concept of education as cultural
momentum, diffusion, and tradition.

If educational history belongs within such a general cultural
context, where do we locate the historical place and function
of educational ideas? Do they not stand a fair chance of becoming lost amid a welter of cultural forces and events? Answers do not come easily here. Intellectual historians have long
sought them with only limited success. For ideas run with society as well as they are prompted or formed by society. Sometimes they lead society; frequently they lag behind. Perhaps
too much profitless speculation has been invested in question-
ing the primacy of ideas over social forces. As with the other
big questions of human history, answers may be found to fit
special historical circumstances. But the answers are usually
elusive and complex. Infinitely varied situations create an infinite variety of circumstances in which ideas can be formulated or received. And since individuals alone have ideas, the
question involves the infinite variety of human nature. Yet
intellectual historians do know that wherever men have tried
to build or to preserve a civilization, the transmission of basic
cultural ideas has been a common concern among men who
otherwise may differ greatly. To seek, to identify, and to understand the effective and durable power of central cultural
ideas is the job of educational historians. In this role they become general cultural historians, an assignment that is easy to
accept but demanding to fill. The ideas they examine are the
cultural impulses of a civilization. These are core ideas.

Theories of education as core ideas are a part of intellectual
history, yet they go beyond it. Most great theories of education
contain a recognizable logic, if not a system. Here they are akin
to academic philosophy or psychology. This kinship is illustrated by the indebtedness of almost all the eighteenth-century
writers in this volume to the epistemology and the psychology

of John Locke, whose educational writings I have not reprinted here because they are completely available elsewhere in inexpensive editions. Surely a study of Lockian psychology alone, or of John Dewey's philosophy in a later age, is a legitimate pastime for the historian of educational theories if this is his bent. Collections of readings in educational history have frequently appeared which try to package human thought very neatly by exhibiting some great thinker's philosophical or pedagogical system as *the* intellectual keynote of his age. There may indeed be ruling ideas in a particular period of academic philosophy or in the history of religious thought. But those who deal with the history of educational thought may see, perhaps even more clearly than those who deal with other aspects of history, the complex if not chaotic condition of human experience wherein formal systems of thought that arise out of abstract reasoning and not out of social experience are but a small part of the story of mankind. This is not to deride the use of reason to reconstruct some degree of order out of the past. It is only to agree with Herbert Butterfield that "we are wrong . . . if we personify ideas in themselves and regard them as self-standing agencies in history." Ever since the appearance of Karl Mannheim's *Ideology and Utopia* (first published in 1929), historians of ideas have not been quite the same as they were with the more direct and logical and formalistic pathway into their subject opened by Arthur O. Lovejoy. The historian of educational theory is more Mannheimian than Lovejovian. To understand the educational force of a total culture, which the ancient Greeks called *paideia,* is his ideal purpose.

The educational historian has available to him, however, a perspective that still sets ideas apart from society. This perspective is offered by the endurance of core ideas over long periods of time. In the long run of western intellectual history, the colonial educational ideas portrayed here about the nature of man and his freedom are only small paragraphs in the larger chapter of custom, memory, and tradition that reaches from the Renaissance to the Enlightenment. The core ideas of a Great Chain of Being or of Natural Law, for example, were ever present no matter what the variations on them through Cambridge Platonism or through Lockian psychology.

This is not to say that educational theories as core ideas exist after all as Platonic ideas or as eternal norms. It is only to say that human society in the West has carried within it core ideas over longer periods of time than our colonial period or indeed in some instances for a longer time than the centuries from the first colonial settlements until today. At times, the balance and the outer wrappings of these core ideas have shifted dramatically or have been shed with the rise of new systems of thought, witnessed in these selections by the dawning American Enlightenment and later by the first movements toward state support and bureaucratization of the schools. But the point here is that the searcher after educational theory need not be tyrannized by the traditional periodization of economic life, politics, church history, or even by the rise and fall of social institutions.

As an illustration we can recall that in 1712, only four years after Cotton Mather praised the "Cheeverian" education, Benjamin Wadsworth published his sermon, *The Well-Ordered Family: or, Relative Duties* (*Selection* 4). This was the clearest and most comprehensive child guidance book of the American eighteenth century until the Revolutionary era. In discussing the basis for mutual obligations between parents and children, husbands and wives, and masters and servants, Wadsworth demonstrated the shifting intellectual baggage of these years by referring to the sanctions of the light of nature as well as of the Scriptures that Mather had cited. Although intellectual and educational historians have tended to see this kind of sermon as standing on the threshold of "enlightenment" thought, the larger and longer-lived core idea, whose vehicle is the family, is that of Social Order. I think this kind of emphasis is more profitable for the historian of educational theory than an emphasis upon the shorter subsidiary systems of thought that support enduring core ideas.

A compelling and pragmatic retort to this suggestion is that colonial educational practice simply did not follow intellectual or educational design, an old story in human affairs. This argument holds that core ideas, if they exist at all, must be sought in experience rather than in formal expressions of thought. The argument maintains that formal plans for education were always inadequate. Men educated for life in a holy commonwealth, for example, found themselves increasingly turning to secular pursuits, or at least relegating the forms and rituals of pious living and learning to a separate part of their lives. Throughout all the colonies the pressing needs of a new society, its openness, and the invitations to break family ties or to settle in westerly or ever newer parts combined to obscure old values learned in youth, to make men grasp and acquire standards of living that their own education had not foreordained or even suggested. Educational theories were ever being rebuilt to tie the training of the mind to the practices of life.

However persuasive the historian of educational ideas may find this point of view, he must question the "practicality" of American education then as now. In the turn of years and decades, from colonial days down to our own, "practical" plans for American education have sometimes been quite impractical in result. The American experience has often nullified educational systems and practices simply because it has run faster than the systems. The pace of American life has usually been more rapid than our plans for it. This continuing dilemma faces us today as it did in the eighteenth century.

The searcher for the core ideas of colonial education can get behind this elusive quality of American educational thought. He can respect the periodization of history without being confined by it. Change within specific time spans is what makes history meaningful. But he would maintain that the *rate* of change for the underlying ideas of western history from around 1500 to around 1800 seldom was as rapid as it was for the subsidiary idea systems and the events of our colonial period. In Poor Richard's day, the ideal of life in a city on a hill had waned and had been replaced by an atmosphere of prudential reality. Yet Poor Richard had come out of that time and place when the ideal of the model city was still forceful in New England, and his maxims for realistic living were indeed a conversion of Calvinist ethics to the bustling life of secular America. Calvin still lived.

Again, the American Revolution brought change to education. But what kind of change was there? The techniques and the means of education shifted to some extent. Our institutions of learning began the nationalization that still continues. To this end, education provided itself with a new rhetoric, as David Ramsay well showed (see *Selection* 14). With the Revolution some of the forms of education were changed; the importance of the classics dropped and the Latin schools waned. But the core of formal learning, the idea of a liberal education through the liberal arts remained, and the central vision of education as a moral enterprise remained. Despite the readjustments in our thinking about nature and human nature that were brought by the Enlightenment, many of the core ideas within educational thought in the colonial period remained with us well down into the nineteenth century, perhaps at least to the publication of Horace Bushnell's *Christian Nurture* in 1847 or even until Charles Darwin's *Origin of Species*.

It is no distortion of Jefferson and the American Enlightenment or of Cotton Mather and the Puritan cosmology to say that they were alike in their concern with the same core ideas within education. They valued order in society, order in the arrangement of knowledge, and order in the advancement of the stages of learning. They respected the idea of the intellectual integrity of teacher and student. They prized the idea of learning as an ethical enterprise. They respected man's mental processes and the discipline of the mind. Above all it seems to me that their paramount idea about education was a concern for the future; this was as true of Ezekiel Cheever as it was a century later of Noah Webster.

To say that some core ideas of the American educational experience have lain in the marrow of western thought for three centuries and longer is a commonplace. If so, however, it is an observation that historians of education these days make too infrequently. And to make this observation is not to replace the concept of pragmatic active ideas working in history with a

Platonic concept of western ideas as eternal norms. Core ideas
—the ancient ideas of truth, beauty, goodness, and justice,
with which members of the School of Athens wrestled, as well
as later ideas of human growth and mental development, of
progress, community, space, time, science, authority, and of
the power of language and of art—are all constantly being re-
moulded and are shedding their outer husks of needless or
subsidiary elements. To maintain this view of core ideas is, in
the final analysis, simply to assert that guidance by utility and
the immediate practical effects of contemporary social agencies
leaves the educational historian with too limited a perspective.
This restricted outlook is the danger that the humanist sometimes sees in the utilitarian norms of the modern social
sciences.

Yet the social sciences and the humanities can come to terms
in the mind of the historian, just as I hope they can come to
terms in the mind of the reader of the following essays. While
the side of the social sciences can hold that educational theories
reflect the means or the agencies by which the transmission of
culture takes place, the side of the humanities can assert that
the means or agencies of education in a given generation are
supported by core ideas that frequently are much older. Core
ideas in this sense then become one of the classic definitions of
education. They are what remains when we have forgotten
everything that we have learned.

Chronology

1635   Founding of Boston Latin School.

1636   Founding of Harvard College.

1638   Printing press set up at Cambridge.

1642   Massachusetts law required selectmen of every town to make periodic inquiries concerning the training of children and apprentices, "especially of their ability to read & understand the principles of religion & the capital lawes of this country."

1643   John Eliot, *New Englands First Fruits.*

1647   Massachusetts law (the "ould deluder, Satan" law) required towns of fifty householders to hire a schoolmaster "to teach all such children as shall resort to him to write & reade." Towns of one hundred householders were to establish Latin grammar schools where students could be prepared "as far as they may be fitted for the university." Similar acts by Connecticut, 1650; Plymouth, 1671; and New Hampshire, 1689.

1655   Charles Chauncy, *God's Mercy, Shewed to His People, in Giving Them a Faithfull Ministry and Schooles of Learning.*

1678   John Bunyan, *Pilgrim's Progress.*

1687   Isaac Newton, *Principia.*

ment and the happiness of mankind, schools and the means of education shall forever be encouraged."

Benjamin Rush, *Thoughts Upon Female Education.*

1789   Founding of first Roman Catholic college at Georgetown, Maryland, by Bishop John Carroll.

Noah Webster, *Dissertations on the English Language.*

1790   Founding of the Massachusetts Historical Society, the first American historical society.

Enactment of law of copyright by Congress.

1791   Robert Coram, *Political Inquiries: To Which Is Added, A Plan for the General Establishment of Schools Throughout the United States.*

1795   Establishment of first permanent public school fund (Connecticut).

Opening of the first state university (North Carolina).

1798   Samuel Harrison Smith, *Remarks on Education.*

1802   Pauper School Act, Pennsylvania.

1805   Founding of the Free School Society of New York.

1806   Establishment of the first Bell-Lancasterian school, New York City.

1812   Gideon Hawley appointed to the superintendency of New York schools.

1817   Opening of law school at Harvard.

Founding of school for the deaf at Hartford, Connecticut, by Thomas Hopkins Gallaudet.

Archibald De Bow Murphey, *Report to the Legislature of North Carolina on a State System of Education.*

1818   Thomas Jefferson, "The Rockfish Gap Report."

1819   Founding of the University of Virginia (opened in 1825).

Dartmouth College v. *Woodward.*

Selected Bibliography

SOURCES

AXTELL, JAMES L., ed. *The Educational Writings of John Locke: A Critical Edition with Introduction and Notes.* Cambridge: Cambridge University Press, 1968.

BEST, JOHN HARDIN, ed. *Benjamin Franklin on Education.* Classics in Education, No. 14. New York: Teachers College Bureau of Publications, 1962.

BREMNER, ROBERT H., ed. *Children and Youth in America, A Documentary History. Volume I, 1600–1865.* Cambridge: Harvard University Press, 1970.

CALHOUN, DANIEL, ed. *The Educating of Americans: A Documentary History.* Boston: Houghton Mifflin, 1969.

COON, CHARLES L., ed. *The Beginnings of Public Education in North Carolina: A Documentary History, 1790–1840.* 2 vols. Raleigh, N.C.: Edwards & Broughton, 1908.

———. *North Carolina Schools and Academies, 1790–1840: A Documentary History.* Raleigh, N.C.: Edwards & Broughton, 1915.

GAY, PETER, ed. *John Locke on Education.* Classics in Education, No. 20, New York: Teachers College Bureau of Publications, 1964.

HOFSTADTER, RICHARD, and SMITH, WILSON, eds. *American*

Higher Education: A Documentary History. 2 vols. Chicago: University of Chicago Press, 1961. Reprinted as a Phoenix Book, 2 vols., 1968. Parts I–V.

KNIGHT, EDGAR W., ed. *A Documentary History of Education in the South before 1860.* 5 vols. Chapel Hill, N.C.: University of North Carolina Press, 1949–1953.

LEACH, ARTHUR, ed. *Educational Charters and Documents, 598 to 1909.* Cambridge, England: Cambridge University Press, 1911.

LEE, GORDON, C., ed. *Crusade Against Ignorance: Thomas Jefferson on Education.* Classics in Education, No. 6. New York: Teachers College Bureau of Publications, 1961.

LOCKE, JOHN. *"Of the Conduct of the Understanding."* Edited by Francis W. Garforth. Classics in Education, No. 31. New York: Teachers College Bureau of Publications, 1966.

MATHER, COTTON. *Bonifacius, An Essay Upon The Good.* Edited by David Levin. Cambridge: Harvard University Press, 1966.

MILLER, PERRY, AND JOHNSON, THOMAS H., eds. *The Puritans: A Sourcebook of Their Writings.* 2 vols. Revised Torchbook Edition. New York: Harper & Row, 1963. Chapter VIII.

The New-England Primer. Edited by Paul Leicester Ford. Classics in Education, No. 13. New York: Teacher's College Bureau of Publications, 1962.

PEACHAM, HENRY. *The Complete Gentleman.* Edited by Virgil B. Heltzel. Ithaca: Cornell University Press, 1962.

RIPPA, S. ALEXANDER, ed. *Educational Ideas in America: A Documentary History.* New York: David McKay, 1969. Part One.

RUDOLPH, FREDERICK, ed. *Essays on Education in the Early Republic.* Cambridge: Harvard University Press, 1965.

SCHNEIDER, HERBERT AND CAROL, eds. *Samuel Johnson, President of King's College: His Career and Writings.* 4 vols. New York: Columbia University Press, 1929. Volume IV.

SIZER, THEODORE R., ed. *The Age of the Academies.* Classics in Education, No. 22. New York: Teachers College Bureau of Publications, 1964.

TYACK, DAVID B., ed. *Turning Points in American Educational History*. Waltham, Mass.: Blaisdell, 1967. Chapters 1–4.

WEBSTER, NOAH. *American Spelling Book*. Edited by Henry Steele Commager. Classics in Education, No. 17. New York: Teachers College Bureau of Publications, 1962.

COLLATERAL READING

ADAMSON, J. W. "The Extent of Literacy in England in the Fifteenth and Sixteenth Centuries: Notes and Conjectures," *The Library*, fourth series, X (September 1929), 163–193.

ARIÈS, PHILIPPE. *Centuries of Childhood: A Social History of Family Life*. Translated from the French by Robert Baldrick. New York: Vintage Books, 1965.

BAILYN, BERNARD. *Education in the Forming of American Society: Needs and Opportunities for Study*. Chapel Hill, N.C.: University of North Carolina Press, 1960. Reprinted as a Vintage Book, 1963.

BRAUER, GEORGE C., JR. *The Education of a Gentleman: Theories of Gentlemanly Education in England, 1660–1775*. New York: Bookman, 1959.

BRIDENBAUGH, CARL. *Vexed and Troubled Englishmen, 1590–1642*. New York: Oxford University Press, 1968. Chapter IX.

BRUCHEY, STUART. *The Roots of American Economic Growth, 1607–1861: An Essay in Social Causation*. London: Hutchinson, 1965. Reprinted as a Harper Torchbook, with a new introduction by the author, 1968. Chapter 8.

BUTTS, R. FREEMAN, AND CREMIN, LAWRENCE A. *A History of Education in American Culture*. New York: Henry Holt, 1953. Chapters 1–7.

CHARLTON, KENNETH. *Education in Renaissance England*. London: Routledge and K. Paul, 1965.

CIPOLLA, CARLO M. *Literacy and Development in the West*. Baltimore: Penguin Books, 1969.

CLARKE, M. L. *Classical Education in Britain, 1500–1900*. Cambridge, England: Cambridge University Press, 1959. Chapters I–V, XI.

COMMAGER, HENRY STEELE. "Leadership in Eighteenth Century America and Today," *Daedalus* (Fall 1961), 652–673. Reprinted in H. S. Commager, *Freedom and Order: A Commentary on the American Political Scene*. New York: Braziller, 1966.

CONANT, JAMES B. *Thomas Jefferson and the Development of American Public Education*. Berkeley and Los Angeles: University of California Press, 1962.

CREMIN, LAWRENCE A. *American Education: The Colonial Experience, 1607–1783*. New York: Harper & Row, 1970.

————. *The Wonderful World of Ellwood Patterson Cubberley: An Essay on the Historiography of American Education*. New York: Teachers College Bureau of Publications, 1965.

CURTIS, MARK H. "The Alienated Intellectuals of Early Stuart England," *Past and Present*, no. 23 (November 1962), 25–41.

————. *Oxford and Cambridge in Transition, 1558–1642: An Essay on Changing Relations Between the English Universities and English Society*. Oxford: Clarendon, Press, 1959.

DEMOS, JOHN. *A Little Commonwealth: Family Life in Plymouth Colony*. New York: Oxford University Press, 1970. Reprinted as a Galaxy Book, 1971.

EGGLESTON, EDWARD. The *Transit of Civilization from England to America in the Seventeenth Century*. New York: D. Appleton, 1900. Reprinted as a Beacon Paperback, with a new introduction by A. M. Schlesinger, 1959.

FLEMING, SANDFORD. *Children & Puritanism: The Place of Children in the Life and Thought of the New England Churches, 1620–1847*. New Haven: Yale University Press, 1933.

GREAVES, RICHARD L. "Puritanism and Science: The Anatomy of a Controversy," *Journal of the History of Ideas*, XXX (July–September 1969), 345–368.

GREVEN, PHILIP J., JR. *Four Generations: Population, Land, and Family in Colonial Andover, Massachusetts.* Ithaca, N. Y.: Cornell University Press, 1970.

GUMMERE, RICHARD M. *The American Colonial Mind and the Classical Tradition: Essays in Comparative Culture.* Cambridge: Harvard University Press, 1963.

HEXTER, J. H. *Reappraisals in History: New Views on History and Society in Early Modern Europe.* Evanston, Ill.: Northwestern University Press, 1961. Reprinted as a Harper Torchbook, 1963. See especially chapter 4, "The Education of the Aristocracy in the Renaissance."

HILL, CHRISTOPHER. *The Century of Revolution, 1603–1714.* London: Thomas Nelson, 1961. Reprinted in The Norton Library, 1966.

HOFSTADTER, RICHARD, AND METZGER, WALTER P. *The Development of Academic Freedom in the United States.* New York: Columbia University Press, 1955. Part One, reprinted as Richard Hofstadter, *Acamedic Freedom in the Age of the College.* Columbia Paperback, 1961.

HOFSTADTER, RICHARD. *Anti-intellectualism in American Life.* New York: Alfred Knopf, 1963. Reprinted as Vintage Book, 1966.

HONEYWELL, ROY J. *The Educational Work of Thomas Jefferson.* Cambridge: Harvard University Press, 1931. Reissued by Russell & Russell, 1964.

JONES, HOWARD MUMFORD. *O Strange New World, American Culture: The Formative Years.* New York: Viking, 1964. Reprinted in Viking Compass edition, 1967.

JORDAN, WILBUR K. *Philanthropy in England, 1480–1660: A Study of the Changing Pattern of English Social Aspirations.* New York: Russell Sage Foundation, 1959.

KIEFER, MONICA. *American Children Through Their Books, 1700–1835.* Philadelphia: University of Pennsylvania Press, 1948.

KLEIN, MILTON M. "Church, State, and Education: Testing the Issue in Colonial New York," *New York History,* XLV (October 1964), 291–303.

KURITZ, HYMAN. "Benjamin Rush: His Theory of Republican Education," *History of Education Quarterly,* VII (Winter 1967), 432–451.

LEWIS, C. S. *English Literature in the Sixteenth Century, excluding Drama.* New York: Oxford University Press, 1954. Introduction.

LOCKRIDGE, KENNETH A. *A New England Town: The First Hundred Years: Dedham, Massachusetts, 1636–1736.* New York: W. W. Norton & Company, Inc., 1970.

MAITLAND, DAVID J. "Puritans and University Reform," *Journal of the Presbyterian Historical Society* (June 1965), 100–123.

MIDDLEKAUFF, ROBERT. *Ancients and Axioms: Secondary Education in Eighteenth-Century New England.* New Haven: Yale University Press, 1963.

MILLER, PERRY. *Errand Into the Wilderness.* Cambridge: Harvard University Press, 1956. Reprinted as a Harper Torchbook with additions by the author, 1964.

MORGAN, EDMUND S. *The Puritan Family: Essays on Religion and Domestic Relations in Seventeenth-Century New England.* Boston: Trustees of the Public Library, 1956. Revised and enlarged as a Harper Torchbook, 1966.

MORISON, SAMUEL ELIOT. *The Puritan Pronaos.* New York: New York University Press, 1936. Reissued as a Cornell Great Seal Book, 1956, and entitled *The Intellectual Life of Colonial New England.*

MURDOCK, KENNETH B. *Literature and Theology in Colonial New England.* Cambridge: Harvard University Press, 1949. Reprinted as a Harper Torchbook, 1963.

MUSGROVE, F. *Youth and the Social Order.* Bloomington, Ind.: University of Indiana Press, 1965.

NORTON, ARTHUR O. "Harvard Text-Books and Reference Books of the Seventeenth Century," *Publications of the Colonial Society of Massachusetts,* XXVIII (1935), 361–461.

NOTESTEIN, WALLACE. *The English People on the Eve of Colonization, 1603–1630.* New York: Harper, 1954. Reprinted as a Harper Torchbook, 1963.

NYE, RUSSELL B. *The Cultural Life of the New Nation, 1776–*

1830. New York: Harper, 1960. Reprinted as a Harper Torchbook, 1962.

PINCHBECK, I. "The State and the Child in Sixteenth Century England," *British Journal of Sociology*, Part I, vol. VII (December 1956), 273–285; Part II, vol. VIII (March 1957), 59–74.

RAND, EDWARD K. "Liberal Education in Seventeenth Century Harvard," *The New England Quarterly*, VI (September 1933), 525–551.

RUDOLPH, FREDERICK. *The American College and University: A History*. New York: Alfred Knopf, 1962. Reprinted as a Vintage Book, 1966.

SHIPTON, CLIFFORD K. "Secondary Education in the Puritan Colonies," *The New England Quarterly*, VII (December 1934), 646–661.

SIMON, JOAN. *Education and Society in Tudor, England*. Cambridge, England: Cambridge University Press, 1966.

————. "The Social Origins of Cambridge Students, 1603–1640," *Past and Present*, no. 26 (November 1963), 58–67.

SIMPSON, ALAN. *Puritanism in Old and New England*. Chicago: University of Chicago Press, 1955. Reprinted as a Phoenix Book, 1961.

SMITH, WILSON. "The Teacher in Puritan Culture," *The Harvard Educational Review*, vol. 36 (Fall 1966), 394–411.

————. *Professors & Public Ethics: Studies of Northern Moral Philosophers Before the Civil War*. Ithaca, N.Y.: Cornell University Press, 1956. Chapters III–IV.

STONE, LAWRENCE. *The Crisis of the Aristocracy, 1558–1641*. Oxford: Clarendon Press, 1965. Abridged edition as a Galaxy Book, 1967.

————. "The Educational Revolution in England, 1560–1640," *Past and Present*, no. 28 (July 1964), 41–80.

————. "Literacy and Education in England, 1640–1900," *Past and Present*, no. 42 (February 1969), 69–139.

WRIGHT, LOUIS B. *The Cultural Life of the American Colonies, 1607–1763*. New York: Harper, 1957. Reprinted as a Harper Torchbook, 1967.

————. *Culture on the Moving Frontier*. Bloomington, Ind.:

Indiana Univerity Press, 1955. Reprinted as a Harper Torchbook, 1961.

ZUCKERMAN, MICHAEL. *Peaceable Kingdoms: New England Towns in the Eighteenth Century.* New York: Alfred A. Knopf, Inc., 1970.

Editor's Note

In preparing these selections for reprinting I have tried to keep them generally in the form of their first publication. This is in keeping with the house rule of Bobbs-Merrill, a rule that I respect on scholarly and aesthetic grounds but regret from the side of readability. Hence the reader will see that the original spelling and punctuation of the selections have been retained, even including their inconsistencies. Occasionally I have employed square brackets in the text to correct obvious printer's errors. If the reader is slowed by the capitalization of almost all nouns and by frequent italics throughout the earlier essays, he may remember that these were standard devices, carefully used and relished by authors and readers of that day for the purpose of literary or rhetorical emphasis. Omissions from the text, usually a repetitive or parenthetical section, or passages irrelevant to the main theme of an essay, are indicated by ellipses.

At various stages in the preparation of this book I was fortunate to have the assistance of Ross W. Beales, Jr., and John W. McDermott, Jr. I am grateful for their help.

W. S.

Davis, California

Theories of
Education in
Early America
1655–1819

1

Charles Chauncy
on Liberal Learning

Many settlers in the back country of Massachusetts Bay Colony, and even some academic men in seventeenth-century England, suspected or opposed the idea of a liberal education for the potential leaders of society. There were those who saw Harvard College and the two older universities in England as nothing but centers of implacable church power, dedicated to the transmission of "useless" learning within a self-perpetuating caste of churchmen and statesmen. So an ancient argument between contenders for applied or practical knowledge and champions of liberal or classical studies pervaded the American educational climate from its outset. This argument in various forms has been a recurring theme in the history of our schools and colleges.

Advocates of liberal learning have often sought to cut the ground from under their "practical" opponents by asserting that a liberal curriculum answers very real social needs if culture is to be maintained and advanced. In this sermon Charles Chauncy (1592–1672), second president of Harvard College and former fellow and classicist of Trinity College, Cambridge, makes such a case for higher learning as an urgently needed ingredient for New England life wherein the "old stock" of ministers soon will wither. His sermon exemplifies Puritan concern for classical learning in the humanist tradition as well as devotion to Biblical authority. Chauncy is specifically taking issue with William Dell, an English antinomian clergyman who, during the Cromwellian period, was for ten years master of Gonville and Caius College, Cambridge. Dell dismayed Cambridge men in 1653 by his reply to the contention of Sidrach Simpson, master of Pembroke College, that classical learning and a

1

university atmosphere were prerequisites to a proper understanding of Scripture for divinity students. Not so, declared Dell, insisting that academic rituals and robes were heathenish and that the university's degree-granting power in divinity is a "power received from Antichrist." Dell wanted universities put under the civil authority. He even went so far as to protest the "monopoly" on humane learning held by Oxford and Cambridge and to propose that a university or college or a center of adult higher learning be established in each great city or town of England. But to Chauncy in New England, more disturbing than these ideas, some three hundred years in advance of their time, was Dell's insistence that clerical training and humane learning should not mix.

To Chauncy, as to most Cantabridgians of his day, Dell's anti-nominan assertion that university theological training is quite unnecessary for divines defied learning itself. As others were doing in England, Chauncy hastened to repudiate this anti-intellectualism before it could gain more partisans in New England.

For besides the Lords former mercyes, in sending in to us the old stock of faithfull ministers, and thrusting out of his labourers into this vineyard, (by the blessing of God upon whose labours, the Gospel of Christ, and the powerful dispensation of Gods Ordinances hath flourished many yeares, to the admiration of all the christian world) I say besides those former mercyes never to be forgotten, the Lord hath graciously superadded this, in *raysing up not only means for this end* (viz: schools of learning) but also from thence *some of our sons & young men to be Prophets & Nazarites*. Is it not so O ye people of God in N-England? And if it be so, see what the Lord expects at our hands in answerable returns of thankfulness unto him, and let us weigh seriously these motives to such thankfulnes.

1. Let us consider *what benefit and comfort all sorts have*

Charles Chauncy, *God's Mercy, Shewed to His People, In Giving Them a Faithfull Ministry and Schooles of Learning, for the Continued Supplyes Thereof. Delivered in a Sermon Preached at Cambridge, the Day After the Commencement. . . . Published with Some Additions Thereto, at the Request of Divers Honoured and Much Respected Friends, for the Publick Benefit, as They Judged.* (Cambridge, 1655), pp. 28–38, 40–44, 46–48.

by us, when as our *sonns & young men* are not only indued with *the seed of knowledg & grace,* but such as are sent forth as seedsmen *to sow the Lord's good seed* in the hearts of others. . . .

2. Consider *the state of the Country where wee live,* which is such, that now the old stock of the country is well nigh worn out, and there is no likelyhood of further supply that way: now you know how Gods people are fastened here, that if there should not be some supply by schools of learning, God's people would soon be left *without a teaching ministry etc.* as 2 *Chron.* 15.2. Is it not so O ye people of N-England?

Object[ion]: But may we not be sufficiently supplyed from among ourselves by the gifts and indowments of gifted brethren?

Answ[er]: I could wish as Moses, *that all God's people were Prophets:* But you shall find it here, as in other trades, that there is a great difference between those that have been bound apprentices to a trade and others that are handy, & have gotten a little skill by the observation of others, this latter will serve to patch or bungle, but wise men will rather choose to deal with those that have been trained up in such a course: Thus from persons educated in good literature we may rather expect that they should be *workmen that need not to be ashamed.* . . .

3. Consider *what helps diverse particular Churches have had* from these schools, in grievous breaches that have been made in them, when any of the precious servants of God have been taken away, from hence others have stood up in their steads & have made up the breaches comfortably. . . .

4. Consider *that this makes for the continuance of the Church & propagation of religion to after ages,* for this was always found true, that *where the vision fails, there the people will be made naked.* Prov. 29.18.—they will be naked Congregations, and naked souls, and naked familyes, and naked posterities; naked of what? naked of the righteousness of Christ which is *put on by faith, and comes by hearing,* and the shame of this nakedness will appear to God & man: naked of the *Christian armour to defend themselves from spirituall enemyes;* and where schools have been put down or ceased, there

churches have been unprovided, and religion hath decayed and great ignorance & errours have succeeded in after ages: but on the contrary this course of the instruction of youth, is the meanes to provide for present & future times. And why do men plant orchards, or preserve the breed of the best cattle? but to provide for future times: but is not the pure religion of more weight, and the providing for the souls of posterityes to the worlds end? this is another benefit of worth. . . .

[5.] Let the *Seperation* consider this, some of whom are averse to schools of learning: that schools are available *to rayse up Nazarites etc. to further an holy seperation,* which is commanded unto *christians.* . . .

Consider how *the Sons of Belsal, papists and hereticks,* they *compass sea and land* to support and spread & fortifie *the Synogogues of Satan,* the *dens of devils, & suburbs of hell?* should not the glory of God and the salvation of souls be deerer unto us, then their destruction & condemnation is to them? all these things should forward our thankfulness to God for these mercys.

But now it is not a verball thankfulness that will serve our turn, (that would be gross hypocrisie) but it must be really expressed, towards the education of youth, & the incouragement of the ministry, and the propagation of the Gospel. . . .

Schools of learning are approved and appointed of God, and of great importance for the benefit of Gods people: Seeing that the Lord works with, & blesseth this means, for the laying up of provision, & making of supplys for the work of the ministry; and the Lord here reckons it up as the chiefest of all the blessings mentioned: and this was always one way (even when there were extraordinary Prophets) of raising up of Prophets etc. And there is much more need of Schools now, when those extraordinary Prophets are wanting. . . .

It will be very needfull upon this occasion for us to consider what weight there is in the objections that diverse in these days have printed against them.

Object 1. Mr. Dell in his answer to *Mr. S[ydrach] Simpson* allowes schooles of the prophets wherin Christian religion is taught, *but against schooles of humane learning this is that that*

makes them Antichrists, seeing they are contrary to, and do op-
pose Christ, this makes the universityes stews of Antichrist,
houses of lyes, and to stinke before God with most loathsome
abomination etc: with a multitude of other reproachfull terms
which Luther & others have loaded Popish Universityes withall.

Answ 1. I do much desire that the opposers of schools & universityes would speak plainly what they mean by humane learning, then wee should easily come to some conclusion. Therfore
let this distinction be premised, that humane learning may
either be taken for all that learning that the heathen Authours
or philosophers have delivered in their writings: or else all
other Arts besides Theology, as they call *physicks, ethicks, poli-*
ticks, etc: take in also the grounds of languages, *Latine, Greek*
& Hebrew. Now in the former sense, if *Mr. D[ell]* do mean by
humane learning, all that learning that the heathen men have
uttered out of the light of nature: It will be a great oversight to
pass such a sentence upon it. 1. Because we find in Scriptures
some testimonies out of humane writers, as *Tit.* 1.12., *Acts*
17.28., I *Cor.* 15.33, etc: which the Spirit of God would not
have alledged, if their writings had been utterly unlawfull to
read. 2. There are certain principles of trueth written, even in
corrupt nature, which heathen authors have delivered unto us,
that doe not cross the holy writ, I *Cor.* 11.14, *doth not nature it*
self teach you etc., and it cannot be denied that all trueth,
whosoever it be that speakes it, comes from the God of truth,
as he is called severall times. And who can deny but that there
are found many excellent & divine morall truths in *Plato, Aris-*
totle, Plutarch, Seneca, etc.: and to condemn all pel-mel, will
be an hard censure, especially to call universities Antichrists
for reading of them. Besides they have treated of the works of
God, most excellently in many places, and the works of God
ought to be *declared by parents to their children,* Psal. 78. 2–6.
Besides they have delivered many excellent sayings of God,
and have attested many Scripture historyes, as might be
shewed by severall instances, out of *Justine, Tacitus, etc:* and
Mr. D[ell] is not ignorant of them, shall all these be thrown
away as antichristian, or as lyes?

Object: But they have much profaness and filthiness in

them, and besides they are made idolls of in our universities, when as *ipse dixit,* and their authority goeth for currant, as Scripture itself amongest them.

Answ: But I. All heathenish writers have not such profaness in them. 2. Those that have, let them be condemned & abhored, & let not youth be poysoned by them. 3. Let God be true & every man a lyer, and let not man, especially any heathen be deified, or his authority be accounted on, or go cheek by jowle with the speaking in the Scriptures: this is indeed to be abhored wheresoever it is received, but *abusus non tollit usum.*

II. But now if humane learning be taken in the second sense, for all those Arts that are commonly taught in Universities, as *Physicks, Ethicks, Politicks, Œconomicks, Rhetorick, Astronomy, etc:* or also for learned tongues of *Latine, Greek, and Hebrew, etc:*

1. I will be bold to affirm that these in the true sense and right meaning thereof are Theological & Scripture learning, and are not to be accounted of as humane learning. For who can deny, that the first & second chapters of *Genesis,* and many chapters in *Job,* and the *Psalms,* and diverse other places of holy Scripture, do afford excellent and sure grounds for natural Philosophy, and a just system thereof. . . ? And where are there to be found such *Ethicall, Politicall, or Morall* precepts, as are to be found in holy Scriptures? or such principles for the ordering of our lifes, families, or common weals? let any man declare it unto us. And where are there such high straines of all sorts of *Rhetoricall Tropes & figures* to be found in any Author, as there are in the writings of the *Prophets & Apostles?* and who can imagine, but that the best & surest Chronology in the world, is to bee found in holy Scriptures, upon which all the computation of times in all ages in the world depends? . . .

Object: *But* [argues Mr. Dell, *ed.*], *there is no necessity of Schools or Universityes, or any humane learning to teach men Divinity, or to make able preachers of the Gospell: the teaching of the Spirit of God alone is sufficient: which Mr. Dell proves by the examples of our Saviour Christ & his Apostles, seeing Christ himself had only the unction of the Spirit.* Isai. 61. 1-4. Luke 4. Mat. 13. 54, 55. *Besides when he would send*

forth preachers into all the world, he chose Fishermen, Pub-
licans, Tent makers, plain men, and [*men*] *of ordinary employ-*
ment in the world, and only put his Spirit upon them. Acts
2.17. . . .

Answ: 1. It is a mervellous mistake to reason from our
Saviour Christ & his Apostles to these times. . . . So the reason
will stand thus. If our Saviour Christ and his Apostles, without
other learning, by the miraculous and extraordinary gifts of the
Spirit, were enabled and furnished sufficiently for the ministry;
Then other ministers in after times (that have no such extraordinary gifts) need no other learning, but the unction of the
Spirit. . . . Then no man need to be an apprentice to learn any
Mechanicall trade, seeing the teaching of the Spirit is sufficient
for any cunning work, who is there that would not account this
reasoning ridiculous? Surely if Mr. D[ell] had not excluded
Logick & reason out of Divinity he would never have made
such collections. . . .

2. I affirm, that the Lord Jesus and his Apostles were learned,
and beyond that which is attainable by ordinary teaching. . . .
It is certain that our Saviour had learning, though never trained
up therin: and also that learning or teaching, is the ordinary
way to attain to learning, yea such learning as our Saviour
manifested in his ministry, (as the Jews conceived). So I may
say of the Apostles, though in a farr inferior degree. . . .

Mr. Dell in his answer to Mr. Simpson.

Object: *Humane learning is rather an hinderance than an*
help to the ministry of the Gospel, and doth rather unfit, than
fit men for it: and the grace and teaching of God only prepares
& enables men to this divine work: learning is so far from
fitting man for this Gospell, and the ministry thereof, that in-
deed there is nothing in greater enmity to Christ crucified nor
more contrary to the WORD of the CROSS than that: Yea
nothing in all the world hath been such an introducer, favourer,
supporter & enlarger of Antichrists kingdom, as humane learn-
ing & Philosophy: This hath brought in all the hypocrisie,
superstition, false worship, sects & schismes etc.:

Answ: It is to be feared that *Mr. D*[ell] hath been tainted
with humane learning, as in some other of his opinions, so in

writing of these things Let the reader remember what approbation hee gave to humane learning before, that he would have
it taught, not only in Universities, but in all Cities & villages:
and yet he hath now so forgot himself, that though for humane
& civill ends, he did allow it, yet now he saith, *that it is enmity
to Christ crucified, and contrary to the word of the cross.* . . .

I. If Mr. Dell had allowed the use of Logick in Divinity, how
should he have dared to have allowed any of these humane
arts, or languages of any end whatsoever? . . .

3. Whereas he saith that humane learning is rather a hinderance, then an help to the ministry of the Gospel, and to all
christianity; Let us consider a little what truth there is in this
assertion. . . .

I. How shall a minister without the knowledg of the Original
tongues, either translate the Scriptures, or when they are translated, maintain them against the popish vulgar, or other diverse
false translations, to be the infallible trueth of God? how shall
he comfort a poor soul that saith he is a reprobate, and proves
it out of 2 Cor. 13.5. Because he knows not *that Jesus Christ is
in him,* if he knows not what *adokimos** means. I might make
innumberable such instances, but I spare. . . .

Yea how shall a man know when a Scripture is wrested, or
falsely applyed, or a false use is made of it, or a false consequence is drawn out of it, or a true, without some principles of
logick, especially to hold forth these things to others he must
needs be a shamefull workman, and many times ridiculous,
neither rightly apprehending, nor dividing the word of trueth,
that hath no knowledg how to interpret the Scripture.

* *adokimos:* neophyte. [Ed.]

2

Cotton Mather
on Teaching Children at Home

Any study of Puritan educational ideas is a study of Puritan life itself. And a study of Puritan life is a study of men dedicated to religious ideals. Some of the most perceptive writing on American history has illuminated the thought and habits of these people. But little of it has emphasized the role of formal education, perhaps because education itself was synonymous with the overall path of one's life. Puritans believed with William Dell in England that "what the youth now is, the whole Commonwealth will shortly be." For this reason the Puritan child, born in sin, must early be trained and indoctrinated by his parents to prepare him for conversion. The preparation might turn out to be a lifelong task, never completed; but still it must be pursued. "Time cuts down all/Both great and small," read the *New England Primer*. Both the venerable "saints" of the New England towns and villages and the children of a land where infant and child mortality rates were rather high were driven by the belief that one's early years were not too soon to begin an uncertain lifetime preparing for salvation.

Hence the family was the place for instructing the young in Christian ways. Puritan fathers concerned themselves in minute detail with the moral and spiritual instruction of their children; their clergymen admonished them repeatedly to foster obedience and attentiveness in their offspring. And parents themselves were fulfilling their own Christian obligation by catechizing little ones and seeking to bring them to an understanding of Scripture and Sabbath sermons. Thus a circle of Christian concern was drawn ever tighter around church members and their families. The educated Puritan's idea of community was an ideal of devout, faith-searching individ-

9

uals, bound together within the authoritative but protective network of kinship and church, always seeking signs of grace within themselves and within each other. The state, too, reinforced this design in the Massachusetts school laws of 1642, 1647, and 1648, whose chief aim was to provide the means in each successive generation for making a literate community of Bible readers. For American educational history, the Puritan ideal of community, above all, encouraged the advancement of learning and cultivation of intellect. If one concedes some key Puritan precepts, he can agree that at no later time have intellect and general commitment to a reasoning way of life been so highly prized by Americans. Even without that concession to faith, modern secular historians agree that Puritan devotion to a singularly educated way of life left its impression upon American thought and institutions. The location and the depth of that imprint have yet to be fully revealed.

For what they accomplished in church, state, letters, and science, Cotton Mather (1663–1728) and his father, Increase, are outstanding in an almost century-long array of orthodox, New England-way Congregational divines. Historians have tended to debate whether Cotton Mather was a medieval man or one who anticipated the moral philosophy of the American Enlightenment, a kind of unwitting precursor of Benjamin Franklin. There are indeed in Mather's writings Augustinian views of man's inquisitive and submissive relationship to God. He possessed some Augustinian convictions about the hierarchy of being, about order and symmetry in the affairs of nature and man, and about the community of souls in the love of the same good, which can create the city of God on earth. But with Cotton Mather these ideas take on a peculiarly Calvinist coloration. Man's thoughts, efforts, and horizons are contained within the concept of the total sovereignty and central place of God as revealed to man by the Bible, not so much by reason or by nature. On the other hand, the claims for Mather's eighteenth-century modernity are put forward on the grounds of his lifelong amateur interest in scientific inquiry, the partial liberalizing of his theology in the 1720's, and the presumably utilitarian cast of his adjurations to goodness after 1710. But what these claims reveal are simply the changing intellectual and social climate of early eighteenth-century New England in which Puritan logic tried to retain its vigor. Cotton Mather's advocacy of inoculation against smallpox in Boston in 1721 must be measured against his scientific though not persecutory implication in the witchcraft delusion of the early 1690s. His hortatory essay on doing good, *Bonifacius* (1710), and his treatise on the *Christian Philosopher* (1721), though no longer the jeremiads of his younger days, are essentially pietistic lessons in glorifying God through one's efforts on earth, not in seeking enlightened self-interest.

By putting Cotton Mather ahead of, or behind his own time, one fails to see Mather as the central Puritan intellect preceding Jonathan Edwards throughout the years that connect the seventeenth and eighteenth centuries. Amid the social changes and the bitter personal disappointments that he experienced when his illustrious father's century came to its close in Massachusetts Bay, Mather remained essentially and firmly committed to the problem of salvation. So too, as he lived and preached into a new century at Boston's Second Church, where he had begun assisting his father in 1680, what we call his "social thought" consisted increasingly of sermons that summoned his people to form the kind of community organizations that could help them save themselves. *Bonifacius* (1710), which Benjamin Franklin later made famous, was Mather's essay "upon the Good that is to be Devised and Designed by Those Who Desire to Answer the Great End of Life and to Do Good while they Live." Life for Mather was a lesson, a long education for the world to come. It is a mistake then to dismiss "Cares About the Nurseries" as a quaint specimen of Puritan authoritarianism, the type of pious exhortation that furnished, at most, a kind of spiritual backbone to later generations of Americans. This sermon, which is an abbreviated version of his "A Family Well-Ordered" (1699), succinctly presents Mather's ideas of the central place of the family and of the places of family members in the Christian community. Upon stable family life are founded the social ideals of discipline, order, and social harmony. The pre-school child, taught the elements of these ideals from Scriptural and parental command, begins in Puritan eyes to be well prepared for this life, which is but a pilgrimage toward the next one.

I Am at this Time to employ the *Public Exhortations* in pressing that Illustrious *Duty,* which we distinguish by the Name of CATECHISING. . . . Learn, O *Parents,* learn this by the way, that if you *Teach* your *Children* the Things that are Good, there

Cotton Mather, *Cares About the Nurseries. Two Brief Discourses. The One, Offering Methods and Motives for Parents to Catechise Their Children While Yet Under the Tuition of Their Parents. The Other, Offering Some Instructions for Children, How They May Do Well, When They Come to Years of Doing for Themselves* (Boston, 1702), pp. 3–6, 8–21, 23–29, 31, 33–34, 37, 41, 45–47, 51–53, 64–66, 69–76, 78–79, 81–86.

is Good hope that they may learn what you Teach them; and if you are *Exemplary* for any Virtue, it may be hoped that your *Children* will follow your *Example. Solomon* was a Son very dear to *David,* and his *Father* expected much Comfort and Credit from him. A *David* can not better express his Endearments than by *Teaching* of his dearest *Solomon.* Of no little Consequence he knew t'would be to a Son of such Expectations. No doubt *Solomon* had as brave Tutors as the whole Nation of *Israel* afforded; the Prophet *Nathan* doubtless was one of them. Nevertheless *David* would himself in his own person take this Charge upon him; he would be the *Teacher* of his own Son himself. What a *Tutor* is here, and what a *Pupil?* A *King* the *Tutor,* the *Pupil* a *Prince!* A lovely sight we have before us; a *David* with a little *Solomon* standing at his Knee; a Mighty *Monarch,* laying aside his Royal *Scepter,* for a *Catechism,* and *Catechising* his little *Son* in the Things of God.

CATECHISING in general, is any *Teaching by word of Mouth.* . . . And it more particularly intends a Familiar *Teaching* in the *first Rudiments* of any Doctrine. Thus far we have a plain Instance of *Catechising* in what our *David* is now a doing. But *Catechising* more strictly, is indeed a more *Interlocutory* way of *Teaching.* It is a way of *Teaching* wherein one puts a *Question* and another gives an *Answer.* To *Examine* another about his Knowledge is to *Catechise* him; to *Catechise* another is to demand from him an *Echo* to what he Enquires of him. . . .

But the Point which you will now readily grant me is This: that it is the Duty of Parents to CATECHISE their Children.

The Case now before us . . . is a Comprehensive one.

What may be proposed, that there may be forwarded among us the Duty of Parental Catechising?

More particularly, what is to be briefly proposed concerning the *Matter* of the Duty, the *Manner* of the Duty, & the *Motive* to the Duty?

I. What is it that *Parents* are to *Teach* their *Children* when they *Catechise* them?

Truly, it must be premised and supposed that *Parents* may do well to *Teach* their *Children,* or see them *Taught,* in as much *Good Knowledge* as ever they can. The more *Liberal*

Education we bestow upon our Children, though we should pinch ourselves for it, and them too, upon other accounts, the greater *Blessings* are they like to prove not only unto *ourselves* while we live, but also unto the *Commonwealth* after we shall be Dead & Gone. Many a man of a *lesser Figure* has brought the *Commonwealth* into his Debt by his even straightening himself to bring up a *Son* fit for a *greater Figure*. Yea, to furnish and adorn our *Children,* as far as ever we can, with the *Knowledge* of all that may *Lawfully* be *known,* is not only *Lawful* but very *Laudable. Philological* and *Philosophical* Knowledge will enable them to *Defend* and *Relieve* themselves; & by all sorts of *Knowledge* they will be qualified for an acceptable *Conversation* with other men. By *Knowledge, the Chambers* of their Souls will be filled with *all precious & pleasant Riches.* The more *Knowledge* our *Children* have, the more *Luxury* we may see in our *Children.* Yea, and *Knowledge* will have this vast *Good* in it, that it will enable them to *Do Good. Knowledge* is *Useful;* the more they *know* the more *Use* may be made of them. O make the little Folks *Redeem* their *Time,* to Learn as much as they can; and some of them will perhaps Learn much in a very *little Time.*

Especially it becomes *Parents* to have their *Children* well *taught* in the *Mysteries* of a *Profitable Calling.* We should be studious to have them *Know* something by which they may *Live.* Yea, and if our *Daughters* too were more *Taught* something more profitable than merely to Rig themselves with Expensive Gaieties, their *Teaching* might be better than a *Portion* unto them. However, the *Knowledge* of some *Art,* in the Exercise whereof our *Sons* may be Beneficial to *Humane Society* and have a claim to the Benefits of the *Society,* let no *Parents* leave their *Children* without it. If any of *you* do so, I'll only tell you it was among some of the Old Pagans a *Law* that the *Children* should be under no obligation to do anything for such *Parents* when a Needy Old Age might overtake them. It may be the Just Hand of Heaven may see some such *Law* Executed on you.

But then, Methinks, a Little *Good Breeding* may do the *Children* some *Good!* They should be *Taught* the *Rules of Be-*

havior: Good Manners do well become the Children of *Good
Christians.* Our *Children* should be *Taught* how to address
their *Superiors* with *Modesty,* their *Inferiors* with *Gentleness,*
their *Equals* with *Decency* & *Inoffensiveness.* I remember when
the Psalmist says of some, *They are full of Children.* The old
version oddly translated it, *They are full of Swine.* Alas, Let
not our *Children* be so brought up as to make the translation
justifiable! *Unmannerly Children* are but a Reproach to their
Feeders and proclaim that they are better *Fed than Taught.*

After all, (nay, *before* all and *above* all) tis the *Knowledge*
of the *Christian Religion* that *Parents* are to *Teach* their *Children* by *Catechising* of them. Tis not only . . . a *Civil Education*
that you must give unto your Children, but also . . . that which
is peculiar to a *Christian.* [Eph. 6:4.] The *Principles* of the
Christian Religion, which are delivered in our ordinary *Catechisms,* these are they wherein our *Children* are to be *Catechised.* The Great God has favored us with that inestimable
Treasure, I Tim. 6, *The Words of our Lord Jesus Christ and the
Doctrine which is according to Godliness.* And if we *Teach* not
these things unto our *Children,* we are ourselves destitute of all
Godliness. The *Knowledge* of other things, though it be never
so desirable an Accomplishment for them, our *Children* may
arrive to Eternal Happiness without it. But the *Knowledge* of
the *Godly Doctrine in the words of the Lord Jesus Christ* is of
a Million times more Necessity for them; without that *Knowledge* our Children are miserable to all *Eternity.* Here, here is
the *Best knowledge* that our *Children* can have. He knows the
best *Grammar* that knows how to season a *Speech* with the
Salt of *Grace.* He knows the best *Rhetoric* that knows how to
Persuade his own Heart unto the service of the Lord Jesus
Christ. He knows the best *Logic* that knows how to conquer
the *Devil* in disputing against his *Temptations.* He knows the
best *Arithmetic* who knows how to *Number his days with wisdom.* He knows the best *Geography* that knows how to
Trample the *Earth* under his Foot. He knows the best *Astron-
omy* who knows how to make sure of *Heaven.* He that knows
God has a better knowledge than he that knows the whole
Creation of God. He that knows *himself* has a better knowledge

than he that knows all other men. He that can *order his own Conversation aright* has a better knowledge than he that knows how to order an Hundred and Twenty Seven Provinces. All of this *Knowledge* we teach our *Children* when we teach them the Christian Religion.

We have in our hands the *Holy Scriptures,* which are a *Storehouse of Saving Truths* and contain all that must be *Known* by all that would be *Saved.* We must now so *Teach* our *Children* that it may be said of them, as it was of a *well-taught Youth,* 2 Tim. 3:15. *From a Child thou hast known the Holy Scriptures, which are able to make thee wise unto Salvation.* But many Servants of the Lord Jesus Christ have been at the pains to Collect from the *Holy Scriptures* the *Principles* of the *Christian Religion* and methodize their Collections into brief CATECHISMS, which have been highly serviceable in the Churches of God. In our Orthodox *Catechisms,* whereof there are (if I be not misinformed) several *Hundreds* of *Sorts* Extant in the world, we have a *Form of sound words,* which we should *Hold Fast,* and then teach our *Children* to do so, that we may not *Lose* our Souls. The sum of what we are to *Teach* our *Children* has been with a sweet variety set before us in our *Catechisms.* And the Judicious *Calvin,* in the beginning of his Incomparable Institutions, refers all to those Two Heads, *The Knowledge of God,* and *The Knowledge of ourselves.* In short, we are to *Teach* our *Children* the *Principles* of the *Christian Religion.* . . .

That these things may be the better Taught unto our *Children* we should also betimes Teach them the *Histories* of the Bible, with some *Instructions* plainly legible in the *Histories. Histories* will strongly Take and Stick with the *Memories* of the *Children;* and we may easily make the *Histories* of the Bible our *Table Talk* with them, or *talk* of them with a daily frequency and fetch from them such Lessons as may be of the First Importance.

And give me leave to add: Should you not Examine your *Children* concerning what they retain of the *Gospel* in the Public Dispensations of it? It is complained that many *Children* are *Scandalous* for *playing at Meeting.* It may be, t'would be Reformed if *Parents* would make the *Children* bring home

some Good Thing from the *Sermon* they heard at the *Meeting*.
The *Children* that are so very Rude seem openly to proclaim
it: '*Our Parents will ask nothing of us when we come home!*'

II. How is it that *Parents* are to *Teach* their *Children* when
they *Catechise* them?

A proper and prudent proceeding in the management of this
Family Exercise will much contribute unto the Advantage of
the *Family*.

First, then, Tis to be taken for granted, O *Parents*, that you
have put an agreeable *Catechism* into the Hands of your *Children* and Charg'd them to get it by Heart. A *Shorter Catechism*
for the Beginners and a *Larger Catechism* for those of a Bigger
Condition and Capacity is *Agreeable*. When you Charge them
to get it into their Memories by convenient portions, which you
may set for them, what if you should also propound an Ingenuous *Recompence* and *Penalty* upon it? A fit *Recompence*
for the Diligent, a fit *Penalty* for the Negligent?

Well A *Time* is now to be taken that you may *See* what they
can *Say*. If this *Time* should not be oftener than once a Week,
yet let it at least be *Once a week*. Tis a *Sabbath-work;* you may
do well to take a *Sabbath-time for* it.

When the *Time* arrives, address yourselves to it with all
suitable *Solemnity*. Let the *Children* be call'd before you and
let the rest of the Family be usually present, and let all see that
you are Solemn and Serious and Earnest in what you have now
to do; *Fervent in Spirit, serving the Lord*.

Hereupon put unto them that *Question* in the *Catechism*
which you would have to be *Answered* and make them Repeat
the *Answer* in the *Catechism* with all Exactness. And what
though the Younger little Things may not fully apprehend the
import of what they *Repeat?* We must not call this a *Taking of
God's Name in Vain*, albeit they have not such Reverent Appre-
hensions of God, as the Elder people have. The *Repetition*
which they make of Divine Things is an *Introduction* and a
Preparation to the further Acknowledgments of God, which
they will one Day make with more of *Reverence*.

But some such *Rules* as these were not amiss to be observed.
First, Be not satisfied with Hearing the *Children* patter out

by Rote the words of the *Catechism* like *Parrots;* but be Inquisitive how far their *Understandings* do take in the Things of
God. When our Lord was *Catechising* His *Family,* He put
this unto them, Mat. 13: 51. *Have ye understood all these
things? They say unto Him, yes, Lord.* Thus we should put this
unto our *Catechumens: My Child, Have you understood what
you have said?* And that we may be sure of it, let us *Try* and
Help their *Understandings* by breaking every *Answer* of the
Catechism into little Parcels, by Questions, whereto Yes, or No,
or one word or two shall be all the *Answer. . . .*

Secondly, Endeavor that the *Children* may not only receive
the *Catechism* into their *Understandings,* but also have their
Affections and *Practices* conformed to what they understand.
. . . When we are *Catechising* our *Children,* we are *Delivering*
unto them a *Form of Doctrine;* and we should contrive all the
Charms imaginable that their *Hearts* and *Lives* may be
Moulded into that *Form.*

As now when we *Teach* our *Children,* what the *Catechism*
says about their *Sin,* their *Original Sin,* their *Actual Sin,* and
the *Wages* of their *Sin,* we may let fall some such Admonition
upon them:

'And *My Child, Is it not a sad thing to be a Sinner? Should
not you seek above all things to be saved from your Sins?*'

When we Teach our *Children* what are the *Offices* or the
Benefits of the Lord Jesus Christ, we may let fall some such
word as this upon them:

'And *Child, would you gladly have this thing done for you?
Or, don't you want such a Favor as this from the Lord Jesus
Christ?*'

When we Teach our *Children* what is *Forbidden* and what
is *Required* in the *Commandments,* we may let fall some such
word as this upon them:

'And *Child, will you beg of God that He would preserve you
from this Evil & assist you to this Good?*'

And thus, by the way, when we Ask our Children *what they
Remember of the Public Sermons?* It were good for us, before
we dismiss them, to ask: 'Well, *Child, what have you now to
pray for?*' When they have told us, then lay the Charge of God

upon them: '*I charge you now to go alone and make that prayer before the Lord.*'

But especially, when we Teach our Children the Nature of the *New Covenant* from their *Catechism*, now, now will be an Opportunity to amplify upon every *Article* of the *Covenant*, and very Distinctly to ask the Consent of their Souls to every *Article*. It may be God will help them to give it, even with Floods of Tears before Him. And if they really do it, from that moment they are *Converted;* unto God, and *United* unto the Lord Jesus Christ. . . . Thus, *O Parents*, you may become *Twice Parents;* your Children may be brought home to the Lord by your means, and be Born again by your happy hands; there may not be so much as one of them left for your Ministers to do any more than to carry on the work whereof you have laid the Foundation in them.

Finally . . . by all means *Pray* over what you do when you *Catechise* your *Children*, especially when the *Fathers*, who are the *Priests* of the *Family*, are thus doing the part of the *Prophets* in it. . . .

III. Why is it that *Parents* are to *Teach* their *Children* by Catechising of them?

The Persuasives to the Duty are neither few nor small. . . .

It must be such a Teaching as the little Folks are capable of even as Nurses cut small Bits for little Children. . . . What we render, *Thou shalt Teach them*, is in the Original, *Thou shalt Whet them*. That is to say, go often over with them, as a man does with his Knife when he whets it on a Whet-stone. Tis the very thing that we do in our *Catechising*. And you see we are but God's *Ushers* in it.

Secondly, Do you consider, O *Parents*, the *Souls* of your poor *Children?* Methinks you should hear the Cries of their *Souls* unto you to be *Cathechised*. . . . *Parents*, Draw out a *Catechism* to your *Young ones:* Give them at least their Milk for Babes. You are worse than the Cruel *Sea-monsters* if you do it not.

Thirdly, the Danger, the Damage, the Mischief of *Ignorance*. O *Parents*, have you considered That? Or, can you cure the

Ignorance of your *Children* without a *Catechism?* . . . You do an infinite *Harm* to your *Children* if you keep them in *Ignorance.* This is very sure, without *Knowledge* the *Soul* itself cannot be *Good* (and some so read the sentence of the *Proverbs*). Though every man be not *Good* that hath *Knowledge,* yet a man cannot be *Good* without *Knowledge.* An *Ignorant Soul* will be a *Vicious* one. The *Devotion* of *Ignorance* is but a *Bastard* sort of *Devotion.* Every *Grace* enters into the Soul through the *Understanding.* They that have their *Understanding darkened* (Eph. 4:18) will be *Alienated from the Life of God.* . . .

Fourthly, Consider, O *Parents,* how much *Good* you may do by *Catechising* of your *Children;* Good both unto your *Children* and unto many others. . . .

What greater Joy, O parents, than to see *Children walking in the Truth!* And I will add this one small consideration unto the rest: you will certainly find your *Families* the more *Tractable* and *Orderly* and *Obedient* for your *Catechising* of them. The more you do your *Duty* to them, the more *Dutiful* they will be to you. By your *Catechising* of them, you will maintain your *Authority* over them. Yea, the People of God in the *Neighbourhood* will have the Good of it. . . .

Nor are you, O Masters, to be Forgetful of this Duty; for *Masters* are a sort of *Parents* to their *Servants.* . . . O do what you can, that your *Servants* may be some of the *Faithful in the Land* and therefore well instructed in the *Faith.* Even *Hire* them to learn their *Catechisms* rather than that they should not. How many *Servants* will to all Eternity Praise God for sending them to live with *Masters* that would *Catechise* them! And the *Masters* of the *School* may do much this way as well as the *Masters* of the *House.* Your little *Scholars* are to be *Catechised.* A *School-Master* is indeed by way of Eminency to be a *Catechist.* Oh let your little *Scholars* be taught something of their *Catechism* as well as of their *Spelling-Book* or of their *Accidence.* But I break off: may these words prove as Great binding Nails to the Intention of Raising *Family Religion* from the Dead among us.

Instructions For Them That Are Past
Their Infancy.

The *Doctrine* which is now to be inculcated is This:

Persons that are come to the Years of doing for themselves must Express the *Graces* and Perform the *Duties* that are *suitable to their Years.*

They that are *come to the Years* of *Men* and *Women* must count it high Time for them to behave themselves as *come to the Years* of *Saints* and *Christians.* They that are come to the Years of Discretion do show no *Discretion* at all if they don't make them the Years of Religion. . . .

Now the Hearers of the *Glorious Gospel* have one *special season* of Life wherein the Admonitions of Religion are to be most livelily and hopefully Address'd unto them. And that *special season* is just when they *come to Years,* even to that *Age* wherein they pass from their *Childhood* unto their *Manhood;* that *Age* wherein they have done saying their *Catechism* to their *Parents* or *Tutors,* and it is expected that ere long they may themselves be *Teachers* of others. If we Preach unto Children, tis with little success. *I said surely* they are too Shallow, too Heedless, too Sportful, to mind our serious counsels or *to know the way of the Lord.* . . . You, our Young Folks, that are just *come to Years* wherein you begin considerately to look about you, you are they that the Calls of the Gospel are likely to do most Good upon. You are in the *Waxy,* the *Ductile* Age, the Age that is most easily *Moulded* into any Form. What, what shall we do, to cast you into the Glorious *Mould* of the Gospel? The Time of peoples' *Transition* from their *Infant-state* unto their *Adult-state* is a Time of a very Critical Importance. . . .

You are no sooner *come to years* but *Satan* will Employ the *Flesh* for to Ensnare you, and the *World* for to Enslave you in the ways of *Sin.* But, O Young People, now call to mind the vast *Obligations* which have been by your *Baptism* laid upon you to Refuse the Delights of the *Flesh,* and to Refuse the Courses of the *World,* and Refuse the whole Service of *Sin* and

Satan. . . . When you first *come to years,* you will be peculiarly in danger of those which are called, 2 Tim. 2:22, *Youthful Lusts.* But, Oh Refuse to gratify those Lusts; and let the Bottom of that Refusal be, *'I have been Baptised, and by Baptism I am lifted under the Banner of the Lord Jesus Christ, and laid under an Oath to fight against those Enemies that would not have Him Reign over me.'* . . .

III. Since you are *come to Years* Capable of coming to the Communion of the Church in all *Special Ordinances,* you should Regularly become *Communicants* at the *Table* of the Lord. . . .

It were well if the *Elders* of the *Churches* would use the best Conduct that may be for the Regular and Orderly Confirmation, (so we may call it) of such as while *Infants* were Baptised in our *Churches.* When our Children *come to Years,* the *Elders* of the *Churches,* methinks, may do well to send for them and Examine them about their *Conversion* to God and their *Preparations* and *Inclinations* to come in a *worthy manner* to the *Table* of the Lord. Those that are found *Ripe* for it may be Excited & Assisted by the *Elders* to proceed unto the Full *Communion* of the Churches in the due methods for it. Those that are found evidently short of a Ripeness for our Highest *Mysteries* may be still detained with agreeable *Instructions,* and *Awakenings* bestowed upon them. Certainly, there is an Ecclesiastical Action which the *Elders* of the *Churches* owe to their Children *when they come to Years!*

If there should be anything Omitted on *their* part, let there be no Omission on *yours,* O our dear *Children.* But come and make an *open profession* of your *Christianity,* and pass from your *Infant-state* unto your *Adult-state* of *Church-Membership.* . . .

IV. Since you are *come to Years* of *Understanding,* you must *Act with Understanding,* and in your Actions proceed with such Exercises of Reason as become your *Years.* You are got out of your *Childhood;* it is now Time for you to say, with him, I Cor. 13:11. *When I was a Child, I spake as a Child, I understood as a Child, I reasoned as a Child; but when I became a Man, I put away Childish things.* The *Years* whereto you are

come are those which we count and call *Years of Understanding*. Let it now be seen that you *Understand* your true Interests.
You are coming to write yourselves *Men and Women*. . . .

At these *Years* tis Time for you to Reflect upon the Errand
which you came into the world upon, and enquire *How far you
have done that Errand*. Every man comes into the world upon
a very weighty *Errand*. His *Errand* is *To Glorify God & the
Lord Jesus Christ, & bear Testimonies unto the Truths & Ways
of the Lord Jesus Christ, & prepare for Everlasting Happiness
in the world to come*. During all the Time of *Childhood,* how
little is this *Errand* thought upon! The wise man complains of
it, Eccl. 11:10, *Childhood is Vanity, Vanity!* That is, it acts for
no *End,* it aims at no *End*. Are you got out of your *Childhood?*
Oh! Tis high time for you to get out of your *Vanity* too; and
think, '*For what am I now to Live!*' . . . Since you are *come to
years* of *Reason,* you must now Regard the *Reason* why God
gives you to *live, move & have your being*. He that lives for
Nothing is one void of *Reason,* & he is *dead while he lives*. He
that lives for *Nothing* but only to partake in the entertainments
of *Sense,* makes himself a *Brute,* rather than a *Reasonable
man*. . . .

At these *Years* tis Time for you to set no little *Price* upon
your Time and see how much of your *Time* is gone. . . . *Children* don't know the worth of *Time,* nor do they know what to
do with their *Time;* they do as if their *Time* would never come
to an end. Very near a *Third part* of our *Years* is irrecoverably
flown away, for the most part, before any of us begin to think
how much of our *Time* is already spent, or that it ever will be
spent at all. . . .

At these *Years* tis Time for you to *put on* the Sobriety and
Solidity belonging to these *Years;* and particularly to *put off* the
Vanities of *Apparel* among other *Childish Vanities*. . . . These
years call for *Gravity*. Tis Time for you to have your Hearts
taken up with better things than the *Toys* that are fit only to
please *Children* and *Babies*. Only I can't prescribe *Habits* for
my *Neighbors*. I'll only say, let them determine to appear *Grave
Christians,* as they that are *come to years* ought to be. Then
they'll soon prescribe for themselves. . . .

V. Since you are *come to years of Discretion,* let it be evident that you are *come to years of Devotion;* being of Age to mind your Temporal Advantage, at this Age also mind your Eternal. . . .

Are you so *come to years* as to set up your *Personal Calling?* Tis Time for you, at these *Years,* to set upon your General Calling. There are *Two Callings* to be followed by *All Christians.* A Christian must have a *Personal Calling,* or that special Employment by which his *Usefulness* in his *Neighborhood* is to be distinguished. . . . But then a Christian hath a *General Calling,* or the Employment of serving the Lord Jesus Christ, and of saving his own Soul, in that Obedience to the Gospel which is incumbent on all the Children of Men. In this we are, as tis said, Heb. 3:1, *Partakers of the Heavenly Calling.* Hear then, O Young People: Are you *come to years* to set up your *Calling?* Tis well you have one. Tis not lawful for a Christian to live without one. A man is a better Christian for not being without one. But this must not be your *only Calling.* Tis Time for you to set upon your *High Calling* and *walk worthy of that Calling.* At these Years I am to tell you that you must set upon the *Work* of daily *Praying* to God, and *Reading* of, and *Musing* on His Word. . . .

Are you so *come to Years* as to hear of *Marrying?* Tis Time for you at these *Years* to come into the Mystical Marriage, whereto the Lord Jesus Christ invites you. . . . Are you *come to Years* wherein a *Marriage* is proper to be prosecuted? Oh, Take not a step towards it, until you are come to a *Marriage* with the Lord Jesus Christ, the King of Heaven, and Lord of Glory; and be astonished at it, O ye Worms of the Dust, be ravished into Astonishment at it, That the King of Kings, and Lord of Lords will vouchsafe to look upon you. . . .

Are you so *come to Years* as to make Provisions for your own Various *Necessities?* Tis Time for you, at these *Years,* to provide those things that are of all, and for all, the most Necessary. While you were in your *Childhood* others did provide for you; but now you are *come to Years* it is fit you should make Provisions for yourselves. . . . Are you of Years to *Labor for the Meat that Perishes?* You are then of Years to *Labor for that which endures to Everlasting Life.* Are you of Years to *Hire* or *Buy* an *House* to Sleep in? You are then of Years to become Owners of the *House not made with Hands, Eternal in the Heavens.* At these Years you are inquisitive how to grow *Rich* in the world. Surely then you are of Years to be inquisitive after *Durable Riches and Righteousness.*

3

"A Master in our Israel"
Cotton Mather on Ezekiel
Cheever and Teaching

Pupil and teacher performed clearly established roles in the Puritan community. Each had his proper place: the pupil was preparing for his own calling in life while the teacher was following his. If student tasks were mechanical, rigorous, and submissive, the teacher's were none the less demanding, narrowly set, and authoritarian.

Historians have not yet etched a full picture of the stages of human growth that Puritans envisioned. We do know that it was not so crude a picture of childhood and youth as is sometimes depicted by the assertion that Puritans held the "medieval" idea of children as simply small adults. This assertion is partly true of the Puritan concept of learning or of filling young minds with knowledge. But it is not true that the Puritan picture of the pre-adult years was without general phases of growth, analogous to what we call infancy, childhood, adolescence, youth or young manhood, and adulthood. These stages can perhaps best be traced through the successive informal steps in the Congregational churches by which young people were advanced into full communion.

Nowhere in their literature is the kind of instruction thought by Puritans appropriate to each stage of childhood and youth revealed so unmistakably as in the writings of Cotton Mather. In his "Cares About the Nurseries" (Selection 2) Mather sets forth the means and the goals of regular instruction at home for the pre-school child. The means of parental authority, catechesis, and repetitive lessons lead to the goals of family harmony, social grace, moral order, and mental discipline. Though preachers are advised by Mather to find a simple common ground of communication with children in their Sabbath sermons, it is in adolescence that youth are to find the catechism replaced regularly by preaching in the meetinghouse. Adolescence, moreover, is in Mather's view the great time of temptation for "our young folks" between baptism and the Devil. It is "the waxy, the ductile age" when the needs for confirmation and communion, for a concern about the "errand" and the calling of one's Christian life are most apparent. Adolescence means the onset of independence and responsibility, a time when the youthful confidence in one's approaching productive years should be mixed realistically and piously with the anticipation of death. Mather's sermons on the instruction of youth were mostly written and preached in the later part of his life, after 1698, when he withdrew from political activities, accepted his fate never to follow his father as president of Harvard College, and turned increasingly to founding voluntary societies for good works. His educational leadership was demonstrated in setting up schools for slaves and the poor, in establishing Indian missions, in distributing tracts, and in continuing his scientific inquiries which won him election to the Royal Society in 1713.

Mather's respect for the school master's calling was developed in his own student years at the Boston Latin School. There he sat under the famous teacher, Ezekiel Cheever (1615–1708), for whose funeral he wrote the following sermon and verse elegy. In calling Cheever the "American Corderius", Mather was referring to Mathurin Cordier (1479–1564), a French scholar who was converted to Protestantism, settled in Geneva, and there wrote his beginner's Latin manual, *Colloquiorum Scholasticorum Libri Quatuor* (1563), or *The Colloquies of Corderius*, well known to seventeenth century English school boys. After coming in 1637 from Emmanuel College, Cambridge, which sent many Puritan scholars to New England, Cheever taught at New Haven, Ipswich, and Charlestown before beginning his thirty-eight years as master of Boston Latin School where he knew or instructed members of notable Massachusetts families. Most skilled as a Latin teacher, Cheever wrote an *Accidence, A Short Introduction to the Latin Tongue* which went through twenty editions by 1785.

Although the Puritan teacher's role was authoritarian, it was not, when skillfully filled, tyrannical. Mather's testimony here bears this out, as do Mather's own words of advice elsewhere to teachers. Indeed, an old stereotype of wooden, artificial, and tyrannical teaching in early America may well need revising. The fact that students were sometimes punished by the rod does not mean that teaching was necessarily unimaginative or lacking in compassion. There is evidence to the contrary insofar as one can find "proof" of the quality of classroom teaching. It may be drawn from such sources as the diary of Michael Wigglesworth, a tutor at Harvard in the 1650's, or from the diary of young John Adams keeping school at Worcester a century later.

Teaching, however, in Puritan eyes was not as important as learning. The reasons for this preference tell us much about the role of education and the place of the schoolman in later American life. Learning, particularly learning to prepare the young for conversion and for their errand in this world, reflected the constant primary concern of Puritans for the future. The chief guide to the future for young people in the seventeenth century New England village was the minister, not the schoolmaster. He was instructor, exhorter, and examiner of all. His position carried the tradition of the teaching ministry, one which Puritans saw as having begun in ancient times when Jesus himself was the great teacher of his disciples and they in turn became teachers to centuries of Christendom. In New England towns whose churches could afford the position, a second minister was called "teacher." It was his duty to explicate the Scriptures. That this basic task of Christian instruction rested with the church leader was an expected state of affairs in the first half-century of New England life. It helps to explain the moral authority and the social deference given by townspeople, including the schoolmaster, to their minister. But in the changing social and intellectual climate of the eighteenth century, teachers increasingly found this to be a community attitude that inhibited their efforts, even though ministers by the second quarter of that century were no longer permitted to promulgate their opinions as school committeemen. A social tradition had been formed. New England school masters never attained the community prestige once held by Puritan ministers.

The *Children* should LEARN TO READ the *Holy Scriptures;* and this, as *Early* as may be. To School therefore with them. Let them not be Loitering *at home,* or playing *abroad,* when they should be at *School.* Be more concerned for their *Schooling,* than for their *Cloathing.* If there be *any,* as I suppose there

---

Cotton Mather, *Corderius Americanus. An Essay Upon the Good Education of Children. And What May Hopefully Be Attempted, for the Hope of the Flock. In a Funeral Sermon upon Mr. Ezekiel Cheever. The Ancient and Honourable Master of the Free-School in Boston. Who Left Off, But When Mortality Took Him Off, in August, 1708, the Ninety-Fourth Year of His Age. With an Elegy and an Epitaph Upon Him. By one that was a Scholar to him.* (Boston, 1708), pp. 11–15, 17–22, 25, 26–32.

cannot be *many,* so necessitous, as to call for it, let us in this
Town go on with our CHARITY-SCHOOLS. When the Children can *Read,* the *Holy Scriptures,* charge them, and cause
them, *every day* to *Read* that *Book of Life. Hire* them to *Remember* what they Read; To get *Select Sentences* of the *Holy
Scriptures* into their *Memories.* And then; Show them, how to
make PRAYERS out of what they *Read.* Help them to turn all
into *Prayers,* That they may be *Wise unto Salvation.* Oh,
Teach them to Pray! . . .

We will . . . Enquire and Declare, WHO it is, that is to
Teach the Children the *knowledge of the Holy Scriptures.*
Come ALL HANDS to the Work.

In particular; The PASTORS of the Flock; They must not
neglect the *Children* of the Flock. . . . O men of God, How
many ways may you *Devise Good,* in this Great Affair; to make
the *Children* under your Charge, *Wise unto Salvation!* In the
midst of many such *Devices,* I will mention one, which the
Excellent Mr. *White,* in his *Manual for Parents,* has proposed;
That *Ministers* would sometimes *Preach at the Schools,* as well
as *Catechise;* Because as he says, *The Preaching of the Word
is the Converting Ordinance.* And when *Sermons* are brought
unto the *Schools,* the Children must needs hear with more
Attention, and hear of such things as do more *immediately
concern* them, which in the Publick Assemblies, are not so
much medled withal; and the Ministers would condescend
unto such *Expressions* as might work most with them, which
would not be so fit for a larger Congregation.

The MASTER and MISTRESS, in the SCHOOL, may do
much in this Noble Work. We read, *The Little Ones have their
Angels.* Truly, to Teach the *Little Ones,* the *Knowledge of the
Holy Scriptures,* and make them *Wise unto Salvation,* it is a
stately work; I had almost call'd it; *A Work for Angels.* It is an
Hard Work to keep a *School;* and hardly ever duly Recom-
pensed. I suppose, It is easier to be at the *Plough* all day, than
in the *School.* But it is a *Good Work:* It is *Gods Plough;* and
God speed it! I would not have you weary of it. . . . Go on with
it Chearfully; And often Teach the Children something of the
Holy Scriptures; often drop some *Honey out of that Rock* upon
them. Who can tell, but you may Teach them the Things that

shall save their Souls, and they shall bless God for you and with you, throughout Eternal Ages. Every time a New *Child* comes to the *School,* Oh! why should you not think! *Here my Glorious LORD sends me another Object, on which I may do something to advance His Kingdom in the World!*

No, nor will we Excuse the very SERVANTS in the Family from this Blessed Work; Even the *Handmaids* in the Family, as they are *Dressing* and *Feeding* the *Children,* O Handmaids of the Lord How much may you do, to instill the *Knowledge of the Holy Scriptures* into the *Children!* If our *Servants* would once come to take pleasure in such a thing, to keep Teaching the *Children* something from the *Holy Scriptures,* O my *Children,* [for such *Servants* are worthy to be called, *Children!*] How much would you *Adorn the Doctrine of God your Saviour!* It was certainly a good Speech, which I find written by a Person of Quality. 'It is certainly, the *Highest Dignity,* if not the *Greatest Happiness,* that Humane Nature is capable of, here in this Vale below, to have a Soul so far Enlightened, as to become the *Mirror,* or *Conduit* or Conveyer of *Gods Truth* to others.['] Now, even a Domestick *Servant,* may arrive to this *Dignity,* this *Happiness.* Yea, Let all Ranks of man aspire after it.

But; *Lastly,* and yet *First of all,* O PARENTS, *Arise: This matter chiefly belongs unto you; we also will be with you.* None, I say, None are so much concerned, as *Parents* to look after it, that their *Children* be taught the *Knowledge of the Holy Scriptures.* . . .

PARENTS, These are the Cries which the Souls of your Children make in your Ears; '*My Head, my Head!* Oh! That you would fill *my Head* with the *Knowledge of the Holy Scriptures! My Heart, my Heart!* It will be a very *Dungeon of Wickedness,* if you do not by the *Knowledge of the Holy Scriptures,* purify it!' . . . There are *Parents,* who so neglect their *Children* that at the Last Day, their miserable Children will cry out, *Parentes sensimus Parricidas:* OUR PARENTS HAVE BEEN OUR MURDERERS! PARENTS, Beware of Coming under so Bitter a Condemnation. . . .

Come, ye Children, Hearken to me, I will teach you, what you ought to do.

You ought, *First,* To be *Willing* to be *Taught the Fear of the*

Lord. When your *Teachers* would learn you something of the *Holy Scriptures*, be *willing* to *Learn*. Be not lothe to wait upon their Teaching. Do not strive to get away from their Teaching. Be not so set upon your Childish & Foolish *Play*, as to count every *minute* a weary Hour under their Teaching. Rather come to your Teachers, and beg it of them, *I pray, Teach me something*. Oh! Count it a *Priviledge*, to be Taught any thing of the *Holy Scriptures*. Prize, Prize the *Sincere Milk of the Word*. Prize, Prize the Word of God, as being *Sweeter than the Honey and the Honey comb*. . . .

Children, 'Tis your *Dawning* Time. It may be your *Dying Time*. A *Child* once grew very Solid, and was more for his *Book* than for his *Play*, and Pray'd unto God more than once every day. Being asked the cause, the Child said, *Why, I was in the Burying-place a while ago, and there I saw a Grave shorter than my self! Children*, Go unto the *Burying-place;* There you will see many a *Grave* shorter than your selves. 'Tis now upon Computation found, *that more than half the Children of men Dy before they come to be Seventeen Years of Age*. And what needs any more be said, for your Awakening, to Learn the *Holy Scriptures!* . . .

Worthy of Honour are the TEACHERS that Convey *Wisdom* unto our *Children; Worthy of Double Honour* the Happy Instruments that Convey *Saving Wisdom* to them! There are some whose peculiar *Profession* it is, to assist the *Education of our Children;* and it is therefore their Endeavour to give them a *Religious Education*. Their *Employment* is to bestow Useful and Various *Learning* on our Children; but they make their Employment, a precious Advantage to Learn them the *Holy Scriptures*, and make them *Wise* for Eternity.

These our SCHOOL-MASTERS, deserve a great Encouragement. We are not *Wise for our Children*, if we do not greatly Encourage them.

The PARTICULAR PERSONS, who have their *Children*, in the Tutelage of the Skilful and Careful *School-Masters*, ought to make them suitable *Recompences*. Their *Stipends* are generally far short of their *Deserts*. They deserve *Additional Compensations*. Their *pains* are not small. What they *DO* is very

Great. And surely our Children are very dear to us; I need not quote *Euripides* to tell you, that they are as the very *Life* and *Soul* unto all Mankind. I can't but observe it with a just Indignation: to *Feed* our Children, to *Cloath* our Children, To do any thing for the *Bodies* of our Children; or perhaps to Teach them some *Trifle* at a *Dancing School,* scarcely worth their Learning, we count no Expence too much; At the same time to have the *Minds* of our Children Enriched with the most valuable *Knowledge,* here, *To what purpose?* is the cry: *a little Expence,* how heavily it goes off! *My Brethren, These things ought not so to be. Well-taught Children* are certainly very much to be accounted of. . . .

And the more *Liberal Provision* the PUBLICK does make for Industrious, well-accomplished, Well-disposed *School-masters,* the more is the *Publick Wisdom* Testified & Propagated!

SCHOOL-MASTERS that have *Used the Office well,* purchase to themselves *A Good Esteem* to *Out-live* their *Death,* as well as Merit for themselves a good *Support* while they Live. 'Tis a Justice to them, that they should be *had* in *Everlasting Remembrance;* And a *Place* and a *Name* among those *Just men,* does particularly belong to that *Ancient* and *Honourable* Man, a *Master in our Israel,* who was with us, the last Time of my Standing here; but is lately Translated unto the *Colledge* of Blessed *Spirits,* in the *Mansions* where the FIRST RESURRECTION is Waited and Longed for. . . . And if I now say a few things, *Concerning the Blessed* CHEEVER, no man who thinks well of *Gratitude,* or likes well to see the *Fifth Commandment* observed, will censure it.

He flourished so long in this Great Work, of bringing our *Sons* to be *Men,* that it gave him an opportunity to send forth many *Bezaleels* and *Aholiabs* for the Service of the *Tabernacle;* and Men fitted for all Good Employments. He that was *my Master,* Seven and Thirty Years ago, was a *Master* to many of my Betters, no less than Seventy Years ago; so long ago, that I must even mention *my Fathers Tutor* for one of them. . . .

Ye have heard, what MY MASTER was, *In the School.* Sir *Walter Rawleigh* commends it as a piece of wisdom, to use great *moderation* when we are treating men with *Commenda-*

tion. I will not forget the Rule, in carrying on my Commendation of *my Master.* But I will say very *much in a Little.* Out of the *School,* he was One, *Antiqua Fide, priscie moribus;* A Christian of the *Old Fashion:* An OLD NEW-ENGLISH CHRISTIAN. And I may tell you, That was as Venerable a Sight, as the World, since the Dayes of *Primitive Christianity,* has ever look'd upon.

He was well Studied in the *Body of Divinity,* An Able Defender of the *Faith and Order of the Gospel;* Notably Conversant and Acquainted with the *Scriptural Prophecies;* And, by Consequence, *A Sober Chiliast.*

He Lived as a *Master,* the Term, which has been for above three thousand years, assign'd for the Life of a *Man;* he continued unto the *Ninety Fourth* year of his Age, an unusual Instance of *Liveliness,* His *Intellectual Force,* as little abated as his *Natural.* He Exemplified the Fulfilment of that word, *As thy Days, so shall thy Strength be;* in the Gloss which the *Jerusalem Targum* has put upon it; *As thou wast in the Dayes of thy Youth, such thou shalt be in thy Old Age.* . . .

An ESSAY on the Memory of
my Venerable MASTER: Ezekiel Cheever.

Augusto perstringere Carmine Laudes.
*Quas nulla Eloquii vis Celebrare queat.**

YOU that are *Men,* & Thoughts of *Manhood* know,
Be Just now to the *Man* that made you so.
Martyr'd by *Scholars* the stabb'd *Cassian* dies,
And falls to cursed Lads a Sacrifice.
Not so my CHEEVER; Not by *Scholars* slain,
But Prais'd, and Lov'd, and wish'd to *Life* again.
A mighty *Tribe* of Well-instructed Youth
Tell what they owe to him, and Tell with Truth.
All the *Eight parts of Speech* he taught to them

* You ought to praise with lofty yet simple verse that life which no power of eloquence can do justice to. [Ed.]

They now Employ to *Trumpet* his Esteem.
They fill *Fames Trumpet,* and they spread a Fame
To last till the *Last Trumpet* drown the same.
Magister pleas'd them well, because 'twas *he*;
They saw that *Bonus* did with it agree.
While they said, *Amo,* they the Hint improve
Him for to make the Object of their *Love.*
No *Concord* so Inviolate they knew
As to pay Honours to their Master due.
With *Interjections* they break off at last,
But, *Ah,* is all they use, *Wo,* and, *Alas!*
We Learnt *Prosodia,* but with that Design
Our Masters Name should in our *Verses* shine.
Our weeping *Ovid* but instructed us
To write upon *his* Death, *De Tristibus.*
Tully we read, but still with this Intent,
That in *his* praise we might be Eloquent.
Our Stately *Virgil* made us but Contrive
As our *Anchises* to keep *him* Alive.
When *Phoenix* to *Achilles* was assign'd
A *Master,* then we thought not *Homer* blind:
A *Phoenix,* which Oh! might his *Ashes* shew!
So rare a Thing we thought *our Master* too.
And if we made a *Theme,* 'twas with Regret
We might not on *his* Worth show all our Wit,
    Go on, ye Grateful Scholars, to proclame
To late Posterity your *Masters* Name.
Let it as many Languages declare
As on *Loretto*-Table do appear.
    Too much to be by any *one* exprest:
    I'll tell my share, and *you* shall tell the rest.
Ink is too vile a Liquor; *Liquid Gold*
Should fill the Pen, by which such things are told.
The Book should *Amyanthus*-Paper be
All writ with *Gold,* from all corruption free.
    A Learned Master of the *Languages*
Which to Rich *Stores* of Learning are the *Keyes*;
He taught us first *Good Sense* to understand

And put the *Golden Keyes* into our Hand,
We but for him had been for Learning *Dumb,*
And had a sort of *Turkish Mutes* become.
Were *Grammar* quite Extinct, yet at his Brain
The *Candle* might have well been lit again.
If *Rhet'rick* had been stript of all her *Pride*
She from his *Wardrobe* might have been Supply'd.
Do but Name CHEEVER, and the *Echo* straight
Upon that Name, *Good Latin,* will Repeat.
A *Christian Terence,* Master of the *File*
That arms the Curious to Reform their *Style.*
Now *Rome* and *Athens* from their Ashes rise;
See their *Platonick Year* with vast surprize:
And in our *School* a *Miracle* is wrought;
For the *Dead Languages* to *Life* are brought.

His *Work* he Lov'd: Oh! had we done the same!
Our *Play-dayes* still to him ungrateful came.
And yet so well our *Work* adjusted Lay,
We came to *Work,* as if we came to *Play.*

Our *Lads* had been, but for his wondrous Cares,
Boyes of my Lady *Mores*[1] unquiet Pray'rs.
Sure were it not for such informing *Schools,*
Our *Lat'ran* too would soon be fill'd with *Owles.*
Tis CORLET's pains, & CHEEVER's, we must own,
That thou, *New-England,* art not *Scythia* grown.
The *Isles* of *Silly* had o're-run this Day
The *Continent* of our *America.*

Grammar he taught, which 'twas his work to do:
But he would *Hagar*[2] have her place to know.

The *Bible* is the Sacred *Grammar,* where
The *Rules of speaking well,* contained are.

He taught us *Lilly,*[3] and he *Gospel* taught;
And us poor Children to our *Saviour* brought.
Master of Sentences, he gave us more

---

[1] Greek: folly. [Ed.]
[2] Mother of Ishmael, or, a bondservant. [Ed.]
[3] William Lily, author of the widely used *Eton Latin Grammar.* [Ed.]

The[n] we in our *Sententiae* had before.
We Learn't Good Things in *Tullies Offices;*
But we from *him* Learn't Better things than these.
With *Cato's* he to us the *Higher* gave
Lessons of JESUS, that our Souls do save.
We Constru'd *Ovid's Metamorphosis,*
But on our selves charg'd, not a *Change* to miss.
Young *Austin*[4] wept, when he saw *Dido* dead,
Tho' not a Tear for a *Lost Soul* he had:
Our Master would not let us be so vain,
But us from *Virgil* did to *David* train,
Textors Epistles[5] would not *Cloathe* our Souls;
Pauls too we heard; we *went to School at Pauls.*

Syrs, Do you not Remember well the Times,
When us he warn'd against our *Youthful Crimes:*
What *Honey dropt* from our old *Nestors* mouth
When with his Counsels he Reform'd our Youth:
How much he did to make us *Wise* and *Good;*
And with what *Prayers,* his work he did conclude.
Concern'd, that when from him we *Learning* had,
It might not *Armed Wickedness* be made!
The *Sun* shall first the *Zodiac* forsake,
And *Stones* unto the *Stars* their Flight shall make:
First shall the *Summer* bring large drifts of *Snow,*
And beauteous Cherries in *December* grow;
E're of those Charges we Forgetful are
Which we, *O man of God,* from thee did hear.

Such *Tutors* to the *Little Ones* would be
Such that *in Flesh* we should *their Angels* see;
Ezekiel should not be the Name of such;

We'd *Agathangelus* not think too much,
Who Serv'd the *School,* the *Church* did not forget;
But Thought, and Pray'd, and often wept for it.
Mighty in Prayer: How did he wield thee, Pray'r!
Thou Reverst Thunder: CHRIST's-Sides-piercing Spear?

---

4 St. Augustine. See *Confessio,* xiii, 21. [Ed.]
5 *Epistles* of Jean Tixier de Ravisi, French humanist. [Ed.]

Soaring we saw the *Bird of Paradise*;
So Wing'd by Thee, for Flights beyond the Skies.
How oft we saw him tread the *Milky Way*,
Which to the Glorious *Throne of Mercy* lay!
    Come from the *Mount,* he shone with ancient Grace.
Awful the *Splendor* of his Aged Face
Cloath'd in the *Good Old Way*, his Garb did wage
A War with the Vain Fashions of the Age.
Fearful of nothing more than hateful *Sin;*
'Twas that from which he laboured all to win,
Zealous; And in *Truths Cause* ne'r known to trim;
No *Neuter Gender* there allow'd by him.
Stars but a *Thousand* did the Ancients know;
On later Globes they *Nineteen hundred* grow;
Now such a *CHEEVER* added to the Sphere;
Makes an Addition to the *Lustre* there.
    Mean time *America* a *Wonder* saw;
A Youth in Age, forbid by *Natures* Law.
    You that in t'other Hemisphere do dwell,
Do of *Old Age* your dismal Stories tell.
You tell of *Snowy Heads* and *Rheumy Eyes*
And things that make a man himself despise.
You say, a *frozen Liquor* chills the Veins,
And scarce the *Shadow* of a *Man* remains.
Winter of Life, that *Sapless Age* you call,
And of all Maladies the *Hospital:*
The *Second Nonage* of the Soul; the *Brain*
Cover'd with Cloud; the *Body* all in pain.
To weak *Old Age,* you say, there must belong
A Trembling Palsey both of *Limb* and *Tongue;*
Dayes all Decrepit; and a Bending *Back,*
Propt by a *Staff*, in *Hands* that ever shake.
    Nay, Syrs, our *CHEEVER* shall confute you all,
On whom there did none of these Mischefs fall.
He *Liv'd,* and to vast Age no Illness knew;
Till *Times Scythe* waiting for him Rusty grew.
He *Liv'd* and *Wrought;* His Labours were Immense;
But ne'r *Declin'd* to *Praeter-perfect Tense.*

A *Blooming Youth* in him at *Ninety Four*
We saw; But, Oh! when such a sight before!
At Wondrous *Age* he did his *Youth* resume,
As when the *Eagle* mew's his Aged plume.
With Faculties of *Reason* still so bright,
And at Good Services so Exquisite;
Sure our sound *Chiliast*,[6] we wondring thought,
To the *First Resurrection* is not brought!
No, He for That was waiting at the Gate
In the *Pure Things* that fit a *Candidate*.
He in Good Actions did his Life Employ,
And to make others Good, he made his Joy.
Thus well-appris'd now of the *Life to Come*,
To *Live here* was to him a *Martyrdom*.
Our brave *Macroebius*[7] Long'd to see the Day
Which others dread, of being *Call'd away*.
So, Ripe with Age, he does invite the Hook,
Which watchful does for its large Harvest look:
Death gently cut the *Stalk*, and kindly laid
Him, where our God His *Granary* has made.

Who at *New-Haven* first began to Teach,
Dying *Unshipwreck'd*, does *White-Haven* reach.
At that *Fair Haven* they all Storms forget;
He there his DAVENPORT[8] with Love does meet.

The *Luminous Robe*, the *Loss* whereof with *Shame*
Our Parents wept, when *Naked* they became;
Those Lovely *Spirits* wear it, and therein
Serve God with *Priestly Glory*, free from Sin.

But in his *Paradisian Rest* above,
To *Us* does the Blest Shade retain his Love.
With *Rip'ned Thoughts* Above concern'd for Us,
We can't but hear him dart his Wishes, thus.

'TUTORS, Be *Strict*; But yet be *Gentle* too:
'Don't by fierce *Cruelties* fair *Hopes* undo.

---

[6] A believer that Christ will reign on earth for 1000 years. [Ed.]
[7] Ambrosius Theodosius (*fl.* 400), Latin author; also in the sense of long-lived. [Ed.]
[8] John Davenport, founder of the New Haven Colony. [Ed.]

'Dream not, that they who are to Learning slow,
'Will mend by Arguments in *Ferio*.
'Who keeps the *Golden Fleece*, Oh, let him not
'A *Dragon* be, tho' he *Three Tongues* have got.
'Why can you not to Learning find the way,
'But thro' the Province of *Severia?*
'Twas *Moderatus*, who taught *Origen;*[9]
'A *Youth* which prov'd one of the Best of men.
'The Lads with *Honour* first, and *Reason* Rule;
'*Blowes* are but for the *Refractory Fool*.
'But, Oh! First Teach them their Great God to fear;
'That you like me, with Joy may meet them here. . . .

[9] Christian theologian and teacher of Alexandria. [Ed.]

4

Benjamin Wadsworth's
Well-Ordered Family

What happens to educational themes and ideas between two dominant periods of national thought? How are cultural moods and programs changed to make acceptable for the schooling of one generation what was unknown or unacceptable to its predecessors? In what ways do parents, schoolmen, churchmen, public men, and all who influence the young blend the new with the old? These questions lie at the heart of education considered as a social function. They involve the question increasingly and sometimes pointlessly asked in our age whether educational agencies lead or follow society.

This sermon by Benjamin Wadsworth (1670–1737) was published in a time of intellectual transition. The High Calvinist texture of Massachusetts thought, illustrated by the writings of the Mathers (see Selections 2, 3), was becoming frayed, though not dissolved, by mundane and practical concerns within the Colony's economic and political life. John Locke would not be read in New England for yet another five years, and the age of American Enlightenment was well over a half century away. But seventeenth-century scientific ideas, particularly a mechanical conception of nature, were becoming a standard part of advanced Puritan thinking. In England, Robert Boyle's work of 1663, reinforced by John Ray's in 1691, set forth in Puritan terms the ancient image of nature as God's clockwork. A divine providence, they argued, had fashioned the clockwork of nature to operate with preordained regularity for all time. Their vague but vivid premise had almost as many elaborations upon it as there were clergymen to propound them. The premise became eighteenth-century natural theology. It was introduced first

to Massachusetts by the correspondence between Boyle and Increase Mather and by the arrival in 1688 of Charles Morton, Boyle's
student from Wadham College, Oxford, as minister at Charlestown.
Though all the leading Puritan divines came to rejoice in "the light
of nature" shed upon the affairs of man, there was ever the crucial
matter of where and how one chose to apply the concept. All agreed
that the light of nature was second to the divine light of Christian
revelation through the Scriptures. But in his argument for the well-
ordered family Wadsworth based his appeal for family piety *first* on
the ground that "the very light of nature" reveals God's ruling providence in governing the affairs of society, of which each family is
itself a small society. Preaching on the same subject two decades
earlier, Cotton Mather had gone first to the sanction of Scriptural
law. Wadsworth emphasized civic stability through family order
here and now for its own sake, whereas Mather had accented civic
stability for community salvation. Though he was as much dedicated
as Mather to home education to prepare his people for conversion
and ultimately for salvation, Wadsworth stressed family piety and
harmony for the sake of "Practical Godliness." Educational change
then, in this instance, emerged from differences of *emphasis* that
learned and conscientious men placed within large issues of general
agreement.

Benjamin Wadsworth's public life is itself a chart to the shifting
tide of late Puritan educational thought. Member of the Harvard
College class of 1690 and for thirty years minister of the First
Church in Boston, Wadsworth came to represent the growing anti-
Mather faction in Massachusetts church politics, not for what he did
but for what Mather said he lacked in ministerial zeal. When John
Leverett, a layman, was elected President of Harvard College in
1708, Cotton Mather was deeply, and perhaps deservedly embit-
tered at not having been offered the post. He and his supporters
thereupon began almost two decades of sniping at the College and
its Overseers. Their cause was permanently defeated in 1725 by
Wadsworth's election to succeed Leverett. Unhappily for Wadsworth's public reputation, he was a fence-sitter in the feud between
the Mather and Leverett church factions. This made him appear to
be a trimmer. He accepted the presidency only after two other men
had declined it. But once in the job, he gave no one reason to doubt
that he was squarely on the side of Leverett's liberal policies. He
saw to it that the College's curriculum kept step with developments
in the new world of science. Isaac Greenwood was appointed the
first Hollis Professor of Mathematics and Natural and Experimental
Philosophy in 1726. Greenwood's teaching not only brought fresh
thinking to the college course; it also helped to adjust Harvard to
the increasing emphasis upon practical subjects among private

academy masters in contrast to the wholly classical training of the grammar schools. Like the times that partially guided Wadsworth's ideas, Harvard students increasingly were succumbing to "worldliness." Wadsworth was sympathetic to them (he and his wife always had young people boarding and studying with them during his ministry), but he was rather ineffective, like many later college presidents, in "controlling" them. He served as president until his death, preferring, as the famous Harvard tutor, Henry Flynt, put it, to "wear out rather than rust out." Plain, practical, and avoiding controversy, Wadsworth himself anticipates the temper of Benjamin Franklin's educated man more than he depicts Cotton Mather's Puritan.

Preface

Good Order in any Society, renders it beautiful and lovely. The upholding of Good Order in it, tends to promote the benefit and comfort, of all the Members of it. This is true of Families, as well as of other Societies. A Family wherein the true Worship of God, good pious Instruction and Government are upheld, is beautiful in the eyes of God himself; he delights to bless such. *He blesseth the Habitation of the Just.* Every Christian (every Gospel Minister especially) should do all he can to promote the Glory of God, & the Welfare of those about him; & the well ordering matters in particular Families, tends to promote these things. I believe the Ignorance, Wickedness (& consequent Judgments) that have prevailed, & still are prevailing among us, are not more plainly owing to any one thing, than to the *neglect* of Family Religion, instruction & government; and the reviving of these things, would yield as comfortable a prospect of our future good, as almost any one thing I can think of. My Prayer to God is, that what I have here offered may be Instrumental to quicken Persons to Family

Benjamin Wadsworth, *The Well-Ordered Family: or, Relative Duties. Being the Substance of Several Sermons, About Family Prayer, Duties of Husbands & Wives, Duties of Parents & Children, Duties of Masters and Servants* (Boston, 1712), preface, pp. 1, 3–5, 16–17, 21–22, 42–51, 53–59, 64–65, 68–69, 90–91, 94–99, 101–115, 117–121.

Prayer, and to carry themselves agreeably to the various Capacities they sustain in Families. If what I have written, may
promote God's Worship, & Good Order in any one Family of
these who shall Read it; I shall not grudge the pains I have
taken. But if none should reap benefit by reading these my
Endeavours, yet I hope I shall not repent of this my Essay; for
(as far as I know my own heart) God's Glory, and the Good of
his People, were chiefly aimed at herein. The consideration that
my Life is short and uncertain, makes me the more desirous, to
do something that may be useful (if God bless it) to the Interests of Religion, after I am gone, and shall be here no more. I
know the things I have here discoursed of are matters of constant Obligation; therefore the Inculcating of them, should
never be thought unseasonable. That God for Christ's sake
would accept these my Endeavours, & make them successful to
promote his Glory, and the good of Souls, is the Prayer of the
Unworthy Author.

Benjamin Wadsworth

The Well-Ordered Family:
or, Relative Duties

1 Cor. 7:24. *Brethren, Let every man wherein he is called,
therein abide with God.*

It should be the Study and Care of Christians to Serve and
Please God, in every Capacity and Relation they sustain; this
seems to be the plain Sense and Import of our Text. . . . *The
Christian Religion does not dissolve or destroy, those various
Relations or Capacities, which are common among men.* It does
not dissolve the Relation between Husbands and Wives, Parents and Children, Masters and Servants, Rulers and Subjects;
It is so far from dissolving, that it rather confirms those Relations, and the Duties thence arising. It teaches the Duties of
those Relations, and presseth the performance of them. Social

Duties and Comforts, are not hindred but furthered by Christianity. The more practical Christianity prevails in any Society, so much the better Relative Duties will be performed, & so much the more Relative Comforts will be promoted. But passing this Note, the *Doctrine* to be insisted on from the words, is this. *Christians should endeavour to Please and Glorifie God, in whatsoever Capacity or Relation they Sustain.*

Under this Doctrine, my design is (by God's help) to say something about *Relative Duties*, particularly in *Families.* I shall therefore endeavour to speak as briefly and plainly as I can, about, (1) *Family Prayer.* (2) *The Duties of Husbands and Wives.* (3) *The Duties of Parents and Children.* (4) *The Duties of Masters and Servants.* Therefore according to this Method, something is to be said.

I. *About Family Prayer.* Now here I shall endeavour: (1) *to show that Family Prayer is a Duty.* (2) *To answer some Objections, that are too apt to be made against this Duty.* (3) *To add something by way of Use.* We are therefore,

To show that Family Prayer is a Duty. Indeed, all particular persons, should maintain a constant practice of *Secret Prayer.* . . . The Families should get together Morning and Evening, and when together, the Head of the Family should Pray to God with them, and for them. That 'tis the Duty of Christians thus to do, seems evident.

From the very light of Nature. That there is a God, that his Providence governs the World which he has made; that Providence bestows Benefits, & inflicts Evils; are things evident from the Light of Nature: therefore this God should be Prayed to and Served. God's Providence governs the Affairs of *Societies* as well as of *Particular Persons;* therefore *Societies* (of which a Family is the first and smallest sort or kind) should acknowledge God, both by way of *Prayer* and *Praise.* A Family should pray to God, for Family Mercies which are needed: and praise him for Family Benefits which are Enjoyed. These things seem very evident from the Light of Nature. . . .

Obj[ection]: *I am so hurried and taken up with much business that I have no time to Pray with my Family.*

Answ[er]: *Tis a shame thou shouldst make this Objection.*

Hast thou time to Eat, Drink, Sleep, to follow thy Outward Affairs; and canst thou spare no time to Pray in? Canst thou find time to receive God's mercies, and none to pray for them, or to give thanks for them? Possibly thou dost spend as much or more time than what's needful for Family prayer, at the Tavern, in idleness, in needless chatting or diversion. And what, canst thou find time thus to throw away, and none to pray with thy Family in? If thou dost not Pray with thy Family, tis not really because thou hast no time for it, but rather because thou hast no heart for it. If thou art so hurried with business, as not to find time for Family Prayer; thou seemest to be a wicked Worldling, and to have thy heart overcharg'd with the cares of this life, and to be hastening to Endless Misery for thy practical Atheism. If thou canst not find time to serve God, do not think that he'l find time to Save thee. . . .

Family Prayer *should be perform'd in due season.* We should indeavour that *all the family be together* to join in God's Holy Worship. And therefore ordinarily (if it may be) Family Prayer should be attended, *before* any go abroad to their Day Labour; and before their minds begin to be hurried with Worldly Business, that so with the more sedateness of Spirit they may Worship God. In the Evening also Prayer should be attended, before persons are overtaken with sleep and drowziness. How unfit are persons to serve the Living God, when through sleepiness they scarce know what they say themselves, or what is said by others? Therefore, Young Persons, Children and Servants, should not be suffered to be abroad from the Family late at night; much less should Heads of Families (unless necessity require it) be out late and unseasonably, lest Family Prayer be thereby neglected, or very sluggishly performed.

When Parents put out their Children to Service, they should take care to put them into Praying Families. If you should put your Children into Prayerless Families, they'll have ill examples set before them; and will be in danger, of being greatly hurt thereby as to their Spiritual Concerns. Take heed therefore, that you don't thus expose or endanger your Children. . . .

II. *About the Duties of Husbands and Wives.* Concerning

the Duties of this Relation, we may assert a few things; and then draw some Inferences therefrom. . . .

The Duties of the Married Estate, should be duly consider'd by Persons before they enter into that Relation. Marriage is one of the weightiest actions of a person's life, and as the Yoke-fellow is suitable or unsuitable, so that Condition is like to be very comfortable or uncomfortable: Yet many enter into the Married State, very rashly and inconsiderately; they are frequently acted by foolish or ill principles, and often smart for it afterwards. If therefore persons would act properly in so great an affair, some regard should be had to the Age of the Relative sought after; a regardlessness of this often brings inconveniences. There should more regard be also had, to the inward qualifications and worth of the person; than to any Riches possessed by the person. Many make Riches their great aim in this weighty affair (and possibly their chief aim, which is very sinful), and they often in one sense or other pay dear for what they have, and it may be are great losers too. None should Marry to such or such for the sake of Riches, Honours, Friends, or any other consideration whatsoever, unless they can have a *real cordial love to them;* for God strictly commands *mutual love* in this relation. Chief regard should be had to the *Vertue and piety* of the person, that both may live as *heirs together of the grace of life.* . . . There is indeed much of the favour and mercy of God, in providing a suitable Husband or Wife; and therefore God should be earnestly sought to in such an affair. Those who have desirable, comfortable Husbands or Wives, should be very thankful to God for so favouring them. And those who have wicked, vicious Yoke–fellows, and sore afflictions thereby, should be humble before God under their trials; and should earnestly pray that they may have grace to do their duty, notwithstanding the temptations they meet with, and that they may be spiritual gainers by all that is uneasy to them.

Parents should act wisely and prudently in the Matching of their Children. . . . And as Parents should be concern'd, to see their children married to suitable persons; so Children should have great regard to the consent and advice of Parents in this great affair. . . . Parents should be as careful, that they dont abuse their power in this matter, in imposing on their Children contrary to their Inclinations, or in needlessly and unreasonably crossing of them. But having thus mentioned the duties of *Husbands & Wives,* we proceed to say something,

III. *About the Duties of Parents and Children.* And here twill be proper to speak (1) About the Duties of Parents to their Children, (2) About the Duties of Children to their Parents. . . .

The very Light and Law of Nature requires, that Parents should *love their Children;* Scripture demands it also. . . . Parents should nourish in themselves a very tender love and affection to their Children; and should manifest it by suitably providing for their outward comfort. . . . Mothers also, if able, should suckle their children. . . . Having given these hints about Mothers, I may say of Parents (comprehending both Father and Mother) they should provide for the Outward Supply and Comfort of their Children. They should *nourish and bring them up,* Isa. 1.2. They should endeavour that their Children may have *Food* suitable for quality and quantity; suitable *Raiment* and *Lodging.* In case of *Sickness, Lameness,* or other Distress on Children; Parents should do all they can for their help, health, or relief. . . . If they can help it, they should not suffer their Children to want any thing that's really good, comfortable and suitable for them, even as to their Outward man. Yet by way of Caution I might say, Let wisdom and prudence sway, more than fond indulgent fancy, in *Feeding* and *Cloathing* your Children. Too much niceness and delicateness in these things is not good; it tends not to make them healthy in their bodies, nor serviceable and useful in their Generations, but rather the contrary. Let not your Children (especially while young and unable to provide for themselves) want any thing needful for their outward comfort.

Parents should bring up their Children, to be diligent in some lawful Business. It's true, time for lawful Recreation now and then, is not altogether to be denied them. . . . Yet for such to do little or nothing else but play in the streets, especially when almost able to earn their living, is a great sin and shame. They should by no means be brought up in Idleness, or merely to learn Fashions, Ceremonious Compliments, and to dress after the newest mode. Such folly as this ruins many Children. *Boys and Girls* should be brought up diligently in such business as they are capable of, and as is proper for them. *Adam* (our First Parent) brought up his two Sons (we first read of) one to *Keep Sheep,* the other to *till the Ground, Gen.* 4:2. Nay, when *Adam* himself was Innocent, God allow'd him not to be *Idle,* but set him to *dress* and *keep the Garden, Gen.* 2:15. *Jacob's* Sons *kept Sheep,* their *Occupation* was about Cattle *from their Youth, Gen.* 37:12, & 46:33, [34]. They were not brought up *Idly when young,* but were imploy'd in business. *David* was at his *Calling,* his business *keeping Sheep,* when God sent to *Anoint him King,* I Sam. 16:13, 11. *Elisha* was *Plowing in the Field* when God call'd him to be a Prophet, I Kings, 19:19–21. *Gideon was threshing,* when called him to *deliver Israel,* Judg. 6:11, 12. *Amos* was taken from his *Particular Calling,* from *following the Flock & gathering Sycamore fruit,* to be a Prophet, *Amos* 7:14, 15. *Peter, Andrew, James and John* were call'd by Christ from following their *Particular Occupation* to be *Apostles,* Mat. 4:18–22. These Godly men, these eminent Saints, were not lazy, idle drones, they had their *Particular Callings,* Trades, were Imploy'd in lawful business; and were so diligent therein, that they would not leave the same to set a Preaching or Prophesying, till they had a plain clear call from God so to do. And from these Instances we might learn by the way, that for men to be diligent in their own proper Calling, Trade, or Business, acting suitably in their own Sphaere; is the way to meet with God's Blessing, and to be advanc'd by God, to be great Blessings to others. *Prov.* 22:29. *Seest thou a man diligent in his business, he shall stand before Kings, he shall not stand before mean men.*

Again, Christians are bid to be, *not slothful in business?* Rom. 12:11. The *Slothful* is called Wicked, Mat. 25:26. If any *would not work, neither should they eat,* 2 Thes. 3:10. *Drowsiness shall cloath a man with rags,* Prov. 23:21. Christians are required, *to work with their hands the thing that is good,* Eph. 4:28. To *do their own business, and work with their own hands,* I Thes. 4:11. And if Christians should be thus diligent in business, surely they should be brought up to it *while Young. Train up a Child, in the way wherein he should go,* Prov. 22:6. This may well refer, to things of a *Civil and Secular,* as well as to those of a religious nature. Would you have your Sons or Daughters, live as lazy, idle drones, as useless, nay, pernicious persons when grown up? If not, then don't bring them up in Idleness. Bring them up to business, some lawful Imployment or other; though you have never so much Estate to give them. It may be they may lose their Estates, (the World is full of such Instances), and how miserable will they be then, if unacquainted with, and uncapable of business? Nay, if they're brought up idly, though they should retain their Estates; it's not likely they should be Serviceable, but very likely they will be hurtful, to the Publick. Therefore let them be brought up to diligence. And when you put them out (if you do put them out) to some Trade or Calling; to be sure [to] see that tis a lawful Calling; and such as suits (as much as may be) the Abilities and Inclinations of your Children. Put them into *Religious Families,* the Heads whereof will say with him, Josh. 24:15, *As for me and my House, we will serve the Lord.* Charge them also to be *dutiful and faithful,* to those under whose care they must be. Some are more fit for a *Studious Life* to serve the Publick with their Heads, Pens, Tongues; and some for a more *Mechannick* Imployment. If you're careful to bring them up diligently in proper business, you take a good method for their comfortable subsistence in this World, (and for their being serviceable in their Generation), you do better for them, then if you should bring them up idly, and yet leave them great Estates. Under this Head I might further add, Parents should (if able) give some portion of Worldly Goods to their Children. . . . When Children first Set up for themselves, their Parents, if able, should give them some Stock, something to begin with; that they may live comfortably, and not be discouraged. . . . By a prudent Will, Parents should also provide, that after their Decease their Estates may be suitably divided among their Children. I don't mean, that they must needs give all they have to their Children; if their Estates are plentiful, they would do well to give something to pious and publick Uses. . . .

Parents should teach their Children good Manners. A civil, respectful, courteous behaviour, is comely and commendable; & Children should be taught such a Carriage. . . . Therefore Parents, teach your Children to be *Mannerly* and *Respectful* to your selves, to Civil Rulers, to Ecclesiastical Rulers, to all Superiors in Age or Office. Yea, teach them to be civil and respectful to all persons whatsoever, according to their Rank and Station: Dont suffer them to be *rude, saucy, provoking* in their words or actions unto any; for this would be a shame to your Children, and to you too. Nay, suffer not your Children to be *Imperious or Domineering,* so much as to the *meanest Servants* in your Houses, for such a base indulgence may embolden them to an ill carriage to others also. But though you should teach your Children to be Mannerly, I don't mean, that they should spend all or great part of their time, in nicely, curiously, critically observing those various, changeable, ceremonious punctilio's of carriage, which some very foolishly affect: this would be time very sinfully spent. A Child may avoid such fooleries and fopperies, and yet be very civil, courteous, mannerly in his words and gestures. . . .

Parents should govern their Children well. Restrain, Reprove, Correct them, as there is occasion. A Christian householder, should *rule well his own house,* I Tim. 3:4. Children should not be left to themselves, to a loose end, to do as they please, but should be *under Tutors and Governours,* not being fit to govern themselves, *Gal.* 4:1, 2. Children being bid to obey their Parents in all things, *Col.* 3:20, Plainly implies, that Parents should give suitable precepts to, and maintain a wise government over their Children; so carry it, as their Children may both *fear* and *love* them. You should restrain your Children from Sin as much as possible, the neglect of this in *Eli,* brought sore Judgments on his house, I *Sam.* 3:13. You should *Reprove* them for their faults; yea if need be *Correct* them too. *Prov.* 13:24: *He that spareth the rod, hateth his Son; but he that loveth him, chasteneth him betimes.* . . . You should by no means carry it ill to them, you should not frown, be harsh, morose, faulting and blaming of them, when they don't deserve it, but do behave themselves well. If you fault and blame your Children, show

your selves displeas'd and discontent, when they do their best
to please you; this is the way to provoke them to wrath and
anger, and to discourage them; therefore you should carefully
avoid such ill carriage to them. Nor should you ever correct
them upon *uncertainties,* without sufficient evidence of their
fault. Neither should you correct them in a *Rage* or *Passion;*
but should deliberately indeavour to *convince* them of their
fault, their sin; and that tis out of love to God's honour and
their good (if they're capable of considering such things) that
you correct them. Again, you should never be *cruel* nor *barbarous* in your corrections; and if *milder* ones will reform them,
more severe ones should never be us'd. Under this head of
Government I might further say, you should refrain your Children *from bad company,* as far as possibly you can *Prov.* 13:20:
A companion of fools shall be destroyed. If you would not have
your Sons and Daughters destroyed, then keep them from ill
company as much as may be. . . . You should not suffer your
Children needlessly to frequent Taverns, nor to be abroad *unseasonably on nights* lest they're drawn into numberless haz-
ards and mischiefs thereby: you can't be too careful in these
matters. . . .

Abraham pray'd for his Son, saying to God, Gen. 17:18, *O
that Ishmael might live before thee.* Surely those Parents have
little or no true love to their Children, who do not daily, constantly, heartily, and earnestly pray to God for his blessing of
them, especially with Spiritual and Heavenly blessings. Having
given these general hints about the *duties of Parents to their
Children,* we may

Give some Directions about the doing of them. Yet the *Directions* (as well as following *Motives*) which I shall mention;
shall be chiefly about *Religion* and what concerns the *Souls* of
their Children. I would therefore say to Parents, by way of
Direction,

*See to it that you instruct Every one of your Children in the
things of God.* The Apostle says, I *Thes.* 2:11, 12, We charged
every one of you as a *Father doth his Children,* that ye walk
worthy of God. Parents should teach *every Child they have* to
know, love, obey God and Jesus Christ. O Parent, look on thy

Children, on all thy Sons and Daughters (if thou has sundry of them) consider their Bodies, consider their Souls; and think, is there any of them, thou couldst be willing should be a Slave to the Devil, an object of divine wrath, a firebrand in hell for ever: couldst thou be willing it should be thus, with any of thy Children? If not, then let not any one of them live uninstructed.

You should keep your Children as much as may be, from those who would poyson their Souls by erronious Doctrines. We read of some *That creep into Houses, and lead captive Silly women, that subvert whole Houses, teaching things that they ought not,* II Tim. 3:6; Tit. 1:11. Therefore keep your Children as much as possible, from those who are known to have erroneous tenets, such as tend to destroy Faith and Godliness. Keep them also as much as may be, from reading vain, foolish, erronious Books; lest thereby they drink in ill principles, or lest some ill Impressions are made on their affections. Indeed there are too many books in the world, which seem greatly fitted and adapted to serve the Devils Interest; they deserve *Burning* rather than *Reading;* let not young ones meddle with such Books.

Warn them particularly against those Sins you see them most peculiarly prone to & in danger of. If you see them peculiarly prone to *rash anger, Revenge, Pride, Calling ill Names, Profane Swearing, Playing on the Sabbath-Day, Stealing, etc.,* you should very particularly warn them against those Sins. Where you see the greatest danger, you should use the greatest care to oppose it, yea, warn against those evils, which many are apt to count Small sins, or it may be *no* sins at all. Possibly some will count, tis no fault for Children to quarrel and *fight;* but surely tis, and you should warn them against it. Possibly some will think, tis scarce a sin for *Children to rob Orchards and Gardens* to get fruit for present eating; but surely tis, and if Children are indulg'd in it, it may lead them to greater transgressions. . . .

Take occasion from the dispensations of Providence to give good Instruction to your Children. How often have you proper opportunities for this? If you hear of great losses any meet with in their estates, how properly might you tell your Children, of the *uncertainty* of earthly Injoyments, & that they are not to be eagerly desir'd, nor at any time trusted in? . . .

Follow your Children with wholesome Counsels, tho' they are grown up. Though they are grown to be Men and Women, yea though they're Married, and live in Families of their own, and you see them but now and then, yet still you are their **Parents,** and twould be proper that you should drop your holy counsels on them. Put them in mind of former Instructions, quicken them to Serve the God of their Fathers; do all you can (as long as you and they live) to further them in a holy heavenly Life.

Be sure to set good Examples before your Children. . . . Walk in Integrity, in Uprightness, setting a blameless heavenly example before your Children; if you would have them blessed after you. Other methods of Instruction, probably will not do much good; if you don't teach them by a godly Example. Dont think your Children will mind the good Rules you give them, if you act contrary to those Rules yourselves. If you bid them *Read, Pray in Secret, attend on God's Ordinances;* and yet neglect these things your selves; if you bid them avoid ill Language, and yet use it your selves; if you thus do, what reason have you to think, that your Counsels and Instructions will do them any good? And you that are Fathers and Mothers, see to it, that you do not quarrel nor contend with one another; and that you don't oppose or contradict one another, in commanding of your Children. If the Father should bid the Child do one thing, and the Mother require another thing at the same time; alas, what an ill example would this be? This would tend to confusion indeed. If your Counsels are good, and your Examples evil; your Children will be more like to be hurt by the latter, than benefitted by the former. See to it therefore, that you dont in word or deed set an ill example before them. . . .

Having said thus much about the *Duties of Parents to their Children,* we are now to say something *about the Duties of Children to their Parents.* And here I shall mention a few things:

Children should love their Parents. . . . *Children should fear their Parents.* . . . *Children should Reverence and Honour their Parents.* . . . *Children should give diligent heed, to the whole-*

some Instructions and Counsels of their Parents. . . . Children should patiently bear, and grow better by, the needful Chastisements and Corrections their Parents give them. . . .

Children should be faithful and obedient to their Parents. They should be faithful to their Interest, and not wrong them in their Estates. It may be some Children are apt to think that what's their Fathers is theirs; and so will make bold to take almost what they please of their Fathers Estates, without their Fathers leave; and will spend, give, or game away the same as they list. But those who are thus free with their Parents Estates, thus waste and diminish them without their Parents leave; they Sin greatly. . . . And as Children should be *faithful* to their Parents Interest, so they should *obey their Commands.* . . . That is, in all *Lawful* things; for if Parents should bid their Children *Lie, Steal, Swear falsely,* or do any thing that's Sinful, they ought not to obey them therein. God is our Supream Lawgiver and Judge; therefore if any should bid us act contrary to his Laws, we ought not to obey them therein. . . . Oh Children, consider these things; they are not light or small matters; lay them seriously to heart. It may be your Parents bid you go to work, bid you do these or those things; but you wont, you disregard what they say. It may be you idle away your time, you'l be abroad very late on Nights, very unseasonably; you'l get into ill Company, frequent Taverns, take to Gaming and other ill practices, and all this quite contrary to the plain commands of your Parents. Is it so? If it is, then you disobey and rebel against God himself. Tis no small evil you're guilty of; you greatly provoke the Holy God, you're in the way to ruine. . . . Alas, Children, if you once become disobedient to Parents, you dont know what vile abominations God may leave you to fall into. When Persons have been brought to die at the *Gallows* for their crimes, how often have they confess'd that *Disobedience to Parents* led them to those crimes? As for my own part, except what's openly irreligious and profane, scarce any thing is more grating and roiling to me than to see Children rude, sawcy, unmannerly, and disobedient to their Parents. . . .

Children should be very willing and ready to Support and Maintain their Indigent Parents. If our Parents are Poor, Aged,

Weak, Sickly, and not able to maintain themselves; we are bound in duty and conscience to do what we can, to provide for them, nourish, support and comfort them. . . . Indeed, Children and Grand children should be ready to feed, nourish, comfort their aged Indigent Parents, and Grand Parents. . . .

Having thus set forth in some general heads, the Duties of Parents and Children, we are (according to the method propos'd) in the last place,

IV. *To say something about the Duties of Masters and Servants.* Under the title of *Masters, Mistresses* also may be comprehended; for they are to be *submitted to,* Gen. 16:9. They are to have an hand *in guiding the house* and governing the Family, *I Tim. 5:14.* And by *Servants* we may understand, *Male* and *Female,* both Men Servants & Maid Servants; for both the one and the other should be under government, and in subjection, *Exod. 20:10.* Under this last head therefore I shall say something, about (1) *The Duties of Masters to their Servants.* (2) *The Duties of Servants to their Masters.*

About the Duties of Masters to their Servants. Here I shall say,

Masters should suitably provide, for the bodily Support and Comfort of their Servants. Servants, are of their household; and if they provide not for such, they're worse than Infidels and have denied the faith, *I Tim. 5:8.* The vertuous Woman allows to her household, both *food and raiment,* Prov. 31:15,21. It's true, sometimes by bargain or agreement, the Servants themselves (or their Parents or Guardians) are to provide them *Cloths;* when 'tis so, then the Master is free from that care and charge. But when Servants are wholly at the finding and allowance of their Masters, then their Masters should provide them *suitable food, raiment, lodging*—such as may be for their *health* and *comfort.* And in case of *Sickness* or *Lameness,* such *Physic* and *careful tendance* as are needful; should be granted to them. . . . For any to pinch their Servants (though *Negro's, Indians,* or any *Slaves*), not allowing them such *Food, Raiment, Sleep* (and careful tendance in case of Sickness) as are needful for them; is an unmerciful, wicked and abominable thing.

Masters should keep their Servants diligently employed. Indeed, they should allow them sufficient time to *Eat, Drink, Sleep;* and on proper occasions some short space for relaxation and diversion, may doubtless be very serviseable. To be sure Servants should be allow'd time, for *Secret Prayer, learning their Catechism, reading the Bible,* and other good books for their Spiritual benefit. The masters dont show much Religion who wont allow their Servants time for such things as these. But tho' time should be allow'd these things, yet we may say in general, Servants should be kept diligently employ'd in business. . . . Idleness is the Devils School; Satan finds work for those, who are not imploy'd for God. No good comes of Idleness. Don't suffer your Servants to be *Idle;* oversee them carefully and inspect their carriage, to prevent their unfaithfulness. On the other hand, *dont be Ægyptian Task masters to them,* dont put them on work beyond their Power and Ability (nor on work improper and unsuitable for that sort of Service they ingag'd for) and dont require an *unreasonable measure* of work from them.

Masters should defend and protect their Servants. Since their Servants are under their care, and imploy'd in their business; if any would wrong or injure them, they should indeavour to protect and defend them. This is *just and equal,* right and reason require it; now Masters should do for their Servants, that which is *just and equal,* Col. 4:1. Masters themselves should not abuse their Servants, nor suffer (if they can prevent it) others to injure them.

Masters should govern their Servants well. They should charge them to obey God's commands, to live soberly, righteously & godlily. They should use their authority, in furthering their Servants in a blameless behaviour; and in restraining them from Sin. They should not suffer *Man Servant* nor *Maid Servant* to profane the Sabbath, *Exod. 20:10.* By the same rule, they should restrain them from all other Sin as far as possibly they can. Therefore they should chasten and correct them, if need so require. *Judgments are prepared for scorners, and stripes for the back of fools,* Prov. 19:29. *A servant will not be corrected by words, for tho' he understand he will not answer,* Prov. 29:19. If he's so fool hardy, high and stout as not to be mended by words; then correction should be us'd for his reformation. Yet you should not correct them (as we said before of children) in rage and passion; nor upon uncertainties, unless you are sure of their faults; nor should your corrections be cruel and unmerciful; if milder ones will do, more severe ones should ever be avoided. Masters should not be tyrannical to their Servants, nor act as tho' they had an Arbitrary, unlimited power over them. They should *not oppress* them, *Deut. 24:14.* Nor *rule them with rigour*, Lev. 25:43. . . . Threatenings should never be immoderate, nor exceed what the crime deserves. Masters should not frown and threaten, when Servants are not in fault; nor for every ignorant slip or mistake neither. Masters should not affect an harsh, rough rigorous way of speaking to their Servants; as though they were another sort of Creatures different from themselves. Masters should be *good and gentle,* I Pet. 2:18. As Masters should govern their Servants well, restraining them from Sin as much as may be; they should incourage and commend them when they do well. Our great Lord (the Master of us all) will say to the faithful, Mat. 25:21, *Well done* thou good and faithful Servant. Surely then, we should say to our Servants, *well done;* we should *commend* and incourage them when they deserve it. Again, when Masters or Mistresses make Promises to Servants, they should faithfully and exactly fulfill them. If we would have Servants faithful to us, we should be so to them. And I might here say as to *hired Servants,* their *Wages* should be duely honestly and seasonably paid them. Col. 4:1. *Masters give to your Servants that which is just and equal; knowing that ye also have a Master in heaven.* If we should wrong our Servants in Word or Deed, possibly in some cases they would scarce know how to right themselves; but shall their helpless condition imbolden us to wrong them? God forbid. We have a Master as well as they, even God in heaven, and we are accountable to him how we carry it to our Servants. God will relieve the oppressed; he will recompense wrongs; the fear of his holy displeasure therefore, should restrain us from any way injuring our Servants. Tho' we are now their Superiors, yet they and we shall soon stand on a level before the Throne of our Judge; who will give to every one according to his ways. Let us not therefore wrong the meanest servant we have; but give what is just and equal; and hear what they can reasonably plead for themselves in any matter. . . .

Masters should Teach and Instruct their Servants well. When Masters take *Apprentices,* to teach them some particular Trade or Occupation; they ought in duty and conscience, to give them all the skill and insight they can, in such their Occupation. If they don't faithfully Instruct them therein, they're unjust and unrighteous to them. But by the way, Masters should not allow themselves in any unfair practices in their Callings, nor teach their servants so to do. If Masters are hired to *Work by the Day* (as in some Trades they often are) they should not be *lazy and idle* (if they are, they do but *Steal* in taking the whole of the Wages agre'd for). They should not do their work slightly or fallaciously; nor teach or suffer their Servants so to do. They should not for the *getting of more custom* (and grasping much more work into their hands) make *fair Promises,* which possibly they have *no prospect nor design to accomplish;* nor should they teach or allow their Servants, in such a vile, wicked, abominable practice. Masters should communicate to their Servants all the honest skill to be us'd in their Trade, but no ill tricks or cheating, fallacious practices. Well, but should not Masters take care of the *Souls of the Servants* and teach them the *Truths and Duties of Religion?* Yes, indeed, they should; tis their indispensable duty so to do; but this was spoken to before, under the head of *Parents bringing up their Children Religiously.* . . . By no means discourage them from any thing that's vertuous and pious; but by good Instructions, counsels, and a blameless example set before them, do your utmost to make them truly religious. Keep them as much as possible from ill company; pray hard for them. You should thus strive that they may be truly religious, for the sake of your own credit, comfort and profit, for the sake of their precious Souls, for the promoting God's glory by the Propagating of Religion in the World. Having thus hinted at the *Duty of Masters to their Servants,* we may,

Say something about the Duty of Servants to their Masters. And here I might say

Servants should fear their Masters. . . . Servants should

Honour their Masters. . . . Servants should in their words and actions, put respect and honour on their Masters; they must not give sawcy, impudent, contradicting Answers to them. If those Servants who pretend and profess to be Christians, are rude and unmannerly to their Masters, carry it as tho' they were their equals; if they are sullen, surly, humoursome so as scarce to give an Answer when spoken to; or if they give ill language, cross provoking impudent words; I say if they do thus, then they expose the Christian Religion (which they profess) to be blasphem'd and ill spoken of. Those who dont honour their Masters, they dishonour God by breaking his plain commands.

Servants should Obey their Masters, be diligent and faithful in their Service and to their interest. . . . You that are *Servants,* take your Bibles, frequently read these plain commands of the Great God; that out of obedience to his supreme indisputable Authority you may be moved and quicken'd, conscientiously to obey your Masters and be faithful to their Interest. And you that are *Masters,* if your Servants are disobedient or unfaithful to you, then read to them these plain commands of the Great God, indeavouring to impress on their Consciences, a sense of God's Authority and their own duty. Tell your Servants not passionately but seriously, that in disobeying your lawful commands, they disobey not only men but God also; because God requires them to obey you. But to proceed, these things plainly show that Servants should be obedient and faithful to their Masters. . . . Servants, are your Masters or Mistresses *froward;* are they peevish, fretful, passionate, unkind, unreasonable in their carriage to you? If they are, that's their Sin, and for it they are accountable to God, their Master and yours too; yet God requires you to obey their lawful commands, and do what you lawfully can to please them, notwithstanding their ill carriage to you. If they don't do their duty to you, yet you should indeavour to do your duty to them. Then when you think they act unreasonably, you may sometimes humbly and modestly suggest your thoughts in the matter, as *Naaman's* Servants did, 2 *King.* 5:13; yet their lawful commands you ought to obey. You, therefore, that are Servants, take heed,

To obey All the Lawful commands of your Masters and Mistresses. . . .

Obey your Masters willingly, heartily, cheerfully. . . . Obey God in obeying your Masters. . . .

Having thus showed, that Servants should honour and obey their Masters, and be faithful to their Interest, we may (before we proceed to other distinct heads) draw a few Inferences from these things:

Servants act very wickedly, when they dishonour or disobey their Masters. It may be some Servants, by telling false tales and stories out of the house, do greatly hurt their Masters and Mistresses in their Credit, Reputation and Business; such are wicked Servants, they disobey and dishonour God, in thus dishonouring those that are over them. Possibly some Servants are very high, proud, stout; they'll scarce bear to be commanded or restrained: they are for much liberty. They must have liberty for their tongues to speak almost what and when they please; liberty to give or receive visits of their own accord, and when they will; liberty to keep what company they please; liberty to be out late on nights, to go & come almost when they will, without telling why or wherefore; such liberty they contend for, they wont be rul'd, govern'd, restrain'd: or it may be the work they are set about, they reckon 'tis beneath and below them, they wont stoop to do it, but will rather disobey Masters or Mistresses; such Servants are very wicked. They are daring in their plain disobedience to God, their abominable rebellion against him: they trample Gods law, his Authority, under their feet.

Servants are very wicked, when they are Lazy and Idle in their Masters Service. . . .

Servants are very wicked, when they Cheat their Masters, or hurt them in their Estate or Interest. When Servants will take *Money, Victuals, Drink,* Cloths, or any goods, any thing belonging to their Masters or Mistresses; and will sell them, give them away, or imploy them in Junkets and Merry meetings, they do very wickedly therein. This is *Theift*, this is *Purloyning. . . .*

Servants do very wickedly, when they run away from their Masters. . . . God has set up Authority and Government in Families; those who throw it off or run from it, rebel against him. Servants are not proper judges, who is fit to go into Publick Service; others are more proper than they, to determine in such a case. Tis not true courage or Publick-Spiritedness, that makes *Servants* (ordinarily) list *Volunteers;* but tis a loose humour, a refractory Spirit; they would be from under the yoke of Family Government. Those Servants who have thus quitted their Masters Service, should be deeply humbled before God for their great Wickedness; they should heartily repent of it. Having thus shewed, that Servants should honour and obey their Masters; and having mention'd a few Inferences there from, we may proceed to say—

Servants should patiently bear, any deserved Chastisements their Masters inflict on them. . . . Tis true, if Masters make a trade of being cruel or unreasonable, in inflicting groundless punishments on their Servants, tis fit such Servants should be reliev'd and help'd by Civil Authority, and that their Masters should be punish'd by the same.

Once more, *Servants should Pray for God's blessing, on their Masters affairs.* Abraham's pious faithful Servant, did so, *Gen. 24·12,* And obtain'd Success in the business his Master set him about. The example of this *Praying Servant,* is fit to be imitated by all Servants. Thus I have mention'd sundry Duties, arising from the various Relations or Capacities, which Christians very often sustain; would to God these Duties might be duely consider'd and practis'd. Tis commonly said, those are not *really good,* who are not *Relatively good.* If we would be *good Christians,* we should obey *All* the commands of Christ, and do the Duties of those several Capacities or Relations he has set us in: then (according to our Text) *wherein we are called, therein we do abide with God.*

Soli Deo Gloria

FINIS

5

John Clarke's
Classical Program of Studies

A provincial schoolmaster in England, John Clarke (1687–1734), did more than any other British educator in the mid-eighteenth century to clarify systematically the ideal curriculum of a Latin grammar school. Trained at St. John's College, Cambridge, Clarke devoted the last fourteen years of his short life to teaching grammar schools at Hull and Gloucester. Writing as John Clarke "of Hull," to distinguish himself from others of the same name, he published several Latin grammars, colloquies, essays on moral philosophy, and this *Essay Upon the Education of Youth in Grammar Schools,* first brought out in 1720 and republished in a second edition in 1730. Like his Latin primers and dialogues, the *Essay* was widely used. It had a third printing in 1740. In America, Hull's *Essay* proved to be more serviceable to grammar school and academy teachers than John Locke's *Some Thoughts Concerning Education* (1693) for two reasons. Clarke advocated instruction in small private schools, which was consonant with the development in America of private academies, and which was a compromise between the old public schools that Locke criticized and the private tutoring that Locke supported. Private tutoring of individual students was simply unworkable in the colonies, except in some of the wealthier, isolated southern planters' families, primarily because qualified tutors were lacking for the job. Schooling in eighteenth-century America, moreover, increasingly meant a collective, not an individual learning situation, especially in New England and the middle Atlantic colonies where the schoolhouse was replacing the family home as the place of formal elementary instruction. For a second and more important reason, Clarke's *Essay,* while giving the reader an admiring view of Locke along with copious quotations from his work, went further than Locke by prof-

fering a detailed plan of studies for a classical grammar school. A
century before normal schools or teacher training institutes, it was the
clearest directive to teachers of classical subjects. Of course, American teachers were no less eclectic than they are now. Although
Clarke's *Essay* seems in the colonies to have been read more than
Locke on education, there is some reason to believe, from the widely
varying quality of local schools and school teachers, that the *Essay*,
when used, served colonial teachers much in the way that "official"
statewide curriculum guides are used eclectically by teachers today.

Still, John Clarke's *Essay* was the first missionary to America for
Lockian ideas of schooling, as distinguished from Locke's works in
philosophy, psychology, moral philosophy, or government. Clarke
elaborated a Lockian *method* of schooling in the popular way that
Isaac Watts (see Document 6) later worked out Locke's description
of the powers of the human mind. In a clear, vernacular style, he
demonstrated that Locke's ideas *about* education could indeed be
revolutionary *within* education. The Lockian precepts upon which
Clarke built his classical studies were to become staple ingredients
of modern schooling. Young people have their own rates of intellectual development. Learning means a progression from the simple
to the complex. It is futile to learn rules without experience. Indis-
criminate corporal punishment kills the initiative of the pupil as
well as the creativity of the teacher. Utility and an economy of time
and effort are indispensable to effective teaching. It was a tribute to
Clarke's powers of argument that he was able to criticize sharply the
traditional or "vulgar" means of teaching Latin by constant memorization, to advocate the use of ponies or trots, and to champion learning rules of grammar sensibly from a teacher rather than "by the
book" without losing his reading public. His *Essay* caught on principally because it stressed the learning of English style rather than the
learning of Latin for its own sake. In the age of the *Spectator* and
the dawn of a new life for England and her colonies, that was what
counted most.

Tho' Nature has not dispensed her Favours with an equal
Hand to all Mankind, but there is a very visible Inequality in

---

John Clarke, *An Essay Upon the Education of Youth in Grammar-
Schools. In Which the Vulgar Method of Teaching Is Examined, and a
New One Proposed, for the More Easy and Speedy Training Up of
Youth to the Knowledge of the Learned Languages; Together with History,
Chronology, Geography, &c.* (2d. ed., with very large additions; London,
1730), pp. 1–17, 20–21, 27–47, 52–54, 56–61, 78–94, 96–99, 102–105,
107, 116–117, 119–120, 123–125, 127–129, 131–138, 141–145, 148–149,
151–152, 167–170, 172–177, 180–185, 187–188.

the natural Parts and Abilities of several Men; yet the greatest Difference amongst them, will be found to arise from the different Use and Improvement of their Faculties, which is chiefly owing to Education. For how many Men are there born into the World with Parts sufficient, had they been duly cultivated, to qualify them for the highest Posts in Church or State; who, for want of that Improvement, never rise above the Talents necessary for the Management of an ordinary Trade, or engrossing to themselves the greatest Share of Talk in common Conversation with Men of their own low Rank? Nay, I think, I may very safely venture to say, that few Men ever attain to any considerable Eminence in Virtue or Knowledge, the only Foundations of all true and solid Greatness, who were not in a great measure indebted to their Education for it.

Children are Strangers in the World, where the first Acquaintance they make is with sensible Objects: Those must store the yet empty Cabinet of the Mind with variety of Ideas, as the Foundation and Materials of their future Knowledge. And as the natural Thirst in the Mind after Happiness, disposes them to pursue with great Eagerness, whatsoever they find capable of ministring to their Pleasure; so it is the Business of Education to watch over that weak and tender Age, that the yet unwary thoughtless Mind, uncapable of seeing into the Nature and Consequences of Things, be not too much led away, and entirely possessed by the deluding Pleasures of Sense; and by due Information and Restraint, to prevent the settling of vicious Habits. Where this is not done, ill Customs are unavoidable, and hardly ever after to be broke. All the Force of Reason and Eloquence from the Pulpit, or the Press, is seldom found sufficient to draw those from the Ways of Vanity and Folly, that have had the Misfortune to be engaged in them from their Childhood. This shews the Necessity of an early Care of Youth, if you design they should be of any Use in the World, either to themselves or their Country.

Tho' the forming the Mind to Virtue is the main thing to be aimed at in Education, yet it is not the only one: Learning, or the Knowledge of Things, is another, and Skill in Languages, at least the Latin, as an Introduction to it. This part is not only necessary, as being highly subservient to the former, but is of the greatest Use and Service in all the most important Stations of Human Life. Virtue stands in need of Knowledge to direct; and a pious Disposition, when misguided by false Notions of Duty, serves oftentimes only to make a Man very mischievous in the World. The mistaken Zealot, the poor blind Bigot, is hurried on to Actions of the most dreadful Consequence to the Peace and Happiness of Mankind, under the Notion of Duty, and to avoid the Penalty of eternal Damnation . . . And perhaps it will not be very easy to determine, whether a misguided Zeal in Matters of Religion, or downright Profaneness, have done more Mischief. Nay, I cannot but think, that whoever will take an impartial Survey of the History of this Part of the World, since the Destruction of the Roman Empire, will find some Reason to be of Opinion, that Men have suffered more in their dearest Interests, by false Notions of Religion, than by all the other Causes or Occasions of Human Misery put together. Besides, the Helps of Learning are necessary, as I said before, in all the most important Stations of Human Life. History, which, as a wise Man observes, ought to be the constant Study of a Gentleman, how necessary is it for the Guidance and Direction of the Stateman and Politician? Those narrow contracted Views of Mankind, he must needs have, that has only his own Experience and Observation to go upon, will frequently misguide him in Matters of the greatest Consequence, to the Peace, Strength, and Security of Kingdoms. But he that keeps a constant Correspondence with the wisest and most judicious Historians, both ancient and modern, will from thence receive such a Knowledge of Men and Things as will enable him to act his Part to the Happiness and Glory of his Country, and his own Honour. The Law of Nature and Nations is another Branch of Literature, necessary for a Gentleman in a Publick Station: And as such Persons should not neglect any proper Means of improving and enlarging their Capacities; Modern Philosophy, I mean the notional Part, together with the Mathematicks, will be highly serviceable to that purpose. Divinity is the common Concern of all Men. And of what Use the Latin Tongue is, which is the common Language of the learned World, is too obvious to be insisted on.

Since therefore a right Method of Education is a Matter of the greatest Importance, it is a Wonder to me, that amidst the great Variety of Books the World is overcharged with, there should have appeared so very few upon this Subject. I know not of any in our Language that are worth the Perusal but Mr. *Locke's,* who has indeed acquitted himself upon this Head with his usual Strength of Reason and Judgment, so far as he has gone. But as the Business of Education is twofold, to rectify the Will, and enlighten the Understanding, he has been as full and particular upon the former Head as could well be desired; but, in my Opinion, deficient in the latter; I mean, as to a Method of reading and attaining the Languages. The Reason of this great Silence upon the Subject, sure is not that a Publick Education is already carried to the highest Pitch it is capable of; far from it! The Vulgar Method that obtains in our Schools, is so miserably trifling, that any one, who duly considers it, will have much ado to forbear thinking, it has been contrived in Opposition to all the Rules of good Method, on purpose to render the Learning of the Languages more tedious than it needs to be: How else were it possible for Boys of good Parts, to spend six or seven Years in a Grammar-School, without attaining so much of the Latin Tongue, as to make Sense of half-a-dozen Lines in the easiest of the Classic Authors? This, which upon Enquiry will be found to be a very common Case, is, I imagine, sufficient to justify the ill Opinion several People have conceived of that Way of Teaching, which is usually follow'd in our Schools.

The great, and I think I may say, the only End, propounded both by Parents and Masters in the common Method, is the Instruction of Youth in the Languages of Latin and Greek: This their whole Time is spent in at School; and if a Boy can but show a very moderate Skill in the Latin, by a Copy of Verses, and a Theme, and make a shift to construe an easy Greek Author indifferently, the Master thinks he has play'd his Part sufficiently, and the Father is very well satisfied with his Son's Proficiency. But how far short this is of what Boys might be brought to by the Age of Sixteen or Seventeen, will appear, I hope, by the Sequel of this Discourse. For my part,

I cannot but wonder, that when it is evident, a great deal of useful Knowledge might be taught them at the same Time they learn the Languages, that advantage should be so little regarded; and the learning of Words made their only Business during the best Part of their Lives.

I shall need no Allowance, I think, for saying that Boys learn nothing but Words, in the useful [usual] Method of the Schools; for a few Scraps of the Greek and Roman History, with as many of the Heathen Mythology, no Man of Sense, I believe, will look upon as any great Accomplishment. This, without a more perfect Acquaintance with those, as well as other Things, is worse than none at all; and serves only to fill their Heads with a vain Conceit of themselves, and renders them oftentimes Pedantick and impertinent, all the Days of their Lives after.

It is not therefore bare Latin and Greek a Boy should spend his whole Time in at School. These must of Necessity go to the making of a Scholar; but then there are other things as necessary, which School-Boys are not only capable of, but may easily be taught, without any Hindrance to their Proficiency in the tongues: I mean History and Geography, both Ancient and Modern, with Chronology, and the most necessary and useful Things in Divinity, &c. These, if a right Method was used with them, might be taught them, to a greater Degree of Perfection than most Men of a Scholastick Education, that apply themselves to Reading, ever attain to. And what a Byass, what an Inclination for Books and Learning, it would give Boys, if they were to leave the School so furnished, I need not say.

I shall therefore, in the first Place, present the Reader with a Detail of those Faults and Blunders, I conceive the common Method is chargeable with, and then proceed to lay down one of my own. The former I shall digest under the following Heads.

I. The Beginning with Grammar, and that a Latin one so ill contriv'd as Lily's is.

II. The want of proper Helps for the Reading of Latin.

III. The want of proper Helps for the Writing and Speaking of it.

IV. The want of due Order and Method in the Reading of Authors.

V. The making Boys get their Lessons in the Poets without Book.

VI. The putting them to too many several Things at the same Time.

VII. The putting them upon Exercise above their Years or Improvement.

VIII. The putting them upon Greek Exercise.

In all these Respects I imagine, the Common Method will be found to be very faulty; and if it be, it will no longer appear a Wonder, Boys should advance so very slowly, and after all, go away so meanly furnished as they do, to the University, when they have so many Clogs and Incumbrances upon them.

I. The First Fault I find with the Common Method of Teaching, is *Beginning with Grammar,* and that a Latin one so ill contrived as Lily's is; whereas, after Boys have got the Declensions of Nouns and Conjugations of Verbs perfectly without Book, they should be immediately entred in the Reading of Authors, and not be troubled with any more of Grammar, till they have made such a Progress, as to be able to read the easier Authors of the Latin Tongue pretty familiarly. I doubt not but a great many People will be shock'd at this, and look upon it as a very preposterous Method of proceeding. I desire their Patience . . . till they hear my Reasons for it; and then let them determine as they see Cause.

1. Boys have no Occasion for *Grammar* for the Reading such Authors as are proper for Beginners, with the Help of *Literal Translations,* such as they should be provided with; and therefore, there is no Necessity however, for their being troubled with any thing of Grammar so soon, besides the Declensions and Conjugations. It will be time enough, after they have, by Reading, gained some Acquaintance with Latin Words, to inform them, how they are to put them together, in order to the Writing and Speaking of Latin.

2. It is not very practicable, I think, to bring a Boy to understand *Grammar* tolerably well, or in any reasonable Time, by making him read the Grammar only over and over again: And

if he must not be entred in his Authors, till he has attained it
either wholly, or in a good Measure that Way, I doubt he will
never come to read a Latin Author at all. This is what every
one that follows that Method must be very sensible of from his
own Experience. And indeed the Practice of our Schools is a
pretty good Proof, that either the Teaching of Grammar is
mis-timed, by putting Boys too soon upon it, before their
Reason is ripe enough to deal with so difficult a Subject; or that
the Way of doing it is not proper, or both: For Boys are everywhere put upon the Reading of Authors, before they understand any thing at all almost of their Grammar, notwithstanding the mighty Pains taken with them, by making them Construe and Parse it over and over again. The going through
the Rules of the Syntax, . . . will never make them understand
it. No body was ever made Master of the Syntax that Way,
nor ever will. The only proper Method for that Purpose, is, to
furnish Boys with Variety of proper English Examples to their
Rules, for them to translate into Latin, beginning with the
easiest first, and advancing by degrees to what is more Difficult. This, with the Parsing their Lessons in the Authors they
read, is the only Means I know of, to bring them to the Knowledge and Practice of their Syntax: the Examples in the Grammar are far short of being sufficient for that Purpose.

3. The Reading of Authors with *Literal Translations* . . . employs nothing but Memory; and consequently is more suitable
to the Capacity of a young Boy, than the Understanding and
Practice of Grammar Rules; which require great Application,
Attention, and Labour of Thought, and for that Reason should
be let alone, till the Mind has been ripened, and improved by
Reading. In the Learning of any Thing, we ought to begin with
what is easiest first, and proceed, as much as may be, by insensible Steps of Difference, to what is more difficult. Thus the
Mind may in Time be brought to master any Thing. To begin
therefore the Learning of the Latin Tongue with the Practice of
Grammar Rules, is quite wrong: And if People would but
consider what a sorry Pittance of Grammar it is that Boys
attain to in four or five Years, at the best of our Schools, where
the common Method of Teaching is followed, notwithstanding

all the Whipping and Spurring made use of to put them forward; they would find Reason to think that Grammar is too difficult for Boys so young. And tho' I do not think it impracticable, to make a Boy of eight or nine Years of Age a pretty good Master of his Syntax, in two Years, or three however; yet I can not but think it much more adviseable to defer it, till he can read an easy Latin Author; because then one fourth Part of the Time will do it. If he begins with Reading, and has the Help above-mentioned, he will lose no Time, because his Business will have no Difficulty in it; but if he must set out with Grammar, he infallibly will. The Mind of a Child of that Age is so little capable of the Consideration and Reflection, necessary for the Understanding and Practice of Grammar Rules; that tho' he has all the Help that Art can give him, yet his Work will go very heavily and slowly forward; and three Parts at least in four of his Time be lost, which might and would be saved, if he was kept to what his Capacity is well enough fitted for, and what is difficult deferr'd, till a greater Ripeness of Sense and Understanding has duly prepared him for it.

But supposing it was necessary to begin with Grammar, yet why must the Grammar needs be in Latin! What can be more ridiculous than to deliver Rules for the Learning of any Thing, in a Language the Learner understands not? This is such a palpable Piece of Absurdity, that I am perfectly at a loss to imagine, what can be alledged in Vindication of it. If Boys must begin with Grammar, in the Name of Wisdom, what is the Meaning of putting Rules upon them in a Language they are going to learn, and consequently as yet know nothing of? Are you afraid they should understand, and make use of them too soon? If not, why are they not in a Language they are acquainted with? . . .

We are, it's true, furnished with an English Syntax in the Accidence, but to what purpose I know not; since it is expected a Boy should learn and make use of the Latin Syntax, before he can understand it, without a construing Book. If not, why has he a construing Book put into his Hands for that purpose? And there is no reason that I know of, why a Boy's Memory should be burdened with two Syntaxes, any more than twenty. And

should any Master depart so far from the vulgar Method of
teaching, as to make use only of the English Rules in the Accidence, it would no doubt be look'd upon as a very grand Defect,
and expose him to suffer in his Reputation and Interest for
it. . . .

II. The next Objection against the common Method of
Teaching, is, the *Want of proper Helps for the Reading of
Authors,* or drawing Beginners over the first Difficulties of the
Latin Tongue, and bringing them to a familiar use of the easier
Authors in that Language. By these Helps, I mean *Translations,*
and those as *Literal* as possible; the great Advantage of which
lies so obvious to common Sense, and is so constantly made use
of in the teaching of other Languages, that it's a perfect Mystery it should be overlook'd in the teaching of Latin. The common Method is, I think, in this Respect, compleatly ridiculous.
For what miserable Pottering Work do the poor Boys make
of it, every where, for the first two or three Years, for want of
this Help so easy to be had, and so visibly necessary, that it's
perfectly amazing they should so long together have been unfurnished with it. It puts me in mind of a Reflection I have
known made upon Schoolmasters, that of all Men they are the
greatest Bunglers in their Profession. . . . Boys commonly spend
one half of their Time, Morning and Afternoon, in poring over
two or three Lines, and teazing first one, and then another of
them, the Master, or some of their School-fellows, perpetually
for their Assistance, who might as well read a Page or more in
the Time, with great Peace and Quietness in their Seats, if they
had but the Help of *a Literal Translation.* This, it's plain, would
save both Master and Boys so much Trouble; would bring the
latter so smoothly, and withal so very expeditiously, to the Reading of the Classicks, that it is the most unaccountable thing in
the World to me, our Schools should be without any Helps of
this Nature. . . .

Translations have been thought so necessary for the Attainment of the Greek Tongue, that for above these hundred and
fifty Years last past, no Authors in that Language have been
published without them. This might, one would think, have
naturally led the World to the pursuit of the same Method, at

least with the easier Authors of the Latin Tongue, for the use of Schools. . . .

Besides, it's a meer Jest to put Boys, so soon as is usually done, upon getting their Lessons by the Dictionary. The looking for their Words does not only make a strange Consumption of their Time, supposing it would do their Business, but, alas! it will not. They are perfectly bewilder'd in that Variety of Significations many Words have, and want Skill to make choice of such as are proper for their Purpose. Whereas the Use of Literal Translations has no difficulty in it: That employs nothing but Memory: Their Words are all ready at hand, and they go smoothly forward, without any Rubs in their Way, or Loss of Time; and with a great deal of Satisfaction, to find their Business so very easy.

All this is so undeniably plain, that I cannot forbear saying again, That it is astonishing to me, our Schools should be to this day without any Helps of this Kind: Nay, so little sensible does the World appear of any thing amiss in this Matter, that we hear no Complaints made of the Want of such Helps. Our Schools are very easy, and our Masters proceed very quietly and contentedly, in a sensless absurd Method of reading Authors, that with the Use of Lily's Grammar, occasions the Loss of at least three of the four first Years Boys spend at School. For this, I think, a Man might safely venture his Reputation upon, That a Boy, by the Help of *Literal Translations,* would do more in one Year, than without them he would in three or four. . . .

III. The next Fault I find with the vulgar Method of Grammar Schools, is, *the Want of proper Helps for the Writing and Speaking of Latin.* The bringing Boys to read a Latin Author, has really no great difficulty in it: Furnish them but with proper Translations, and see they do not saunter away their Time, and you will find your Business done, much sooner than without Tryal you would imagine. But the bringing Boys to a true Latin Style, is really Matter of great Difficulty, and the greatest of all Difficulties the Master has upon his hands. This requires Art and Method, and a great deal of Pains both from Master and Scholar. . . . It is not the Reading twenty or thirty Pages in two or three of the Latin Classicks in Prose, with the Scribling a few Lines of Latin Exercise every Night, by the help of a Dictionary, such as we are yet furnish'd with however, will do the Business. The Latin is a large copious Language, that abounds with Variety of Words, very various in their Significations: And to imagine that Boys should make any tolerable Acquaintance with them, in that poor Pittance of the Classick Authors in Prose (from which alone they are to learn a Style) is a Jest that can never enter into the Head of any Man of Understanding, that considers the Matter. . . .

The first Step towards the Attainment of a Latin Style, should be a Collection of proper *English Examples,* for the Reducing the Latin Syntax to Practice. . . .

Boys are left to make their Latin by the Dictionary; but were our Dictionaries as well contrived as they are otherwise, it would be impossible for Boys so young to make use of them: Much less can they make use of such sort of English-Latin Dictionaries as we yet have, without Blundering perpetually in the Choice of their Words. I am sure it is a fair Wager of two to one against them, they chuse amiss, almost every time they have occasion to consult their Dictionary. To leave them therefore to the Use of that so soon, is the Way to spoil them, by filling their Heads with infinite Mistakes, as to the proper Import and Signification of Words. The Master must be at the pains to supply them with the Words they want, and for that purpose should read them at least one Lesson every Day, in the Book they use for Exercise, into Latin, which they must go over again amongst themselves till they are perfect in it. This Method is to be pursued till they have got a pretty good Acquaintance with Words and can acquit themselves tolerably well in the Translation of the Pantheon, or any such plain easy Book. After which, the most proper Way of proceeding with them, in my Opinion, will be to make them translate some easy Author, such as Cæsar, Justin, or Cornelius Nepos, by way of Exercise in the Evenings, and oblige them to get their Translations to read back again into the very Original Latin of their Author. Thus they will kill two Birds with one Stone, improve in both Languages at once, and by seeing the Idiom of the Latin and English go constantly together, make a much greater Progress in Style than will easily be imagined by one that has not tried this Method. But then you must not let them put you off with a bald Literal Translation, but oblige them to turn their Author into proper English; for which purpose some Rules and Directions may be given them which will easily enough offer themselves to any one that will be at the pains to exercise himself in Translation now and then; or compare any good Translation of a Classic Author with the Original. I would advise the Master to help them a little at first setting out in this Way by reading them their Author into proper English, tho' with as little Variation too from the Letter of the Latin as is consistent with a tolerable English Style. As they improve in each Language by this Exercise, they may take more Liberty; till at last they must be left to their utmost Freedom in their Way of Expression, provided they keep but up to the Sense of their Author. . . .

Another Help wanting for the due and speedy Improvement of Youth in the Writing and Speaking of Latin is a *Good Set of Latin Dialogues, upon all the usual Topicks of common Conversation, with a proper English Translation;* not for the understanding them, for I propose not this; but for the use of such Boys as have made some progress in Reading of Authors, and are therefore capable of understanding such a Book pretty well without Help. But I would have them read their Translation into Latin. This would bring them on apace towards Style, and be of other kind of use to their Speaking of Latin, than their talking barbarously among themselves; which is the Way, forsooth! of bringing Boys to the Speaking of Latin in some Schools, but, in my mind, a very strange one, unless the talking badly with those that cannot inform them better, can be supposed to be the Way to talk well. There is no properer Method of improving in any Language, for those that already have a Smattering in it, than Conversation with such as talk it well; and on the other hand, nothing worse than Conversation with those that talk it but badly. Boys therefore must not be put upon this Task of Speaking Latin, till they can write it pretty well, and are Judges of the Latin Idiom; that is to say, in almost all Schools never at all.

When Boys have attained to something of a Mastery in the easier Classics, then, instead of Reading the Latin Prose Authors into English, I think it would be proper to make them read the best Translations of them that are Public, into Latin; I mean that of the Authors themselves, by making them read the Original and Translation together, till they can render the latter into the former exactly. In this Way of Proceeding, they will have these three great Advantages: 1. Of Understanding their Latin Authors more compleatly, and more readily than they could do without the Translation. 2. Of Improving in the English Tongue, whilst they are getting the Latin, and that perhaps in the most proper Way that could be thought of. And, 3. Of attaining much quicker to an Imitation of the Stile of the best Authors in the Latin Tongue, than they would do by reading the Originals alone. All which is so very visible, that I think I need not enlarge upon this Head.

IV. A fourth Objection against the usual way of Proceeding in our Schools, is, *The Want of due Order and Method in the Reading of Authors:* For when Boys are thought fit to be enter'd in the Classics, they commonly begin with the Poets; some with *Ovid de Tristibus,* some with his *Metamorphoses,* and some with both; a very great Absurdity certainly: For none sure that knows what Poetry means, can make a doubt of it, whether the Style of Prose be not ordinarily more easy than that of the Poets. . . .

Let any one dip into a Poet and an Historian at the same time, and compare the first Passages he lights on together, and it will give him full Satisfaction, if he wants it. The one abounds with Figure, and the whole Turn of his Expression is quite out of the common Road, while the Historian generally delivers his Mind in proper Terms, and in a Way and Manner agreeable to common Conversation. In short, they have so visibly the Advantage of the Poets, with respect to Perspicuity and Plainness of Style, that I cannot but wonder how the latter came to take place of the former, in the common Method of the Schools. This looks something like teaching young Children to stand upon their Hands, before know how to make use of their Legs. . . .

For the Style of Poetry is so remote from the vulgar Manner of Expression, that to imitate it in Prose, would be the most ridiculous thing in the World; and he would be sure to set every body a laughing at him, that should pretend to write a History in the Strain of Virgil's Æneid, or Horace's Lyricks. To prevent therefore their confounding those two different Styles, it will be necessary to make them read the Historians well in the first place: By so doing, they will learn the genuine and proper Signification of Words, and use them accordingly: They will not be misled by the figurative Use of Words, Phraseology, and Forms of Construction proper only for Poetry; nor need they fear to imitate the Language of their Authors: Whereas in the Reading of the Poets, the Case would be quite otherwise; there they could borrow nothing, without rendering their Style very bombastick and ridiculous.

V. Another Oversight in the common Method of Teaching, is *making Boys get their Lessons in the Poets without Book* [by heart—Ed]. If this be proper, why is it not equally so, to take the same Method with them in Prose, and make them commit to Memory every Lesson they read there too? But if this be absurd, as I suppose every body will readily grant, why is not the other so too? For what is it that Boys do in getting any thing without book, but learn the Order of the Words? . . . But as Mr. *Locke* has very well exposed this simple Custom, in his Thoughts of Education [sic], and has said all upon the Point that I think can well be said, I shall, I hope, oblige my Reader much more by presenting him with the Words of that great Master of Education, than by enlarging my self upon the Matter. They are as follows.

> Another thing very ordinary in the vulgar method of grammar schools there is, of which I see no Use at all, unless it be to baulk young Lads in the Way to learning Languages, which, in my Opinion, should be made as easy and pleasant as may be; and that which was painful in it, as much as possible, quite removed. That which I mean, and here complain of, is, their being forced to

learn by heart, great Parcels of the Authors which are taught them; wherein I can discover no Advantage at all, especially to the Business they are upon. Languages are to be learnt only by Reading and Talking, and not by Scraps of Authors got by heart. . . .

I do not mean hereby, that there should be no Exercise given to Childrens Memories: I think their Memories should be employ'd, but not in learning by rote whole Pages out of Books, which, the Lesson being once said, and that Task over, are delivered up again to Oblivion, and neglected for ever. This mends neither the Memory nor the Mind. . . . They should learn by heart out of Authors . . . such wise and useful Sentences . . . they should never be suffered to forget again, but be often call'd to an account for them; whereby, besides the Use those Sayings may be to them in their future Life, as so many good Rules and Observations, they will be taught to reflect often, and bethink themselves what they have to remember, which is the only Way to make the Memory quick and useful. The Custom of frequent Reflection will keep their Minds from running adrift, and call their Thoughts home from useless unattentive Roving: And, therefore, I think, it may do well, to give them something every Day to remember; but something still that is in it self worth the remembring, and what you would never have out of Mind whenever you call, or they themselves search for it. This will oblige them often to turn their Thoughts inwards, than which you cannot wish them a better intellectual Habit."

VI. Another thing that in the common Method of our Schools proves a great Impediment to the Progress of Boys, is, *The putting them on too many several things at the same Time.* Thus 'tis usual for them to be engaged in the Reading of half a dozen Authors, or more, and almost as many several sorts of Exercise at once. Nay, I know a publick School, and in no obscure Place, where the Boys, by that time they reach Virgil, are plyed with such a Multiplicity of Authors, that *poor Virgil* takes his turn but for one Lesson a Week amongst them: A most admirable Method, to be sure, to make Boys understand that admirable Author! I am clearly of Opinion, that such a Man deserves more to be whipt for his Folly, than any Boy he teaches. Would not any one be thought half crazed, that should pretend to carry on his Studies in so confused a manner, by engaging in ten or a dozen Authors at a time? And shall that be a proper Method to be taken with Boys, that would pass for little less than Madness in a Man? I could never yet hear any Reason alledged for this wonderful way of proceeding. . . .

But the putting Boys too soon to the Reading of *Greek,* is, I think, one of the greatest Grievances of the common Method. It is very frequent to enter them in the *Greek Grammar,* before they have Skill enough in Latin to understand the Rules of it, than which nothing can be more ridiculous. This is design'd sure to impose upon the Parents, by making them believe their Sons are wonderful Scholars, rather than for the Childrens Improvement. The Father oftentimes understands not so much as the Character of that Language: And how can he chuse but take his Son for a downright Conjurer, when he finds him able to read a Book he cannot tell a Letter in, to his great astonishment? Tho' there be no more Mystery in the matter, than in the Reading of English. His Son is a brave Scholar, the Master an incomparable Man, and the Father very happy in the mighty Conceit he has of both; when the poor Child all this while is a mere Ignoramus in the most common Rules of Grammar: And as for the Reading a Latin Author, knows little more of it than the Father, who himself knows nothing at all. Something of this nature, I imagine, has given rise to this silly senseless Custom of our Schools. Besides, this Piece of ill Method is attended with this woful Misfortune upon such Boys as are design'd for Trades, and therefore stay not long enough to go thorough [sic] the School; that they spend their time there (which is often six or seven Years) to no manner of purpose at all. Whereas, were it not for this Custom of putting Boys upon the *Greek Tongue,* before they understand any thing of Latin, such Boys might attain to a pretty competent Skill in the latter, or however go away much better Latinists than they do. By which means they would be enabled to understand what they read, if they have a mind to apply themselves to reading, much better than they could do without it. And as most of your genteeler Tradesmen have a great deal of time upon their hands for Reading, why they should not be encourag'd to it, and prepar'd for it at School, I do not understand. For how much soever some People may ridicule the Custom of sending Boys to Grammar-Schools, that are design'd for Trades; yet certainly a familiar Acquaintance with the Latin Tongue, Chronology and Geography, all which might be attain'd in less time than such Boys usually spend at School to no manner of purpose, would be of vast Advantage to those that have time enough upon their hands for Reading, and the most likely means to tempt them to it, and make them in love with a Book.

VII. *The putting Boys upon Exercise above their Years or Improvement, is another unhappy Oversight in the common Method of Education.* They usually begin much too soon with Dialogues and Epistles, for which they cannot be supposed duly prepared, till they have pretty well digested their Grammar Rules. If you set them to such Work sooner, the Invention of Matter will so employ and perplex their Thoughts, that they will not be at liberty to reflect upon, and consider their Rules: And thus, whilst one thing justles out another, they must needs make a very slow progress. But whatsoever may be said in vindication of the common Method, as to this particular; I am sure, the putting Boys upon the Exercise of *Themes* and *Verses*, so soon as is usually done, is capable of no manner of Defence. These Exercises are thought of absolute necessity in the Education of a Scholar, with which the poor Boys are so unmercifully teazed, that by the Time they spend in them, and the great Noise and Bustle made about them, one would be tempted to think, sure all the Happiness of Heaven and Earth depended upon the Success of their Endeavours that way; or at least, that those Exercises were a wonderful Improvement to a Boy's Parts: And yet having consider'd the Matter for some time, I cannot but be much of Mr. *Locke's* Mind, with respect to versifying however. I will grant, if you please, it may not be amiss to employ Boys now and then, in making little Discourses upon the Passions, Virtues, Vices, or any Moral Subject, when their Minds are by the Reading of Latin and Greek Authors, and the Master's Discourses upon them, when any Points of Morality come in his way, furnish'd with a pretty competent Knowledge of those Things, and they can express themselves pretty properly and handsomely in the Latin

Tongue. But to put Boys upon such sort of Work, before they are well able to read a plain Latin Author, and are so far from writing any thing tolerably well in that Language, that they have scarce digested the plainest and most necessary and useful Rules of their Syntax, is perhaps one of the most absurd ridiculous things in the world. It is not only an Egyptian Tyranny, as Mr. *Locke* properly calls it, but devours their time to no purpose, when they are obliged in the frequent returns of this dismal Task, to beat their Brains hours together, to hammer out a little nonsense in very ill Language, which might be spent to a thousand times better purpose, in the Reading of Authors, or other Exercises more suitable to their Years and Improvement, and more proportionate to the Parts of young Boys, than Themes and Verses; which require the Sense and Understanding of a grown Man, to perform tolerably well. . . .

VIII. The eighth and last Charge against the vulgar Method of Teaching, is, the *putting Boys upon Greek Exercise*, as is frequently done in our Schools; but to what purpose, I must own, I am not able to comprehend; unless it be to mispend their time, in what is never like to be of any manner of use to them. For what sort of Business, or what kind of Company is it, I wonder, that can ever make the Writing or Speaking of Greek, necessary? Who ever writes Greek, unless a whimsical Fellow to shew his Learning sometimes in a Copy of Verses? Which, I suppose, the World was never yet the better for, nor ever will. And whether this be the most likely way to the Reputation of something more than ordinary amongst the Men of Letters, or to expose the Pride and Vanity of a Man's Heart, to such as have the Sense to distinguish betwixt solid, useful Knowledge, and a fantastical kind of Learning, of no manner of use to Mankind; I leave to the Consideration of such as have an Itch to be shewing their parts that way. For since Latin is by common Consent become the Language of the learned World, and no more than one is, or can be necessary, to keep up a free Commerce and Intercourse betwixt the Men of Letters in the several parts of it; I should be very glad to be informed, how the Writing or Speaking of Greek can be any ways useful. . . . All the time Boys have to spend at School, is little enough for the attaining of but a tolerable Latin Style, and I doubt the Number is but very small of those that do arrive to it. What therefore can be the Meaning of those Gentlemen that will needs pretend to make Boys Masters of a Greek Style as well as the Latin? I am afraid it is a sign they themselves must be ignorant in both; or they would hardly attempt a thing so impossible to be attain'd. . . . It is therefore sufficient to bring Boys to the Reading of an easy Author in Greek; that is all that can be done for them at School, with respect to that Language: to pretend to make them write it, when they have not time so much as to attain to a familiar Reading of it, is a vain ridiculous Attempt, and utterly impracticable. . . .

Having thus demolished an ugly old Building, thrown away the Rubbish, and cleared the Ground, we shall now proceed to the erecting of one more regular, beautiful, and convenient. . . .

The first thing a Boy is to be instructed in at a Grammar-School is the Declension of Nouns. . . .

After a Boy is pretty perfect in the Examples of his Declensions, he must proceed to the *Verbs*, and get the Examples of the four Conjugations in the Active and Passive Voice, perfectly without Book. . . .

I have already declared my self against putting any more Grammar upon Boys, till they begin to read the easier Classics pretty well; and having given my Reasons for it, I shall therefore now proceed . . . to inform the Reader, what Authors I judge most proper for Boys to read, and in what Order. . . .

The Book Boys begin with in many Schools, is *Sententiæ Pueriles;* but it may very justly be questioned, whether a Book, consisting wholly of a Parcel of dry, moral Sayings, be altogether so convenient for the use of Children, as old Men. Upon which account, I think, it might more properly be called *Sententiæ Seniles*, than *Pueriles*, as being better suited to the Reading of those of that Age, than young Boys, who have no Apprehension, or Relish for such kind of things. The Matter of

Cordery's Colloquies is such kind of Tittle-Tattle for the most part, as passes betwixt Boys, and therefore finds a more easy Entrance into their Minds, and is therefore most proper for them to begin with. The Classic Authors are, I think, all too difficult for them. We want indeed an Introduction to the Classics. For tho' *Cordery*, and *Erasmus*, are Books proper enough for them to read, in order to bring them acquainted with the most common Words of the Language; yet perhaps something further would be convenient to prepare them more effectually for the Reading of the Classic Authors. For all the Parts of their Business should be so contrived, that one might be an Inlet or Introduction to another, and the Boys proceed all along by insensible Steps of Difference, from what is more easy, to what is more difficult. But the Subject Matter of Cordery, and Erasmus, has so very little Affinity with that of the Classick Authors that are to follow them, that is, the Historians, that they do not prepare them so well as might be wished for the Reading of them. They come to them Strangers to the most trite and common Words and Phrases in them. I could wish therefore we had some Piece of useful History compiled in a plain, easy, Latin Style, with the Words placed in their natural Order, that is, the same they have in the English Tongue, with a Translation as literal as possible. Till such a Help can be had, about a Hundred of *Cordery's Colloquies*, and eight or ten of the most comical, diverting Dialogues in *Erasmus*, I think they should read before they meddle with a Classick Author.

When they have done with Erasmus, it will be time to enter them in the *Classicks*. And here care must be taken to begin with the easiest first. I know none plainer than *Cæsar's Commentaries*. The Style of them is as Natural and Easy, as any thing in good Latin can well be, without Dress, or Affectation, rhetorical Flourishes, or studied Turns to disguise the Sense. . . . When Cæsar begins to grow easy, and you find they generally understand him pretty well, without the help of their Translation; you may enter them in *Justin*, and make them read the first Books as far as the Death of Alexander the Great. . . . *Cornelius Nepos* I would recommend as most proper to be made use of in the next place. The Reading this Author will bring to mind several things in Justin: And enlarge their Acquaintance with the History of Greece. After him, let them proceed to the Roman History, beginning with *Eutropius,* which must be follow'd by *Florus.* . . . The more important Transactions and memorable Occurrences must be inculcated upon them by a reiterated and frequent Perusal of them. Such, for instance, as the Life of Cyrus, the Founder of the Persian Monarchy; Xerxes's Expedition into Greece; the great Actions of Epaminondas; Philip of Macedon and Alexander the Great; the Building of Rome; the Expulsion of the Tarquins; the Institution of the Decemviri, and the Tribunes of the Commons; the Burning of Rome by the Gauls; the Carthaginian and Civil Wars, etc.

After they have read Florus over, it may be convenient to enter them in *Terence;* an Author whose Style is of a different Complexion from the former; occasion'd by the different Nature of the Subjects he treats upon. His Language being very pure, and just such as was spoke by Persons of the best Quality in Rome, in Matters of common Conversation, will be of great use to them in the writing of Dialogues, and speaking Latin. . . .

This Advice will, I doubt not, appear shocking to such as are prejudiced in behalf of the vulgar Method of proceeding, that Boys should read so much Prose, and ten times more than is usually read at School, by such as go from thence to an University, without ever meddling all the while with any more of Grammar, than the Declension of Nouns and the Formation of Verbs, &c. But how wide soever this is of the common Method of proceeding, it is nevertheless just and reasonable, as a little Consideration may satisfy any reasonable Man. There are two things requisite in the learning of a Language: The Knowledge of Words, and Skill to put them together in Writing or Speaking. The former is, beyond all question, much the more easy of the two; and by consequence ought to go first; and to intermix any foreign Stuff, as Grammar, with it, is throwing a rub in Boys way, and hindering their Progress. They are to be kept to but one thing at once, as much as may be. To trouble them with Variety at the same time, unless by way of refreshing their Memories, or to prevent their forgetting what they have already learnt, is, I think a grand Mistake in Education, and one main occasion of that miserable work Boys make of it, in most Schools. . . .

After Boys have done with Terence, it will be time to think of entering them in *Geography.* . . . *Geography* is so useful and pleasant a part of Learning, and withal so necessary for a Scholar, that I cannot but wonder it should be so little regarded as it is; especially since Boys will learn it with a great deal of Ease and Pleasure: For the Sight of a *Map* is as entertaining to them as a picture. . . . It will be the master's fault only, if they are not considerable proficients, both in *ancient and modern geography*, before they leave school . . . .

When they have read Terence well twice over, it may be time to enter them in the Poets, beginning with *Ovid's Metamorphoses*, not only as the easiest, but likewise an Introduction to the rest, by giving an Account of those Fictions and Fables so often alluded to, and hinted at by them. . . .

After they have done with Ovid, they may proceed to the *Greek Grammar*, and keep to that only, till they have master'd their Nouns and Verbs . . . . After they are pretty perfect in their Nouns and Verbs, they must be enter'd in the *Greek Testament*, and kept to that only, till it begins to grow something easy to them; then they may proceed to *Virgil*, reading that and the Greek Testament by turns, and so continue to read one Greek and one Latin Author alternately. . . .

When Boys have read the Gospels and Acts in Greek, (for I do not think it necessary they should go over the Epistles too) they may proceed to *Herodian*, and after they have read him over, go on in *Zosimus*, for their further Improvement in the History of the Romans. As for Poets in this Language, *Homer* ought to lead the Van; not only as the most ancient and necessary for the understanding of the Poets, Historians, and other Authors in both Languages, who frequently allude to him; but as the most easy too. Ten or twelve Books in his *Iliad*, well read twice over, will enable them to read that Author almost every where extempore. After him may follow *Heriod* and *Theocri-tus,* which, I think, will be Greek enough for them at School.

Having thus laid before the Reader what Authors I judge most proper for Boys to read at School, together with the Order in which they are to be read, I proceed now to say something of Exercise. . . .

The *Making of Latin* is to Boys the most difficult Part of their Business; and therefore great Allowances must be made for weak and tender Minds, not capable of that Attention and Labour of Thought required in the Matter, for the Consideration of so many several things at once. The right Management of Children, and the carrying it in a due Mean betwixt a rigorous Severity, on the one side, and too slack a Hand, on the other, is a nice Point. It is hard to distinguish betwixt such Faults in their Latin, as are to be imputed to a blameable Neglect, or wilful Carelessness on the one hand, or the natural Weakness and Unsteadiness of their Minds, on the other, that it will require a good Share of Prudence in the Master to do it to any tolerable degree. He must be content to correct a great many Mistakes in their Exercise, without whipping, or so much as chiding them for them; for those are never to be made use of, but for the amending of some visible and notorious Fault in them. But then you'll say, it is to be feared that Boys eager of their Game will take the advantage of the Master's Easiness, and put him off with any thing. This is indeed to be feared; and here lies the Difficulty; for which it is so hard to prescribe Rules, that the Matter must be left to the Master's Discretion: Only I would caution him against leaning too much on the side of Severity, as I doubt is too commonly done. It's hard indeed to conceive it possible for Boys to commit so many Oversights as they usually do, against Rules they know very well, and have for a long time made use of, without being very careless, and upon that account justly liable to Punishment; and yet it's plain such Slips will scape them, tho' they understand their Rules perfectly well; and that in spite of all the chiding and whipping that can be used. This in the main therefore is not to be imputed to want of Care in them; for it's certain, there is nothing made of Flesh and Blood could undergo such a Discipline, as I fear Boys do in many places, for a Fault that was easily mended. The Master may take it for granted they cannot help far the greatest part of the Blunders they commit. They cannot reflect upon all the Variety of Rules they have occasion for, without Confusion; and it's in-vain to expect it from them, till long Practice has opened and enlarged their Minds, and settled in them a Habit of tranferring their Thoughts with Ease and Quickness, to so many various Considerations as are necessary in the Writing of Latin.

I know there are some People in the World altogether against the Learning of Languages by *Grammar;* and Mr. *Locke* in his *Thoughts of Education,* [sic], advises the Learning of Latin by use only, without the Perplexity of Rules: But I could never yet see any great reason to be of his Opinion. Not that in a private Education, where a young Gentleman has a Tutor that is a good Master of the Language, and speaks it well, he would not more readily attain the use of the Latin Tongue that way, than if he was to proceed in the common Method of the Schools: Yet I believe he would do it much sooner, if with constant use, he had the Assistance of some plain and easy Rules, and was made to proceed methodically, from such as are most easy, and of most general use, reducing them to Practice, by the Translation of proper English, given him for that purpose. . . . I am apt to think, it was only that abominable loss of time, occasioned by an ill use of an ill-contrived Grammar in Latin, that prejudiced so great a Man as Mr. *Locke* against the use of any Grammar at all. . . .

After they have attained a pretty good Stock of proper Words and Phrases, for common Conversation, they may be advanced to the making of *Epistles,* both *English* and *Latin.* This, of all the Exercises Boys are put upon at School, is perhaps the most useful and necessary; and what they should be kept pretty constantly to, after they once begin, till their leaving the School. I propose the Writing of *English Epistles* as well as *Latin,* for their Improvement in their own Language; a thing to be regarded and taken care of, as of infinitely more Use and Importance than the Writing and Speaking of *Latin.*

And it's a surprizing thing, that tho' we have the Example of the old Greeks and Romans for this, who were at a world of pains to bring themselves to an easy, proper, elegant Use of their own Language; and tho' the Reason of the thing speaks aloud of itself, there should be no manner of Care taken of Youth as to this matter; but the English Tongue laid aside, as a sorry, silly, insignificant thing; and their whole Time taken up betwixt Latin and Greek: But I am prevented upon this head by Mr. *Locke*, and therefore to him I refer my Reader. . . .

The last sort of Exercise Boys are to be put upon at School, is *Themes*. . . . This, I say, ought to be the last sort of Exercise they are to be set to at School; for they cannot be reasonably supposed in any tolerable measure qualified for it, till they have in good degree attain'd the Idiom, and have got the peculiar Turn of a Latin Style; till they begin to think and write something like Men. Then perhaps it may not be wholly useless to exercise them that way, not so much for their Improvement in the Latin Tongue (for the other Exercises are more proper for that purpose) as for the cultivating their Reason, by obliging them to study Morality, the most useful of all the Sciences, to form their Minds, and by giving them a right Sense of Things, to prepare them to act their parts like Men when they come to appear upon the Stage of the World. . . .

But if Boys are to be put to this sort of Exercise, the most proper way of entering them in it, would be, I think, for the Master to put into their hands *Themes* of his own Composing, for their perusal and imitation . . . . *Tully's Offices*, as well as *Seneca*, should be recommended to their private Reading at home, as Books that will furnish them with Thoughts and Language proper for their Purpose, in the Making of Themes. . . .

But of all Books, I know none so proper to be put into their hands, as the *Spectators*. They will not only furnish them with just and fine Thoughts, upon a great Variety of moral Subjects, very proper to enter into their Compositions of this kind, but will be of great service to them, in other respects. They will not only receive a great Advantage from the frequent Perusal of them, with regard to their Improvement in their own Language, but become acquainted with the World, before they go into it. And as they have there the various Vices, Follies, and Whimseys of Mankind, very finely, and elegantly, exposed, and ridiculed, the Mind may from thence receive an early Tincture, and contract a timely Aversion, for what it ought to hate, before it has been imposed upon by Custom and Fashion. . . .

And to prevent that Confusion and Want of Clearness, so visible in your Men of Oratory and Declamation, let the Minds of Boys, as soon as capable of it, be furnish'd with *clear and distinct Ideas,* of the things they read; especially in *Divinity* and *Morality,* as being, above all other parts of Literature, of the greatest Concern to Mankind. They should be frequently warn'd against that Abuse of Language which consists in using Words, through Want of Care, for Ideas different from those to which common Use has annexed them, or without any settled determinate Meaning at all; a Fault which Men, even Authors that make a very great Noise in the World; and are look'd upon as the very Standards of Truth and good Language, are apt to be guilty of. This Caution is of the greatest Use to enable a Man to steer his Course aright towards Truth, and true Happiness. And it is to the Want of it chiefly, we must impute the various Errors, which make such wild Distraction and Confusion in the World. Let but the Mind be furnished with clear and distinct Ideas upon such Subjects, as are of the greatest Concern to Men to be inform'd in; and the way to the weightiest Truths, upon which depend the Peace and good Order of this World, with the Happiness of the next, will be made smooth and easy. The Master cannot therefore be too careful to implant in the Minds of Youth, an habitual Cautiousness against a careless Use of Words, inuring them to reflect upon those they make use of; by asking them now and then, what they mean by them; letting them understand, that it is too common a Practice for Men to have Words in their Mouths without any distinct Meaning; and that therefore, it behoves them to have a care of being guilty of the Folly of talking like Parrots.

By that time Boys are fit to be enter'd in Greek, or sooner, it may be convenient to bring them acquainted with the *Pub-lick-News*, by making them read the *Evening-Post*, or some other *News-Paper constantly*. . . .

Whilst Boys are getting the Greek Tongue, it will not be amiss to put into their hands *Dionysius Petavius's Rationarium Temporum:* From the second Part of which, the Master may quickly teach them as much *Chronology* as will be necessary for the more orderly digesting what History they read in their Memories. I rather recommend this than *Strauchius;* because, besides the Epochs made use of in History, and other things of that nature, it contains a succinct and methodical Account of the Affairs of Mankind, down from the Creation of the World, to the last Century, which will be of great use to them; not only to revive the Memory, of what they read in their Greek and Roman Authors, but likewise to acquaint them with the most remarkable Revolutions and Transactions, that have been in the World, since the Dissolution of the Roman Empire. Perhaps it may be convenient, to acquaint them more particularly with the History of their Native Country, by putting into their hands such a Book as *Medulla Historiæ Anglicanæ*. These they should be ordered to read at spare Hours by themselves at home, that they may not interrupt the Course of their other Business in the School; only the *Technical* Part of *Chronology* will require a little of the Master's Assistance.

Nor will Boys, if rightly managed, be so averse to spend their Time, when out of the Master's sight, after this manner. It is the Fault of an ill Method of Education, I am apt to believe, generally speaking, and not the Boys, that they have no greater Inclination for Books and Study. They understand so little, I believe, for the most part, of what they read, perfectly well, and as they should do, and are so hardly and severely used withal, that it is no wonder, if they have so little stomach to what they cannot but look upon as the Occasion of all their Woe. And they would, no doubt of it, have as great a Dislike to their best beloved Sports and Diversions, as they have to their Books, if they should procure them as much ill Usage for eight or ten Years together, as the latter usually do. Let but Boys be gently managed without such abundance of Whipping and

Scourging for their Books: Let them proceed regularly, and by insensible steps of Difference, from what is easy and suited to their tender Capacities, to what is more difficult, without being puzzled and perplexed by the use of Authors or Exercise, above their Years or Improvement; see they have every thing made as smooth, easy, and delightful as possible; that they be gently help'd over the Difficulties and Rubs that are in their way, without Blows and ill Language: Let their Minds be satisfied with a perfect Comprehension of what they read, and I am confident, you will find the Aversion they usually have to Study and Application, is not to be imputed to Nature, but something else. Knowledge is naturally grateful and acceptable to the Mind, and nothing almost could render the Charms of Learning ineffectual, but the slavish Discipline of the Rod.

I say not this, that I think that Instrument of Correction is never to be made use of; it will be necessary at least for the Punishment of Vice. . . . But this I shall be bold to say, That for once a Boy, in the common Management of the Schools, suffers for any Fault in his Business, really his own, he is punished twice at least for those of his Master, or the Method he makes use of. For till I see a Reformation in the vulgar Manner of educating Youth, I must be of opinion, that for one Blunder a Boy is really to blame for, he must commit several, which are to be charged upon want of Method, or a due Way of proceeding in the Master. And if the Money laid out in Rods, was but duly distributed amongst the diligent and orderly Boys, for their Encouragement; such at least as have any great share of Parts, and Ingenuity withal, would by that means be as effectually moved to behave well, and mind their Books, as by whipping and lashing, I should think; with this great Advantage beside, that they will hereby be made in love with their Master, and their Books too: whereas the rough Discipline of the Lash, will be sure to create in them an utter Aversion for both.

Another Method to prevent the Use and Necessity of the Lash, is for the Master to commend and caress those that do well, and advance them according to their Merit. . . . The Master must be sure to act with the utmost Impartiality: Nothing must ever entitle a Boy to any distinguishing Favour, but Diligence, and an orderly Carriage. The poorest and meanest must be in this case always upon a level with those of the highest Quality. Nothing is here to be regarded but Merit. Partiality will spoil all, give the Boys an ill opinion of their Master, and breed ill Blood and Quarrels amongst them. But a steady Impartiality will prevent all murmuring, and raise such a Spirit of innocent Emulation and Industry, as will make the use of the Rod almost wholly needless. . . .

Another Contrivance the Master may make use of to spur up Boys to Industry and good Behaviour, and thereby spare the Rod, is to give them now and then *leave to play*, when they behave better than ordinary. This, from the natural Gaiety of their Tempers, and that strong Desire in them of being Masters of their Time, they are hugely fond of, that to gratify now and then that Inclination in them, sweetens their Humour, and obliges them beyond expression. . . .

If therefore Boys can be brought by gentle Methods to the use of a good degree of Application to their Business, and to acquit themselves pretty handsomely, tho' they do not do their utmost, or exert all that Diligence, which by the dint of hard whipping they might be brought to; I think it will be best to let the rugged Discipline of the Lash quite alone, the Remedy being, to my Apprehension, much worse than the Disease it is design'd to cure.

When a Man comes from a Life of Ease and Pleasure in an University, or from some undisturbed way of passing his Hours in a Curacy, or a Living, to engage in the teaching of a Grammar-School, he is got into a new World, where every Hour presents him with various Occasions of Chagrine and Vexation. The Roguishness of one Boy, the Dulness of another, the Stubbornness of a third, and the Carelessness or Giddiness of all, disturb him beyond all patience. And if he be a Man of quick Resentment, as Men of Parts, and a lively brisk Temper (a very useful Ingredient in the Composition of a School-Master) usually are, the first Thought is to lay about him, in order to be revenged upon the troublesome Company he finds himself engaged in, and procure a little Quiet, if possible. This has some little Effect, it may be, for the Removal of some Causes of Uneasiness, for the present; which are soon breaking out again, and then cured again in the same manner. But there are some constant Occasions of Disturbance, that will not give way to all the Thunder of his Tongue, or the Heaviness of his Arm. Giddiness and Dulness still continue in defiance to both. These, which have their Root and Foundation in Nature, and are therefore not to be wholly removed, he, for want of Experience in Children, calls Idleness or Carelessness, and therefore immediately resolves upon a constant Course of thrashing, and like an honest Man, determines to whip those Vices out of them, cost what Leather it will, since he stands to no Repairs. Years, it may be, are spent in this fruitless Pursuit of Ease and Success, which seem to fly before him, as fast as he can follow, till at last wearied with a Pursuit, which he finds to very little purpose, he drops his Industry and Severity together; and laying aside all Care and Concern for his Charge, lets all go at Sixes and Sevens, and gives himself up to a lazy, indolent Life. This, I fear, is too oft another ill Consequence of an indiscreet Use of the whipping Method; and therefore to prevent that, . . . too much Care and Contrivance cannot be used, to avoid the Necessity of coming to that dangerous and woful Extremity.

I shall say no more upon this Head, but refer my Reader to *that great Master of the Art of Education, Mr. Locke.* His Book deserves to be well read and consider'd by every School-Master. For tho' most of the Lessons he gives are adapted to a private Education, and therefore not practicable in a School; yet there are here and there some things, which a prudent Master may make his advantage of. But that Book, in my Opinion, above all others, deserves the most serious Consideration of all sober thinking Gentlemen, that are in good earnest concern'd for the Welfare of their own Children, and the Nation too. If the Method there laid down for a private Education (which is certainly the most proper for a Gentleman) was duly followed by those whose Circumstances very well enable them to bear the Expence, it would produce, I believe, another kind of Reformation in the World, than any Means yet made use of,

ever did. For, as that Great Man rightly observes in the Dedication of his Book, "If the Gentlemen are by their Education
once set right, they will quickly bring all the rest into Order."

Virtue, as I took notice in the Beginning, should be the
principal Thing aim'd at in Education, since every thing else
Youth are to be instructed in, receives its Value from it; and is
of little Use, nay for the most part dangerous and mischievous
without it: Learning in a vicious Man being something like a
Sword in the Hands of a mad Man. And tho' the Care of Youth,
in this Particular, does more properly belong to the Parents and
Ministers, than the Master, no more being usually expected
from him, than that he should give the Boys due Correction,
whenever he catches them in any Vice at School; yet, I think,
it may very well become him, to concern himself a little further,
in a Matter of so much Consequence; where all his Care and
Instruction, joined to that of the Parents and Ministers, will be
little enough to prevent the Contagion of Vice, and the Growth
of evil Habits. For this purpose, right Notions of *God* and
Religion should be instill'd into their Minds now and then, as
Occasion may offer, in the reading of Authors. . . .

The Idea of an *Almighty Being,* that made and governs the
World, sees and knows every thing, and from whom no Secrets
are hid, should be form'd in them, and inculcated betimes, as
the Foundation of all Religion. For, how innate soever some
People may imagine it to be; 'tis certain, if due care be not
taken to implant this Idea in the Minds of Youth, the Generality will but have very odd Thoughts of him, and such as will
derogate very much from the infinite Grandeur and Majesty of
that Eternal Being, and have little more Influence upon them
than none at all. . . .

I would likewise have the Arguments upon which the Credi-
bility of the Christian Religion is founded, laid before
them. . . .

I am well aware, it will be a great Surprize upon some
People, to hear talk of Boys at School being troubled with
Things of this nature. This they'll say is to confound the Busi-
ness of a School-Master, with that of a Divinity Professor. I

cannot help it, if it be; this I am sure of, that these are Things of the greatest Concern to them, with respect to the Life they are to lead here upon Earth, as well as that to come, and therefore, if they are in any measure capable of understanding them before they leave the School, as, in this Method of Education, I think they will: there can be no Objection against what I have advised, worth an Answer. . . .

It will not be foreign to the Design of an Essay upon Education, to say something here, concerning *the Qualifications requisite in a School-master*. For which purpose it is necessary to reflect upon the great End of Education, which is to instill into the Minds of Youth a Love of Virtue and Knowledge; and to give them such an Insight into the learned Languages, Geography, History, Chronology, &c. as may enable them to proceed therein by themselves, with ease and pleasure. From hence it follows, that a School-master ought to be,

1. In the first place, a Man of *Virtue*. For . . . it be the main End of Education to make virtuous Men. . . .

2. A School-master ought to have *a pretty large Acquaintance with the Latin Tongue;* by which I mean, that he ought at least to have made all the Classick Authors, that are ever read in Schools, very familiar to him, by a frequent and often-repeated Perusal of them, with the Notes of the best Criticks upon them. This is a Qualification, which every one, upon the least Reflection, must allow to be absolutely necessary; and yet how few are there, concerned in the Education of Youth, that have gone even this short length? For short it is, in comparison of the Extent of the Latin Tongue, and the Number of the Number of the Classick Authors, which are far more than either are, or can be read in Grammar-Schools. The business of teaching . . . is generally in the hands of such as were designed for, and are actually engaged in, other Work; who betwixt both Employs, must have little or no Time to spare for the Study of the Classicks. Men so engaged usually content themselves with what they read at School, as indeed they must, if they are faithful in the Discharge of the double Task they have upon their hands. The business of teaching School, if it is attended as it

ought to be, leaves but little time for Study, and less Inclination, unless a Man have a singular Constitution both of Body and Mind. But when to that Business the Cure of Souls is added, he must have a great deal less, if he minds both as he should do, and that indeed be possible, which I make some question of; for in my poor Judgment, either of them alone is Business enough for one Man.

3. A School-Master should be able *to talk the Latin Tongue pretty readily and properly.* . . .

4. As for the *Greek Tongue,* I do not think it absolutely necessary, a Master should have as extensive a Knowledge of it as Latin. For as that is a Language not at all necessary for a Gentleman as such, but only for those that are to live by their Learning, as Tutors, School-masters, and Clergymen; and besides, as Youth have not Time at School, to make any great Progress in it, the less of it may suffice a Master. If he can read the *Greek Testament, Homer's Iliad,* and some other few easy Authors, such as are commonly read at Schools, well, that may perhaps be all that is very necessary. . . .

5. A School-master ought, in my opinion, *to be a Philosopher.* I do not mean that it is necessary he should be profoundly skilled in the Mathematicks, with their Application to Nature, and experimental Philosophy; but I would have him well read in the finest Treatises of *Logick* and *Morality,* and very conversant in the Writings of such great Masters of the Art of Reasoning, as *Episcopius, Chillingworth,* and *Locke.* By this means he will attain to think and talk clearly upon Subjects of the highest Importance, and so be better enabled to descant upon Authors, and furnish his Scholars with useful Reflections upon them, for their Improvement in Morality, and the Conduct of Life: which a Man must needs be but indifferently qualified for, that has taken no care for the Improvement of his Reason. For Men are not born to the Faculties of Thinking, and Talking clearly: those valuable Endowments will not come in course with Years and Conversation, but are principally the Product of Study, and Exercise, and no otherwise attainable to any great degree. And of the two, I must own, I would rather have a Man deficient in the Languages than in

this Qualification: for the former without the latter will signify not very much; but the latter, without a masterly Skill in the former, may signify a great deal, and enable a Man to acquit himself to much better purpose, in the Instruction of his Charge, than the Critique of a shallow confused Head, stuffed with little else besides Words. The Art of Reasoning well, is the greatest and noblest Endowment of a human Mind, next to Virtue itself; and the Man that is happy in the Enjoyment of that Talent, will ever distinguish himself in all the Business he engages in. And as a rational Method of proceeding is no where more necessary, or of more importance, than in the Affair of Education, a Master of a strong clear Head, tho' his Knowledge of the Languages be but moderate, will yet have vastly the advantage of, and acquit himself in his Profession with much better Success, than a meer Grammarian or Critick possibly can.

6. A School-master ought *to be a good Master of his own Language,* or Mother-Tongue . . . .

7. A School-master should *be well acquainted with the old and new Geography, and know something of Chronology.* I mention not *History,* because so much of it as he can have any great occasion for, will be got in qualifying himself with a competent Knowledge of the Latin and Greek Tongues, most of the Books he must read for the purpose being historical, and all together making up a pretty good System of ancient History, as much as will be necessary for a School-master, tho' indeed he can never have too much of it. . . .

From what has been said above, I think we may infer, that the Number of those that are duly qualified for the Business of a School-Master, is not so great, as perhaps is usually supposed. It is not every Stripling from the University, tho' of a sober, regular Behaviour, that can or ought to be looked upon, as well enough fitted for the important Charge of educating Youth. . . . A Man must sit close to his Studies for some Years, after he has left a College, before he can be handsomely qualified for it. And yet where is the Man to be met with, that ever pursues his Studies with such a View? Men educated to Letters, as well as the World about them, usually think the Learning that has been acquired at School and University together, abundantly sufficient for the purpose. And therefore but few perhaps are to be found, among such as engage in the Profession of teaching a Grammar-School, that follow their Studies, with any direct Intention of fitting themselves for it. They take it for granted their Education has already done that sufficiently, and therefore but seldom, I fear, trouble their heads much further about the matter. For indeed a School is usually looked upon as a Step into the World only, which a Man of Parts may content himself with for a while, till he can attain to more easy, and more profitable Preferment; but few such undertake that sort of Work, with a design to make it the Business of their Lives, nor are those that do not, to be therefore blamed at all. It is too rugged and barren an Employment, to engage Men of Sense and Learning for Life, that have any possibility of arriving at the means of greater Ease and Plenty, as such Persons usually have. A Man well qualified for the teaching of a Grammar School, is qualified for better Preferment; and when that falls out, unless his Passion for Gain be very strong in him, he will certainly quit so laborious and fruitless an Employment, as that generally is. For the Encouragement thereto is almost everywhere trifling, far from a reasonable Compensation for the Trouble and Vexation that attends it; in which respect, no sort of Business that Men of Letters, as such, are engaged in, is to be compared with it. . . .

In my opinion, it is neither for the Honour or Interest of the Kingdom, that an Employment which might be rendered so exceedingly useful to the Publick, should be so little regarded and encouraged. The Profession undoubtedly requires Men of uncommon Attainments, not to be come at, but by the use of good Parts, in a close Application to Study, Men of ingenuous Minds, Lovers of Knowledge and Virtue, and of indefatigable Industry. Now for such Men, besides the continual teazing and plague of their Business, to be cramped in their Fortunes, and to be so far from being in a Condition of making any decent handsome Provision for their Families, that they cannot, over above the scanty Supply of present Wants, afford to furnish a single Room, a Study, I mean, in a proper manner, for the Entertainment of their leisure Hours, and their further Improvement in the Business of their Profession; is certainly a very great Hardship, so miserable a Situation in Life to a Man of an ingenuous Mind, elevated with a Passion for Letters, as he can never be easy with, but will be sure to exert his utmost Endeavours to quit, as soon as possible. Whether this may not be the reason, why many of our Schools are no better provided with Masters, I shall leave the Reader to judge.

6

Isaac Watts on Improving the Mind

Isaac Watts (1674–1748), like John Clarke, devoted much of his life to systematizing ideas of education for his country men. Few writers on education excelled him in illustrating, by the style and arrangement of their works, the exceptional orderliness of the eighteenth-century cultivated English mind. He brought twenty years of reflection and self-inquiry to his renowned essay on *The Improvement of the Mind* (1741). Although he had much to say about teaching young people, he was writing for literate people of all ages who were concerned with acquiring "useful knowledge." His leading principle was that "all persons are under some obligation to improve their understanding." In the section of his treatise first reprinted here, he describes the five primary means of acquiring knowledge: observation, reading, attending lectures, conversation, and study. At the outset Watts stresses the fundamental Lockian thesis that experience through sensation and reflection furnishes knowledge for the mind, which at birth is "an empty cabinet." In his section on teaching, next reprinted here, he emphasizes reason and understanding, the two primary faculties of the mind that he would have the teacher cultivate in his students like "a skilful gardener"—an analogy that was to crop up often in the American child study literature of the nineteenth century. Indeed, the theme that the teacher must well understand the characteristics of youth and tailor his methods to "the temper and inclination of the child" is Lockian, liberal, and modern.

Watts in his lifetime was an independent minister and a liberal, or anti-Trinitarian, in the Arian controversy, which put his theology at odds with English and American Puritans. Though lacking university training, he had been well prepared in classical studies at Stoke Newington, one of the excellent dissenting academies, for his short active ministry followed by many years of study and writing.

His dissenting conscience blocked his path to church preferment. Beside his interest in logic and in analyzing other men's ideas, especially John Locke's, he was a religious poet who showed his greatest talent in writing about six hundred hymns. Although he was not nearly so profound in theology and philosophy as some of the great English divines and schoolmen of his age, his name has lived on in the Protestant world as the composer of, among other hymns, "O God, Our Help in Ages Past," and the Christmas hymn, "Joy To the World!"

There is some measure of the contrast between his age and the intellectual and educational temper of the last hundred years when one reads Leslie Stephen's appraisal of Watts. Stephen, who anticipated the ascendancy of secular libertarian and scientific thought in our day through his description of English thought in the eighteenth century, wrote in 1876 that Watts was a part of the powerful "religious reaction" of the emotions upon the intellect. The name of Watts, Stephen declared, though that of a man whose "Psalms and Hymns" for many years ran to 50,000 copies annually and whose influence "must have been greater than that of many legislators," has however "contracted a faint flavour of the ludicrous."

Watts's writings on education went out of style in America only after a century of use. His treatise, generally known as "Watts on the Mind," had an extraordinary public: between 1793 and 1849 there were twelve American editions of *The Improvement of the Mind*. It was the most influential popularization in America of Locke's *Essay on Human Understanding*. And by 1819 Watts's *Logick* (1725), a preceding companion volume, went through six editions from a single publisher in the United States. The combination of Lockian psychology with rigorous morality, set within the context of broadly Protestant belief, produced writing that served the educational needs of expanding America for several generations. (See also Section 7.)

Part I

Chap. II.

OBSERVATION, READING, INSTRUCTION BY LECTURES, CONVERSATION, AND STUDY, COMPANY.

There are five eminent means or methods whereby the mind is improved in the knowledge of things; and these are observa-

Isaac Watts, *The Improvement of the Mind, To Which Is Added, A Discourse on the Education of Children and Youth* (London, 1751), pp. 25–

tion, reading, instruction by lectures, conversation, and meditation; which last, in a most peculiar manner, is called study.

Let us survey the general definitions or descriptions of them
all.

I. Observation is the notice that we take of all occurrences
in human life, whether they are sensible or intellectual,
whether relating to persons or things, to ourselves or others. It
is this that furnishes us, even from our infancy, with a rich
variety of ideas and propositions, words and phrases: it is by
this we know that fire will burn, that the sun gives light, that a
horse eats grass, that an acorn produces an oak, that man is a
being capable of reasoning and discourse, that our judgment is
weak, that our mistakes are many, that our sorrows are great,
that our bodies die and are carried to the grave, and that one
generation succeeds another. All those things which we see,
which we hear or feel, which we perceive by sense or consciousness, or which we know in a direct manner, with scarce
any exercise of our reflecting faculties or our reasoning powers,
may be included under the general name of observation.

When this observation relates to any thing that immediately
concerns ourselves, and of which we are conscious, it may be
called experience. So I am said to know or experience that I
have in myself a power of thinking, fearing, loving, etc., that I
have appetites and passions working in me, and many personal
occurrences have attended me in this life.

Observation therefore includes all that Mr. Locke means by
sensation and reflection.

When we are searching out the nature or properties of any
being, by various methods of trial, or when we apply some
active powers, or set some causes to work, to observe what
effects they would produce, this sort of observation is called
experiment. So when I throw a bullet into water, I find it sinks;
and when I throw the same bullet into quicksilver, I see it
swims; but if I beat out this bullet into a thin hollow shape, like

---

28, 36–37, 68–71, 234–241. First edition, entitled *The Improvement of
the Mind: or, a supplement to the Art of Logick, etc.* (London, 1741),
published without *A Discourse on . . . Education.*

a dish, then it will swim in the water too. So when I strike two flints together, I find they produce fire; when I throw a seed into the earth, it grows up into a plant.

All these belong to the first method of knowledge, which I shall call observation.

II. Reading is that means or method of knowledge, whereby we acquaint ourselves with what other men have written, or published to the world, in their writings. These arts of reading and writing are of infinite advantage; for by them we are made partakers of the sentiments, observations, reasonings, and improvements, of all the learned world, in the most remote nations, and in former ages, almost from the beginning of mankind.

III. Public or private lectures are such verbal instructions as are given by a teacher while the learners, attend in silence. This is the way of learning religion, from the pulpit; or of philosophy or theology, from the professor's chair; or of mathematics, by a teacher showing us various theorems or problems, i. e. speculations or practices by demonstration and operation, with all the instruments of art necessary to those operations.

IV. Conversation is another method of improving our minds, wherein, by mutual discourse and inquiry, we learn the sentiments of others, as well as communicate our sentiments to others, in the same manner. Sometimes indeed, though both parties speak by turns, yet the advantage is only on one side, as when a teacher and a learner meet and discourse together; but frequently the profit is mutual. Under this head of conversation, we may also rank disputes of various kinds.

V. Meditation or study includes all those exercises of the mind, whereby we render all the former methods useful for our increase in true knowledge and wisdom. It is by meditation we come to confirm our memory of things that pass through our thoughts, in the occurrences of life, in our own experiences, and in the observations we make. It is by meditation that we draw various inferences, and establish in our minds general principles of knowledge. It is by meditation that we compare the various ideas which we derive from our senses, or from the operations of our souls, and join them in propositions. It is by meditation that we fix in our memory whatsoever we learn, and form our own judgment of the truth or falsehood, the strength or weakness, of what others speak or write. It is meditation or study that draws our long chains of argument, and searches and finds deep and difficult truths which before lay concealed in darkness.

It would be a needless thing to prove that our solitary meditations, together with the few observations that the most part of mankind are capable of making, are not sufficient, of themselves, to lead us into the attainment of any considerable proportion of knowledge, at least in an age so much improved as ours is, without the assistance of conversation and reading, and other proper instructions that are to be attained in our days. Yet each of these five methods have their peculiar advantages, whereby they assist each other; and their peculiar defects, which have need to be supplied by the other's assistance. . . .

By a survey of these things, we may justly conclude that he who spends all his time in hearing lectures, or poring upon books, without observation, meditation, or converse, will have but a mere historical knowledge of learning, and be able only to tell what others have known or said on the subject: he that lets all his time flow away in conversation, without due observation, reading, or study, will gain but a slight and superficial knowledge, which will be in danger of vanishing with the voice of the speaker: and he that confines himself merely to his closet and his own narrow observation of things, and is taught only by his own solitary thought, without instruction by lectures, reading, or free conversation, will be in danger of a narrow spirit, a vain conceit of himself, and an unreasonable contempt of others; and, after all, he will obtain but a very limited and imperfect view and knowledge of things, and he will seldom learn how to make that knowledge useful.

These five methods of improvement should be pursued jointly, and go hand in hand, where our circumstances are so happy as to find opportunity and conveniency to enjoy them all; though I must give my opinion that two of them, viz, reading and meditation, should employ much more of our time than public lectures, or conversation and discourse. As for observation, we may be always acquiring knowledge that way, whether we are alone or in company. . . .

Chap. VI.

OF LIVING INSTRUCTION AND LECTURES, OF TEACHERS AND LEARNERS.

I. There are few persons of so penetrating a genius and so just a judgment, as to be capable of learning the arts and sciences, without the assistance of teachers. There is scarcely any science so safely and so speedily learned, even by the noblest genius and the best books, without a tutor. His assistance is absolutely necessary for most persons; and it is very useful for all beginners. Books are a sort of dumb teachers; they point out the way of learning; but if we labour under any doubt or mistake, they cannot answer sudden questions, or explain present doubts and difficulties: this is properly the work of a living instructor.

II. There are very few tutors who are sufficiently furnished with such universal learning, as to sustain all the parts and provinces of instruction. The sciences are numerous, and many of them lie far wide of each other; and it is best to enjoy the instructions of two or three tutors at least, in order to run through the whole encyclopædia or circle of sciences, where it may be obtained; then we may expect that each will teach the few parts of learning which are committed to his care, in greater perfection. But where this advantage cannot be had with convenience, one great man must supply the place of two or three common instructors.

III. It is not sufficient that instructors be competently skilful in those sciences which they profess and teach; but they should have skill also in the art or method of teaching, and patience in the practice of it.

It is a great unhappiness indeed, when persons, by a spirit of party, or faction, or interest, or by purchase, are set up for tutors, who have neither due knowledge of science, nor skill in the way of communication. And, alas! there are others who, with all their ignorance and self-sufficiency, have self-admiration and effrontery enough to set up themselves; and the poor pupils fare accordingly, and grow lean in their understandings.

And let it be observed also, there are some very learned men who know much themselves, but have not the talent of communicating their own knowledge; or else they are lazy, and will take no pains at it. Either they have an obscure and perplexed way of talking, or they show their learning uselessly, and make a long periphrasis on every word of the book they explain, or they cannot condescend to young beginners, or they run presently into the elevated parts of the sciences, because it gives themselves greater pleasure, or they are soon angry and impatient, and cannot bear with a few impertinent questions of a young inquisitive and sprightly genius; or else they skim over a science in a very slight and superficial survey, and never lead their disciples into the depths of it.

IV. A good tutor should have characters and qualifications very different from all these. He is such a one as both can and will apply himself with diligence and concern, and indefatigable patience, to effect what he undertakes; to teach his disciples, and see that they learn; to adapt his way and method, as near as may be, to the various dispositions, as well as to the capacities, of those whom he instructs, and to inquire often into their progress and improvement.

And he should take particular care of his own temper and conduct, that there be nothing in him or about him which may be of ill example; nothing that may savour of a haughty temper, or a mean and sordid spirit; nothing that may expose him to the aversion or to the contempt of his scholars, or create a prejudice, in their minds, against him and his instructions; but, if possible, he should have so much of a natural candour and sweetness mixed with all the improvements of learning, as might convey knowledge into the minds of his disciples with a sort of gentle insinuation and sovereign delight, and may tempt them into the highest improvements of their reason by a resistless and insensible force. . . .

V. The learner should attend with constancy and care on all the instructions of his tutor; and if he happens to be at any time unavoidably hindered, he must endeavour to retrieve the loss, by double industry for time to come. . . .

VI. A student should never satisfy himself with bare attendance on the lectures of his tutor, unless he clearly takes up his sense and meaning, and understands the things which he teaches. A young disciple should behave himself so well as to gain the affection and ear of his instructor, that, upon every occasion, he may, with the utmost freedom, ask questions, and talk over his own sentiments, his doubts and difficulties, with him, and in a humble and modest manner desire the solution of them.

VII. Let the learner endeavour to maintain an honourable opinion of his instructor, and heedfully listen to his instructions, as one willing to be led by a more experienced guide; and, though he is not bound to fall in with every sentiment of his tutor, yet he should so far comply with him as to resolve upon a just consideration of the matter, and try to examine it thoroughly with an honest heart, before he presume to determine against him: and then it should be done with great modesty, with a humble jealousy of himself, and apparent unwillingness to differ from his tutor, if the force of argument and truth did not concern him.

VIII. It is a frequent and growing folly in our age, that pert young disciples soon fancy themselves wiser than those who teach them: at the first view, or upon a very little thought, they can discern the insignificancy, weakness, and mistakes, of what their teacher asserts. The youth of our day, by an early petulancy, and pretended liberty of thinking for themselves, dare reject, at once, and that with a sort of scorn, all those sentiments and doctrines which their teachers have determined, perhaps after long and repeated consideration, after years of mature study, careful observation, and much prudent experience.

IX. It is true, teachers and masters are not infallible, nor are they always in the right; and it must be acknowledged, it is a matter of some difficulty for younger minds to maintain a just and solemn veneration for the authority and advice of their parents and the instructions of their tutors, and yet at the same time to secure to themselves a just freedom in their own thoughts. We are sometimes too ready to imbibe all their sentiments, without examination, if we reverence and love them; or, on the other hand, if we take all freedom to contest their opinions, we are sometimes tempted to cast off that love and reverence to their persons, which God and nature dictate. Youth is ever in danger of these two extremes.

X. But I think I may safely conclude thus: Though the authority of a teacher must not absolutely determine the judgment of his pupil, yet young and raw and unexperienced learners should pay all proper deference that can be to the instructions of their parents and teachers, short of absolute submission to their dictates. Yet still we must maintain this, that they should never receive any opinion into their assent, whether it be conformable or contrary to the tutor's mind, without sufficient evidence of it first given to their own reasoning powers.

Part II

Chap. I.

METHODS OF TEACHING, AND READING LECTURES.

He that has learned anything thoroughly, in a clear and methodical manner, and has attained a distinct perception and an ample survey of the whole subject, is generally best prepared to teach the same subject in a clear and easy method; for, having acquired a large and distinct idea of it himself, and made it familiar to him by frequent meditation, reading, and occasional discourse, he is supposed to see it on all sides, to grasp it, with all its appendices and relations, in one survey, and is better able to represent it to the learner, in all its views, with all its properties, relations, and consequences. . . .

But it is not every one who is a great scholar, that always becomes the happiest teacher; even though he may have a clear conception, and a methodical as well as an extensive survey, of the branches of any science. He must also be well acquainted with words, as well as ideas, in a proper variety, that, when his disciple does not take in the ideas in one form of expression, he may change the phrase into several forms, till at last he hits the understanding of his scholar, and enlightens it in the just idea of truth.

Besides this, a tutor should be a person of a happy and condescending temper, who has patience to bear with a slowness of perception or want of sagacity in some learners. He should also have much candour of soul, to pass a gentle censure on their impertinencies, and to pity them in their mistakes, and use every mild and engaging method for insinuating knowledge into those who are willing and diligent in seeking truth, as well as reclaiming those who are wandering into error. . . .

A very pretty and useful way to lead a person into any particular truth is by questions and answers which is the Socratical method of disputation. . . .

But the most useful, and perhaps the most excellent way of instructing students in any of the sciences, is by reading lectures, as tutors in the academy do to their pupils.

The first work is to choose a book well written, which contains a short scheme or abstract of that science. . . . Let a chapter or section of this be read daily by the learner, on which the tutor should paraphrase in this manner; namely,

He should explain both words and ideas more largely; and especially what is dark and difficult should be opened and illustrated. . . .

Where the arguments are strong and cogent, they should be enforced by some further paraphrase; and the truth of the inferences should be made plainly to appear. Where the arguments are weak and insufficient, they should be either confirmed, or rejected as useless; and new arguments, if need be, should be added to support that doctrine.

What is treated very concisely in the author, should be amplified; and where several things are laid closely together, they must be taken to pieces, and opened by parts.

Where the tutor differs from the author which he reads, he should gently point out and confute his mistakes.

Where the method and order of the book is just and happy,

it should be pursued and commended: where it is defective and irregular, it should be corrected.

The most necessary, the most remarkable and useful, parts of that treatise, or of that science, should be peculiarly recommended to the learners. . . .

The various ends, uses, and services of that science, or of any part of it, should be also declared and exemplified as far as the tutor hath opportunity and furniture to do it; particularly in mathematics and natural philosophy.

And if there be any thing remarkably beautiful or defective in the style of the writer, it is proper for the tutor to make a just remark upon it. . . .

Let the teacher always accommodate himself to the genius, temper, and capacity, of his disciples, and practice various methods of prudence, to allure, persuade, and assist everyone of them in their pursuit of knowledge.

Where the scholar has less capacity, let the teacher enlarge his illustrations; let him search and find out where the learner sticks, what is the difficulty, and thus let him help the labouring intellect.

Where the learner manifests a forward genius and a sprightly curiosity by frequent inquiries, let the teacher oblige such an inquisitive soul, by satisfying those questions, as far as may be done with decency and conveniency; and where these inquiries are unseasonable, let him not silence the young inquirer with a magisterial rebuff, but with much candour and gentleness postpone those questions, and refer them to a proper hour.

Curiosity is a useful spring of knowledge: it should be encouraged in children, and awakened by frequent and familiar methods of talking with them. It should be indulged in youth, but not without a prudent moderation. In those who have too much, it should be limited by a wise and gentle restraint or delay, lest, by wandering after every thing, they learn nothing to perfection. In those who have too little, it should be excited, lest they grow stupid, narrow-spirited, self-satisfied, and never attain a treasure of ideas or an amplitude of understanding. . . .

A teacher should not only observe the different spirit and humour among his scholars, but he should watch the various efforts of their reason and growth of their understanding. He should practise in his young nursery of learning, as a skilful gardener does in his vegetable dominions, and apply prudent methods of cultivation to every plant. . . .

The tutor should take every occasion to instil knowledge into his disciples, and make use of every occurrence of life, to raise some profitable conversation upon it; he should frequently inquire something of his disciples, that may set their young reason to work, and teach them how to form inferences, and to draw one proposition out of another.

Reason being that faculty of the mind which he has to deal with in his pupils, let him endeavour by all proper and familiar methods, to call it into exercise, and to enlarge the powers of it. He should take frequent opportunities to show them when an idea is clear or confused, when the proposition is evident or doubtful, and when an argument is feeble or strong. And by this means their minds will be so formed, that whatsoever he proposes with evidence and strength of reason they will readily receive.

When any uncommon appearances arise in the natural, moral, or political world, he should invite and instruct them to make their remarks on it, and give them the best reflections of his own, for the improvement of their minds.

He should by all means make it appear that he loves his pupils, and he seeks nothing so much as their increase of knowledge, and their growth in all valuable acquirements: this will engage their affection to his person, and procure a just attention to his lectures.

And indeed there is but little hope that a teacher should obtain any success in his instructions, unless those that hear him have some good degree of esteem and respect for his person and character. And here I cannot but take notice, by the way, that it is a matter of infinite and unspeakable injury to the people of any town or parish, where the minister lies under contempt. If he has procured it by his own conduct, he is doubly criminal, because of the injury he does to the souls of them that hear him; but if this contempt and reproach be cast upon him by the wicked, malicious, and unjust censures of men, they must bear all the ill consequences of receiving no good by his labours, and will be accountable hereafter to the great and divine Judge of all.

It would be very necessary to add, in this place (if tutors were not well apprised of it before) that, since learners are obliged to seek a divine blessing on their studies, by fervent prayer to the God of all wisdom, their tutors should go before them in this pious practice, and make daily address to Heaven, for the success of their instructions.

7

Isaac Watts on the Prudential Education of Youth

A wide reading public for the works of Isaac Watts (1674–1748) was created by developments in eighteenth-century English life. Commercial and mercantile classes were expanding and formulating their own social values; the cultural tempo of the great English cities was heightening; there was a rise in adult male literacy, continuing from the previous century, among tradesmen, artisans, and yeomen; the printing, marketing, and use of newspapers, journals, and books were increasing spectacularly; academies and independent schools for the children of the middle classes were multiplying; the nation was awakening to its needs for "useful learning" as it looked to its ventures and possessions overseas; toleration and liberal theology were coming into the Church of England while evangelical groups were attracting ever larger memberships. Amid all this there was growing demand for instructional and inspirational manuals. If there had been no Isaac Watts, Englishmen would have had to invent someone like him. His treatises on improving the mind (see Selection 6), on logic, on the education of young people, and surely his psalms and hymns were all tuned to the growth of a popular middle class culture characterized by its liberal piety, meaning a greater concern with moral conduct than with theology, and its desire for self-improvement through formal and informal schooling. The style, the tone, and the intellectual stance of Watts's books were simple; over a century later Leslie Stephen was to call them almost "childish." Yet the English people thrived on his works. And so too did Americans. His *Discourse on the Education of Children and Youth*, a portion of which is here reprinted from the first edition of 1751, published posthumously, was usually printed in the same volume with *The Improvement of the Mind* (1741). Although there were no separate American editions of the *Discourse*, the two essays were published in America as one volume in 1793, 1812, and 1819. These dates fall in the half century after the American Revolution when American cultural expansion had many of the characteristics and motivations of eighteenth-century English popular culture.

As in his books on improving the mind and on logic, Watts offered Lockian directives in the *Discourse*. The child's curiosity must be stimulated by showing him how to observe the world around him. His memory must be trained. Judgment and reasoning must be taught the child, based upon his own experiences and his reflections upon them. And education can be considered truly effective only when it is promoted within a religious context.

But what of the contention that Watts's educational prescriptions, like Locke's, were not "democratic"? How do we square his ideas about educating the child for a "proper" rank and station in life with his cordial reception in an America that was making its way toward the white equalitarian Age of Jackson? In the first place, we should not make this into more of a present-minded inconsistency than past-mindedness will allow. Watts was Lockian in wanting to get away from the old "vulgar" method of rigid memorization in learning ancient languages. But, unlike Locke, he realized that private tutoring to realize this method in classical studies was simply unworkable, mainly on the ground that a lot more young people than just the sons of the nobility should have the benefit of such training for good citizenship. Further, Watts, like John Clarke (see Selection 5), favored the study of more "useful" modern languages, rather than Latin and Greek, for "persons of the lower and middle station" in life. There was then in Watts's mind a design of classical studies somewhat more suitable than Locke's to the realities of changing English life. But more important is the fact that, in speaking of a "proper" place in life for students, Watts was not pleading for retention of some firm social *status quo*. Surely he subscribed to the eighteenth-century idea of a society with rather clearly marked class distinctions. But the point is that he was writing for people who were aspiring *to* what could be their "proper" station in life, not only for those who were already *in* their "proper" place. Englishmen, and for many years Americans too, were a deferential people in matters of political representation. But the advent of an industrial age and the mobility of people into a rewarding life of trade, craft, or commerce, if not alone the *expectation* of that life, were the circumstances that Watts recognized and that indeed brought his works into popularity. The "rules of prudence" laid down in this *Discourse* could not have been more compatible with social developments of his time in England or with those in America from the Revolution until the time of Jackson. That England was a political monarchy with an aristocratic and stratified society, or that post-Revolutionary America was a deferential republic that only slowly took on democratic traits have really little to do with the reasons for Watts's great influence in both countries. We may remind ourselves, finally, that Watts gave his educational designs the kind of religious sanction that in some ways served the function of political equalitarianism. Just as the Puritans had preached that all men were "equal" as sinners in the sight of God, so too, for Watts, were eighteenth-century men made "equal," so to speak, by piously educating themselves to a calling in life that could through their industry gain them economic and material equality with each other. Thus the Protestant Ethic merged with the myths and the reality of expectant capitalism. What Benjamin Franklin advised, Isaac Watts had already proposed.

Introduction.

OF THE IMPORTANCE OF EDUCATION, AND THE DESIGN OF THIS DISCOURSE, WITH A PLAN OF IT.

The Children of the present age are the hope of the age to come. We who are now acting our several parts in the busy scenes of life, are hasting off the stage apace: months and days are sweeping us away from the business and the surface of this earth, and continually laying some of us to sleep underground. The circle of thirty years will plant another generation in our room: another set of mortals will be the chief actors in all the greater and lesser affairs of this life, and will fill the world with blessings or with mischiefs, when our heads lie low in the dust.

Shall we not then consider with ourselves, What can we do now to prevent those mischiefs, and to entail blessings on our successors? What shall we do to secure wisdom, goodness, and religion, amongst the next generation of men? Have we any concern for the glory of God, in the rising age? Any solicitude for the propagation of virtue and happiness to those who shall stand up in our stead?

Isaac Watts, *The Improvement of the Mind, To Which Is Added, A Discourse on the Education of Children and Youth* (London, 1751), pp. 295–297, 317–336.

Let us then hearken to the voice of God and Solomon, and we shall learn how this may be done: the all-wise God and the wisest of men join to give us this advice: 'Train up a child in the way that he should go, and when he is old he will not depart from it.' The sense of it may be expressed more at large in this proposition, namely, Let children have a good education given them in the younger parts of life, and this a most likely way to establish them in virtue and piety in their elder years.

In this discourse, I shall not enter into any inquiries about the management of children in the two or three first years of their life: I leave that tender age entirely to the care of the mother and the nurse. . . .

I begin with children when they can walk and talk, when they have learned their mother tongue, when they begin to give some more evident discoveries of their intellectual powers, and are more manifestly capable of having their minds formed and moulded into knowledge, virtue, and piety.

Now the first and most universal ingredient which enters into the education of children, is an instruction of them in those things which are necessary and useful for them in their rank and station, and that with regard to this world and the world to come.

I limit these instructions, especially such as relate to this world, by the station and rank of life in which children are born, and placed by the providence of God. Persons of better circumstances in the world should give their sons and their daughters a much larger share of knowledge, and a richer variety of instruction, than meaner persons can or ought. But since every child that is born into this world hath a body and a soul; since its happiness or misery in this world and the next depends very much upon its instructions and knowledge, it hath a right to be taught by its parents, according to their best ability, so much as is necessary for its well-being both in soul and body, here and hereafter.

It is true that the great God our Creator hath made us reasonable creatures: we are by nature capable of learning a million of objects: but as the soul comes into the world, it is unfurnished with knowledge: we are born ignorant of every good and useful thing: we know not God, we know not ourselves, we know not what is our duty and our interest, nor where lies our danger; and, if left entirely to ourselves, should probably grow up like the brutes of the earth: we should trifle away the brighter seasons of life, in a thousand crimes and follies, and endure the fatigues and burdens of it, surrounded with a thousand miseries; and at last we should perish and die without knowledge and hope, if we have no instructors.

All our other powers of nature, such as the will and the various affections, the senses, the appetites, and the limbs, would become

wild instruments of madness and mischief, if they are not governed
by the understanding; and the understanding itself would run into
a thousand errors, dreadful and pernicious, and would employ all
the other powers in mischief and madness, if it hath not the happiness to be instructed in the things of God and men. And who is
there among all our fellow-creatures so much obliged to bestow this
instruction on us, as the persons who, by divine providence, have
been the instruments to bring us into life and being? It is their duty
to give their young offspring this benefit of instruction, as far as
they are able, or at least to provide such instructors for them, and
to put their children under their care. . . .

Section IV.

THE COMMON ARTS OF READING AND WRITING.

Writing is almost a divine art, whereby thoughts may be communicated without a voice, and understood without hearing.
To these I would add some small knowledge of arithmetic and
accounts, as the practice of it is, in a manner, so universal in
our age, that it does almost necessarily belong to a tolerable
education.

The knowledge of letters is one of the greatest blessings that
God ever bestowed on the children of men: by this means,
mankind are enabled to preserve the memory of things done
in their own times, and to lay up a rich treasure of knowledge
for all succeeding generations.

By the art of reading, we learn a thousand things which our
eyes can never see, and which our thoughts would never have
reached to; we are instructed, by books, in the wisdom of
ancient ages; we learn what our ancestors have said and done,
and enjoy the benefit of the wise and judicious remarks which
they have made through their whole course of life, without the
fatigue of their long and painful experiments. By this means,
children may be led, in a great measure, into the wisdom of
old age. It is by the art of reading, that we can sit at home, and
acquaint ourselves with what has been done in distant parts of
the world. The histories and the customs of all ages and all

nations are brought as it were to our doors. By this art, we are
let into the knowledge of the affairs of the Jews, the Greeks,
and the Romans; their wars, their laws, and their religion; and
we can tell what they did in the nations of Europe, Asia, and
Africa, above a thousand years ago.

But the greatest blessing that we derive from reading, is the
knowledge of the holy scriptures. . . .

It must be confessed that, in former ages, before printing was
invented, the art of reading was not so common, even in polite
nations, because books were much more costly, since they must
be all written with a pen, and were therefore hardly to be obtained by the bulk of mankind: but since the providence of
God has brought printing into the world, and knowledge is so
plentifully diffused through our nation at so cheap a rate, it is
a pity that any children should be born and brought up in
Great Britain, without the skill of reading; and especially since,
by this means, every one may see, with his own eyes, what God
requires of him, in order to eternal happiness.

The art of writing also is so exceedingly useful, and is now
grown so very common, that the greatest part of children may
attain it at an easy rate; by this means, we communicate our
thoughts, and all our affairs. . . . We maintain correspondence
and traffic with persons in distant nations; and the wealth and
grandeur of Great Britain is maintained by this means. . . .

I might add here also, true spelling is such a part of knowledge as children ought to be acquainted with; since it is a matter of shame and ridicule, in so polite an age as ours, when
persons who have learned to handle the pen, cannot write three
words together without a mistake or blunder, and when they
put letters together in such an awkward and ignorant manner,
that it is hard to make sense of them, or to tell what they mean.

Arithmetic, or the art of numbers is . . . to be reckoned also a
necessary part of a good education. Without some degrees of
this knowledge, there is indeed no traffic among men. And
especially it is more needful at present, since the world deals
much more upon trust and credit than it did in former times;
and therefore the art of keeping accounts is made, in some
measure, necessary to persons even in meaner stations in life,

below the rank of merchants or great traders. A little knowledge of the art of accounts is also needful, in some measure, in order to take a survey, and make a just judgment of the common expenses of a person or a family; but this part of learning, in the various degrees of it, is more or less useful and needful, according to the different stations and business for which children are designed.

As the sons of a family should be educated in a knowledge of writing, reading, spelling, and accounts, so neither should the daughters be trained up without them. Reading is as needful for one sex as the other. Nor should girls be forbid to handle the pen, or to cast up a few figures; since it may be very much for their advantage, in almost all circumstances of life, except in the very lowest rank of servitude or hard labour. . . .

Section V.

OF TRADE OR EMPLOYMENT.

In a good education, it is required also that children, in the common ranks of life, be brought up to the knowledge of some proper business or employment, for their lives; some trade or traffic, artifice or manufacture, by which they may support their expenses, and procure for themselves the necessaries of life, and by which they may be enabled to provide for their families, in due time. In some of the eastern nations, even persons of high rank are obliged to be educated to some employment or profession; and perhaps that practice has many advantages in it: it engages the younger years in labour and diligence, and secures from the mischievous effects of sloth, idleness, vanity, and a thousand temptations.

In our nation, I confess it is the custom to educate the children of noblemen, and the eldest sons of the gentry, to no proper business or profession, but only to an acquaintance with some of the ornaments and accomplishments of life, which I shall mention immediately. But perhaps it would be far happier for some families, if their sons were brought up to busi-

ness, and kept to the practice of it, than to have them exposed
to the pernicious inconveniences of a sauntering and idle life,
and the more violent impulse of all the corrupt inclinations of
youth.

However, it is certain that the far greater part of mankind
must bring up their children to some regular business or profession, whereby they may sustain their lives, and support a
family, and become useful members to the state. Now, in the
choice of such a profession or employment for children, many
things are to be consulted.

1. The circumstances and estate of the parent: whether it
will reach to place out the child as an apprentice, to provide
for him materials for his business or trade, and to support him
till he shall be able to maintain himself by his profession.
Sometimes the ambition of the parent and the child hath fixed
on a trade far above their circumstances, and in consequence of
which the child hath been exposed to many inconveniences,
and the parent to many sorrows.

2. The capacity and talents of the child must also be considered. If it be a profession of hard labour, hath the child a
healthy and firm constitution, and strength of body equal to
the work? If it be a profession that requires the exercise of
fancy, skill, judgment, or much study, or contrivance, then the
question will be, Hath the lad a genius capable of thinking
well, a bright imagination, a solid judgment? Is he able to
endure such an application of mind as is necessary for the
employment?

3. The temper and inclination of the child must be brought
into this consultation, in order to determine a proper business
for life. If the daily labour and business of a man be not agreeable to him, he can never hope to manage it with any great advantage or success. I knew a bricklayer who professed that he
had always an aversion to the smell of mortar; and I was acquainted once with a lad who began to learn Greek at school,
but he complained that it did not agree with his constitution. I
think the first of these ought to have been brought up to work
in glass or timber, or any thing rather than in bricks; as for the
other, to my best remembrance, he was wisely disposed of to a
calling wherein he had nothing to do with Greek.

And here I would beg leave to desire that none might be encouraged to pursue any of the learned professions, that is, divinity, law, or physic, who have not the signs of a good genius, who are not patient of long attention and close application to study, who have not a peculiar delight in that profession which they choose, and withal a pretty firm constitution of body; for much study is a weariness to the flesh, and the vigour of nature is sooner impaired by laborious thoughtfulness, than by the labour of the limbs.

4. It should be also the solicitous and constant care of parents, when they place out their children in the world, to seek out masters for them who profess serious religion, who practise all moral virtues, and keep good order and good hours in their family. The neglect of this concern has been the ruin of a thousand youths in our day; and, notwithstanding the sensible mischief arising from this negligence, yet there is still too little care taken in a matter of so great importance.

What business of life must daughters be brought up to? I must confess, when I have seen so many of the sex who have lived well in their childhood, grievously exposed to many hardships and poverty upon the death of their parents, I have often wished there were more of the callings or employments of life peculiarly appropriated to women, and that they were regularly educated in them, that there might be a better provision made for their support. . . .

It is the custom of the nation, and indeed it hath been the custom of most nations and ages, to educate daughters in the knowledge of things that relate to the affairs of the household, to spin and to use the needle, both for making garments and for the ornaments of embroidery: they have been generally employed in the preparation of food, in the regular disposal of the affairs of the house, for the conveniences and accommodations of human life, in the furniture of the rooms and the elegancies of entertainment. . . .

Some of these things are the constant care and labour of women in our day, whereby they maintain themselves: the most laborious parts of them belong to the poor. And it is the opinion of the best judges that even in superior and wealthy circumstances, every daughter should be so far instructed in them as to know when they are performed aright, that the servant may not usurp too much power, and impose on the ignorance of the mistress. Nature and Providence seemed to have designed these offices for the sex, in all ages and in all nations, because, while the men are engaged in harder and more robust labours, and are often called abroad in business, the women are more generally accustomed to keep house and dwell at home; and the word of God, as well as the custom of human life, recommends it. Tit. ii. 5; 1 Tim. v. 14.

Section VI.

RULES OF PRUDENCE.

All children should have some instruction given them in the conduct of human life, some necessary rules of prudence, by which they may regulate the management of their own affairs, and their behaviour towards their fellow-creatures. Where all other sorts of knowledge are conferred upon children, if this be wanting they make but a contemptible, figure in the world, and plunge themselves into many inconveniences.

Some of these rules of prudence are of a general nature, and necessary at all times, and upon all occasions: others are more particular, and are proper to be used according to the various occurrences of life.

If I were to inquire what are the foundations of human prudence, I should rank them under these three heads:

1. A knowledge of ourselves. Here every one should be taught to consider within himself, "What is my temper and natural inclination? what are my most powerful appetites, and my prevailing passions? what are my chief talents and capacities, if I have any at all? what are the weaknesses and follies to which I am most liable, especially in the days of youth? what are the temptations and dangers which attend me? what are my circumstances in the world? and what my various relations to mankind round about me? what are my constant, and what my occasional duties? what are the inward or outward advantages

that attend me, or the disadvantages under which I labour? A wise and just survey of all these things, and keeping them always in mind, will be of unspeakable use to us in the conduct of life, that we may set our chief guard upon our weak side, and where our greatest danger lies; that we may employ our talents aright, and seize all advantages to improve them for the best purpose, and proceed in the shortest way to piety, usefulness, and peace.

2. The knowledge of mankind is also necessary to acquire prudence. . . .

3. The knowledge of the things of the world, and the various affairs of human life, must be included as one of the chief foundations of prudence. . . .

Prudence consists in judging well what is to be said, and what is to be done on every new occasion; when to lie still, and when to be active; when to keep silence, and when to speak; what to avoid, and what to pursue; how to act in every difficulty; what means to make use of to compass such an end; how to behave in every circumstance of life, and in all companies; how to gain the favour of mankind, in order to promote our own happiness, and to do the most service to God and the most good to men, according to that station we possess, and those opportunities which we enjoy.

For this purpose, there is no book better than the Proverbs of Solomon. Several of the first chapters seem to be written for young men, under the name of Solomon's son: and all the rest of them should be made familiar to youth by their frequent converse with them, and treasuring them up in their head and heart. . . .

Section VII.

THE ORNAMENTS AND ACCOMPLISHMENTS OF LIFE.

The last part of instruction which I include in the idea of a good education, is an instruction of youth in some of the useful ornaments and accomplishments of life.

It has been the custom of our nation, for persons of the middle and lower ranks of life, who design their children for trades and manufactures, to send them to the Latin and Greek schools. There they wear out four or five years of time, in learning a number of strange words, that will be of very little use to them in all the following affairs of their station: and this very learning is also generally taught in a very tiresome and most irrational method, when they are forced to learn Latin by grammars and rules written in that unknown tongue. When they leave the school, they usually forget what they have learned; and the chief advantage they gain by it is to spell and pronounce hard words better, when they meet with them in English: whereas this skill of spelling might be attained in a far shorter time, and at an easier rate, by other methods; and much of life might be saved and improved to better purposes.

As for the sons of those who enjoy more plentiful circumstances in the world, they may be instructed in the Latin and Greek languages, for several valuable ends in their station; and especially those who are designed for the learned professions ought thoroughly to understand them: and such as pursue the study of divinity must be acquainted also with Hebrew and Chaldee, that they may read the Old Testament in its original language, as well as the New.

The French is now-a-days esteemed also an accomplishment to both sexes. . . . There are many words now introduced in the English language, borrowed and derived from thence, as well as from the Latin and Greek; so that it may not be improper for an English gentleman to learn these tongues, that he may understand his own the better. . . .

In short, it is a thing of far greater value and importance that youth should be perfectly well skilled in reading, writing, and speaking, their native tongue, in a proper, a polite, and graceful manner, than in toiling among foreign languages. It is of more worth and advantage to gentlemen and ladies to have an exact knowledge of what is decent, just, and elegant, in English, than to be a critic in foreign tongues. . . .

Thus far concerning the knowledge of words. But the knowledge of things is of much more importance.

1. The young gentry of both sexes should be a little acquainted with logic, that they may learn to obtain clear ideas; to judge by reason and nature of things; to banish the prejudices of infancy, custom, and humour; to argue closely and justly on any subject; and to cast their thoughts and affairs into a proper and easy method.

2. Several parts of mathematical learning are also necessary ornaments of the mind, and not without real advantage. . . .

Besides the common skill in accounts which is needful for a trader, there is a variety of pretty and useful rules and practices in arithmetic, to which a gentleman should be no stranger: and if his genius lie that way, a little insight into algebra would be no disadvantage to him. It is fit that young people, of any figure in the world, should see some of the springs and clues whereby skilful men, by plain rules of reason, trace out the most deep, distant, and hidden questions; and whereby they find certain answers to those inquires which, at first view, seem to lie without the ken of mankind, and beyond the reach of human knowledge. It was for want of a little more general acquaintance with mathematical learning in the world, that a good algebraist and a geometrician were accounted conjurors, a century ago; and people applied to them to seek for lost horses and stolen goods.

They should know something of geometry. . . . The world is now grown so learned in mathematical science, that this sort of language is often used in common writings and in conversation, far beyond what it was in the days of our fathers. And besides, without some knowledge of this kind, we cannot make any farther progress towards an acquaintance with the arts of surveying, measuring, geography, and astronomy, which are so entertaining and so useful an accomplishment to persons of a polite education.

Geography and astronomy are exceedingly delightful studies. The knowledge of the lines and circles of the globes, of heaven and earth, is counted so necessary in our age, that no person of either sex is now esteemed to have an elegant education without it. Even tradesmen and the actors in common life should, in my opinion, in their younger years, learn something of these sciences, instead of vainly wearing out seven years of drudgery in Greek and Latin. . . .

3. Natural philosophy, at least in the more general principles and foundations of it, should be infused into the minds of youth. This is a very bright ornament of our rational natures, which are inclined to be inquisitive into the causes and reasons of things. A course of philosophical experiments is now frequently attended by the ladies, as well as the gentlemen, with no small pleasure and improvement. God and religion may be better known, and clearer ideas may be obtained of the amazing wisdom of our Creator, and of the glories of the life to come, as well as of the things of this life, by the rational learning and knowledge of nature that is now so much in vogue. . . .

4. History is another accomplishment of youth, and ornament of education. The narratives of the various occurrences in nations, as well as in the lives of particular persons, slide into younger minds with pleasure. These will furnish the soul in time with a treasure of knowledge, whence to derive useful observations, inferences, and rules of conduct. These will enable us to gratify our acquaintance, by rehearsing such narratives at proper seasons, and render our own company agreeable and useful to mankind.

5. Nor can our education be called completely elegant without something of poesy, in so very polite an age as this. . . .

The thing, therefore, which I here recommend to persons of a polite education, is some acquaintance with good verse. To read it in the best authors, to learn to know, and taste, and feel, a fine stanza, as well as hear it, and to treasure up some of the richest sentiments and expressions of the most admired writers, is all that I mean in this advice. . . .

But it is time to descend, and mention some of the accomplishments of animal nature. The first of this kind, and perhaps the nearest to poesy, is the art of singing; a most charming gift of the God of nature, and designed for the solace of our sorrows, and the improvement of our joys. Those young persons who are blest with a musical ear and voice, should have some instruction bestowed on them, that they may acquire this delightful skill. I am sorry that the greatest part of our songs, whereby young gentlemen and ladies are taught to practise this art, are of the amorous kind, and some of them polluted too. Will no happy genius lend a helping hand to rescue music from all its defilements, and to furnish the tongue with nobler and more refined melody? But singing must not be named alone.

Various harmony, both of the wind and string, were once in use in divine worship, and that by divine appointment. It is certain, then, that the use of these instruments in common life, is no unlawful practice. . . .

Shall I be allowed, after this, to mention drawing and painting as agreeable amusements for polite youth? Where the genius leads that way, it is a noble diversion and improves the mind. . . .

Shall I now name the art of fencing, and of riding the managed horse, as an accomplishment for gentlemen? These are exercises of a healthy kind, and may be useful in life. Shall I speak of dancing, as a modish accomplishment of both sexes? I confess I know no evil in it. This is also a healthy exercise, and gives young persons a decent manner of appearance in company. . . .

But where it is much beloved and indulged, it has most sensible dangers, especially in mixed dancing. It leads youth too often and too early into company: it may create too much forwardness and assurance in the sex whose chief glory is their modesty: it may kindle vain and vicious inclinations, and raise in young minds too great a fondness for the excessive gaieties and licentious pleasures of the age. . . .

But among all the accomplishments of youth, there is none preferable to a decent and agreeable behavior among men, a modest freedom of speech, a soft and elegant manner of address, a graceful and lovely deportment, a cheerful gravity and good humour, with a mind appearing ever serene under the ruffling accidents of human life: add to this, a pleasing solemnity and reverence when the discourse turns upon anything sacred and divine, a becoming neglect of injuries, a hatred of calumny and slander, a habit of speaking well of others, a pleasing benevolence and readiness to do good to mankind, and special compassion to the miserable, with an air and countenance, in a natural and unaffected manner, expressive of all these excellent qualifications.

Some of these I own are to be numbered among the duties and virtues, rather than among the ornaments, of mankind: but they must be confessed to be ornaments as well as virtues. They are graces in the eye of man as well as of God. These will bespeak the affection of all that know us, and engage even an ill-natured world betimes in our favour. These will enable the youth of both sexes, who are, so happy to attain them, to enter upon the stage of life with approbation and love; to pass through the world with ease, as far as ease may be expected in so degenerate and unhappy a state of things; to finish the scenes of action on earth with applause, and to leave behind them the monument of a good name, when their bodies sleep in the dust, and their souls dwell with God.

8

Lord Kames's
Educated Man Anticipates
the Jeffersonian View

At the age of eighty-five, Henry Home, Lord Kames (1696–1782), wrote his *Loose Hints Upon Education, Chiefly Concerning the Culture of the Heart.* The hints were "loose" because Kames knew that he had little time left and could not produce a systematic treatise on education. He wanted to distill the reflections of his own lifetime in Scotland as jurist, gentleman farmer, and writer on aesthetics, law, and moral philosophy. The result was a book that found its way into the private libraries of educated Americans who earlier had been influenced by Kames in their thinking on ethics and criticism. *Loose Hints* is displayed at Mount Vernon as part of George Washington's library, while Thomas Jefferson's *marginalia* in Kames's *Essays on the Principles of Morality and Natural Religion* (1751) reveal his intellectual indebtedness to its author. Although there was no American edition of Kames on education, the book is in part reprinted here because it neatly summarizes the principles Kames set forth in his larger work on moral philosophy and in his famous *Elements of Criticism* (3 vols., 1762), which was reprinted and widely used in American academies and colleges well into the nineteenth century. Kames conceived the *Loose Hints Upon Education* to be more a general guide to self-improvement outside formal schooling and more a sketch of the well-educated man's attitude toward learning than a manual of instruction *per se.*

Kames's ideas on education broadly conceived were especially attractive to two Americans who became the pacesetters of American educational style as the eighteenth century waned and the nineteenth matured. Benjamin Franklin, self-educated like Lord Kames, first met Kames in 1759 on a trip to Scotland. Franklin found a man devoted to inculcating "right habits" in young people (particularly in his own children) and to teaching them the "art" of orderly thinking. He and Kames corresponded for about ten years. Thomas Jefferson owed his idea of an innate moral sense in man to reading Kames's *Essays on the Principles of Morality.* A moral sense was the ingredient that John Locke had not given human beings at birth. Eighteenth-century Scottish philosophy added it to Lockian man. Jefferson and most Americans after him used the idea to advantage by insisting with Kames that the moral sense is always being developed and refined like other powers and faculties of the mind. This belief set the moral sense in a social and historical context and made it, above all, supremely useful for the optimistic mood of the new nation and of nineteenth-century America. (See Selection 21.) Since Jefferson viewed the moral sense as an instinctive part of man's heart, not of his head, he posed the problem of an anti-intellectual basis for morality. The problem is always well illustrated by Jefferson's dictum that a plowman will often judge a moral case better than a professor because the former "has not been led astray by artificial rules." Yet there was in this Jeffersonian point of view something rationally advantageous to later American democratic thought beyond its explicit romantic equalitarianism. It stems from Scottish philosophy which generally taught that, since man is by his nature a social creature, his perfection consists in his becoming a worthy part of his community. Or to put it another way: to esteem virtue is to love men. This was the Kamesian position. And for Kames, who became famous in America as a reliable guide to genteel behavior, gentlemanly conduct was based not so much upon one's inheritance or social place as it was tested by one's attempts to become a harmonious member of society, relying upon the heart as one's guide to virtue. Jefferson turned this view into his American definition of virtue. He attributed the improvement of the moral sense in Americans to their closeness to the land. Or to put it another way: to esteem virtue is to love men of the land.

Yet neither Jefferson nor Kames, as this selection demonstrates, were followers of Rousseau. They were basically Lockian in their educational outlook. Kames stressed the power of habit and the need for early discipline in the formation of character. Jefferson agreed with Kames that moulding "the heart and the affections" is as important as moulding the understanding (reason), particularly in the very young. The issues of "permissiveness" in education were as important to them as they have become in our age. Although they were together with Rousseau in holding that genuine virtue is often sacrificed to manners and to "the varnish of politeness," they parted with him in believing that training in morality and in tolerance of others should precede, not follow maturity and the training of the understanding. Kamesian principles of morality were, moreover, Lockian, and their teaching was grounded upon the Enlightenment view of God as the great designer—benevolent, benign, and rewarding of virtue. Though steering clear of any theological basis for his educational views, Jefferson shared with Kames the historical perspective of the Enlightenment that religion is not itself morality, but is rather the greatest support of morality.

In America these views were far removed from Puritan educational precepts. Family education, for example, should be carried on for "society and happiness," wrote Lord Kames, not for spiritual salvation. Kames and Jefferson truly represent the mainstream of educational thought in the eighteenth-century English-speaking world. Yet their emphasis upon developing man's innate moral sense through education and their concern for the heart and the head of man make these two figures of the British and American Enlightenment singularly prescient of nineteenth-century educational theories.

Introduction.

The mind of man is a rich soil, productive equally of flowers and weeds. Good passions and impressions are flowers which ought carefully to be cultivated: bad passions and impressions are weeds which ought to be suppressed, if they cannot be totally rooted out. Such moral culture is no slight art: it requires a complete knowledge of the human heart, of all its mazes, and of all its biases.

As impressions made in childhood are the deepest and the most permanent, the plan of our Creator for giving access to the heart, even in that early period, cannot be too much admired. The first thing observable is an innate sense that enables us to discover internal passions from their external signs*. As that sense is of prime use in every period of life, it early attains to full exercise; indeed as early as the senses of seeing and hearing do. An infant on the

---

Lord Kames, *Loose Hints Upon Education, Chiefly Concerning the Culture of the Heart* (Edinburgh, 1781), 1–12, 14–15, 20–37, 40–41, 268–273, 281–284, 299–305, 307–309.
* Elements of Criticism, edit. 5. vol. I. p. 441.
The Head is the seat of thinking, deliberating, reasoning, willing, and of all other internal actions. The Heart is the seat of emotions and passions; and of moral perceptions, such as right and wrong, good and bad, praise and blame, &c. See *Elements of Criticism*, edit. 5. vol. II. page 507.

breast discerns good or bad humour in its nurse, from their external signs on her countenance, and from the different tones of her voice. Next, these signs and tones affect the infant differently: a song or a smile, cheers it: a harsh look or tone makes it afraid or keeps it in awe.

By these means the human heart lies open to early instruction; and is susceptible of having proper notions stamped on it, such as those of right and wrong, of praise and blame, of benevolence and selfishness, of yours and mine. The great utility of such notions will appear from opposing them to various absurd notions and opinions which never could have prevailed in the world, had they not been inculcated during infancy. Take the following instance. Stories of ghosts and hobgoblins heard for the first time by one grown up make no impression unless it be of laughter; but stamped on the mind of a child, they harrass it incessantly, and are never totally obliterated. . . . When notions that have no foundation in nature take such hold of the mind it cannot be doubted but that notions grafted on some natural principle or affection will be equally permanent. Therefore, let it be the first care of parents to instill into their children right notions, which can be done by looks and gestures even before a child is capable of understanding what is said to it. With regard to families of distinction in particular, this branch of education is of the highest importance. Even before the age of seven, notions of rank, of opulence, of superiority in the children of such families, begin to break out and to render them less obsequious to discipline than in their more tender years; and if admitted to take peaceable possession, adieu to education of any sort.

Rousseau advances a strange opinion, that children are incapable of instruction before the age of twelve. This opinion, confined to the understanding, is perhaps not far from truth. But was it his opinion that children before twelve are incapable of being instructed in matters of right and wrong, of love and hatred, or of other feelings that have an original seat in the heart? If it was, gross must have been his ignorance of human nature. And yet that this was really his opinion, appears from his insisting that a child ought not to be punished for telling a lie; which can have no foundation other than that a child is not conscious of doing wrong when it tells a lie, more than when it tells truth. If the difference between truth and falsehood be innate, which it surely is, why ought not a child to be punished for telling a lie, if the vice cannot be restrained by gentler means?

Infancy is a busy scene, and yet little attended to, except for the sake of health. As this period is short, every opportunity ought to be taken for instilling right notions and making proper impressions. The infant at the same time is busy in gathering for itself a stock of ideas from the various objects of the external senses, ready to be uttered as soon as it can speak, which commonly is before the age of two. The difficulty it has to struggle with is not want of ideas, but want of words. It is wonderful to what degree of understanding some children arrive very early. A child named Martha, three years old, had been told jocularly that Martha or Mattie was an ugly name, and that she ought to have been called Matilda. The child was overheard saying to a younger sister, who had not yet got the use of her tongue, "When you can speak, you must not call me Mattie, which is an ugly name, but Matilda." There are instances without number of the same kind; and in tracing the progress of the mind they deserve well to be recorded.

The education of girls is by nature entrusted to the mother; and of boys, till they are fit for regular discipline at school. The father occasionally may give a helping hand, but it can only be occasionally.

Thus the culture of the heart during childhood, the most precious time for such culture, is a task with which females only are charged by providence, a vocation that ought to employ their utmost sagacity and perseverance, a vocation not inferior in dignity, as will appear afterward, to any that belongs to the other sex. Yet children during that precious time are commonly abandoned to nurses and servants. The mother is indeed attentive to the health of her child and flatters herself that nothing further is required from her. But it cannot be expected that early education will be regarded by a mother who is ignorant of its advantages.

This is deplorable, especially as there are several obstacles to a remedy. One is that there is no school, public or private, for teaching the art of cultivating the heart. Nor is it an art of a slight kind: few arts are more complicated or more profound. Another is that this art, as the world goes, appears to be little in request; and I believe is seldom thought of in choosing a wife. A young man inclined to avarice discovers no virtue in a young woman but a plentiful fortune. Another addicted to the pleasures of sense regards beauty only. A prudent man, having nothing in view but an agreeable companion, is satisfied with a sweet temper and affable manners. The art of training up children is never thought of, though of all the most essential in a mother.

Zeal to have such obstacles removed, suggested to me the following Essay. . . . Were it generally understood that the education of children is the mother's peculiar province, an important trust committed to her by her Maker, education during that early period would, I am persuaded, be carried on more accurately than it is at present. With respect to the education of female children in particular, genteel accomplishments such as music and dancing need not be rejected; but in order to accomplish them as mothers, the knowledge of human nature and the art of improving the heart would chiefly be insisted on. This art would have a beneficial influence on the conduct of married women. Instead of roaming abroad for want of occupation at home, the dignified occupation of educating their children would be their most charming amusement. The husband, happy in his wife and in his children, would in no other place find the comfort of his own house. The children, early inspired with morality and religion, would be prepared to perform with alacrity every duty and to stand firm against every temptation.

How distant from such a state are persons in high life who, in great cities, are engaged in a perpetual round of pleasure! Take for instance routs and card-assemblies. Excepting those at the card-tables, who make but a small part of the company, the rest saunter about, looking at one another, wishing in vain to have something to say. Whether frequency does not render such meetings woefully insipid, I appeal to those who pass much of their time in them. And yet for such pastime married women not only neglect domestic economy, but even the education of their children.—Unhappy mortals to be thus enslaved by a mere shadow! Their only resource for their children is a boarding school; which is not a little hazardous for girls, who by their number escape strict attention and who, in the most ticklish period of life, are more apt to follow bad example than good. Young ladies of rank, carried from the boarding school to the dissipation of high life, are not likely to behave better than their mothers did before them. The fruits of such education are but too apparent. Formerly, neither divorce nor separation were much heard of: they have now become so frequent as scarce to make a figure in a newspaper. . . .

It appears unaccountable that our teachers generally have directed their instructions to the head, with very little attention to the heart. From Aristotle down to Locke, books without number have been composed for cultivating and improving the understanding: few in proportion for cultivating and improving the affections. Yet surely as man is intended to be more an active than a contemplative being, the educating a young man to behave properly in society is of still greater importance than to make him even a Solomon for knowledge. Locke has broached the subject and Rousseau has furnished many ingenious hints. The following Loose Thoughts on the same subject are what have occurred to me occasionally. . . .

Few articles concerning government are of greater importance than good education. Our moral duties are circumscribed within precise bounds and therefore may be objects of law. But manners, depending on an endless variety of circumstances, are too complex for law; and yet upon manners chiefly depends the well-being of society. . . . To give vigor to the censorian office, it indispensably must be exercised by men of dignity, eminent for patriotism, and of a character above exception. . . . Our only resource for exercising that important office are fathers and mothers. Let it sink into their hearts that we have no reliance but upon them for preventing universal corruption and of course dissolution of the state. . . . Much need, alas! is there, . . . considering the defective state of education in this island. So little notion have the generality of its importance that if a young heir get but a smattering of Latin or of French he is held to be an accomplished gentleman, qualified for making a figure. What if a person who hath carefully bred up a family and added to the society a number of virtuous citizens, male and female, should be distinguished by some mark of honor which, at the same time, would add lustre to every individual of the family? What if men of genius were encouraged by suitable rewards to give us good systems of education? When a man has taught a public school for 12 or 15 years with success and applause, why not relieve him from his fatigue by a handsome pension, enabling him to confine his attention to a few select scholars? I offer these as hints only. It will not be difficult to multiply them.

It is of the utmost importance to the nation, and to the King and his ministers, that young men who may serve in parliament should be carefully educated, and in particular be fairly initiated in the science of politics. Were the members, in general, of the two houses expert in that science there would be no such woeful division among them as at present. A clear sight of the public good would at least damp the vile appetite for the loaves and fishes that governs many of them. . . . It would be a . . . solid plan to engage tutors of colleges and other teachers to instil into their pupils a due submission to government and to teach them this useful lesson, that the public never suffers so much from an unskilful minister as from a factious opposition to him. Why not schools for teaching the science of politics, erected at the expence of the public, as schools are for teaching the art of war? Such an institution, inconsistent, indeed, with absolute monarchy, would suit admirably the constitution of Britain. . . .

Parents! your children are not your property. They are entrusted to you by Providence, to be trained up in the principles of religion and virtue; and you are bound to fulfil the sacred trust. You owe to your Maker obedience; you owe to your children the making of them virtuous; you owe to your country good citizens; and you owe to yourselves affectionate children who, during your gray hairs, will be your sweetest comfort and firmest support.

In gathering materials for this work, I have adhered strictly to the system of nature, and have given no place to any observation or conjecture but what appeared clearly founded upon that system, upon some noted principle, feeling, or faculty. Rousseau has unhappily too much imagination to be confined within so narrow bounds: he builds castles in the air, and in vain endeavors to give them a foundation. His *Emile,* however, with all its imperfections, is a work of great genius; and he has given many hints that deserve to be prosecuted. Compare his performance with others on the same subject, and its superiority will appear in a striking light. Compare it with a book intitled, *Instructons for educating a Daughter,* attributed, I must believe, unjustly, to an excellent writer, the most virtuous of men, Fenelon, Archbishop of Cambray. The following passage will by contrast, do honour to my favourite author.

> The substance of the brain is in children soft and tender; but it hardens every day. By this softness, every thing is easily imprinted on it. It is not only soft but moist, which being joined with a great heat, give the child a continual inclination to move, whence proceeds the agitation of children who are no more able to fix their mind on any one object than their body in any one place. The first images, engraven while the brain is soft, are the deepest and harden as age dries the brain, and consequently become indefaceable by time. Hence it is that when old we remember many things done in youth, and not what were done in riper age; because the brain at that age is dried and filled with other images. But if in childhood the brain be adapted for receiving images, it is not altogether so for the regular disposal of them, or for reasoning. For though the moisture of the brain renders the impressions easy, yet, by being joined with too great a heat, it makes a sort of agitation which breaks the series of rational deductions.

What a rant is this; words without any meaning! Here man is reduced to be a mere machine, everything explained from soft and hard, moist and dry, hot and cold; causes that have no imaginable connection with the effects endeavored to be explained. Books of this kind may be pored on without end, and the reader be not a jot the wiser. Why from the same principles does not this most profound philosopher deduce the light of the sun, the circulation of the blood, or, what is no less difficult, the mathematical regularity of an egg?

Authority of Parents.

The faculty of reason is bestowed on man for controling his appetites and passions, and for giving them a proper direction.

This faculty is indeed born with us; but as it is feeble like the body during the first stage of life, parental authority supplies the want of reason during that period. And, as no work of God is left imperfect, children are directed by instinct to obey their parents; and if children be not unkindly treated, their obedience is not only voluntary but affectionate. This is not a picture of imagination: everyone who has given attention to the infant state will bear witness that a child clings to its mother, and is fonder of her than of all the world beside. By this admirable plan children, who have no reason, are commonly better governed than adult persons who possess a considerable share of it: the former are entirely obsequious to the reason of another; the latter not always to their own.

That the authority of parents must be absolute is evident because in the nature of things it cannot be subject to any control. And it is equally evident that the same authority must be transferred to the keeper, where the parents are dead or at a distance. But much art and delicacy are requisite in the manner of exercising it. I absolutely prohibit severity, which will terrify the child and reduce it to dissimulation, the worst of habits. If such severity be exercised as to alienate the child's affection, there is an end to education; the parent or keeper is transformed into a cruel tyrant over a trembling slave. . . . Some children begin early to show a keenness for what touches their fancy. Lose not a moment to repress that keenness, not by bluntness or roughness, but by informing the child that it is improper. If from infancy it have been trained to obedience, it will submit pleasantly. The effect of this discipline is not confined to childhood: it is an excellent preparation for bearing crosses and disappointments in all the stages of life. . . .

The absolute dependence on parents that nature puts children under has, when rightly exercised, two effects extremely salutary. One is that it produces a habit of submission to authority, a fine preparation for the social life. The authority of the magistrate succeeds to that of the parent; and the submission paid to the latter is readily transferred to the former. . . . Another effect is that the habit of submission to parental authority introduces naturally a habit of submission to self-authority, or, in other words, a habit of submission to the authority of conscience. Youth is liable to the seduction of passion, and a dangerous period it is to those who have been neglected in childhood. But a young man, obedient from infancy to his parents, submits with as little hesitation to the dictates of his own conscience; and if happily, at his entrance into public life, he escape temptations that are difficult to be resisted, he becomes fortified by habit to resist every temptation.

Though parental authority well tempered fits us thus for society and happiness, yet that eminent writer Rousseau, rejecting the system of nature, declares for emancipating children from all subjection, indulging them in every fancy, provided only they do no mischief to others. I cannot really conjecture upon what imagined principle in human nature this doctrine is founded. A child is incapable to judge for itself, and yet it must not be directed by its parents. "Pray Sir, hold off, there ought to be "no authority, the child must be left to "itself." This is a strange notion. Can it be improper to tell a child that what it desires is wrong or that the doing what it desires would make it despised or hated? If the child be not so far advanced as to understand that language, nothing remains but plain authority, which the child submits to readily and pleasantly. Rousseau maintains, that you must not pretend to have any authority over your pupil, but only that you are the stronger, and can subject him by force*. Is not this to teach him that right depends on force, and that he may lawfully subject every one who is weaker than himself? Was it Rousseau's intention to breed his pupil a tyrant and oppressor? he could not take a more effectual method.

Rousseau . . . could not mean that parents should stand by and suffer their children to hurt themselves. His doctrine thus reformed resolves in giving children full liberty in matters indifferent, such as can neither hurt themselves nor others; to which restriction I willingly subscribe. And thus a doctrine ushered in with solemnity as a leading principle in the educa-

---

* Emile, vol. I. p. 95.

tion of children and seeming at first view of great importance, does upon a more narrow inspection vanish into smoke. . . .

Opinion and Belief Less Influenced by Reason than by Temper and Education

A courageous person under-rates danger: to the indolent the slightest obstacle appears unsurmountable. A person of veracity, relying on the veracity of others, is easy of belief: where a man's veracity is so supple as to bend to his interest, he will be suspicious of evidence and hard of belief. Hence it is that upon the benevolent and humane the arguments for the goodness of the Deity make a deeper impression, than on the sullen and morose.

How important then is the art of education when upon it in a great measure depends not only our behavior and conduct, but even our judgment and understanding, by which chiefly we are elevated above the brute creation! What can be more interesting to human beings, than their conviction of the existence of a benevolent Deity, their Maker, their Father, their Protector? Did parents seriously consider, that this conviction depends in some measure upon our disposition, they would neglect no opportunity of sweetening the temper of their children and improving their benevolence. The time for such discipline is confined to pupillage, when the mind, like wax, is deeply susceptible of impressions. At maturity, it becomes inflexible like the body, and then culture comes too late. Against passions and prejudices that never have been controlled, the most cogent reasons signify little. Arguments that accord with a man's taste are greedily swallowed, while the unpalatable are rejected with disgust. He is therefore no adept in logic who hopes to convince others by arguments that have weight with himself. He ought to study the temper of the person he would convince, and urge the arguments that are suited to that temper. . . .

Seeing then that our opinions and belief depend greatly on

passion and prepossession, little upon reason, and not at all upon will, how extravagant is the attempt to force conviction by rewards and punishments! . . . What then shall be thought of persecution for difference of opinion in points of faith? Often in perusing histories of persecution I have started up as from sleep and imagined that all the while I had been dreaming. And yet in fact that monster Persecution, the offspring of wild bigotry, has shed more blood than the fiercest wars for power and glory. Considering that to believe is not in our power, more than to be hot or cold, would one imagine it possible that by misguided education a rational being can be made to believe the most palpable absurdities? . . . Such . . . perverse education, tending to eradicate the faculty of reason and to make us blindly submissive to the crafty and designing, ought to call forth the most fervent zeal of parents to have their children properly educated. It is not sufficient that they are taught morality and the rules of conduct; their rational powers ought to be exercised and fortified in order to lay a foundation for proper opinions upon every subject, and for judging what they ought to believe and what they ought not to believe. What a heavy charge then lies against those parents who, instead of instructing their children in the principles of reason, the noblest faculty of man, leave them open to every wrong impression that may be stamped on the tender mind by chance or by the depravity of people about them!

Differences in Opinion Make the Cement of Society

It appears to me the utmost perversion of human nature that people differing in opinion, even with respect to religion, cannot live peaceably together, not to say happily. . . . There are indeed certain opinions that ought to be universal because they are grafted on our nature. I would persecute every opinion contradictory to the following propositions: that there is a Deity to whom we owe gratitude and worship; and that there is a right and a wrong in actions which ought to regulate the conduct of every human being. But I would persecute the opinions only, not the persons who hold them: they are the objects of pity, not of persecution. It is not in the power of man to eradicate his opinions, more than his feelings or his appetites. How absurd then is it to punish a man for what he cannot help? There is not in science a principle more evident than that now mentioned, which every man must assent to when fairly stated. Yet such is the influence of passion and prejudice as to have rendered that principle invisible for many ages. What rancor, distress, and bloodshed would have been prevented even among Christians, had the absurdity of persecution been displayed to them in open daylight? This doctrine ought to be carefully instilled into young minds hitherto free from bias. Let it be inculcated early into both sexes, that men are not accountable for their opinions more than for their faces; and that a wry opinion, even in matters of religion, is not the subject of punishment more than a wry shape. It is indeed a sort of Herculean labor to eradicate notions that from infancy have been held fundamental. But the mind of a child is white paper ready to receive any impression, good or bad. This is the precious time for impressions, though too early for regular instruction. Let it not be trifled away, for it never can be recalled. Good impressions stamped on the mind at that early age sink deep and never are obliterated. Therefore, neglect no opportunity of setting virtue and vice before your child in their proper colours: repeat to it often that if it be good, every person will love it; if naughty, that every person will hate it; and, in a word, that happiness is the result of virtue; misery of vice. Give me the naming of the tutor, and the pupil shall partake of the angelic nature or of the nature of a beast of prey.

I finish with observing historically that the art of Printing, among its other advantages, has had an influence to eradicate persecution by spreading everywhere knowledge and rational principles. Even those who are the most prone to persecution begin to hesitate. Reason, resuming her sovereign authority, will banish it altogether. It is true that no farther back than the beginning of the present century Mr. Locke, even by Protestants, was held grossly heterodox for maintaining toleration. I am however hopeful that within the next century it will be thought strange that persecution should have prevailed among social beings. It will perhaps even be doubted whether it ever was seriously put in practice.

Association of Ideas

A man while awake is constantly thinking. Ideas pass successively in his mind without a gap or interval, forming a succession of related thoughts or ideas, following one another according to an established law of nature. Our external actions are in a great measure governed by this succession, there being an intimate connection between thought and action. Did our thoughts flow on without any mutual relation and without any relation to our external actions, we should be hurried from thought to thought and from action to action entirely at the mercy of chance*. It is of importance in the education of youth that this succession be preserved entire, free from ill–sorted ideas that have originally no relation. Any unlucky bias by which unrelated ideas are conceived to be related is sufficient to disturb the regular course of actions and to throw all into confusion. Nature is faithful in displaying to us things as they exist: our erroneous conceptions are the result of misguided education or of unhappy biases contracted during childhood. The harsh treatment, for example, of a tender boy by a merciless pedagogue may produce an intimate connection between study and distress so as to give an aversion to books never to be conquered. Inculcate into a boy that his fate depends on the motion of the planets: in spite of reason he will be addicted to judicial astrology. There are men who from some unlucky impression made on them when children are as much afraid of a harmless cat as of a fierce lion.

One of Mr. Locke's most beautiful chapters is upon association of ideas. He shows the bad effects that certain ideas un-

---

* Elements of Criticism, chap. 1.

happily connected or associated have upon the understanding and upon the affections. . . . Mr. Locke has given a fine opening to the subject of ill founded associations and it deserves well to be prosecuted. It ought to be a chief concern in the tutor to prevent in his pupil an association between truth and error. Truth is in great danger from such an association: error cannot forever stand its ground against reason; and if it happen to be detected, the whole tumbles down together like the cemented parts of an old fabric. Thus it has fared with the Christian religion. . . . Unhappily, the absurd doctrines grafted on revelation have led many well meaning persons to reject it totally. Opinions associated by education and confirmed by custom are, as Mr. Locke expresses it, so coupled in the mind as not to be separated more than if they were but one idea. Had the Christian Revelation been preserved in its original purity, promulgating immortality to the world, with a distribution of rewards and punishments in a future state, I am confident that it would have been embraced by the wisest and the best men, and adhered to by all without hesitation, not even excepting such as may entertain doubts or scruples about the strength of the evidence. . . .

Associations . . . tend to mislead people from a just way of thinking. Formerly this nation was over-run with imaginary ghosts and apparitions; for simple people give a ready ear to wonders; and the more wonderful the more firm is their belief. A child in the nursery listens greedily to a dreadful story. It believes and trembles; and, if not of a bold spirit, is domineered by the impression for life. I could name persons whom even the most profound philosophy has not delivered from the fancied association of terror with darkness. What skill then does not the cultivation of the heart and head require when, after the ordinary discipline of school and college, men of all ranks are found to be infected with wrong biases and irregular associations which stand firm even against the most solid reasoning! Let this consideration actuate those who preside over the education of youth. How deep are the impressions, good or bad, that are made in childhood! As this is the proper period for impressions what have not teachers to answer for who neglect that period. With respect to religion in particular, the most important branch of education, it is in the power of a sensible tutor to instil into his pupil notions so just and clear as to secure him against every hurtful error. Above all, let it be inculcated that religion is the great support of morality, that it is our strongest safeguard against the distresses of life, that it is consistent with every rational enjoyment; and upon the whole that its direct tendency is to make its votaries happy.

9

Livingston and Smith
The Challenge to
Sectarian Education

The founding of King's College (later Columbia University) in New York City reveals the interplay between ideas and institutions that makes educational history conceived as intellectual history unique. In 1753, three young Presbyterian lawyers led an attack upon the design for Anglican sectarian control of the proposed college. They were William Livingston, John Morin Scott, and William Smith, Jr. All three were graduates of Yale College and had come to New York to study law with William Smith, Sr. and with James Alexander, advocate of Peter Zenger's case over freedom of the press in 1734. Together with William Peartree Smith, another Yale graduate who joined them briefly, they published the *Independent Reflector,* a weekly journal that placed their Presbyterian Whiggish views before New Yorkers.

William Livingston (1723–1790), the senior and leading contributor to the journal, had been concerned since 1749 with the need for a nonsectarian college in the province. But the Anglicans, who resented Harvard and Yale as "nurseries of sedition," had already been planning a college for several decades. Funds for the college were raised by lottery between 1746 and 1751; a substantial majority of Episcopalians was appointed to trusteeship of the funds; and the Reverend Samuel Johnson (1696–1772) of Connecticut, famed for his conversion to episcopacy when a tutor at Yale College, was selected as first president of King's College. Livingston and his colleagues feared that these steps were pointing toward an Anglican establishment in the province. The Anglicans in turn thought that their Presbyterian critics meant only to weaken the proposed college so that the recently established College of New Jersey (later Princeton University) would be without competition.

Sectarian rivalry and suspicion turned into political warfare. But King's College was chartered and opened despite the *Independent Reflector*. The college had liberal direction under Samuel Johnson. Its first board of control was interdenominational. Yet it never really flourished before the Revolution because Presbyterian and anti-gubernatorial groups in the provincial assembly denied it support.

In later years, after settling in New Jersey, Livingston became governor of that state and a leader of the Revolution. John Morin Scott (1730–1784) had a distinguished career at the New York bar and in the Revolutionary cause. But William Smith, Jr., jurist and historian, decided for the Loyalist side in the Revolution upon the outbreak of violence, though he had been a popular Whig leader in New York, which suggests that we should not read these essays of the 1750s as inevitable pathmarkers toward revolution. Nor should we read them as strictly Presbyterian statements. Though all four collaborators in the *Independent Reflector* were graduates of Thomas Clap's Yale, none was a strong Calvinist or disciple of Clap (see Selection 10). Embroiled in urban politics, these young men were more concerned with the political uses of church membership than with specific theology, not an uncommon circumstance for men in American public life then or later. Most significantly for the cultural life of New York City, the four Yale graduates, through their many civic activities, performed much the same function of stirring up the sleepy intellectual life of their town that Benjamin Franklin was performing almost alone in Philadelphia (see Selections 11–12).

The defense of intellectual freedom in the *Independent Reflector* is generally Miltonian and Lockian in tone. Specifically, it echoes the anticlericalism and the Protestant latitudinarianism of eighteenth-century English Whiggism, particularly the writings of Thomas Gordon and John Trenchard, two pamphleteers whose essays widely influenced American political thought before the Revolution. While it cannot be claimed that the *Independent Reflector* anticipated the arrival of modern secular and scientific arguments for academic freedom, these essays clearly portray the changing premises of higher learning that were forged out of the struggle for sectarian equality and religious freedom. Their argument that the state should favor no one church or sect over another comes as much out of the circumstances of sectarian rivalry in which the essayists found themselves as it does out of Lockian theory about religious toleration. And it is this argument for governmental impartiality toward all sects, elaborated in William Smith's final proposal (Number XXI), that does indeed anticipate the consensus that created the first American state universities.

More significant in retrospect is the academic philosophy of the essays. They advocate the toleration of varying creeds and biblical interpretations within a Protestant context that served to modify Calvinism and to give a truly "American" character to education in British North America. This philosophy or, better stated, way of looking at education would linger at least until the age of Jackson. Morality over theology; prudence over absolute norms of behavior; the combination of humane, scientific, and practical subjects over traditional classical learning; preparation for public life rather than for the ministry—these became the standard of American colleges. That this intellectual development occurred in some colleges that were founded out of the evangelical fervor of the mid-eighteenth century Great Awakening and that it continued in many more small denominational colleges of the next century is not merely an illustration of the gradual liberalization of orthodox Calvinism. It once again demonstrates the tendency of American education to reflect or to follow the changing forces and circumstances of its society.

Number XVII

[Thursday, March 22, 1753]

Remarks on Our Intended College

The true Use of Education, is to qualify Men for the different Employments of Life, to which it may please God to call them. 'Tis to improve their Hearts and Understandings, to infuse a public Spirit and Love of their Country; to inspire them with the Principles of Honour and Probity; with a fervent Zeal for Liberty, and a diffusive Benevolence for Mankind; and in a Word, to make them the more extensively serviceable to the Common-Wealth. Hence the Education of Youth hath been the peculiar Care of all the wise Legislators of Antiquity, who

---

The Independent Reflector: or, Weekly Essays on Sundry Important Subjects. More particularly adapted to the Province of New-York. . . . New-York: Printed (until tyrannically suppressed) in MDCCLIII. These excerpts are taken from a bound volume of the *Independent Reflector* in the New York Public Library. An earlier, modernized reprinting of these selections may be found in Herbert and Carol Schneider, eds., *Samuel Johnson, His Career and Writings* (New York, 1929), IV, 119–146. The only reprinting of the complete *Independent Reflector* is edited and annotated by Milton M. Klein: *The Independent Reflector* (Belknap Press: Cambridge, 1963). These excerpts may be found there at pp. 172–204.

thought it impossible to aggrandize the State, without imbuing the Minds of its Members with Virtue and Knowledge. Nay, so sensible of this fundamental Maxim in Policy, were PLATO, ARISTOTLE, and LYCURGUS, and in short all the ancient Politicians who have delivered their Sentiments on Government, that they make the Education of Youth, the principal and most essential Duty of the Magistrate. And, indeed, whatever literary Acquirement cannot be reduced to Practice, or exerted to the Benefit of Mankind, may perhaps procure its Possessor the Name of a Scholar, but is in Reality no more than a specious Kind of Ignorance. This, therefore, I will venture to lay down for a capital Maxim, that unless the Education we propose, be calculated to render our Youth better Members of Society, and useful to the Public in Proportion to its Expence, we had better be without it. As the natural Consequence of this Proposition, it follows, that the Plan of Education the most conducive to that End is to be chosen, and whatever has a Tendency to obstruct or impede it, ought carefully to be avoided.

The Nature, End and Design of such Seminaries, is to teach the Students particular Arts and Sciences, for the Conduct of Life, and to render them useful Members of the Community. "*Science* in Propriety of Language signifies, a clear and certain Knowledge of any Thing, founded on self-evident Principles or Demonstration: Tho' in a more particular and imperfect Sense, it is used for a System of any Branch of Knowledge, comprehending its Doctrine, Reason and Theory, without an immediate Application thereof to any Uses or Offices of Life. . . ."

The vast Influence of any Education upon the Lives and Actions of Men, and thence by a kind of political Expansion, on the whole Community, is verified by constant Experience. Nay, it discriminates Man from Man, more than by Nature he is differenced from the Brutes: And beyond all doubt much greater was the Disparity between the renowned Mr. *LOCKE*, and a common Hottentot, than between the latter and some of the most sagacious of the irrational Kingdom. But the Influence of a Collegiate Education, must spread a wider Circle proportionate to the Number of Students, and their greater Progress in Knowledge.

The Consequences of a liberal Education will soon be visible throughout the whole Province. They will appear on the Bench, at the Bar, in the Pulpit, and in the Senate and unavoidably affect our civil and religious Principles. . . .

There is no Place where we receive a greater Variety of Impressions, than at Colleges. Nor do any Instructions sink so deep in the Mind as those that are there received. . . . The Students not only receive the Dogmata of their Teachers with an implicit Faith, but are also constantly studying how to support them against every Objection. The System of the College is generally taken for true, and the sole Business is to defend it. Freedom of Thought rarely penetrates those contracted Mansions of systematical Learning. But to teach the establish'd Notions, and maintain certain Hypotheses, *hic Labor hoc opus est.* Every Deviation from the beaten Tract, is a kind of literary Heresy; and if the Professor be given to Excommunication, can scarce escape an Anathema. Hence that dogmatical Turn and Impatience of Contradiction, so observable in the Generality of Academics. To this also is to be referred, those voluminous Compositions, and that learned Lumber of gloomy Pedants, which hath so long infested and corrupted the World. In a Word, all those visionary Whims, idle Speculations, fairy Dreams, and party Distinctions, which contract and embitter the Mind, and have so often turn'd the World topsy-turvy.

I mention not this to disparage an academical Education, from which I hope I have myself received some Benefit, especially after having worn off some of its rough Corners, by a freer Conversation with Mankind. The Purpose for which I urge it, is to shew the narrow Turn usually prevailing at Colleges, and the absolute Necessity of teaching Nothing that will afterwards require the melancholy Retrogradation of being unlearned.

From this Susceptibility of tender Minds, and the extreme Difficulty of erasing original Impressions, it is easy to conceive, that whatever Principles are imbibed at a College, will run thro' a Man's whole future Conduct, and affect the Society of which he is a Member, in Proportion to his Sphere of Activity; especially if it be considered, that even after we arrive to Years of Maturity, instead of entering upon the difficult and disagreeable Work of examining the Principles we have formerly entertained, we rather exert ourselves in searching for Arguments to maintain and support them.

Tho' I have sufficiently shewn the prodigious Influence of a College upon the Community, from the Nature and Reason of the Thing, it may not be improper, for its farther Corroboration, to draw some Proofs from Experience and History.

At *Harvard* College in the *Massachusetts-Bay*, and at *Yale* College in *Connecticut*, the Presbyterian Profession is in some sort established. It is in these Colonies the commendable Practice of all who can afford it, to give their Sons an Education at their respective Seminaries of Learning. While they are in the Course of their Education, they are sure to be instructed in the Arts of maintaining the Religion of the College, which is always that of their immediate Instructors; and of combating the Principles of all other Christians whatever. When the young Gentlemen, have run thro' the Course of their Education, they enter into the Ministry, or some Offices of the Government, and acting in them under the Influence of the Doctrines espoused in the Morning of Life, the Spirit of the College is transfused thro' the Colony, and tinctures the Genius and Policy of the public Administration, from the Governor down to the Constable. Hence the Episcopalians cannot acquire an equal Strength among them, till some new Regulations, in Matters of Religion, prevail in their Colleges, which perpetually produce Adversaries to the heirarchical System. Nor is it to be question'd, that the Universities in *North* and *South-Britain,* greatly support the different Professions that are establish'd in their respective Divisions. . . .

Z.

[William Livingston]

Number XVIII

[Thursday, March 29, 1753]

I shall now proceed to offer a few Arguments, which I submit to the Consideration of my Countrymen, to evince the Necessity and Importance of constituting *our* College upon a Basis the most catholic, generous and free.

It is in the first Place observable, that unless its Constitution and Government, be such as will admit Persons of all protestant Denominations, upon a perfect Parity as to Privileges, it will itself be greatly prejudiced, and prove a Nursery of Animosity, Dissention and Disorder. The sincere Men of all Sects, imagine their own Profession, on the whole, more eligible and scriptural than any other. It is therefore very natural to suppose, they will exert themselves to weaken and dimish all other Divisions, the better to strengthen and enlarge their own. To this Cause must in a great Measure be ascribed, that Heat and Opposition, which animate the Breasts of many Men of religious Distinctions, whose intemperate and misapplied Zeal, is the only Blemish that can be thrown upon their Characters. Should our College, therefore, unhappily thro' our own bad Policy, fall into the Hands of any one religious Sect in the Province: Should that Sect, which is more than probable, establish its religion in the College, shew favour to its votaries, and cast Contempt upon others; 'tis easy to forsee, that Christians of all other Denominations amongst us, instead of encouraging its Prosperity, will, from the same Principles, rather conspire to oppose and oppress it. Besides *English* and *Dutch* Presbyterians, which perhaps exceed all our other religious Professions put together, we have Episcopalians, Anabaptists, Lutherans, Quakers, and a growing Church of Moravians all equally zealous for their discriminating Tenets: Which-soever of these has the sole Government of the College, will kindle the Jealousy of the Rest, not only against the Persuasion so preferred, but the College itself. Nor can any Thing less be expected, than a general Discontent and Tumult; which, affecting all Ranks of People, will naturally tend to disturb the Tranquility and Peace of the Province.

In such a State of Things, we must not expect the Children of any, but of that Sect which prevails in the Academy will ever be sent to it: For should they, the established Tenets must either be implicitly received, or perpetual religious War necessarily maintained. Instead of the liberal Arts and Sciences, and such Attainments as would best qualify the Students to be useful and ornamental to their Country, Party Cavils and Disputes about Trifles, will afford Topics of Argumentation to their incredible Disadvantage, by a fruitless Consumption of Time. Such Gentlemen, therefore, who can afford it, will give their Sons an Education abroad, or at some of the neighbouring Academies, where equally imbibing a Zeal for their own Principles, and furnished with the Arts of defending them, an incessant Opposition to all others, on their Return, will be the unavoidable Consequence. Not to mention, that Youth may become strongly attached to the Places at which they are educated. At this season of Life they receive the deepest Impressions: And, for the sake of a Wife or a Friend, and a thousand other Reasons that cannot now be enumerated, a Gentleman may turn his Back upon the Place of his Birth, and take up his Residence where the Morning of Life has been agreeably passed. Hence, besides the Expence of such Education prejudicial to us, we may frequently lose the Hopes of our Country, lose perhaps a Man every Way qualified to defend its Interests, and advance its Glory.

Others, and many such there may be, who not able to support the Expence of an Education abroad, but could easily afford it at Home, thro' a Spirit of Opposition to the predominant Party, will rather determine to give their Children no Educaat all. From all which it follows, that a College under the sole Influence of a Party, for want of suitable Encouragement, being but indifferently stocked with Pupils, will scarce arrive to the Usefulness of a *Schola illustris,* which being inferior to a College is, I hope, much short of what is intended by Ours.

Another Argument against so pernicious a Scheme is, that it will be dangerous to Society. The extensive Influence of such a Seminary, I have already shewn in my last Paper. And have we not reason to fear the worst Effects of it, where none but the Principles of one Persuasion are taught, and all others depressed and discountenanced? Where, instead of Reason and Argument, of which the Minds of the Youth are not capable, they are early imbued with the Doctrines of a Party, enforced by the Authority of a Professor's Chair, and the combining Aids of the President, and all the other Officers of the College? That religious Worship should be constantly maintained there, I am so far from opposing, that I strongly recommend it, and do not believe any such Kind of Society, can be kept under a regular and due Discipline without it. But instructing the Youth in any particular Systems of Divinity, or recommending and establishing any single Method of Worship or Church Government, I am convinced would be both useless and hurtful. Useless, because not one in a Hundred of the Pupils is capable of making a just Examination, and reasonable Choice. Hurtful, because receiving Impressions blindly on Authority, will corrupt their Understandings, and fetter them with Prejudices which may everlastingly prevent a judicious Freedom of Thought, and infect them all their Lives, with a contracted turn of Mind.

A Party-College, in less than half a Century, will put a new Face upon the Religion, and in Consequence thereof affect the Politics of the Country. Let us suppose what may, if the College should be entirely managed by one Sect, probably be supposed. Would not all possible Care be bestowed in tincturing the Minds of the Students with the Doctrines and Sentiments of that Sect? Would not the Students of the College, after the Course of their Education, exclusive of any others, fill all the Offices of the Government? Is it not highly reasonable to think, that in the Execution of those Offices, the Spirit of the College would have a most prevailing Influence, especially as that Party would perpetually receive new Strength, become more fashionable and numerous? Can it be imagined that all other Christians would continue peaceable under, and unenvious of, the Power of that Church which was rising to so exalted a Pre-eminence above them? Would they not on the Contrary, like all other Parties, reflect upon, reluct at, and vilify such an odious Ascendency? Would not the Church which had that Ascendency be thereby irritated to repeated Acts of Domination, and stretch their ecclesiastical Rule to unwarrantable and unreasonable Lengths? Whatever others may in their Lethargy and Supineness think of the Project of a Party-College, I am convinced, that under the Management of any particular Persuasion, it will necessarily prove destructive to the civil and religious Rights of the People: And should any future House of Representatives become generally infected with the Maxims of the College, nothing less can be expected than an Establishment of one Denomination above all others, who may, perhaps, at the good Pleasure of their Superiors, be most graciously favoured with a bare Liberty of Conscience, while they faithfully continue their annual Contributions, their Tythes and their Peter-Pence. . . .

Shall the Government of the College be delivered out of the Hands of the Public to a Party! They who wish it, are Enemies to their Country: They who ask it, have, besides this *Anti-Patriotism*, a Degree of Impudence, Arrogance, and Assurance unparallel'd. And all such as are active in so iniquitous a Scheme, deserve to be stigmatized with Marks of everlasting Ignominy and Disgrace. Let it, therefore, ever remain where it is, I mean under the power of the Legislature: The Influence, whether good or bad, we shall all of us feel, and are, therefore, all interested in it. It is, for that Reason, highly fit, that the People should always share in the Power to enlarge or restrain it: That Power they will have by their Representatives in Assembly; and no Man who is a Friend to Liberty, his Country and Religion, will ever rejoice to see it wrested from them.

It is farther to be remarked, that a public Academy is, or ought to be a mere civil Institution, and cannot with any tolerable Propriety be monopolized by any religious Sect. The Design of such Seminaries, hath been sufficiently shewn in my last Paper, to be entirely political, and calculated for the Benefit of Society, as a Society, without any Intention to teach Religion, which is the Province of the Pulpit: Tho' it must, at the same Time, be confessed, that a judicious Choice of our Principles, chiefly depends on a free Education.

Again, the Instruction of our Youth, is not the only Advantage we ought to propose by our College. If it be properly regulated and conducted, we may expect a considerable Number of Students from the neighbouring Colonies, which must, necessarily, prove a great Accession to our Wealth and Emolument. For such is our Capacity of endowing an Academy; that if it be founded on the Plan of a general Toleration, it must, naturally, eclipse any other on the Continent, and draw many Pupils from those Provinces, the Constitution of whose Colleges is partial and contracted: From *New-England,* where the *Presbyterians* are the prevailing Party, we shall, undoubtedly, be furnished with great Numbers, who, averse to the Sect in vogue among them, will, unquestionably, prefer the free Constitution, for which I argue, to that of their Colleges in which they cannot enjoy an equal Latitude, not to mention that such an Increase by foreign Students, will vastly augment the Grandeur of our Academy.

Add to all this, that in a new Country as ours, it is inconsistent with good Policy, to give any religious Profession the Ascendency over others. The rising Prosperity of *Pennsylvania,* is the Admiration of the Continent; and tho' disagreeing from them, I should always, for political Reasons, exclude *Papists* from the common and equal Benefits of Society. Yet, I leave it to the Reflections of my judicious Readers, whether the impartial Aspect of their Laws upon all Professions, has not, in a great Degree, conduced to their vast Importation of religious Refugees, to their Strength and their Riches: And whether a like Liberty among us, to all Protestants whatsoever, without any Marks of Distinction, would not be more commendable, advantageous, and politic.   A.

[William Smith, Jr.]

Number XIX

[Thursday, April 5, 1753]

It has in my last Papers been shewn, what an extensive and commanding Influence the Seat of Learning will have over the whole Province, by diffusing its Dogmata and Principles thro' every Office of Church and State. What Use will be made of such unlimited Advantages, may be easily guessed. The civil and religious Principles of the Trustees, will become universally established, Liberty and Happiness be driven without our Borders, and in their Room erected the Banners of spiritual and temporal Bondage. My Readers may, perhaps, regard such Reflections as the mere Sallies of a roving Fancy; tho', at the same

Time, nothing in Nature can be more real. For should the Trustees be prompted by Ambition, to stretch their Authority to unreasonable Lengths, as undoubtedly they would, were they under no Kind of Restraint, the Consequence is very evident. Their principal Care would be to chuse such Persons to instruct our Youth, as would be the fittest Instruments to extend their Power by positive and dogmatical Precepts. Besides which, it would be their mutual Interest to pursue one Scheme. Their Power would become formidable by being united: As on the Contrary, a Dissention would impede its Progress. Blind Obedience and Servility in Church and State, are the only natural Means to establish unlimited Sway. Doctrines of this Cast would be publicly taught and inculcated. Our Youth, inured to Oppression from Infancy, would afterwards vigorously exert themselves in their several Offices, to poison the whole Community with Slavish Opinions, and one universal Establishment become the fatal Portion of this now happy and opulent Province. . . .   B.

[William Livingston]

Number XX

[Thursday, April 12, 1753]

Instead of a Charter, I would propose, that the College be founded and incorporated by Act of Assembly, and that not only because it ought to be under the Inspection of the civil Authority; but also, because such a Constitution will be more permanent, better endowed, less liable to Abuse, and more capable of answering its true End. . . .

To a Matter of such general, such momentous Concern, our Rulers can never too particularly apply their Thoughts, since under their Protection alone Learning must flourish, and the Sciences be improved: It may indeed be urged, that the Nature of their Employment forbids them to spend their Time in the Inspection of Schools, or directing the Education of Youth: But are the Rise of Arts, the Improvement of Husbandry, the

Increase of Trade, the Advancement of Knowledge in Law, Physic, Morality, Policy, and the Rules of Justice and civil Government, Subjects beneath the Attention of our Legislature? In these are comprehended all our public and private Happiness; these are Consequences of the Education of our Youth, and for the Growth and Perfection of these, is our College designed.

Another Reason that strongly evinces the Necessity of an Act of Assembly, for the Incorporation of our intended Academy, is, that by this Means that Spirit of Freedom, which I have in my former Papers, shewn to be necessary to the Increase of Learning, and its consequential Advantages, may be rendered impregnable to all Attacks. While the Government of the College is in the Hands of the People, or their Guardians, its Design cannot be perverted. As we all value our Liberty and Happiness, we shall all naturally encourage those Means by which our Liberty and Happiness will necessarily be improved: And as we never can be supposed wilfully to barter our Freedom and Felicity, for Slavery and Misery, we shall certainly crush the Growth of those Principles, upon which the latter are built, by cultivating and encouraging their Opposites. Our College therefore, if it be incorporated by Act of Assembly, instead of opening a Door to universal Bigotry and Establishment in Church, and Tyranny and Oppression in the State, will secure us in the Enjoyment of our respective Privileges both civil and religious. For as we are split into so great a Variety of Opinions and Professions; had each Individual his Share in the Government of the Academy, the Jealousy of all Parties combating each other, would inevitably produce a perfect Freedom for each particular Party.

Should the College be founded upon an Act of Assembly, the Legislature would have it in their Power, to inspect the Conduct of its Governors, to divest those of Authority who abused it, and appoint in their Stead, Friends to the Cause of Learning, and the general Welfare of the Province. Against this, no Bribes, no Solicitations would be effectual: No Sect or Denomination plead an Exemption: But as all Parties are subject to their Authority; so would they all feel its equal Influence in this Particular. Hence should the Trustees pursue any Steps but those that lead to public Emolument, their Fate would be certain, their Doom inevitable: Every Officer in the College being under the narrow Aspect and Scrutiny of the civil Authority, would be continually subject to the wholesome Alternative, either of performing his Duty, with the utmost Exactness, or giving up his Post to a Person of superior Integrity. By this Means, the Prevalence of Doctrines destructive of the Privileges of human Nature, would effectually be discouraged, Principles of public Virtue inculcated, and every Thing promoted that bears the Stamp of general Utility. . . .　　　B.

[William Livingston]

Number XXI

[Thursday, April 19, 1753]

I shall now proceed to point out those Things which in my Judgment, are necessary to be inserted in the incorporating Act, for the Advancement of the true Interest of the College, and rendering it really useful to the Province. Such Things as will effectually prevent its being prejudicial to the Public, and guard us against all the Mischiefs we so justly apprehend, should it ever unhappily fall into the Hands of a Party.

First: That all the Trustees be nominated, appointed, and incorporated by the Act, and that whenever an Avoidance among them shall happen, the same be reported by the Corporation to the next Sessions of Assembly, and such Vacancy supplied by Legislative Act. That they hold their Offices only at the good Pleasure of the Governor, Council and General Assembly: And that no Person of any Protestant Denomination be, on Account of his religious Persuasion, disqualified for sustaining any Office in the College.

In Consequence of this Article we shall have the highest Security, that none will be dignified with that important and honourable Office, but such as are really qualified for executing it, agreeable to the true Design of its Institution. Should either

Branch, or any two Branches of the Legislature, propose and elect a Candidate obnoxious to the Third, the Negative of the latter is sufficient to prevent his Admission. The three Branches concurring in every Election, no Party can be disobliged, and when we consider the Characters of the Electors, all Possibility of Bribery and Corruption, seems to be *entirely excluded.*

Secondly: That the President of the College be elected and deprived by a Majority of the Trustees, and all the Inferior Officers by a Majority of the Trustees with the President; and that the Election and Deprivation of the President, be always reported by the Trustees, to the next Session of Assembly, and be absolutely void, unless the Acts of the Trustees in this Matter, be then confirmed by the Legislature.

By this Means the President, who will have the supreme Superintendency of the Education of our Youth, will be kept in a continual and ultimate Dependence upon the Public; and the Wisdom of the Province being his only Support, he will have a much greater Security, in the upright Discharge of his Duty, than if he depended solely on the Trustees, who are likely to oust him of his Office and Livelihood thro' Caprice or Corruption. That Station being therefore more stable, will at the same Time be more valuable; and for this Reason we have the stronger Hopes of filling the President's Chair, with a Man of Worth and Erudition, upon whose good Qualifications and Conduct, the Success and Improvement of the Students, will eminently depend.

Thirdly: That a Majority of the President and Trustees, have Power to make By-Laws not repugnant to the Act of Incorporation, and the Law of the Land: That all such By-Laws be reported to the House of Representatives at their next succeeding Session, *in hæc Verba,* under the seal of the College, and the Hands of the President and five Trustees; and that if they are not reported, or being reported are not confirmed, they shall be absolutely void.

Hence it is easy to conceive, that as on the one Hand there will be a great Security against the arbitrary and illegal Rule of the President and Trustees; so on the other, the immediate Governors of the College will have all proper Authority to make such salutary Rules as shall be necessary to advance the Progress of Literature, and support a Decorum and Police in the Academy,— as well as maintain the Dignity and Weight which the Superiors of it ought undoubtedly to be enabled to preserve over their Pupils.

Fourthly: That the Act of Incorporation contain as many Rules and Directions for the Government of the College as can be forseen to be necessary.

As all our Danger will arise from the Mis-Rule of the President and Trustees; so all our Safety consists in the Guardianship of the Legislature. Besides, the Advantage herefore, of being by this Article secured from arbitrary Domination in the College; the Business of the Trustees and President will be less, and they with their Subordinates, more at Leisure to concert the Advancement of the College.

The Fifth Article I propose is, that no religious Profession in particular be established in the College; but that both Officers and Scholars be at perfect Liberty to attend any Protestant Church at their Pleasure respectively: And that the Corporation be absolutely inhibited the making of any By-Laws relating to Religion, except such as compel them to attend Divine Service at some Church or other, every Sabbath, as they shall be able, lest so invaluable a Liberty be abused and *made a Cloak for Licenciousness.*

To this most important Head, I should think proper to subjoin,

Sixthly: That the whole College be every Morning and Evening convened to attend public Prayers, to be performed by the President, or in his Absence, by either of the Fellows; and that such Forms be perscribed and adhered to as all Protestants can freely join in.

Besides the Fitness and indisputable Duty of supporting the Worship of God in the College; obliging the Students to attend it twice every Day, will have a strong Tendency to preserve a due Decorum, Good Manners and Virtue amongst them, without which the College will sink into Profaness and Disrepute. They will be thereby forced from the Bed of Sloth, and being brought before their Superiors, may be kept from Scenes of Wickedness and Debauchery, which they might otherwise run into, as hereby their Absence from the College will be better detected.

With Respect to the Prayers, tho' I confess there are excellent Forms composed to our Hands, it would rather conduce to the Interest of our Academy, if, instead of those, new Ones were collected, which might easily be done from a Variety of approved Books of Devotion among all Sects; and perhaps it may be thought better to frame them as near as possible in the Language of Scripture. . . .

Seventhly: That Divinity be no Part of the public Exercises of the College. I mean, that it be not taught as a Science: That the Corporation be inhibited from electing a Divinity Professor; and that the Degrees to be conferred, be only in the Arts, Physic, and the Civil Law.

Youth at a College, as I have remarked in a former Paper, are incapable of making a judicious Choice in this Matter; for this Reason the Office of a theological Professor will be useless: Besides, Principles obtruded upon their tender Minds, by the Authority of a Professor's Chair, may be dangerous. But a main Reason in support of this Clause, is the Disgust which will necessarily be given to all Parties that differ in their Professions from that of the Doctor. The Candidate for the Ministry will hereby in his Divinity Studies, whenever he is fit for them, be left to the Choice and Direction of his Parents or Guardians. Besides, as most of the Students will be designed for other Employments in Life, the Time spent in the Study of Divinity, may be thought useless and unnecessary, and therefore give Umbrage to many. Nor will their whole Course of Time at the College, be more than sufficient for accomplishing themselves in the Arts and Sciences, whether they are designed for the Pulpit, or any other learned Profession. And it may justly be doubted, whether a Youth of good Parts, who has made any particular Proficiency in the Elements, or general Branches of Knowledge (his Instruction in which is the true and proper Business of a collegiate Education) would not be able to qualify himself for the Pulpit, by a Study of the Scriptures, and the best Divinity Books in the College Library, as well without as with the Aid of a Professor; especially if it be enacted,

Eighthly: That the Officers and Collegians have an unrestrained Access to all Books in the Library, and that free Conversation upon polemical and controverted Points in Divinity, be not discountenanced; whilst all public Disputations upon the various Tenets of different Professions of Protestants, be absolutely forbidden.

Ninthly: That the Trustees, President, and all inferior Officers, not only take and subscribe the Oaths and Declaration appointed by Statute, but be also bound by solemn Oath, in their respective Stations, to fulfil their respective Trusts, and preserve inviolate the Rights of the Scholars, according to the fundamental Rules contained in the Act. And that an Action at Law be given and well secured to every inferior Officer and Student, to be brought by himself, or his *Guardian*, or *prochein Amy*, according to his Age, for every Injury against his legal Right so to be established.

And in as much as artful Intrigues may hereafter be contrived to the Prejudice of the College, and a Junto be inleagued to destroy its free Constitution, it may perhaps be thought highly expedient, that the Act contain a Clause

Tenthly: That all future Laws, contrary to the Liberty and Fundamentals of this Act, shall be construed to be absolutely void, unless it refers to the Part thus to be altered, and expressly repeals it; and that no Act relating to the College, shall hereafter pass the House of Representatives, but with the Consent of the Majority of the whole House; I mean all the Members of Assembly in the Province.

Nor would it be amiss to prescribe,

Eleventhly: That as all Contests among the inferior Officers of the College, should be finally determined by the Majority of the Members of the Corporation, so the latter should be determined in all their Disputes, by a Committee of the whole House of Representatives, or the major Part of them.

These are the Articles which in my Opinion, should be incorporated in the Act for the Establishment of the College; and without which we have the highest Reason to think, the Advantages it will produce, will at best fall short of the Expence it will create, and perhaps prove a perpetual Spring of public Misery. . . .   A.

[William Smith, Jr.]

10

Thomas Clap
Defends the Sectarian College

Even as King's College was being directed toward interdenominational control (see Selection 9), Thomas Clap (1703–1767), President of Yale College, was writing this systematic defense of the idea that a college should be organized and rigorously controlled by a single sect. For the next century of American higher education Clap's argument was to prevail. To be sure, most of the colonial colleges followed the examples set by King's College and by the College of Philadelphia (later the University of Pennsylvania) in having an interdenominational representation on their first boards of trustees. In Philadelphia even the Roman Catholic priest was included on the board. But Clap's ideal of institutional control was fulfilled in the majority of small American colleges founded by Protestant denominations from the 1790s to the mid-nineteenth century.

For good or ill, two longer lasting traditions of American higher education were established by Clap at Yale during his tenure from 1740 to 1766. They are the self-perpetuating, single board of college or university control and the strong presidency. They have had remarkable influence upon the American theory of higher education. After only five years at Yale as Rector, Clap, a Harvard graduate, changed his relatively weak office into the powerful one of president. For the next twenty-one years Yale was *his* institution. Highhanded, petulant, dogmatic in his orthodox Calvinism, and a bully who loved theological battle, Clap fought Arminians and Anglicans to keep Yale pure, first for Old Light then for New Light Congregationalism. Though successful in guiding the physical expansion of Yale and in some ways acting the sagacious administrator, Clap followed a policy of making Yale a fortress of orthodoxy. He set down a test act for tutors and a loyalty oath for members of the Yale Corporation. He censored the college library; he searched the collections of students for "lascivious books"; and he rusticated some students for heterodoxy.

Clap's interest in Newtonian science, particularly observational astronomy, has tempted some historians to characterize him as a man who nicely balanced science and theology. This characterization is unfair to Clap's basic affirmations of faith and to New England Calvinism. True, Clap did make Yale College a center for science and mathematics. But his faith always came first. To read his scientific pursuits as the equal of his theological is to miss the primacy of his Calvinism. Moreover, such a reading of Clap can distort one's reading of the intellectual daring, toleration, and faith of Ezra Stiles, the later Yale president (1778–1795) who epitomizes the Enlightenment in American academic life and who was, in Edmund S. Morgan's phrase, a far "gentler" Puritan than Clap. There were, in sum, varying degrees of Calvinism and various shadings of scientific relativism in the colleges of later eighteenth-century America.

The Universities, in Scotland, have as great, or greater Privileges, than those in England. . . . Their Worship, is wholly under their own Regulation, and they are not subject, to any particular Parish, or Presbytery; but only to the general Assembly, of the Church of *Scotland;* to which, they send a President, or Professor, in the Quality of a Minister, as Presbyteries do. p. 32.

Religious Worship, Preaching, and Instruction on the Sabbath, being one of the most important Parts, of the Education of Ministers; it is more necessary, that it should be under the Conduct, of the Authority, of the College, than any other Part of Education. The Preaching, ought to be adapted, to the superior Capacity, of those, who are to be qualified, to be *Instructors of others;* and upon all Accounts *Superior,* to that, which is ordinarily to be expected, or indeed requisite, in a common Parish.

Thomas Clap, *The Religious Constitution of Colleges* (New London, Connecticut, 1754), pp. 5–8, 10–20.

There are many different Principles, in Religion, and Kinds of Preaching, which, when they are in any Degree faulty, cannot always be easily remedied, by Complaint, to any other Authority. And therefore, every *religious Society,* naturally chooses, as far as may be, to have, the Nomination of their own Minister. And this is much more necessary in a *College,* where the Preaching, is of such general Importance, to a whole Country; and such special Care, should be taken, that it be, upon all Accounts, of the *best Kind.* And it cannot be reasonable, nor safe, that any particular Parish, especially, that which happens to be the nearest to a College, should appoint the Minister for it. . . .

And where, as it generally happens, there are sundry Places of Worship, in the City, where a College is; if the Students should disperse to all, and every one of them, this would break up all order in the Society, and defeat the Religious Design, and Instructions of it. . . .

YALE-COLLEGE in *New-Haven;* does not come up, to the Perfection, of the Ancient Established Universities, in *Great Britain;* yet, would endeavour, to Imitate them, in most things, as far, as its present State, will admit of.

It was *Founded,* A. D. 1701. By *Ten Principal Ministers,* in the Colony of *Connecticut;* upon the Desire, of many other Ministers, and People in it; with the *License, and Approbation, of the General Assembly.* Their main Design, in that *Foundation,* was to *Educate Persons, for the Ministry of these* Churches, commonly called *Presbyterian* or *Congregational,* according to their own *Doctrine, Discipline,* and *Mode of Worship.* . . .

The present Governors, of the College; esteem themselves, bound by *Law,* and the more *sacred Ties of Conscience, and Fidelity to their Trust, committed to them, by their Predecessors;* to pursue, and carry on, the pious Intention, and Design, of the *Founders;* and to improve, all the *College Estate,* descended to them, for that purpose. And therefore, about seven Years ago; began, to lay a Fund for the Support of a *Professor, of Divinity,* in the College; and being, of late Years, more sensible, of the *Necessity* of it; from, the unhappy, divided

Circumstances, of *New-Haven;* and having receiv'd, some large
Donations . . . have determined, to settle, such a Professor; as
soon, as, by Leasing more of the said Land, or other ways, a
competent Support, can be obtained.

In the mean Time, they have desired, the *President;* with
some Assistance, from themselves, and others; to carry on the
Work, of a Professor, of Divinity; by Preaching, in the College
Hall, every Lord's Day. Being hereunto, sufficiently warranted,
from, the original Nature, Design, and Practice of Colleges, and
Universities; (which are, superior Societies, for Religious Purposes); and, the several special Clauses, in the Acts, of the
General Assembly; That so, the Students, may have the Advantage, of such Preaching, and Instruction, as is *best adapted, to
their Capacity, State, and Design.*

The Governors, of the College, cannot, consistent, with the
Trust committed, to them; give up, the ordinary, public Instruction, of the Students; especially, in Matters of Divinity; to
any, but their *own Officers* and *Substitutes.* For, they can have,
no sufficient Security, as such Governors, that others, who are
not, of their Nomination, and under their Authority, will Teach,
or Instruct, according, to the Design, of the *Founders:* and, if
they should deviate from it; the Governors, could have, no
Authority, to prevent it. And, upon that account, it is more
necessary, that the Governors of the College, should nominate
the Preacher to it, than any *other Officer,* or Instructor.

Particularly, it cannot be reasonable; that, either of the three,
religious Assemblies, in *New-Haven,* should choose, a Minister,
for the College; or that, the College, should be *obliged, to attend* upon such Preaching, as they, or either of them, should
choose. They would not allow, that the College, should choose
a Minister for *them;* much less, is it reasonable, that they,
should choose a Minister, for the *College;* which is a religious
Society, of a superior, more general, and more important
Nature.

This would be, to subject the College, to a Jurisdiction out of
itself; in the most important Point, of it's Institution, and Design. And no Society, or Body Politick, can be *safe,* but only, in
it's having, a Principle of self-Preservation; and a Power, of

Providing, every thing necessary, for it's own Subsistance, and Defence.

Indeed, as the College, receives it's Charter, and Part, of it's Support, from the *Government;* it is necessarily, *dependent* upon them; and under their Direction; and must choose, such a Minister as is agreeable to them; or otherwise, they may, withdraw their special Protection, and Support. And it cannot, reasonably, be suppos'd that, the General Assembly, would neglect, this part, of their Superintendency; and suffer it, to be exercised, by any, particular Parish. For, by this means, it might easily happen, that the College, might be subjected, to such Preaching, as would be contrary, to the Minds, of the Generality, of the Colony; as well, as, the Design, of the *Founders.*

Some indeed, have supposed, that, the only Design of Colleges, was to teach the Arts, and Sciences; and that Religion, is no part, of a College Education: And therefore, there ought to be, no religious Worship upheld, or enjoined, by the Laws of the College; but every Student, may Worship, where, and how, he pleaseth; or, as his Parents, or Guardian, shall direct.

But, it is probable, that there is not a College, to be found upon Earth, upon such a Constitution; without any Regard, to Religion. And we know, that Religion, and the Religion of these Churches, in particular; both, as to *Doctrine,* and *Discipline,* was the main Design, of the *Founders,* of this College; (agreeable, to the minds, of the *Body, of the People;*) and, this Design, their Successors, are bound in Duty, to pursue. And indeed, Religion, is a matter, of so great Consequence, and Importance; that, the Knowledge, of the Arts, and Sciences, how excellent soever, in themselves, are comparatively, worth but little, without it. . . .

And, if Parents, have a *Right,* to order, what Worship, their Children shall attend, at College; it would take, the Power, wholly out, of the Hands, of the Authority, of College, as to matters of Religion; and there may be, as many Kinds, of Religious Worship, at College; as there are, different Opinions, of Parents.

And, if Parents, give the *Law;* they must also, affix the *Pen-*

alty; and indeed, *inflict it themselves.* But Parents, at a Distance, cannot, Govern, their Children, at College; neither, is it practicable, that, they should give, such, a just *System of Rules,* as the Authority, of College *can,* or *ought,* to put in Execution.

For, we may suppose, for Instance; that, there may be, an Assembly, of *Jews,* or *Arrians,* in *New Haven;* and then, the Authority, of College, may be obliged, to punish, the Students, for not attending, such a Worship, as they esteem, to be *worse than none;* and such, as they are obliged, by the Statutes, of the *Founders,* not to permit, the Students, to attend upon.

It has been said; that, *Liberty of Conscience,* ought, to be allowed to all; to Worship, as they please.

Upon which, it has been considered; that, the College acts, upon the Principles, of Liberty, of Conscience, in the *fullest Sense;* and suppose, that any Man, under the Limitations of the Law; may Found a College, or School, for such Ends, and Purposes; and upon such Conditions, and Limitations, with Respect to those, who are allow'd, the Benefit of it, *as he in his Conscience,* shall think best. And that *his* Conscience, who has the Property, of a Thing; or gives, it, upon Conditions; ought to Govern, in all Matters, relating to the Use, of that thing; and not, his Conscience, who is allowed, to take the Benefit; who, has *no Right* to it, but according to the *Will,* and Conditions of the Proprietor, or Donor. And Liberty of Conscience in, him, who is allow'd, to take the Benefit, extends no further, than to determine, whether he will accept it upon those Conditions. And to challenge the Benefit, without complying with the Conditions, would be, to rob the Proprietor, (or Feoffee in Trust,) of his Property; and Right of Disposal.

The great Design, of Founding this School, was to Educate Ministers in our *own Way;* and in order to attain this End; the *Founders,* and *their Successors,* apprehend it to be necessary, that the Students, should ordinarily attend, upon the *same Way of Worship:* and should they give up, that Law, and Order; the College would serve Designs, and Purposes, *contrary* to that, for which it was *originally Founded:* which, in *Point of Conscience,* and Fidelity, to their Trust; *they cannot permit.* And in this Point, the College, Exercises, no kind of *Power,* or *Author-*

ity; but only that, which Results, from the *natural Liberties,* and Privileges of all free, and *Voluntary Societies* of Men; which is to determine, *their own Design,* amongst themselves; and the Conditions, of their own Favors, and Benefits to *others.*

Yet the Governors of the College, have always freely admitted, Protestants, of all Denominations, to enjoy the Benefit, of an Education in it; they attending upon, (as they always have done,) our Way of Worship; while they are there.

It has also been said; that, all the Students, ought to attend, the Worship, of the Church of *England;* or so many of them, as shall see Cause; or, as their Parents shall order, or permit.

That, the Church of England, is the *Established Religion,* of this Colony; and that those, who do not conform to it, are *Schismaticks.*

Upon which, it has been consider'd, that the Act of Parliament, in the Common Prayer Book, for the Establishment, of the Church of *England,* is expressly limitted, to *England, and Wales, and the Town of Berwick, upon Tweed.* And it is, a well known Maxim in the Law; *that the Statutes of England, do not extend to the Plantations; unless, they are Expressly mentioned.* . . .

It has also been said; that, Governor *Yale,* and Bishop *Berkley,* who were Church Men, made large *Donations,* to this College.

Upon which, it has been consider'd that; when any Donation is given, after the Foundation is laid, the Law presumes, that it was the Intention, of the *Donors,* that their Donations, should be improved, according, to the Design, of the *Founders.* The Law presumes, that every Man, knows the Law, in that thing, wherein he Acts: And since, by Law, the Statutes of the Founders, cannot be altered, it presumes, that the Donor, had not any Design to do it. And there is not, the least Reason to suppose, that the Governor, or Bishop, intended, or Expected, that, upon their Donations, any alteration should be made, in the Laws of the College; or any Deviation, from the Design, of the Founders, towards *the Church of England or* any other way.

If it was so; it seems, as if they intended, to *Buy* the College, rather than make a *Donation,* to it. And if there was Evidence, that they made their Donations, upon that *Condition;* the College would *Resign* them back again.

And since, there is not, the least Reason to suppose that, they, expected, or desired, that, upon their Donations, any Alteration should be made, in the Laws of College; we see no Obligation to do it, in Point of *Gratitude.* . . .

Yet, we have a just Sense, of the Generosity, of those Gentlemen; and for that, and many other Reasons, are Willing to do, all that we can, to gratify, the Gentlemen, of the Church of England; consistant with the Design and Statutes, of the Founders; and particularly, have given Liberty, to those Students, who have been educated, in the Worship, of the Church of England; and are, of that Communion; to be absent, at those Times, when the Sacrament is Administered, in that Church; and upon Christmas; and, at some such other Times, as will not be, an Infraction upon, the general, and *standing Rules,* of College.

It has been further said, that there are, a Number of Church Men, in this Colony; who, in the annual public Taxes, contribute something, towards the Support, of the College.

Upon which, it has been consider'd; that, when a Community, are jointly, at some public Charge; it is equitable, that the Benefit, of each Individual, should be consulted, so far, as it is consistant, with the general Design, and Good of the whole, or the Majority. And tho' it is impossible, that such a Benefit, should be Mathematically proportioned, to each Individual; yet this College, has educated, as many Episcopal Ministers, and others, as they desired, or stood in need of; which has been a sufficient Compensation, for their Paying, about, a Half Peny Sterling, per Man; in the annual Support, of the College.

And it may still continue to be, as serviceable, to the Church of England, as it has been, if they please; for the Orders of it, remain in Substance, just the same.

It may further be consider'd, that this College, was Founded, and in a good measure, Indowed, many Years, before there were any Donations made, by Church-Men; or so much, as one Episcopal Minister, in the Colony. And if Mens contributing, something, towards the Support of the College; gives, them a

Right, to order, what Worship, their Children shall attend upon, while at College; it gives the same Right, to Parents, of all other Denominations; which to admit, as was before Observ'd, would defeat the Design of the *Founders;* and destroy, the religious Order, of the College; which ought, *sacredly,* to be observed.

11

Benjamin Franklin and the
Theme of Self-Improvement

Four years after Benjamin Franklin (1706–1790) arrived in Philadelphia in 1723 at the age of seventeen, he and a group of his
"ingenious Acquaintances" organized a club for mutual self-improvement and assistance. Assuming leadership, as he did in many
civic activities, Franklin patterned the Junto after recommendations
made in 1710 by Cotton Mather, which had deeply influenced him
when a young apprentice printer in Boston. One of Mather's
schemes in his *Essays to do Good*, or *Bonifacius* (see Selection 2),
was the formation of what we today call adult education groups.
Their purpose was the promotion of religion and civic morality. The
purposes of Franklin's Junto were distinctly practical and specific,
as is demonstrated by these "Queries" put by the members to one
another. To Franklin's mind, however, the Junto's proceedings were
none the less moral than Mather's proposals. Members discussed
such applied scientific questions as the nature of sound, the phe-
nomenon of vapors, an explanation of tides, the curbing of smoky
chimneys, or an explanation of the shape of a candle flame. And
they put political and philosophical questions such as the proper
form of government, the wisdom of paper money, truth as defense
against libel, the power of self-interest, or whether philosophy
should eradicate the passions.

It is Franklin's self-appraisal and dedicated pursuit of his daily
business affairs, together with the constant improvement of his
mind through reading, reflection, conversation, and, above all,
through his recognition of prudent and tactful experiences that have
made the first half of his life synonymous with his educational ideas.
It is all described in the language of common sense throughout his
famed *Autobiography*. As a Junto member or as the "Poor Richard"

of his *Almanack* (1732–1757), Franklin not only was articulating the advice of Cotton Mather in New England and of Isaac Watts in old England (see Selection 7), but also he was speaking for two American ways of thought, the puritan and the pragmatic—the one formed long before his time and the other promulgated long after him. These two channels of thought, so opposed to each other as formal "systems" of ideas, cut deeply into the American character and into American schooling.

Unhappily for American educational history, Franklin of the Junto, the *Almanack*, or of the innovative proposals for secondary and technical schooling (see Selection 12) is virtually the only Franklin whom America has claimed for its intellectual past. Though he may be pictured in some textbooks as a bespectacled experimental scientist, flying his kite in an electrical storm, Franklin the man of Newtonian scientific thought, the man who conversed or corresponded on equal terms with the great contemporary minds of France and Britain, is not the Franklin most Americans have known or have been taught. This myopia toward Franklin the Renaissance, or broadly learned man, and the Enlightened, or empirically guided man in one person is symptomatic of two chronic infirmities in the history of American schools. One is a curricular parochialism, often sustained by complacent folk anti-intellectualism, that has championed "practical" or applied knowledge and skills over liberal learning and theory. The second problem was recognized by American Transcendentalists in the Jacksonian Age and by academic humanists since the 1920s. It was most vigorously exposed in 1923 from his singular point of view by the Englishman D. H. Lawrence, who condemned the Franklin model of life as education for a narrow, machine-like morality eliciting the virtues of temperance, order, frugality, industry, and so forth, like so many tunes from an automatic piano. Franklin, Lawrence charged, "this dry, moral, utilitarian little democrat," has imprisoned the free soul of man the "moral animal," who in the "American corral" has become only "a moral machine."

Recent scholarship on Franklin as scientist, statesman, and political thinker has sought to absolve him from this indictment. But the dominant image of Franklin in American schools remains, like the folk hero, the man of self-improvement, utilitarian inventions, and practical affairs.

Previous question, to be answer'd at every meeting.

Have you read over these queries this morning, in order to

Leonard W. Labaree *et al.*, eds., *The Papers of Benjamin Franklin* (13 vols. to date; New Haven: Yale University Press, 1959), I, 256–259. Reprinted by kind permission of Yale University Press.

consider what you might have to offer the Junto [touching] any one of them? viz.

1. Have you met with any thing in the author you last read, remarkable, or suitable to be communicated to the Junto? particularly in history, morality, poetry, physic, travels, mechanic arts, or other parts of knowledge.

2. What new story have you lately heard agreeable for telling in conversation?

3. Hath any citizen in your knowledge failed in his business lately, and what have you heard of the cause?

4. Have you lately heard of any citizen's thriving well, and by what means?

5. Have you lately heard how any present rich man, here or elsewhere, got his estate?

6. Do you know of any fellow citizen, who has lately done a worthy action, deserving praise and imitation? or who has committed an error proper for us to be warned against and avoid?

7. What unhappy effects of intemperance have you lately observed or heard? of imprudence? of passion? or of any other vice or folly?

8. What happy effects of temperance? of prudence? of moderation? or of any other virtue?

9. Have you or any of your acquaintance been lately sick or wounded? If so, what remedies were used, and what were their effects?

10. Who do you know that are shortly going voyages or journies, if one should have occasion to send by them?

11. Do you think of any thing at present, in which the Junto may be serviceable to *mankind?* to their country, to their friends, or to themselves?

12. Hath any deserving stranger arrived in town since last meeting, that you heard of? and what have you heard or observed of his character or merits? and whether think you, it lies in the power of the Junto to oblige him, or encourage him as he deserves?

13. Do you know of any deserving young beginner lately set up, whom it lies in the power of the Junto any way to encourage?

14. Have you lately observed any defect in the laws of your *country,* [of] which it would be proper to move the legislature for an amendment? Or do you know of any beneficial law that is wanting?

15. Have you lately observed any encroachment on the just liberties of the people?

16. Hath any body attacked your reputation lately? and what can the Junto do towards securing it?

17. Is there any man whose friendship you want, and which the Junto or any of them, can procure for you?

18. Have you lately heard any member's character attacked, and how have you defended it?

19. Hath any man injured you, from whom it is in the power of the Junto to procure redress?

20. In what manner can the Junto, or any of them, assist you in any of your honourable designs?

21. Have you any weighty affair in hand, in which you think the advice of the Junto may be of service?

22. What benefits have you lately received from any man not present?

23. Is there any difficulty in matters of opinion, of justice, and injustice, which you would gladly have discussed at this time?

24. Do you see any thing amiss in the present customs or proceedings of the Junto, which might be amended?

Any person to be qualified, to stand up, and lay his hand on his breast, and be asked these questions; viz.

1. Have you any particular disrespect to any present members? *Answer.* I have not.

2. Do you sincerely declare that you love mankind in general, of what profession or religion soever? *Answ.* I do.

3. Do you think any person ought to be harmed in his body, name or goods, for mere speculative opinions, or his external way of worship? *Ans.* No.

4. Do you love truth for truth's sake, and will you endeavour impartially to find and receive it yourself and communicate it to others? *Answ.* Yes.

12

Benjamin Franklin's Useful English Curriculum

Benjamin Franklin (1706–1790) first wrote in 1743 about the need for an academy in Philadelphia. He worked toward its establishment with his friends from the Junto (see Selection 11), and in 1749 he published the first of two essays to publicize the academy. *Proposals Relating to the Education of Youth in Pensilvania* emphasized in general terms the subjects to be studied. Franklin's theme was that it would be well if the students "could be taught *every Thing* that is ornamental: But Art is long, and their Time is short. It is therefore propos'd that they learn those Things that are likely to be *most useful* and *most ornamental,* Regard being had to the several Professions for which they are intended."

The second essay, his *Idea of the English School* (1751), was built upon Franklin's conviction that a good command of writing the English language, stressing thought and expression, is the cornerstone of a useful education. With the term "English school," he was using the explicit name of his day for a school that distinguished its curriculum from the traditional Latin and Greek preparatory studies. His rejection of ancient languages was lifelong: as a young apprentice printer in Boston he satirized classical learning and social exclusiveness at Harvard College; and in his last years he labeled Greek and Latin "the quackery of literature."

Although the *Idea of the English School,* reprinted here, is not as well known as Franklin's *Proposals,* it was more specific about a practical program of studies for the academy. The *Idea* was largely adopted in 1753 when the school opened with Franklin as first president of an interdenominational board of trustees. This program of studies not only pointed the institution toward vernacular training, but it also overcame Franklin's fear that English would become secondary in Philadelphia to the German language then widely spoken. Indeed, because of the ethnic and commercial diversity of its people, Philadelphia was, as Henry Adams later observed, the most cosmopolitan and hence the most democratic American city of the late colonial and early national periods. A utilitarian English curriculum offered common academic ground on which the city's young people could meet. In this respect, Franklin's scheme anticipated the linguistic nationalism advocated later by Noah Webster (see Selection 16).

Franklin's designs for a new academy also merged readily with the developing educational ideas of two men whose work had far-reaching effects. Franklin visited and corresponded in 1750 with Samuel Johnson (1696–1772), soon to become first president of King's College in New York City where there was some of the cosmopolitan and interdenominational air of Philadelphia. The utilitarian part of Franklin's *Idea of the English School* also attracted the attention of William Smith (1727–1803), a Scot tutoring on Long Island, who worked Franklin's ideas into his own model for schooling entitled *A General Idea of the College of Mirania* (1753). This essay won a teaching job for Smith at the Philadelphia Academy. When the Academy was expanded in 1755 to become The College, Academy, and Charitable School of Philadelphia (even later the University of Pennsylvania), Smith was made first Provost. Although Smith gradually subordinated the English to the classical part of the curriculum and later became Franklin's political enemy, the utilitarian *Idea of the English School* was prototypical of much that changed the course of American secondary schooling.

If the Age of the Academy marked American formal schooling after the Revolution, that age was born in the practical studies, the secular though intensely moral ethos, and the socially liberal style of Franklin's academy. Although estimates of their total number in the early nineteenth century are hard to determine, academies became, from Franklin's time to the Civil War, the most prevalent and effective institutions for educating young people beyond the elementary level. They displaced the Latin grammar school as the chief means of secondary education. They usually were sponsored by, and chartered in response to some local organizing group, rather than individual. Frequently a local church or its regional authority was the sponsor, although everywhere secular sponsorship became more common. They were "public" though not "free" schools in their admissions policies. They offered broader curricula than the old college-directed Latin schools, emphasizing English grammar, ethics though not theology, practical mathematics, commercial subjects, and foreign languages. In these respects they anticipated the modern public high school, but above all they anticipated it in their design and popularity as institutions responding to the manifold cultural needs of a locality or region.

Idea of the English School Sketch'd out for the Consideration of the Trustees of the Philadelphia Academy

It is expected that every Scholar to be admitted into this School, be at least able to pronounce and divide the Syllables in Reading, and to write a legible Hand. . . .

FIRST OR LOWEST CLASS.

Let the first Class learn the *English Grammar* Rules, and at the same time let particular Care be taken to improve them in *Orthography*. Perhaps the latter is best done by *Pairing* the Scholars, two of those nearest equal in their Spelling to be put together; let these strive for Victory, each propounding Ten Words every Day to the other to be spelt. He that spells truly most of the other's Words, is Victor for that Day; he that is Victor most Days in a Month, to obtain a Prize, a pretty neat Book of some Kind useful in their future Studies. This Method fixes the Attention of Children extreamly to the Orthography of Words, and makes them good Spellers very early. 'Tis a shame for a Man to be so ignorant of this little Art, in his own Language, as to be perpetually confounding Words of like Sound and different Significations; the Consciousness of which Defect, makes some Men, otherwise of good Learning and Understanding, averse to Writing even a common Letter.

Richard Peters, *A Sermon on Education. Wherein Some Account Is Given of the Academy, Established in the City of Philadelphia. Preach'd at the Opening Thereof, on the Seventh Day of January, 1750–1* (Philadelphia: B. Franklin and D. Hall, 1751)

Let the Pieces read by the Scholars in this Class be short, such as [Samuel] Croxall's Fables [of Aesop], and little Stories. In giving the Lesson, let it be read to them; let the Meaning of the difficult Words in it be explained to them, and let them con it over by themselves before they are called to read to the Master, or Usher; who is to take particular Care that they do not read too fast, and that they duly observe the Stops and Pauses. A Vocabulary of the most usual difficult Words might be formed for their Use, with Explanations; and they might daily get a few of those Words and Explanations by Heart, which would a little exercise their Memories; or at least they might write a Number of them in a small Book for the Purpose, which would help to fix the Meaning of those Words in their Minds, and at the same Time furnish every one with a little Dictionary for his future Use.

THE SECOND CLASS TO BE TAUGHT

Reading with Attention, and with proper Modulations of the Voice according to the Sentiments and Subject.

Some short Pieces, not exceeding the Length of a *Spectator,* to be given this Class as Lessons (and some of the easier *Spectators* would be very suitable for the Purpose.) These Lessons might be given over Night as Tasks, the Scholars to study them against the Morning. Let it then be required of them to give an Account, first of the Parts of Speech, and Construction of one or two Sentences; this will oblige them to recur frequently to their Grammar, and fix its principal Rules in their Memory. Next of the *Intention* of the Writer, or the *Scope* of the Piece; the Meaning of each Sentence, and of every uncommon Word. This would early acquaint them with the Meaning and Force of Words, and give them that most necessary Habit, of Reading with Attention.

The Master then to read the Piece with the proper Modulations of Voice, due Emphasis, and suitable Action, where Action is required; and put the Youth on imitating his Manner.

Where the Author has us'd an Expression not the best, let it be pointed out; and let his Beauties be particularly remarked to the Youth.

Let the Lessons for Reading be varied, that the Youth may be made acquainted with good Stiles of all Kinds in Prose and Verse, and the proper Manner of reading each Kind. Sometimes a well-told Story, a Piece of a Sermon, a General's Speech to his Soldiers, a Speech in a Tragedy, some Part of a Comedy, an Ode, a Satyr, a Letter, Blank Verse, Hudibrastick, Heroic, &c. But let such Lessons for Reading be chosen, as contain some useful Instruction, whereby the Understandings or Morals of the Youth, may at the same Time be improv'd.

It is requir'd that they should first study and understand the Lessons, before they are put upon reading them properly, to which End each Boy should have an English Dictionary to help him over Difficulties. When our Boys read English to us, we are apt to imagine *they* understand what *they* read because *we* do, and because 'tis their Mother Tongue. But they often read as Parrots speak, knowing little or nothing of the Meaning. And it is impossible a Reader should give the due Modulation to his Voice, and pronounce properly, unless his Understanding goes before his Tongue, and makes him Master of the Sentiment. Accustoming Boys to read aloud what they do not first understand, is the Cause of those even set Tones so common among Readers, which when they have once got a Habit of using, they find so difficult to correct: By which Means, among Fifty Readers we scarcely find a good One. For want of good Reading, Pieces publish'd with a View to influence the Minds of Men for their own or the publick Benefit, lose Half their Force. Were there but one good Reader in a Neighbourhood, a publick Orator might be heard throughout a Nation with the same Advantages, and have the same Effect on his Audience, as if they stood within the Reach of his Voice.

THE THIRD CLASS TO BE TAUGHT

Speaking properly and gracefully, which is near of Kin to good Reading, and naturally follows it in the Studies of Youth.

Let the Scholars of this Class begin with learning the Elements
of Rhetoric from some short System, so as to be able to give an
Account of the most usual Tropes and Figures. Let all their
bad Habits of Speaking, all Offences against good Grammar, all
corrupt or foreign Accents, and all improper Phrases, be
pointed out to them. Short Speechs [sic] from the Roman or
other History, or from our *Parliamentary Debates*, might be got
by heart, and deliver'd with the proper Action, &c. Speeches and
Scenes in our best Tragedies and Comedies (avoiding every
Thing that could injure the Morals of Youth) might likewise be
got by Rote, and the Boys exercis'd in delivering or acting
them; great Care being taken to form their Manner after the
truest Models.

For their farther Improvement, and a little to vary their
Studies, let them now begin to read *History*, after having got
by Heart a short Table of the principal Epochas in Chronology.
They may begin with [Charles] Rollin's *Antient and Roman
Histories*, and proceed at proper Hours as they go thro' the
subsequent Classes, with the best Histories of our own Nation
and Colonies. Let Emulation be excited among the Boys by
giving, Weekly, little Prizes, or other small Encouragements to
those who are able to give the best Account of what they have
read, as to Times, Places, Names of Persons, &c. This will make
them read with Attention, and imprint the History well in their
Memories. In remarking on the History, the Master will have
fine Opportunities of instilling Instruction of various Kinds,
and improving the Morals as well as the Understandings of
Youth.

The Natural and Mechanic History contain'd in [Noël A.
Pluche] *Spectacle de la Nature*, might also be begun in this
Class, and continued thro' the subsequent Classes by other
Books of the same Kind: For next to the Knowledge of *Duty*,
this Kind of Knowledge is certainly the most useful, as well as
the most entertaining. The Merchant may thereby be enabled
better to understand many Commodities in Trade; the Handi-
craftsman to improve his Business by new Instruments, Mix-
tures and Materials; and frequently Hints are given of new

Manufactures, or new Methods of improving Land, that may be set on foot greatly to the Advantage of a Country.

THE FOURTH CLASS TO BE TAUGHT

Composition. Writing one's own Language well, is the next necessary Accomplishment after good Speaking. 'Tis the Writing-Master's Business to take Care that the Boys make fair Characters, and place them straight and even in the Lines: But to *form their Stile,* and even to take Care that the Stops and Capitals are properly disposed, is the Part of the English Master. The Boys should be put on Writing Letters to each other on any common Occurrences, and on various Subjects, imaginary Business, &c. containing little Stories, Accounts of their late Reading, what Parts of Authors please them, and why. Letters of Congratulation, of Compliment, of Request, of Thanks, of Recommendation, of Admonition, of Consolation, of Expostulation, Excuse, &c. In these they should be taught to express themselves clearly, concisely, and naturally, without affected Words, or high-flown Phrases. All their Letters to pass through the Master's Hand, who is to point out the Faults, advise the Corrections, and commend what he finds right. Some of the best Letters published in our own Language, as Sir William Temple's, those of Pope, and his Friends, and some others, might be set before the Youth as Models, their Beauties pointed out and explained by the Master, the Letters themselves transcrib'd by the Scholar.

Dr. Johnson's *Ethices Elementa,* or first Principles of Morality, may now be read by the Scholars, and explain'd by the Master, to lay a solid Foundation of Virtue and Piety in their Minds. And as this Class continues the Reading of History, let them now at proper Hours receive some farther Instructions in Chronology, and in that Part of Geography (from the Mathematical Master) which is necessary to understand the Maps and Globes. They should also be acquainted with the modern Names of the Places they find mention'd in antient Writers.

The Exercises of good Reading and proper Speaking still continued at suitable Times.

FIFTH CLASS.

To improve the Youth in *Composition,* they may now, besides continuing to write Letters, begin to write little Essays in Prose; and sometimes in Verse, not to make them Poets, but for this Reason, that nothing acquaints a Lad so speedily with Variety of Expression, as the Necessity of finding such Words and Phrases as will suit with the Measure, Sound and Rhime of Verse, and at the same Time well express the Sentiment. These Essays should all pass under the Master's Eye, who will point out their Faults, and put the Writer on correcting them. Where the Judgment is not ripe enough for forming new Essays, let the Sentiments of a *Spectator* be given, and requir'd to be cloath'd in a Scholar's own Words; or the Circumstances of some good Story, the Scholar to find Expression. Let them be put sometimes on abridging a Paragraph of a diffuse Author, sometimes on dilating or amplifying what is wrote more closely. And now let Dr. [Samuel] Johnson's *Noetica,* or first Principles of human Knowledge, containing a Logic, or Art of Reasoning, &c. be read by the Youth, and the Difficulties that may occur to them be explained by the Master. The Reading of History, and the Exercises of good Reading and just Speaking still continued.

SIXTH CLASS.

In this Class, besides continuing the Studies of the preceding, in History, Rhetoric, Logic, Moral and Natural Philosophy, the best English Authors may be read and explain'd; as Tillotson, Milton, Locke, Addison, Pope, Swift, the higher Papers in the *Spectator* and *Guardian,* the best Translations of Homer, Virgil and Horace, of *Telemachus, Travels of Cyrus,* &c.

Once a Year, let there be publick Exercises in the Hall, the

Trustees and Citizens present. Then let fine gilt Books be given as Prizes to such Boys as distinguish themselves, and excel the others in any Branch of Learning. . . .

The Hours of each Day are to be divided and dispos'd in such a Manner, as that some Classes may be with the Writing-Master, improving their Hands, others with the Mathematical Master, learning Arithmetick, Accompts, Geography, Use of the Globes, Drawing, Mechanicks, &c. while the rest are in the English School, under the English Master's Care.

Thus instructed, Youth will come out of this School fitted for learning any Business, Calling or Profession, except such wherein Languages are required; and tho' unaquainted with any antient or foreign Tongue, they will be Masters of their own, which is of more immediate and general Use; and withal will have attain'd many other valuable Accomplishments; the Time usually spent in acquiring those Languages, often without Success, being here employ'd in laying such a Foundation of Knowledge and Ability, as, properly improv'd, may qualify them to pass thro' and execute the several Offices of civil Life, with Advantage and Reputation to themselves and Country.

B. F.

13

John Witherspoon on Training Children and Their Parents

From the time of Cotton Mather's sermons on child-rearing until the publication of Horace Bushnell's *Views of Christian Nurture* in 1847, few American books appeared on child development or on preschool child training. Although Americans increasingly wrote books about formal schooling, their reading on child nurture was restricted mainly to the writings of Englishmen such as Isaac Watts (see Selections 6–7) who were popularizers of John Locke's educational ideas. In this field, America was culturally an English colony long after independence. The slowness of Americans to advance their own theories of child development and behavior until about the 1830s was generally due to what today are called the "underdeveloped" conditions of a new country. No educational system was organized when the Republic was founded. Industrial and technological developments that would require school training in skills or expertise were then in their earliest stages. Great urban cultural centers had not yet matured where middle and upper economic classes would prolong childhood through formal schooling and would invent the adolescence of modern times. An agrarian nation needed its young out of school and in the labor force as soon as possible. In these circumstances, it is suggestive of the enduring connection in the American mind between children and religion that the second wave of child training literature finally came under the moralistic and religious reform impulses of the 1830s. Unlike its European counterpart, it did not arise directly from the Enlightenment. And the relatively late arrival of this kind of literature on the American scene is a reminder that modern American fascination with the ways of children and youth does not have a long heritage.

Although John Witherspoon's *Letters on Education* are among the few essays on child training from the early national period, their success is somewhat puzzling. They were not written for an American audience since they were addressed in 1765 to an unknown "gentleman of rank" in Scotland. Nor were they built upon original ideas or composed in vivid prose. The prestige and fame of their author must account for their being reprinted five times by 1822 after their first appearance in the Pennsylvania Magazine in 1775. Indeed, few men in the early Republic matched Witherspoon's eminence in several ways. Following a famous ministry in Scotland, Witherspoon (1723–1794) came in 1768 to the presidency of the College of New Jersey (later Princeton University) where he served till the end of his days. A leader in the movement toward American independence, he sat in the New Jersey legislature, represented his state in Congress through most of the Revolution, signed the Declaration of Independence, and helped to ratify the Constitution. He led in unifying and nationalizing the Presbyterian Church in America. Nassau Hall was truly Witherspoon's college. It prospered under his direction before the Revolutionary War, and by 1794 it graduated an astonishing number of church, civic, and educational leaders. Witherspoon's pupils were leading clergymen throughout the middle and southern states; they became college presidents in eight different states as well as they tutored or taught in academies and colleges in even more. James Madison and Aaron Burr reached the highest national positions, while other graduates of Witherspoon's time number six members of the Continental Congress, thirty-nine federal congressmen, twenty-one senators, twelve state governors, fifty-six state legislators, and thirty judges, including three members of the Supreme Court. Through the preaching, teaching, and writing of these men and many others, Witherspoon's common sense morality became a widespread educational and cultural standard. The *Letters on Education* are not written by an exceptional mind. They are written by an exceptional public man and teacher. If the old American tradition of viewing college presidents as local or even national sages had any historical merit, surely Witherspoon was one good reason for its durability.

The *Letters* illustrate an accommodation of religious belief to secular social conditions that characterizes American education from the pre-Revolutionary years through the mid-nineteenth century. This accommodation advanced academic moral philosophy (and its practitioners like John Witherspoon) to the forefront of intellectual activities. Witherspoon, the Presbyterian descendant of John Knox, is professedly concerned with the religious upbringing of children. But what really emerges from his pages is counsel on the behavior of parents toward their children to fit a culture that was increasingly secular, interdependent, urban, and upwardly mobile though still deferential toward the established or chosen leaders of society. The result is advice that mixes traditional Calvinist doctrine with some Enlightenment concepts of child-rearing. The Bible is no longer a primary authority; it is a support. Child and parent must seek divine approval, but there is little talk of salvation or damnation, aside from the assertion that the reality of hell must not be concealed from the child. The injunctions and rewards of a good life are essentially social, this-worldly, and humane. One must live, Witherspoon advises, so as to make religion appear respectable. A religious spirit is seen in children who are taught to follow parental examples of social grace, kindness, humility, generosity, and dignity. Piety and politeness merge. Witherspoon turns child-training from a religious to a moral process.

There is much that is derivative of Locke and similar to Watts and Kames in the *Letters*. They are partial to Lockian inductive logic. Their assertion that it is safer in reasoning "to trace facts upward than to reason downward," together with their tone of everyday good sense, mark almost everything that Witherspoon wrote or taught in America. His methods of early parental discipline over the child are also Lockian. For authority, he prefers solemnity to severity, though, when necessary, "the rod itself is an evidence of love." The point for the modern reader, however, is that parental discipline, dispensed without passion or resentment, must be dictated by a sense of duty and by conscience. For it is man's innate conscience, or his moral faculty, that distinguishes Witherspoon's model from Locke's. An innate moral faculty was a keystone of Scottish Common Sense academic philosophy, whose first and chief spokesman in American was Witherspoon. The presence of the moral sense in small children should make them all the more susceptible to good example. Thus a recalcitrant child should have his conscience awakened by discipline. Even parents of "irregular lives," whose consciences are guided only by "natural light" and not by piety, must see that a religious home atmosphere, especially for the pious rural family of little means, is conducive to humanity, good will, and "a decency of sentiment."

Religion, Witherspoon maintains, "is the great polisher of the common people." His appeal to the equalitarian power of evangelical religious sentiment helps us to understand how his comments could be palatable to those who, even in a deferential society, did not accept his easy acquiescence in social distinctions. Moreover, like Watts, he was read by people who were expecting to better themselves and their children, though many of his readers were already employers of servants or holders of slaves.

Above all, Witherspoon's *Letters* were addressed to fathers and mothers who guide their children toward social harmony. Despite their piety, the *Letters* do not emphasize education for salvation in the Puritan way. It was precisely their appeal to the present condition of the child and his future place in this world, written with the tone of old religious authority, that made them well received in their day and that makes them today a fair example of popular sentiment on child nurture when the nation began.

Letter I.

After so long a delay, I now set myself to fulfil my promise of writing to you a few thoughts on the education of children.— Though I cannot wholly purge myself of the crimes of laziness and procrastination, yet I do assure you, what contributed not a little to its being hitherto not done, was, that I considered it not as an ordinary letter, but what deserved to be carefully meditated on, and thoroughly digested. The concern you show on this subject, is highly commendable: for there is no part of your duty, as a Christian, or a citizen, which will be of greater service to the public, or a source of greater comfort to yourself.

The consequence of my thinking so long upon it, before committing my thoughts to paper, will probably be the taking the thing in a greater compass than either of us at first intended, and writing a series of letters, instead of one. With this view I begin with a preliminary to the successful education of children, viz. that husband and wife ought to be entirely one upon this subject, not only agreed as to the end, but as to the means to be used, and the plan to be followed, in order to attain it. It ought to encourage you to proceed in your design, that I am persuaded you will not only meet with no opposition to a rational and serious education of your children, but great assistance from Mrs. S——   ❖   ❖   ❖   ❖   ❖   ❖   ❖   ❖   ❖

The Works of the Rev. John Witherspoon, D.D., L.L.D., Late President of the College at Princeton, New Jersey. To which Is Prefixed An Account of the Author's Life, in a Sermon occasioned by his Death, by the Rev. Dr. John Rodgers, of New York. 3 vols. (Philadelphia, 1800), vol. III, pp. 497–531.

The erased lines contained a compliment, written with great sincerity: but recollecting that there are no rules yet settled for distinguishing true compliment from flattery, I have blotted them out: on which, perhaps, you will say to yourself, "He is fulfilling the character which his enemies give him, who say, it is the nature of the man to deal much more in satire, than in panegyric." However, I content myself with repeating, that certainly husband and wife ought to conspire and co-operate in every thing relating to the education of their children; and if their opinions happen, in any particular, to be different, they ought to examine and settle the matter privately by themselves, that not the least opposition may appear either to children or servants. When this is the case, every thing is enforced by a double authority, and recommended by a double example: but when it is otherwise, the pains taken are commonly more than lost, not being able to do any good, and certainly producing very much evil.

Be pleased to remember, that this is by no means intended against those unhappy couples, who, being essentially different in principles and character, live in a state of continual war. It is of little advantage to speak either to, or of such persons. But even differences incomparably smaller, are of very bad consequence: when one, for example, thinks a child may be carried out, and the other thinks it is wrong; when one thinks a way of speaking is dangerous, and the other is positive there is nothing in it. The things themselves may indeed be of little moment; but the want of concurrence in the parents, or the want of mutual esteem and deference, easily observed even by very young children, is of the greatest importance.

As you and I have chiefly in view the religious education of children, I take it to be an excellent preliminary, that parental affection should be purified by the principles, and controled or directed by the precepts of religion. A parent should rejoice in his children, as they are the gift of a gracious God; should put his trust in the care of an indulgent Providence for the preservation of his offspring, as well as himself; should be supremely desirous that they may be, in due time, the heirs of eternal life; and, as he knows the absolute dependence of every creature upon the will of God, should be ready to resign them at what time his Creator shall see proper to demand them. This happy qualification of parental tenderness, will have a powerful influence in preventing mistakes in the conduct of education. It will be the most powerful of all incitements to duty, and at the same time a restraint upon that natural fondness and indulgence, which, by a sort of fascination of fatality, makes parents often do or permit what their judgment condemns, and then excuse themselves by saying, that no doubt it is wrong, but truly they cannot help it.

Another preliminary to the proper education of children, is a firm persuasion of the benefit of it, and the probable, at least, if not certain success of it, when faithfully and prudently conducted. This puts an edge upon the spirit, and enables the christian not only to make some attempts, but to persevere with patience and diligence. I know not a common saying either more false or pernicious, than "that the children of good men are as bad as others." This saying carries in it a supposition, that whereas the force of education is confessed with respect to every other human character and accomplishment, it is of no consequence at all as to religion. This, I think, is contrary to daily experience. Where do we expect to find young persons piously disposed but in pious families? The exceptions, or rather appearances to the contrary, are easily accounted for, in more ways than one. Many persons appear to be religious, while they are not so in reality, but are chiefly governed by the applause of men. Hence their visible conduct may be specious, or their public performances applauded, and yet their families be neglected.

It must also be acknowledged that some truly well–disposed persons are extremely defective or imprudent in this part of their duty, and therefore it is no wonder that it should not succeed. This was plainly the case with Eli, whose sons we are told, made themselves vile, and he restrained them not. However, I must observe, if we allow such to be truly good men, we must at the same time confess that this was a great drawback upon their character; and that they differed very much from the father of the faithful, who had this honorable testimony given him by God, "I know him, that he will command his children and his houshold after him, that they serve me." To this we may add, that the child of a good man, who is seen to follow dissolute courses, draws the attention of mankind more upon him, and is much more talked of, than any other person of the same character. Upon the whole, it is certainly of moment, that one who desires to educate his children in the fear of God, should do it in a humble persuasion, that if he was not defective in his own duty, he will not be denied the blessing of success. I could tell you some remarkable instances of parents who seemed to labor in vain for a long time, and yet were so happy as to see a change at last; and of some children in whom even after the death of the parents, the seed which was early sown, and seemed to have been entirely smothered, has at last produced fruit. And indeed no less seems to follow from the promise, annexed to the command. "Train up a child in the way he should go, and when he is old he will not depart from it."

Having laid down these preliminaries, I shall say a few things upon the preservation of the health of children. Perhaps you will think this belongs only to the physician: but though a physician ought to be employed to apply remedies in dangerous cases, any man, with a little reflection, may be allowed to form some judgment as to the ordinary means of their preservation; nay, I cannot help being of opinion, than any other man is fitter than a physician for this purpose. His thoughts are so constantly taken up with the rules of his art, that it is an hundred to one he will prescribe more methods and medicines than can be used with safety.

The fundamental rules for preserving the health of children, are cleanliness, liberty, and free air. By cleanliness, I do not mean keeping the outside of their clothes in a proper condition to be seen before company, nor hindering them from fouling their hands and feet, when they are capable of going abroad, but keeping them dry in the night time, when young, and frequently washing their bodies with cold water, and other things of the same nature and tendency. The second rule is liberty. All persons young and old, love liberty: and as far as it does them no harm, it will certainly do them good. Many a free born subject is kept a slave for the first ten years of his life; and is so much handled and carried about by women in his infancy, that the limbs and other parts of his body, are frequently mishapen, and the whole very much weakened; besides, the spirits, when under confinement, are generally in a dull and languishing state. The best exercise in the world for children, is to let them romp and jump about, as soon as they are able, according to their own fancy. This in the country is best done in the fields; in a city a well aired room is better than being sent into the streets under the care of a servant, very few of whom are able so far to curb their own inclinations, as to let the children follow theirs, even where they may do it with safety. As to free air there is nothing more essentially necessary to the strength and growth of animals and plants. If a few plants of any kind are sown in a close confined place, they commonly grow up tall, small, and very weak. I have seen a bed of beans in a garden, under the shade of a hedge or tree, very long and slender, which brought to my mind a young family of quality, trained up in a delicate manner, who if they grow at all, grow to length, but never to thickness. So universal is this, that I believe a body of a sturdy or well built make, is reckoned among them a coarse and vulgar thing.

There is one thing with regard to servants, that I would particularly recommend to your attention. All children are liable to accidents; these may happen unavoidably; but do generally arise from the carelessness of servants, and to this they are almost always attributed by parents. This disposes all servants, good or bad, to conceal them from the parents, when they can possibly do it. By this means, children often receive hurts in falls or otherwise, which if known in time, might be easily remedied, but not being known either prove fatal, or make them lame or deformed. A near relation of mine has a high shoulder and a distorted waist from this very cause. To prevent such accidents, it is necessary to take all pains possible to acquire the confidence of servants, to convince them of the necessity of concealing nothing. There are two dispositions in parents, which hinder the servants from making discoveries; the first is when they are very passionate, and apt to storm and rage against their servants, for every real or supposed neglect. Such persons can never expect a confession, which must be followed by such terrible vengeance. The other is, when they are tender-hearted, or timorous to excess, which makes them show themselves deeply affected or greatly terrified upon any little accident that befals their children. In this case, the very best servants are unwilling to tell them through fear of making them miserable. In such cases, therefore, I would advise parents, whatever may be their real opinions, to discover them as little as possible to their servants. Let them still inculcate this maxim, that there should be no secrets concerning children, kept from those most nearly interested in them. And that there may be no temptation to such conduct, let them always appear as cool and composed as possible, when any discovery is made, and be ready to forgive a real fault, in return for a candid acknowledgment.

Letter II.

If I mistake not my last letter was concluded by some remarks on the means of trying servants to be careful of the safety of children, and ready to discover early and honestly any accidents that might happen to befal them. I must make some farther remarks upon servants. It is a subject of great importance, and inseparably connected with what I have undertaken. You will find it extremely difficult to educate children properly, if the servants of the family do not conspire in it; and impossible, if they are inclined to hinder it. In such a case, the orders issued, or the method laid down, will be neglected, where that is possible and safe; where neglect is unsafe, they will be unsuccessfully or improperly executed, and many times, in the hearing of the children, they will be either laughed at, or complained of and disapproved. The certain consequence of this is, that children will insensibly come to look upon the directions and cautions of their parents, as unnecessary or unreasonable restraints. It is a known and very common way for servants to insinuate themselves into the affections of children, by granting them such indulgences as would be refused them by their parents, as well as concealing the faults which ought to be punished by parents, and they are often very successful in training them up to a most dangerous fidelity in keeping the secret.

Such is the evil to be feared, which ought to have been more largely described: let us now come to the remedy. The foundation, to be sure, is to be very nice and careful in the choice of servants. This is commonly thought to be an extremely difficult matter, and we read frequently in public papers the heaviest complaints of bad servants. I am, however, one of those who think the fault is at least as often in the masters. Good servants may certainly be had, and do generally incline of themselves to be in good families, and when they find that they are so, do often continue very long in the same, without desiring to remove. You ought, therefore, to be exceedingly scrupulous, and not without an evident necessity, to hire any servant but who seems to be sober and pious. Indeed, I flatter myself, that a pious family is such, as none but one who is either a saint or a hypocrite will be supposed to continue in. If any symptoms of the last character appear, you need not be told what you ought to do.

The next thing, after the choice of servants, is to make conscience of doing your duty to them, by example, instruction, admonition and prayer. Your fidelity to them will naturally produce in them fidelity to you and yours, and that upon the very best principles. It will excite in them a deep sense of gratitude, and at the same time fill them with sentiments of the highest and most unfeigned esteem. I could tell you of instances (you will however probably recollect some yourself) of servants who from their living comfortably, and receiving benefits in pious families, have preserved such a regard and attachment to their masters, as have been little short of idolatry. I shall just mention one—a worthy woman in this place, formerly servant to one of my predecessors, and married many years since to a thriving tradesman, continues to have such an undiminished regard to her master's memory, that she cannot speak of him without delight; keeps by her to this hour the newspaper which gives an account of his death and character, and, I believe, would not exchange it for a bill or bond, to a very considerable sum.

But the third and finishing direction with regard to servants, is to convince them, in a cool and dispassionate manner, of the reasonableness of your method of proceeding, that as it is dictated by conscience, it is conducted with prudence. Thence it is easy to represent to them that it is their duty, instead of hindering its success by opposition or negligence, to co-operate with it to the utmost of their power. It is not below any man to reason in some cases with his servants. There is a way of speaking to them on such subjects, by which you will lose nothing of your dignity, but even corroborate your authority. While you manifest your firm resolution, never to depart from your right and title to command: you may, notwithstanding, at proper seasons, and by way of condescension, give such general reasons for your conduct, as to show that you are not acting by mere caprice or humor. Nay, even while you sometimes insist, that your command of itself shall be a law, and that you will not suffer it to be disputed, nor be obliged to give a reason for it, you may easily show them that this also is reasonable. They may be told that you have the greatest interest in the welfare of your children, the best opportunity of being apprised as to the means of prosecuting it, and that there may be many reasons for your orders which it is unnecessary or improper for them to know.

Do not think that all this is excessive refinement, chimerical or impossible. Servants are reasonable creatures, and are best governed by a mixture of authority and reason. They are generally delighted to find themselves treated as reasonable, and will sometimes discover a pride in showing that they understand, as well as find a pleasure in entering into your views. When they find, as they will every day by experience, the success and benefit of a proper method of education, it will give them a high opinion of, and confidence in, your judgment; they will frequently consult you in their own affairs, as well as implicitly follow your directions in the management of yours. After all, the very highest instance of true greatness of mind, and the best support of your authority, when you see necessary to interpose it, is not to be opinionative or obstinate, but willing to acknowledge or remit a real mistake, if it is discreetly pointed out, even by those in the lowest stations. The application of these reflections will occur in several of the following branches of this subject.

The next thing I shall mention as necessary, in order to the education of children, is, to establish as soon as possible, an entire and absolute authority over them. This is a part of the subject which requires to be treated with great judgment and delicacy. I wish I may be able to do so. Opinions, like modes and fashions, change continually upon every point; neither is it easy to keep the just middle, without verging to one or other of the extremes. On this, in particular, we have gone in this nation in general, from one extreme to the very utmost limits of the other. In the former age, both public and private, learned and religious education was carried on by mere dint of authority. This, to be sure, was a savage and barbarous method, and was in many instances terrible and disgusting to the youth. Now, on the other hand, not only severity, but authority, is often decried; persuasion, and every soft and gentle method, is recommended, in such terms as plainly lead to a relaxation. I hope you will be convinced that the middle way is best, when you find it is recommended by the Spirit of God in his word, Prov. xiii. 24. xix. 18. xxii. 15. You will also find a caution against excess in this matter, Col. ii. 21.

I have said above, that you should "establish as soon as possible an entire and absolute authority." I would have it early, that it may be absolute, and absolute that it may not be severe. If parents are too long in beginning to exert their authority, they will find the task very difficult. Children, habituated to indulgence for a few of their first years, are exceedingly impatient of restraint, and if they happen to be of stiff or obstinate tempers, can hardly be brought to an entire, at least to a quiet and placid submission; whereas, if they are taken in time, there is hardly any temper but what may be made to yield, and by early habit the subjection becomes quite easy to themselves.

The authority ought also to be absolute, that it may not be severe. The more complete and uniform a parent's authority is, the offences will be more rare, punishment will be less needed, and the more gentle kind of correction will be abundantly sufficient. We see every where about us examples of this. A parent that has once obtained, and knows how to preserve authority, will do more by a look of displeasure, than another by the most passionate words and even blows. It holds universally in families and schools, and even the greater bodies of men, the army and navy, that those who keep the strictest discipline, give the fewest strokes. I have frequently remarked that parents, even of the softest tempers, and who are famed for the greatest indulgence to their children, do, notwithstanding, correct them more frequently, and even more severely, though to very little purpose, than those who keep up their authority. The reason is plain. Children, by foolish indulgence, become often so froward and petulent in their tempers, that they provoke their easy parents past all endurance; so that they are obliged, if not to strike, at least to scold them, in a manner as little to their own credit, as their childrens profit.

There is not a more disgusting sight than the impotent rage of a parent who has no authority. Among the lower ranks of people, who are under no restraint from decency, you may sometimes see a father or mother running out into the street after a child who is fled from them, with looks of fury and words of execration; and they are often stupid enough to imagine that neighbors or passengers will approve them in this conduct, though in fact it fills every beholder with horror. There is a degree of the same fault to be seen in persons of better rank, though expressing itself somewhat differently. Ill words and altercations will often fall out between parents and children before company; a sure sign that there is defect of government at home or in private. The parent stung with shame at the misbehavior or indiscretion of the child, desires to persuade the observers that it is not his fault, and thereby effectually convinces every person of reflection that it *is*.

I would therefore recommend to every parent to begin the establishment of authority much more early than is commonly supposed to be possible: that is to say, from about the age of eight or nine months. You will perhaps smile at this: but I do assure you from experience, that by setting about it with prudence, deliberation, and attention, it may be in a manner completed by the age of twelve or fourteen months. Do not imagine I mean to bid you use the rod at that age; on the contrary, I mean to prevent the use of it in a great measure, and to point out a way by which children of sweet and easy tempers may be brought to such a habit of compliance, as never to need correction at all; and whatever their temper may be, so much less of this is sufficient, than upon any other supposition. This is one of my favorite schemes; let me try to explain and recommend it.

Habits in general may be very early formed in children. An association of ideas is, as it were, the parent of habit. If then, you can accustom your children to perceive that your will must always prevail over theirs, when they are opposed, the thing is done, and they will submit to it without difficulty or regret. To bring this about, as soon as they begin to show their inclination by desire or aversion, let single instances be chosen now and then (not too frequently) to contradict them. For example, if a child shows a desire to have any thing in his hand that he sees, or has any thing in his hand with which he is delighted, let the parent take it from him, and when he does so, let no consideration whatever make him restore it at that time. Then at a considerable interval, perhaps a whole day is little enough, especially at first, let the same thing be repeated. In the mean time, it must be carefully observed, that no attempt should be made to contradict the child in the intervals. Not the least appearance of opposition, if possible, should be found between the will of the parent and that of the child, except in those chosen cases, when the parent must always prevail.

I think it necessary that those attempts should always be made and repeated at proper intervals by the same person. It is also better it should be by the father than the mother or any female attendant, because they will be necessarily obliged in many cases to do things displeasing to the child, as in dressing, washing, &c. which spoil the operation; neither is it necessary that they should interpose, for when once a full authority is established in one person, it can easily be communicated to others, as far as is proper. Remember, however, that mother or nurse should never presume to condole with the child, or show any signs of displeasure at his being crossed; but on the contrary, give every mark of approbation, and of their own submission, to the same person.

This experiment frequently repeated will in a little time so perfectly habituate the child to yield to the parent whenever he interposes, that he will make no opposition. I can assure you from experience, having literally practised this method myself, that I never had a child of twelve months old, but who would suffer me to take any thing from him or her, without the least mark of anger or dissatisfaction; while they would not suffer any other to do so, without the bitterest complaints. You will easily perceive how this is to be extended gradually and universally, from one thing to another, from contradicting to commanding them. But this, and several other remarks upon establishing and preserving authority, must be referred to another letter.

Letter III.

DEAR SIR,

The theory laid down in my last letter, for establishing an early and absolute authority over children, is of much greater moment than, perhaps, you will immediately apprehend. There is a great diversity in the temper and disposition of children; and no less in the penetration, prudence and resolution of parents. From all these circumstances, difficulties arise, which increase very fast as the work is delayed. Some children have naturally very stiff and obstinate tempers, and some have a certain pride, or if you please, greatness of mind, which makes them think it a mean thing to yield. This disposition is often greatly strengthened in those of high birth, by the ideas of their own dignity and importance, instilled into them from their mother's milk. I have known a boy not six years of age, who made it a point of honor not to cry when he was beat even by his parents. Other children have so strong passions, or so great sensibility, that if they receive correction, they will cry immoderately, and either be, or seem to be, affected to such a degree, as to endanger their health or life. Neither is it uncommon for the parents in such a case to give up the point, and if they do not ask pardon, at least they give very genuine marks of repentance and sorrow for what they have done.

I have said this is not uncommon, but I may rather ask you whether you know any parents at all, who have so much prudence and firmness as not to be discouraged in the one case, or to relent on the other? At the same time it must always be remembered, that the correction is wholly lost which does not produce absolute submission. Perhaps I may say it is more than lost, because it will irritate instead of reforming them, and will instruct or perfect them in the art of overcoming their parents, which they will not fail to manifest on a future opportunity. It is surprising to think how early children will discover the weak side of their parents, and what ingenuity they will show in obtaining their favor or avoiding their displeasure. I think I have observed a child in treaty or expostulation with a parent, discover more consummate policy at seven years of age, than the parent himself, even when attempting to cajole him with artful evasions and specious promises. On all these accounts, it must be a vast advantage that a habit of submission should be brought on so early, that even memory itself shall not be able to reach back to its beginning. Unless this is done, there are many cases in which, after the best management, the authority will be imperfect; and some in which any thing that deserves that name will be impossible. There are some families, not contemptible either in station or character, in which the parents are literally and properly obedient to their children, are forced to do things against their will, and chidden if they discover the least backwardness to comply. If you know none such, I am sure I do.

Let us now proceed to the best means of preserving authority, and the way in which it ought to be daily exercised. I will trace this to its very source. Whatever authority you exercise over either children or servants, or as a magistrate over other citizens, it ought to be dictated by conscience, and directed by a sense of duty. Passion or resentment ought to have as little place as possible; or rather, to speak properly, though few can boast of having arrived at full perfection, it ought to have no place at all. Reproof or correction given in a rage, is always considered by him to whom it is administered, as the effect of weakness in you, and therefore the demerit of the offence will be either wholly denied or soon forgotten. I have heard some parents often say, that they cannot correct their children unless they are angry; to whom I have usually answered, Then you ought not to correct them at all. Every one would be sensible, that for a magistrate to discover an intemperate rage in pronouncing sentence against a criminal, would be highly indecent. Ought not parents to punish their children in the same dispassionate manner? Ought they not to be at least equally concerned to discharge their duty in the best manner, one case as in the other?

He who would preserve his authority over his children, should be particularly watchful of his own conduct. You may as well pretend to force people to love what is not amiable, as to reverence what is not respectable. A decency of conduct, therefore, and dignity of deportment, is highly serviceable for the purpose we have now in view. Lest this, however, should be mistaken, I must put in a caution, that I do not mean to recommend keeping children at too great a distance by an uniform sternness and severity of carriage. This, I think, is not necessary, even when they are young; and it may, to children of some tempers, be very hurtful when they are old. By and by you shall receive from me a quite contrary direction. But by dignity of carriage, I mean parents showing themselves always cool and reasonable in their own conduct; prudent and cautious in their conversation with regard to the rest of mankind; not fretful or impatient, or passionately fond of their own peculiarities; and though gentle and affectionate to their children, yet avoiding levity in their presence. This, probably, is the meaning of the precept of the ancients, *Maxima debetur pueris reverentia.* I would have them cheerful, yet serene. In short, I would have their familiarity to be evidently an act of condescension. Believe it, my dear Sir, that which begets esteem, will not fail to produce subjection.

That this may not be carried too far, I would recommend every expression of affection and kindness to children when it is safe, that is to say, when their behavior is such as to deserve it. There is no opposition at all between parental tenderness and parental authority. They are the best supports to each other. It is not only lawful, but will be of service that parents should discover the greatest fondness for children in infancy, and make them perceive distinctly with how much pleasure they gratify all their innocent inclinations. This, however, must always be done when they are quiet, gentle, and submissive in their carriage. Some have found fault with giving them, for doing well, little rewards of sweetmeats and playthings, as tending to make them mercenary, and leading them to look upon the indulgence of appetite as the chief good. This I apprehend, is rather refining too much: the great point is, that they be rewarded for doing good, and not for doing evil. When they are cross and froward, I would never buy peace, but force it. Nothing can be more weak and foolish, or more destructive of authority, than when children are noisy and in an ill humor, to give them or promise them something to appease them. When the Roman emperors began to give pensions and subsidies to the Northern nations to keep them quiet, a man might have foreseen without the spirit of prophecy, who would be master in a little time. The case is exactly the same with children. They will soon avail themselves of this easiness in their parents, command favors instead of begging them, and be insolent when they should be grateful.

The same conduct ought to be uniformly preserved as children advance in years and understanding. Let parents try to convince them how much they have their real interest at heart. Sometimes children will make a request, and receive a hasty or froward denial: yet upon reflection the thing appears not to be unreasonable, and finally it is granted; and whether it be right or wrong, sometimes by the force of importunity, it is extorted. If parents expect either gratitude or submission for favors so ungraciously bestowed, they will find themselves egregiously mistaken. It is their duty to prosecute, and it ought to be their comfort to see, the happiness of their children; and therefore they ought to lay it down as a rule, never to give a sudden or hasty refusal; but when any thing is proposed to them, consider deliberately and fully whether it is proper—and after that, either grant it cheerfully, or deny it firmly.

It is a noble support of authority, when it is really and visibly directed to the most important end. My meaning in this, I hope, is not obscure. The end I consider as most important is, the glory of God in the eternal happiness and salvation of children. Whoever believes in a future state, whoever has a just sense of the importance of eternity to himself, cannot fail to have a like concern for his offspring. This should be his end both in instruction and government; and when it visibly appears that he is under the constraint of conscience, and that either reproof or correction are the fruit of sanctified love, it will give them irresistible force. I will tell you here, with all the simplicity necessary in such a situation, what I have often said in my course of pastoral visitation in families, where there is in many cases, through want of judgment, as well as want of principle, a great neglect of authority. "Use your authority for God, and he will support it. Let it always be seen that you are more displeased at sin than at folly. What a shame is it, that if a child shall, through the inattention and levity of youth, break a dish or a pane of the window, by which you may lose the value of a few pence, you should storm and rage at him with the utmost fury, or perhaps beat him with unmerciful severity; but if he tells a lie, or takes the name of God in vain, or quarrels with his neighbors, he shall easily obtain pardon: or perhaps, if he is reproved by others, you will justify him, and take his part."

You cannot easily believe the weight that it gives to family authority, when it appears visibly to proceed from a sense of duty, and to be itself an act of obedience to God. This will produce coolness and composure in the manner, it will direct and enable a parent to mix every expression of heart-felt tenderness, with the most severe and needful reproofs. It will make it quite consistent to affirm, that the rod itself is an evidence of love, and that it is true of every pious parent on earth, what is said of our Father in heaven: "Whom the Lord loveth, he chasteneth, and scourgeth every son whom he receiveth. If ye endure chastening, God dealeth with you as with sons: for what son is he whom the Father chasteneth not? But if ye are without chastisement, whereof all are partakers, then ye are bastards and not sons." With this maxim in your eye, I would recommend, that solemnity take the place of, and be substituted for severity. When a child, for example, discovers a very depraved disposition, instead of multiplying stripes in proportion to the reiterated provocations, every circumstance should be introduced, whether in reproof or punishment, that can either discover the seriousness of your mind, or make an impression of awe and reverence upon his. The time may be fixed before hand—at some distance—the Lord's day—his own birth-day—with many other circumstances that may be so special that it is impossible to enumerate them. I shall just repeat what you have heard often from me in conversation, that several pious persons made it an invariable custom, as soon as their children could read, never to correct them, but after they had read over all the passages of scripture which command it, and generally accompanied it with prayer to God for his blessing. I know well with what ridicule this would be treated by many, if publicly mentioned; but that does not shake my judgment in the least, being fully convinced it is a most excellent method, and that it is impossible to blot from the minds of children, while they live upon earth, the impressions that are made by these means, or to abate the veneration they will retain for the parents who acted such a part.

Suffer me here to observe to you, that such a plan as the above requires judgment, reflection, and great attention in your whole conduct. Take heed that there be nothing admitted in the intervals that counteract it. Nothing is more destructive of authority, than frequent disputes and chiding upon small matters. This is often more irksome to children than parents are aware of. It weakens their influence insensibly, and in time makes their opinion and judgment of little weight, if not wholly contemptible. As before I recommended dignity in your general conduct, so in a particular manner, let the utmost care be taken not to render authority cheap, by too often interposing it. There is really too great a risk to be run in every such instance. If parents will be deciding directly, and censuring every moment, it is to be supposed they will be sometimes wrong, and when this evidently appears, it will take away from the credit of their opinion, and weaken their influence, even where it ought to prevail.

Upon the whole, to encourage you to choose a wise plan, and to adhere to it with firmness, I can venture to assure you, that there is no doubt of your success. To subdue a youth after he has been long accustomed to indulgence, I take to be in all cases difficult, and in many impossible; but while the body is tender, to bring the mind to submission, to train up a child in the nurture and admonition of the Lord, I know is not impossible: and he who hath given the command, can scarcely fail to follow it with his blessing.

Letter IV.

Dear Sir,

Having now finished what I proposed to say on the means of establishing and preserving authority, I shall proceed to another very important branch of the subject, and beg your very particular attention to it, viz. *example.* Do not, however, suppose that I mean to enter on that most beaten of all topics, the influence of example in general, or to write a dissertation on the common saying, that "example teaches better than precept." An able writer, doubtless, might set even this in some new lights, and make it a strong argument with every good man to pay the strictest attention to his visible conduct. What we see every day has a constant and powerful influence on our temper and carriage. Hence arise national characters, and national manners, and every characteristic distinction of age and place. But of this I have already said enough.

Neither is it my purpose to put you in mind of the importance of example to enforce instruction, or of the shamefulness of a man's pretending to teach others what he despises himself. This ought in the strongest manner to be laid before pastors and other public persons, who often defeat habitually by their lives, what they attempt to do occasionally in the execution of their office. If there remains the least suspicion of your being of that character, these letters would have been quite in another strain. I believe there are some persons of very irregular lives, who have so much natural light in their consciences, that they would be grieved or perhaps offended, if their children should tread exactly in their own steps: but even these, and much less others, who are more hardened, can never be expected to undertake or carry on the system of education, we are now endeavoring to illustrate. Suffer me, however, before I proceed, to make one remark: when I have heard of parents who have been watched by their own children, when drunk, and taken care of, lest they should meet with injury or hurtful accidents—or whose intemperate rage and horrid blasphemies, have, without scruple, been exposed both to children and servants—or who, as has been sometimes the case, were scarcely at the pains to conceal their criminal amours, even from their own offspring—I have often reflected on the degree of impiety in principle, or fearedness of conscience, or both united, necessary to support them in such circumstances. Let us leave all such with a mixture of pity and disdain.

By mentioning example, therefore, as an important and necessary branch of the education of children, I have chiefly in view a great number of particulars, which, separately taken, are, or at least are supposed to be, of little moment; yet by their union or frequent repetition, produce important and lasting effects. I have also in view to include all that class of actions, in which there is, or may be, a coincidence between the duties of piety and politeness, and by means of which, the one is incorporated with the other. These are to be introduced under the head of example, because they will appear there to best advantage, and because many of them can hardly be taught or understood in any other way.

This, I apprehend, you will readily approve of, because,

though you justly consider religion as the most essentially necessary qualification, you mean at the same time that your children should be fitted for an appearance becoming their station in the world. It is also the more necessary, as many are apt to disjoin wholly the ideas of piety and politeness, and to suppose them not only distinct, but incompatible. This is a dangerous snare to many parents, who think there is no medium between the grossest rusticity, and giving way to all the vanity and extravagance of a dissipated life. Persons truly pious have often by their conduct given countenance to this mistake. By a certain narrowness of sentiment and behavior they have become themselves, and rendered their children, unfit for a general intercourse with mankind, or the public duties of an active life.

You know, Sir, as much as any man, how contrary my opinion and conduct have been upon this subject. I cannot help thinking that true religion is not only consistent with, but necessary to the perfection of true politeness. There is a noble sentiment to this purpose illustrated at considerable length in the Port-Royal Essays, viz. "That worldly politeness is no more than an imitation or imperfect copy of Christian charity, being the pretence or outward appearance, of that deference to the judgment, and attention to the interest of others, which a true Christian has as the rule of his life, and the disposition of his heart."* I have at present in my mind the idea of certain persons, whom you will easily guess at, of the first quality; one or two of the male, and twice that number at least of the female sex, in whom piety and high station are united. What a sweetness and complacency of countenance, what a condescension and gentleness of manners, arising from the humility of the gospel being joined to the refined elegance inseparable from their circumstances in life!

Be pleased to follow me to the other extreme of human society. Let us go to the remotest cottage of the wildest country,

---

* The authors of these essays, commonly called by writers who make mention of them, the gentlemen of Port-Royal, were a society of Jansenists in France, who used to meet at that place; all of whom were eminent for literature, and many of them of high rank, as will be evident by mentioning the names of Pascal, Arnaud, and the Prince of Conti. The last was the author of the essay from which the above remark is taken.

and visit the family that in habits it. If they are pious, there is a certain humanity and good will attending their simplicity, which makes it highly agreeable. There is also a decency in their sentiments, which, flowing from the dictates of conscience, is as pleasing in all respects as the restraint imposed by the rules of good-breeding, with which the persons here in view have little opportunity of being acquainted. On the contrary, unbred country people, when without principle, have generally a savageness and brutality in their carriage, as contrary to good manners as to piety itself. No one has a better opportunity of making observations of this kind, than I have from my office and situation, and I can assure you, that religion is the great polisher of the common people. It even enlarges their understanding as to other things, Having been accustomed to exercise their judgment and reflection on religious subjects, they are capable of talking more sensibly on agriculture, politics, or any common topic of indifferent conversation.

Let me not forget to speak of the middle ranks of life. Here, also, I scruple not to affirm, that whatever sphere a man has been bred in, or attained to, religion is not an injury but an addition to the politeness of his carriage. They seem indeed to confess their relation to one another, by their reciprocal influence. In promiscuous conversation, as true religion contributes to make men decent or courteous, so true politeness guards them effectually from any outrage against piety or purity. If I were unhappily thrown into mixed or dangerous company, I should not apprehend any thing improper for me to hear from the most wicked man, but from the greatest clown. I have known gentlemen who were infidels in principle, and whose lives, I had reason to believe, were privately very bad, yet in conversation they were guarded, decent and improving; whereas if there come into company a rough, unpolished country gentleman, no man can promise that he will not break out into some profane exclamation or obscene allusion, which it would be wrong to attribute to impiety, so much as to rudeness and want of reflection.

I have been already too long in the introduction, and in giving the reasons for what I propose shall make a part of this branch of the subject, and yet I must make another preliminary remark: there is the greater necessity for uniting piety and politeness in the system of family example, that as piety is by that means inculcated with the greatest advantage, so politeness can scarcely be attained in other way. It is very rare that persons reach a higher degree of politeness, than what they have been formed to in the families of their parents and other near relations. True politeness does not consist in dress, or a few motions of the body, but in a habit of sentiment and conversation: the first may be learned from a master, and in a little time; the last only by a long and constant intercourse with those who possess, and are therefore able to impart it. As the difficulty is certainly greatest with the female sex, because they have fewer opportunities of being abroad in the world, I shall take an example from among them.

Suppose a man of low birth living in the country, by industry and parsimony has become wealthy, and has a daughter to whom he desires to give a genteel education. He sends her to your city to a boarding school, for the other which is nearer me, you are pleased not to think sufficient for that purpose. She will speedily learn to buy expensive and fashionable clothes, and most probably be in the very height and extravagance of the fashion, one of the surest signs of a vulgar taste. She may also, if her capacity is tolerable, get rid of her rustic air and carriage; and if it be better than ordinary, learn to discourse upon whatever topic is then in vogue, and comes in immediately after the weather, which is the beginning of all conversation. But as her residence is only for a time, she returns home; where she can see or hear nothing but as before. Must she not relapse speedily in the same vulgarity of sentiment, and perhaps the same provincial dialect, to which she had been accustomed from her youth? Neither is it impossible that she may just retain as much of the city ceremonial, as by the incongruous mixture, will render her ridiculous. There is but one single way of escape, which we have seen some young women of merit and capacity take, which is to contract an intimacy with persons of liberal sentiments and higher breeding, and be as little among their relations as possible. I have given this description to convince you that it is in their father's house and by the conversation and manners, to which they are there accustomed, that children must be formed to politeness, as well as to virtue. I carry this matter so far, that I think it a disadvantage to be bred too high, as well as too low. I do not desire, and have always declined any opportunities given me of having my children reside long in families of high rank. I was afraid they would contract an air and manner unsuitable to what was to be their condition for the remainder of their lives. I would wish to give my children as just, as noble, and as elegant sentiments as possible, to fit them for rational conversation, but a dress and carriage suited to their station, and not inconsistent with the meekness of the gospel.

Though the length of this digression, or explanatory introduction, has made it impossible to say much in this letter on forming childrens' character and manners by example, before I conclude I will give one direction which is pretty comprehensive. Give the utmost attention to the manner of receiving and entertaining strangers in your family, as well as to your sentiments and expressions with regard to them when they are gone. I am fully persuaded that the plainest and shortest road to real politeness of carriage, and the most amiable sort of hospitality, is to think of others just as a Christian ought, and to express these thoughts with modesty and candor. This will keep you at an equal distance from a surly and morose carriage on the one hand, and a fawning cringing obsequiousness, or unnecessary compliment and ceremony on the other. As these are circumstances to which children in early life are very attentive, and which occur constantly in their presence, it is of much moment what sentiments they imbibe from the behavior of their parents. I do not mean only their learning from them an ease and dignity of carriage, or the contrary; but also, some moral or immoral habits of the last consequence. If they perceive you happy and lifted up with the visit or countenance of persons of high rank, solicitous to entertain them properly, submissive and flattering in your manner of speaking to them, vain and apt to boast of your connection with them: and if, on the contrary, they perceive you hardly civil to persons of inferior stations, or narrow circumstances, impatient of their company, and immediately seizing the opportunity of their departure to despise or expose them; will not this naturally lead the young mind to consider riches and high station as the great sources of earthly happiness? Will it not give a strong bias to their whole desires and studies, as well as visibly affect their behavior to others in social life. Do not think that this is too nice and refined: the first impressions upon young persons, though inconsiderable in themselves, have often a great as well as lasting effect.

I remember to have read many years ago, in the Archbishop of Cambray's Education of a Daughter, an advice to parents to let their children perceive that they esteem others, not according to their station or outward splendor, but their virtue and real worth. It must be acknowledged that there are some marks of respect due to men, according to their place in civil life, which a good man would not fail to give them, even for conscience sake. But it is an easy matter, in perfect consistency with this, by more frequent voluntary intercourse, as well as by our usual manner of speaking, to pay that homage which is due to piety, to express our contempt or indignation at vice, or meanness of every kind. I think it no inconsiderable addition to this remark, that we should be as cautious of estimating *happiness* as *virtue* by outward station; and keep at the same distance from envying as from flattering the great.

But what I must particularly recommend to you, is to avoid that common but detestable custom of receiving persons with courtesy, and all the marks of real friendship in your house; and the moment they are gone, falling upon their character and conduct with unmerciful severity. I am sensible there are some cases, though they are not numerous, in which it may be lawful to say of others behind their back, what it would be at least imprudent or unsafe to say in their own presence. Neither would I exclude parents from the advantage of pointing out to their children the mistakes and vices of others, as a warning or lesson of instruction to themselves. Yet as detraction in general is to be avoided at all times; so of all others the most improper season to speak to any man's prejudice, is, after you have just received and treated him in an hospitable manner, as a friend. There is something mean in it, and something so nearly allied to hypocrisy and disingenuity, that I would not choose to act such a part even to those whom I would take another opportunity of pointing out to my children, as persons whose conversation they should avoid, and whose conduct they should abhor.

In every station, and among all ranks, this rule is often transgressed; but there is one point in which it is more frequently and more universally transgressed than in any other, and that is by turning the absent into ridicule, for any thing odd or aukward in their behavior. I am sorry to say that this is an indecorum that prevails in several families of high rank. A man of inferior station, for some particular reason is admitted to their company. He is perhaps not well acquainted with the rules of politeness, and the presence of his superiors, to which he is unaccustomed, increases his embarrassment. Immediately on his departure, a petulent boy or giddy girl will set about mimicking his motions and repeating his phrases, to the great entertainment of the company, who apparently derive much self-satisfaction from a circumstance in which there is no merit at all. If any person renders himself justly ridiculous, by effecting a character which he is unable to sustain, let him be treated with the contempt he deserves. But there is something very ungenerous in people treating their inferiors with disdain, merely because the same Providence that made their ancestors great, left the others in a lower sphere.

It has often given me great indignation to see a gentleman or his wife, of real worth, good understanding, but simple manners, despised and ridiculed for a defect which they could not remedy, and that often by persons the most insignificant and frivolous, who never uttered a sentence in their lives that deserved to be remembered or repeated. But if this conduct is ungenerous in the great, how diverting is it to see the same disposition carried down through all the inferior ranks, and showing itself in a silly triumph of every class over those who are supposed to be below them? I have known many persons, whose station was not superior to mine, take great pleasure in expressing their contempt of *vulgar ideas* and *low life;* and even a tradesman's wife in a city, glorying over the unpolished manners of her country acquaintance.

Upon the whole, as there is no disposition to which young persons are more prone than derision, or, as the author I cited above, Mr. Fenelon, expresses it, *un esprit mocqueur et malin*—and few that parents are more apt to cherish—under the idea of its being a sign of sprightliness and vivacity—there is none which a pious and prudent parent should take greater care to restrain by admonition, and destroy by a contrary example.

Letter V.

Dear Sir,

Let us now proceed to consider more fully what it is to form children to piety by example. This is a subject of great extent, and, perhaps, of difficulty. The difficulty, however, does not consist either in the abstruseness of the arguments, or uncertainty of the facts upon which they are founded, but in the minuteness or trifling nature of the circumstances, taken separately, which makes them often either wholly unnoticed or greatly undervalued. It is a subject, which, if I mistake not, is much more easily conceived than explained. If you have it constantly in your mind, that your whole visible deportment will powerfully, though insensibly, influence the opinions and future conduct of your children, it will give a form or colour, if I may speak so, to every thing you say or do. There are numberless and nameless instances in which this reflexion will make you speak, or refrain from speaking, act, or abstain from some circumstances of action, in what you are engaged in; nor will this be accompanied with any reluctance in the one case, or constraint in the other.

But I must not content myself with this. My profession gives me many opportunities of observing, that the impression made by general truths, however justly stated or fully proved, is seldom strong or lasting. Let me, therefore descend to practice, and illustrate what I have said by examples. Here again a difficulty occurs. If I give a particular instance it will perhaps operate no farther than recommending a like conduct in circumstances the same, or perhaps perfectly similar. For example. I might say, in speaking to the disadvantage of absent persons, I beseech you never fail to add the reason why you take such liberty, and indeed never take that liberty at all, but when it can be justified upon the principles of prudence, candor and charity. A thing may be right in itself, but children should be made to see why it is right. This is one instance of exemplary caution, but if I were to add a dozen more to it, they would only be detached precepts; whereas I am anxious to take in the whole extent of edifying example. In order to this, let me range or divide what I have to say, under distinct heads. A parent who wishes that his example should be a speaking lesson to his children, should order it so as to convince them, that he considers religion as necessary, respectable, amiable, profitable, and delightful. I am sensible that some of these characters may seem so nearly allied, as scarcely to admit of a distinction. Many parts of a virtuous conduct fall under more than one of these denominations. Some actions perhaps deserve all the epithets here mentioned, without exception and without prejudice one of another. But the distinctions seem to me very useful, for there is certainly a class of actions which may be said to belong peculiarly, or at least eminently, to each of these different heads. By taking them separately, therefore, it will serve to point out more fully the extent of your duty, and to suggest it when it would not otherwise occur, as well as to set the obligation to it in the stronger light.

1. You should, in your general deportment, make your children perceive that you look upon religion as absolutely necessary. I place this first, because it appears to me first both in point of order and force. I am far from being against taking all pains to show that religion is rational and honorable in itself, and vice the contrary; but I despise the foolish refinement of those, who, through fear of making children mercenary, are for being very sparing of the mention of heaven or hell. Such conduct is apt to make them conceive, that a neglect of their duty is only falling short of a degree of honor and advantage, which,

for the gratification of their passions, they are very willing to relinquish. Many parents are much more ready to tell their children such or such a thing is mean, and not like a gentleman, than to warn them that they will thereby incur the displeasure of their Maker. But when the practices are really and deeply criminal, as in swearing and lying, it is quite improper to rest the matter there. I admit that they are both mean, and that justice ought to be done to them in this respect, but I contend that it should only be a secondary consideration.

Let not human reasonings be put in the balance with divine wisdom. The care of our souls is represented in Scripture as the one thing needful. He makes a miserable bargain, who gains the whole world and loses his own soul. It is not the native beauty of virtue, or the outward credit of it, or the inward satisfaction arising from it, or even all these combined together, that will be sufficient to change our natures and govern our conduct; but a deep conviction, that unless we are reconciled to God, we shall without doubt perish everlastingly.

You will say, this is very true and very fit for a pulpit—but what is that class of actions that should impress it habitually on the minds of children? Perhaps you will even say, what one action will any good man be guilty of—much more habitual conduct—that can tend to weaken their belief of it? This is the very point which I mean to explain. It is certainly possible that a man may at stated times give out that he looks upon religion to be absolutely necessary, and yet his conduct in many particulars may have no tendency to impress this on the minds of his children. If he suffers particular religious duties to be easily displaced, to be shortened, postponed or omitted, upon the most trifling accounts, depend upon it, this will make religion in general seem less necessary, to those who observe it. If an unpleasant day will keep a man from public worship, when perhaps a hurricane will not keep him from an election meeting—if he chooses to take physic, or give it to his children on the Lord's day, when it could be done with equal ease on the day before or after—if he will more readily allow his servants to pay a visit to their friends on that day than any other, though he has reason to believe they will spend it in junketing and idleness—it will not be easy to avoid suspecting that worldly advantage is what determines his choice.

Take an example or two more on this head. Supposing a man usually to worship God in his family; if he sometimes omits it —if he allow every little business to interfere with it—if company will make him dispense with it, or shift it from its proper season—believe me, the idea of religion being every man's first and great concern, it is in a good measure weakened, if not wholly lost. It is a very nice thing in religion to know the real connection between, and the proper mixture of spirit and form. The form without the spirit is good for nothing; but on the other hand, the spirit without the form, never yet existed. I am of opinion, that punctual and even scrupulous regularity in all those duties that occur periodically, is the way to make them easy and pleasant to those who attend them. They also become, like all other habits, in some degree necessary; so that those who have been long accustomed to them, feel an uneasiness in families where they are generally or frequently neglected. I cannot help also mentioning to you, the great danger of paying and receiving visits on the Lord's day, unless when it is absolutely necessary. It is a matter not merely difficult, but wholly impracticable, in such cases, to guard effectually against improper subjects of conversation. Nor is this all, for let the conversation be what it will, I contend that the duties of the family and the closet are fully sufficient to employ the whole time; which must therefore be wasted or misapplied by the intercourse of strangers.

I only further observe, that I know no circumstance from which your opinion of the necessity of religion will appear with the greater clearness, or carry it in greater force, than your behavior towards and treatment of your children in time of dangerous sickness. Certainly there is no time in their whole lives when the necessity appears more urgent, or the opportunity more favorable, for impressing their minds with a sense of the things that belong to their peace. What shall we say then of those parents, who, through fear of alarming their minds, and augmenting their disorder, will not suffer any mention to be made to them of the approach of death, or the importance of

eternity? I will relate to you an example of this. A young
gentleman of estate in my parish, was taken ill of a dangerous
fever in a friend's house at a distance. I went to see him in his
illness, and his mother, a widow lady, intreated me not to say
anything alarming to him, and not to pray with him, but to go
to prayer in another room, wherein she wisely observed, it
would have the same effect. The young man himself soon found
that I did not act as he had expected, and was so impatient
that it became necessary to give him the true reason. On this he
insisted, in the most positive manner, that all restriction should
be taken off, which was done. What was the consequence? He
was exceedingly pleased and composed; and if this circumstance did not hasten, it certainly neither hindered nor retarded
his recovery.

Be pleased to remark, that the young gentleman here spoken
of, neither was at that time, nor is yet, so far as I am able to
judge, truly religious; and therefore I have formed a fixed
opinion, that in this, as in many other instances, the wisdom of
man disappoints itself. Pious advice and consolation, if but
tolerably administered in sickness, are not only useful to the
soul, but serve particularly to calm an agitated mind, to bring
the animal spirits to an easy flow, and the whole frame into
such a state as will best favor the operation of medicine, or
the efforts of the constitution, to throw off or conquer the
disease.

Suffer me to wander a little from my subject, by observing
to you, that as I do not think the great are to be much envied
for any thing, so they are truly and heartily to be pitied for the
deception that is usually put upon them by flattery and false
tenderness. Many of them are brought up with so much delicacy, that they are never suffered to see any miserable or
afflicting object, nor, so far as can be hindered, to hear any
affecting story of distress. If they themselves are sick, how
many absurd and palpable lies are told them by their friends?
and as for physcians I may safely say, few of them are much
conscience bound in this matter. Now, let the success of these
measures be what it will, the only fruit to be reaped from
them is to make a poor dying sinner mistake his or her condi-

tion, and vainly dream of earthly happiness, while hastening to the pit of perdition. But, as I said before, men are often taken in their own craftiness. It oftentimes happens that such persons, by an ignorant servant, or officious neighbor, or some unlucky accident, make a sudden discovery of their true situation, and the shock frequently proves fatal.—Oh! how much more desirable is it—how much more like the reason of men, as well as the faith of christians—to consider and prepare for what must inevitably come to pass? I cannot easily conceive any thing more truly noble, than for a person in health and vigor, in honor and opulence, by voluntary reflection to sympathize with others in distress; and by a well founded confidence in divine mercy, to obtain the victory over the fear of death.

2. You ought to live so as to make religion appear respectable. Religion is a venerable thing in itself, and it spreads an air of dignity over a person's whole deportment. I have seen a common tradesman, merely because he was a man of true piety and undeniable worth, treated by his children, apprentices and servants, with a much greater degree of deference and submission, than is commonly given to men of superior station, without that character. Many of the same meannesses are avoided, by a gentleman from a principle of honor, and by a good man from a principle of conscience. The first keeps out of the company of common people, because they are below him—the last is cautious of mixing with them, because of that levity and profaneness that is to be expected from them. If, then, religion is really venerable when sincere, a respectable conduct ought to be maintained, as a proof of your own integrity, as well as to recommend it to your children. To this add, if you please, that as reverence is the peculiar duty of children to their parents, any thing that tends to lessen it is more deeply felt by them than by others who observe it. When I have seen a parent, in the presence of his child, meanly wrangling with his servant, telling extravagant stories, or otherwise exposing his vanity, credulity or folly, I have felt just the same proportion of sympathy and tenderness for the one, that I did of contempt or indignation at the other.

What has been said, will, in part, explain the errors which a parent ought to shun, and what circumstances he ought to attend to, that religion may appear respectable. All meannesses, whether of sentiment, conversation, dress, manners, or employment, are carefully to be avoided. You will apply this properly to yourself. I may, however, just mention, that there is a considerable difference in all these particulars, according to mens' different stations. The same actions are mean in one station, that are not so in another. The thing itself, however, still remains; as there is an order and cleanliness at the table of tradesmen, that is different from the elegence of a gentleman's, or the sumptuousness of a prince's or nobleman's. But to make the matter still plainer by particular examples. I look upon talkativeness and vanity to be among the greatest enemies to dignity. It is needless to say how much vanity is contrary to true religion; and as to the other, which may seem rather an infirmity than a sin, we are expressly cautioned against it, and commanded to be swift to hear, and slow to speak. Sudden anger, too, and loud clamorous scolding, are at once contrary to piety and dignity. Parents should, therefore, aquire as much as possible, a composure of spirit, and meekness of language; nor are there many circumstances that will more recommend religion to children, when they see that this self command is the effect of principle, and a sense of duty.

There is a weakness I have observed in many parents, to show a partial fondness for some of their children, to the neglect, and in many cases approaching to a jealousy or hatred of others. Sometimes we see a mother discover an excessive partiality to a handsome daughter, in comparison of those that are more homely in their figure. This is a barbarity, which would be truly incredible, did not experience prove that it really exists. One would think they should rather be excited by natural affection, to give all possible encouragement to those who labor under a disadvantage, and bestow every attainable accomplishment to balance the defects of outward form. At other times we see a partiality which cannot be accounted for at all, where the most ugly, peevish, froward child of the whole family, is the favorite of both parents. Reason ought to counteract these errors; but piety ought to extirpate them entirely. I do not stay to mention the bad effects that flow from them, my purpose being only to show the excellence of that character which is exempted from them.

The real dignity of religion will also appear in the conduct of a good man towards his servants. It will point out the true and proper distinction between condescension and meanness. Humility is the very spirit of the gospel. Therefore, hear your servants with patience, examine their conduct with candor, treat them with all the humanity and gentleness that is consistent with unremitted authority; when they are sick, visit them in person, provide remedies for them, sympathize with them, and show them that you do so; take care of their interests; assist them with your counsel and influence to obtain what is their right. But, on the other hand, never make yourself their proper companion: do not seem to taste their society; do not hear their jokes, or ask their news, or tell them yours. Believe me, this will never make you either beloved or esteemed by your servants themselves; and it will greatly derogate from the dignity of true religion in the eyes of your children. Suffer me also to caution you against that most unjust and illiberal practice, of exercising your wit in humorous strokes upon your servants, before company, or while they wait at table. I do not know any thing so evidently mean, that is at the same time so common. It is I think, just such a cowardly thing as to beat a man who is bound; because the servant, however happy a repartee might occur to him, is not at liberty to answer, but at the risk of having his bones broken. In this, as in many other particulars, reason, refinement, and liberal manners, teach exactly the same thing with religion, and I am happy in being able to add, that religion is generally the most powerful, as well as the most uniform principle of decent conduct.

I shall have done with this particular, when I have observed, that those who are engaged in public, or what I may call political life, have an excellent opportunity of making religion appear truly respectable. What I mean is, by showing themselves firm and incorruptible, in supporting those measures that appear best calculated for promoting the interest of

religion, and the good of mankind. In all these cases, I admire
that man who has principles, whose principles are known, and
whom every body despairs of being able to seduce, or bring
over to the opposite interest. I do not commend furious and intemperate zeal. Steadiness is a much better, and quite a different thing. I would contend with any man who should speak
most calmly, but I would also contend with him who should
act most firmly. As for your placebo's, your prudent, courtly,
compliant gentlemen, whose vote in Assembly will tell you
where they dined the day before, I hold them very cheap
indeed, as you very well know. I do not enter further into this
argument, but conclude at this time, by observing, that public
measures are always embraced under pretence of principle;
and therefore an uniform uncorrupted public character is one
of the best evidences of real principle. The free thinking gentry
tell us, upon this subject, that "every man has his price." It
lies out of my way to attempt refuting them at present, but it
is to be hoped there are many whose price is far above their
reach. If some of my near relations, who took so much pains
to attach me to the interest of evangelical truth, had been
governed by court influence in their political conduct, it had
not been in my power to have esteemed their character, or
perhaps to have adhered to their instructions. But as things
now stand, I have done both from the beginning, and I hope
God will enable me by his grace, to continue to do so to the
end of life.

14

David Ramsay on the Arts and Sciences in a New Republic

A clear and enduring educational development of the early nation was the emergence of cultural nationalism in the life and purpose of the schools. At its ideological center the American Revolution increasingly signified a desire for republican government. After the war, leaders who had reluctantly begun and painfully won a struggle for republican rule contined to press upon a receptive peacetime citizenry the claims of republican ideology. They were leaders who set forth broad and necessarily simple principles of the good life for a largely agrarian people embarked upon an exciting but uncertain experiment. Though they found republicanism hard to define, public men generally agreed that it meant life without monarchical rule in a land of representative and limited government. It entailed rational political participation in self-government by free men who owned property (usually land) and who respected other people's property as they respected the law itself. The republican attitude rejected aristocratic or hereditary privileges, yet it was deferential toward the "natural" leadership of talented, self-made, or well-educated men. These loosely formulated but firmly and popularly held concepts helped to put the European Enlightenment into American terms. Republican civic leaders generated and supported American schools from the 1770s to around 1825. For the most part, these statesmen, not schoolmen, were then the agents of educational change. Their aims and axioms promulgated a sense of republican cultural unity, which became in effect the first national credo of American education. To the nation's fathers, a republican system of government was in itself an educational policy because in it men of intelligence and virtue came to the fore. Several outstanding spokesmen set the tone of republican education, but none was more insistent, purposive, or clearer in expressing his ideas than Thomas Jefferson. In terms of later national developments and ideals anticipated by the educational thought and work of one man, the half-century down to 1820 can most meaningfully be called The Age of Jefferson.

This oration by David Ramsay (1749–1815) brings to the modern reader the sense of excitement and of enthusiasm that opened the new educational era. Its theme is the promise of American arts and letters after independence. Despite the youthful bombast of its author and the fact that older men were more cautious than Ramsay in their predictions, the speech is a prototype of the proud cultural nationalism heard later in the more famous and illuminating speeches of Charles Jared Ingersoll in 1823 and of Edward Everett in 1824. For Ramsay, the immediate tasks of education were to instill patriotism and to create a sense of national unity. Liberally and classically educated men were needed—men skilled in debate, gifted in oratory, able to sway public sentiment, dedicated to public service and to a life of conspicuous example.

The times indeed produced the kind of men Ramsay sought. Public leadership and patriotic enterprise were taken up by men who possessed or acquired the advantages of talent, learning, or wealth. They looked upon public service as the avenue of duty for the well-educated man, as indeed it was virtually the only area of endeavor open in this new country to men of superior talents. The democratic impulse of later years would demand that educational opportunity and leadership itself be opened to far greater numbers of men. But in the constitutional period Ramsay's ideal proved immensely serviceable to the young republic.

Ramsay himself typified the educated leader of whom he spoke. Graduate of John Witherspoon's Nassau Hall and later a son-in-law of Witherspoon, Ramsay studied medicine at the College of Philadelphia with Benjamin Rush; then went to settle in Charleston, South Carolina, where he became a leading physician and patriot. He represented Charleston in the South Carolina legislature throughout the Revolution and his state in the Continental Congress, 1782–1785. Beside scholarly medical treatises, Ramsay's publications include one of the first histories of his state (2 vols., 1809) and of the American Revolution (2 vols., 1789), in which he once again emphasized the dutiful leadership assumed by classically educated men during a conflict for republican independence.

Our present form of government is every way preferable to the royal one we have lately renounced. It is much more favorable to purity of morals, and better calculated to promote all our important interests. Honesty, plain-dealing, and simple manners, were never made the patterns of courtly behavior . . . Republics are favorable to truth, sincerity, frugality, industry, and simplicity of manners. Equality, the life and soul of commonwealth, cuts off all pretensions to preferment but those which arise from extraordinary merits . . . .

The arts and sciences, which languished under the low prospects of subjection, will now raise their drooping heads, and spread far and wide, till they have reached the remotest parts of this untutored continent. It is the happiness of our present constitution, that all offices lie open to men of merit, of whatever rank or condition; and that even the reins of state may be held by the son of the poorest man, if possessed of abilities equal to the important station. . . . The independence of our country holds forth such generous encouragement to youth, as cannot fail of making many of them despise the syren calls of luxury and mirth, and pursue heaven-born wisdom with unwearied application. A few years will now produce a much greater number of men of learning and abilities, than we could have expected for ages in our boyish state of minority, guided by the leading strings of a parent country.

How trifling the objects of deliberation that came before our former legislative assemblies, compared with the great and important matters, on which they must now decide! They might then, *with the leave of the king*, his governors and councils, make laws about *yoking hogs, branding cattle, or making rice;* but they are now called upon to determine on peace and war, treaties and negociations with foreign states,

---

David Ramsay, M.D., *An Oration on the Advantages of American Independence, Spoken Before a Public Assembly of the Inhabitants of Charlestown, in South-Carolina, On the Second Anniversary of that Glorious Era* (Charleston, 1778). Reprinted in the *Pennsylvania Gazette*, January 20, 1779. Reprinted here from Hezekiah Niles, *Principles and Acts of the Revolution in America* (Baltimore, 1822), pp. 64–67, 69–72.

and other subjects interesting to the peace, liberty, sovereignty, and independence of a wide extended empire. No wonder that so little attention has been paid to learning; for ignorance was better than knowledge, while our abject and humiliating condition so effectually tended to crush the exertions of the human mind, and to extinguish a generous ardor for literary preeminence.

The times in which we live, and the governments we have lately adopted, all conspire to fan the sparks of genius in every breast, and kindle them into flame. When, like children, we were under the guardianship of a foreign power, our limited attention was naturally engrossed by agriculture, or directed to the low pursuit of wealth. In this state, the powers of the soul, benumbed with ease and indolence, sunk us into sloth and effeminacy. Hardships, dangers, and proper opportunities give scope to active virtues; and rouse the mind to such vigorous exertions, as command the admiration of an applauding world. Rome, when she filled the earth with the terror of her arms, sometimes called her generals from the plough: In like manner, the great want of proper persons to fill high stations, has drawn from obscurity many illustrious characters, which will dazzle the world with the splendor of their names. The necessities of our country require the utmost exertions of all our powers; from which vigorous, united efforts, much more improvement of the human mind is to be expected, than if we had remained in a torpid state of dependence.

Eloquence is the child of a free state. In this form of government, as public measures are determined by a majority of votes, arguments enforced by the arts of persuasion, must evermore be crowned with success: The rising patriot, therefore, who wishes the happiness of his country, will cultivate the art of public speaking. In royal governments, where the will of one or a few has the direction of public measures, the orator may harangue, but most probably will reap prosecution and imprisonment, as the fruit of his labor: Whereas, in our present happy system, the poorest school boy may prosecute his studies with increasing ardor, from the prospect, that in a few years he may, by his improved abilities, direct the determinations of public bodies, on subjects of the most stupendous consequence.

Thus might I go through the whole circle of the arts and sciences, and shew that while we remained British subjects, cramped and restrained by the limited views of dependence, each one of them would dwindle and decay, compared with the perfection and glory in which they will bloom and flourish, under the enlivening sunshine of freedom and independence. . . .

The attention of thousands is now called forth from their ordinary employments to subjects connected with the sovereignty and happiness of a great continent. As no one can tell to what extent the human mind may be cultivated, so no one can foresee what great events may be brought into existence, by the exertions of so many minds expanded by close attention to subjects of such vast importance.

The royal society was founded immediately after the termination of the civil wars in England. In like manner, may we not hope, as soon as this contest is ended, that the exalted spirits of our politicians and warriors will engage in the enlargement of public happiness, by cultivating the arts of peace, and promoting useful knowledge, with an ardor equal to that which first roused them to bleed in the cause of liberty and their country? Their genius, sharpened by their present glorious exertions, will naturally seek for a continuance of suitable employment. Having, with well tried swords and prudent counsels, secured liberty and independence for themselves and posterity, their great souls will stoop to nothing less than concerting wise schemes of civil polity and happiness—instructing the world in useful arts—and extending the empire of science. I foresee societies formed of our heroes and statesmen, released from their present cares; some of which will teach mankind to plough, sow, plant, build, and improve the rough face of nature; while others critically examine the various productions of the animal, vegetable, and mineral kingdoms, and teach their countrymen to "look through nature up to nature's God." Little has been hitherto done towards completing the natural history of America, or for the improvement of agriculture, and the peaceful arts of civil life; but who will be sur-

prised at this, who considers that during the long past night of
150 years, our minds were depressed, and our activity benumbed by the low prospects of subjection? Future diligence
will convince the candid world, that past inattention was the
effect of our dependent form of government.

Every circumstance concurs to make it probable, that the
arts and sciences will be cultivated, extended, and improved,
in independent America. They require a fresh soil, and always
flourish most in new countries. A large volume of the book of
nature, yet unread, is open before us, and invites our attentive
perusal. Many useful plants, unknown to the most industrious
botanist, waste their virtues in our desert air. Various parts of
our country, hitherto untrod by the foot of any chymist,
abound with different minerals. We stand on the shoulders of
our predecessors, with respect to the arts that depend on
experiment and observation. The face of our country, inter-
sected by rivers, or covered by woods and swamps, gives ample
scope for the improvement of mechanics, mathematics, and
natural philosophy. Our free governments are the proper
nurseries of rhetoric, criticism, and the arts which are founded
on the philosophy of the human mind. In monarchies, an
extreme degree of politeness disguises the simplicity of nature, and "sets the looks at variance with the thought;"
in republics, mankind appear as they really are, without any
false coloring. In these governments, therefore, attentive observers have an opportunity of knowing all the avenues to the
heart, and of thoroughly understanding human nature. The
great inferiority of the moderns to the ancients in fine writing,
is to be referred to this veil cast over mankind by the artifical
refinements of modern monarchies. From the operation of
similar causes, it is hoped, that the free governments of America will produce poets, orators, critics and historians, equal to
the most celebrated of the ancient commonwealths of Greece
and Italy.

Large empires are less favorable to true philosophy, than
small, independent states. The authority of a great author is
apt, in the former case, to extinguish a free enquiry, and to
give currency to falsehood unexamined. The doctrines of Con-

fusius were believed all over China, and the philosophy of Descartes, in France: But neighboring nations, examining them without partiality or prepossession, exploded them both. For the same reason, our separate states, jealous of the literary reputation of each other, and uninfluenced by any partial bias, will critically pry into the merit of every new opinion and system, and naught but truth will stand the test, and finally prevail.

In monarchies, favor is the source of preferment; but, in our new forms of government, no one can command the suffrages of the people, unless by his superior merit and capacity.

The weight of each state, in the continental scale, will ever be proportioned to the abilities of its *representatives in congress:* Hence, an emulation will take place, each contending with the other, which shall produce the most accomplished statesmen. From the joint influence of all these combined causes, it may strongly be presumed, that literature will flourish in America; and that our independence will be an illustrious epoch, remarkable for the spreading and improvement of science.

A zeal for promoting learning, unknown in the days of our subjection, has already begun to overspread these United States. In the last session of our assembly, three societies were incorporated for the laudable purpose of erecting seminaries of education. Nor is the noble spirit confined to us alone. Even now, amidst the tumults of war, literary institutions are forming all over the continent, which must light up such a blaze of knowledge, as cannot fail to burn, and catch, and spread, until it has finally illuminated, with the rays of science the most distant retreats of ignorance and barbarity. . . .

Our independence will naturally tend to fill our country with inhabitants. Where life, liberty, and property, are well secured, and where land is easily and cheaply obtained, the natural increase of people will much exceed all European calculations. Add to this, the inhabitants of the old world, becoming acquainted with our excellent forms of government, will emigrate by thousands. In their native lands, the hard-earned fruits of uninterrupted labor are scarcely equal to a scanty supply of their natural wants, and this pittance is held on a very precarious tenure: while our soil may be cheaply purchased, and will abundantly repay the toil of the husbandman, whose property no rapacious landlord dare invade. Happy America! whose extent of territory, westward, is sufficient to accommodate with land thousands and millions of the virtuous peasants, who now groan beneath tyranny and oppression in three quarters of the globe. Who would remain in Europe, a dependent on the will of an imperious landlord, when a few years industry can make him an independent American freeholder?

Such will be the fruits of our glorious revolution, that in a little time gay fields, adorned with yellow robes of ripening harvest, will smile in the remotest depths of our western frontiers, where impassable forests now frown over the uncultivated earth. The face of our interior country will be changed from a barren wilderness into the hospitable abodes of peace and plenty. Cities too will rise majestic to the view, on those very spots which are now howled over by savage beasts and more savage men. . . .

Our independent constitutions, formed on the justest principles, promise fair to give the most perfect protection to life, liberty and property, equally to the poor and the rich. . . . None can tell to what perfection the arts of government may be brought. May we not therefore expect great things from the patriots of this generation, jointly co-operating to make the new born republic of America as complete as possible? Is it not to be hoped, that human nature will here receive her most finished touches? That the arts and sciences will be extended and improved? That religion, learning, and liberty, will be diffused over this continent? and in short, that the American editions of the human mind will be more perfect than any that have yet appeared? Great things have been achieved in the infancy of states; and the ardor of a new people, rising to empire and renown, with prospects that tend to elevate the human soul, encourages these flattering expectations.

Should any puny politician object, that all these prospects are visionary, till we are certain of independence, I reply, that we have been in possession of it for two years, and are daily more able to support it, and our enemies less able to overset it. . . .

I congratulate you on our glorious prospects. Having for three long years weathered the storms of adversity, we are at length arrived in view of the calm haven of peace and security. We have laid the foundations of a new empire, which promises to enlarge itself to vast dimensions, and to give happiness to a great continent. It is now our turn to figure on the face of the earth, and in the annals of the world. The arts and sciences are planted among us, and, fostered by the auspicious influence of equal governments, are growing up to maturity; while truth and freedom flourish by their sides. Liberty, both civil and religious, in her noon-tide blaze, shines forth with unclouded lustre on all ranks and denominations of men.

Ever since the flood, true religion, literature, arts, empire and riches, have taken a slow and gradual course from east to west, and are now about fixing their long and favorite abode in this new western world. Our sun of political happiness is already risen, and hath lifted its head over the mountains, illuminating our hemisphere with liberty, light, and polished life. Our independence will redeem one quarter of the globe from tyranny and oppression, and consecrate it the chosen seat of truth, justice, freedom, learning and religion. We are laying the foundation of happiness for countless millions. Generations yet unborn will bless us for the blood-bought inheritance, we are about to bequeath them. Oh happy times! Oh glorious days! Oh kind, indulgent, bountiful Providence, that we live in this highly favored period, and have the honor of helping forward these great events, and of suffering in a cause of such infinite importance!

15

Thomas Jefferson's Bill
for the Diffusion of Knowledge

Thomas Jefferson (1743–1826) epitomized the concern of republican statesmen for an educated citizenry. His ideas of government and of education were almost inseparable. His conception of life in a new republic, wherein each generation comes fresh to its own education guided but unfettered by the past and confident of its own capacities, made his the most liberal educational mind of his time. His quest for present liberty written into the Declaration of Independence and his pursuit of open scientific inquiry became central features of the Jeffersonian temper to which later Americans would turn for intellectual renewal. No nation in a state of civilization, he maintained, can be ignorant and free. He insisted further that the only safe guardians of liberty are a free press and a majority of intelligent and reading people. Because he was also a lifelong advocate of informal education in the ways of "natural" virtue to be gained by living on the land, he supported federal measures during his Presidency (1801–1809) that would safeguard and strengthen the agrarian and hence to him virtuous character of the American people. His sentiments have made Jefferson, the thinker and man of universal interests, an unfailingly stimulating figure to those who interpret education broadly as a social process or as the transmission of culture. They have many documents from Jefferson's pen to study. But he did not systematize his ideas, and he left no great works on education. His ideas for the most part are found only in his vast correspondence and in his *Notes on the State of Virginia* (1785). Nor has Jefferson the historical figure been found by scholars to be beyond criticism. There were lapses from his Miltonian stance on freedom of the mind, particularly when he proscribed Federalist writings at his own university. His educational ideas paid little attention to women and none to slaves—two short-comings that in the temper of his times were overshadowed by what he strove to accomplish. Yet in retrospect no better confession of faith sums up the best of his republican age and links it to later democratic aspirations for education than his resolution: "I have sworn upon the altar of God, eternal hostility against every form of tyranny over the mind of man."

If Jefferson's republicanism symbolized his theory of education, that theory was made real and formalized through his institutional accomplishments. While largely directed to his own state of Virginia, his practical efforts for schooling were nevertheless aimed at enhancing the republican identity of the entire nation. He hoped that other states would follow the example of Virginia in their educational designs, and they ultimately did so. As a young state legislator in December, 1778, he drew up and sponsored the legislative bill, partly reprinted here, that would have created a statewide system of public instruction in Virginia. He was responsible for reorganizing and partially secularizing the curriculum of his *alma mater*, William and Mary College. He renewed the Library of Congress, destroyed by fire in 1814, by selling to it his personal library of some 6,500 books. Most memorable of all were his long efforts, from 1800 to 1825, to plan and to build the University of Virginia. (See Selection 22.)

Jefferson's *Bill for the More General Diffusion of Knowledge* proposed a state supported ladder of primary, secondary, and higher learning that was secular. "Public" schooling in the sense of state required schools had existed in America since the early Massachusetts school laws of the 1640s. But public elementary schooling in the modern sense, carrying an entirely secular motivation and bias, and free to all for three years, was a departure that Jefferson thought would ensure the health of the republic. His secular intent not only reflected the temper of the Enlightenment, but also revealed his preference for the educational aims of the ancient Greek republics, long studied by him and the statesmen of his age.

There are two more aspects of Jefferson's *Bill* that make it worthy of inclusion in a book about *theories* of education even though the *Bill*, except its notable preamble, deals with the structure, not the ideas of schooling. For one, it meant to systematize schooling. In this obvious but important respect it anticipated later developments in many other states which made American education synonymous with the efficient organization and dispersal of schools over wide areas. It was, then, a practical theory, which is characteristic of Jefferson's ideas as indeed it is characteristic of most educational ideas Americans have put into practice. Secondly, the *Bill* would have made elementary schooling widely available to the free white youth of Virginia. Here again it anticipated developments of the 1830s and later. The charge leveled against it in our time that it was an "elitist" program is only evidence of how far America has moved into democracy since then. Nothing was said in the *Bill* about the education of slaves or of free black people. And to modern eyes there is an intellectual, though not an economic elitism in its method of selecting or winnowing out only the ablest scholars for advancement up the educational ladder. Nevertheless, had it been put into operation, Jefferson's plan would have opened schoolroom doors at that early date to many boys and girls who otherwise would not even have seen them. And this opportunity became reality for some young Virginians who entered the University when it opened in 1825. As for Jefferson in 1778, he was convinced, as he wrote later to John Adams (see Selection 20), that this *Bill*, like his successful bills to establish religious freedom and to abolish primogeniture, would have "laid the axe to the root of pseudo-aristocracy." Had the *Bill* passed, he asserted, "worth and genius would . . . have been sought out from every condition of life, and completely prepared by education for defeating the competition of wealth and birth for public trusts." (For an elaboration of these sentiments and for a full discussion of Jefferson's republican philosophy of education, the reader is urged next to read Selections 20, 21, and 22.)

Although his *Bill* was finally defeated *in toto* by the legislature in 1786, Jefferson in 1818 still had hopes for its revival (see Selections 20 and 22). That part of his scheme providing for elementary schools was enacted into law in 1796, but it took effect only at the instigation of the courts; and the idea of his state university came to fruition in 1825. All along the way, political Federalists and religious sectarians in the legislature blocked Jefferson's path. Provision for secondary schools to link the two extreme rungs of his state educational ladder was never made in his lifetime in Virginia or elsewhere. Several decades would pass before any American state provided free schooling for its young people from primary grades to university.

A Bill for the More General Diffusion of Knowledge.

Whereas it appeareth that however certain forms of government are better calculated than others to protect individuals in the free exercise of their natural rights, and are at the same time

---

Julian P. Boyd *et al.*, eds., *The Papers of Thomas Jefferson* (17 vols. to date; Princeton, New Jersey, 1950), II, 526–529, 531–533. Reprinted by kind permission of the editor and Princeton University Press.

themselves better guarded against degeneracy, yet experience hath shown, that even under the best forms, those entrusted with power have, in time, and by slow operations, perverted it into tyranny; and it is believed that the most effectual means of preventing this would be, to illuminate, as far as practicable, the minds of the people at large, and more especially to give them knowledge of those facts, which history exhibiteth, that, possessed thereby of the experience of other ages and countries, they may be enabled to know ambition under all its shapes, and prompt to exert their natural powers to defeat its purposes; And whereas it is generally true that people will be happiest whose laws are best, and are best administered, and that laws will be wisely formed, and honestly administered, in proportion as those who form and administer them are wise and honest; whence it becomes expedient for promoting the publick happiness that those persons, whom nature hath endowed with genius and virtue, should be rendered by liberal education worthy to receive, and able to guard the sacred deposit of the rights and liberties of their fellow citizens, and that they should be called to that charge without regard to wealth, birth or other accidental condition or circumstance; but the indigence of the greater number disabling them from so educating, at their own expence, those of their children whom nature hath fitly formed and disposed to become useful instruments for the public, it is better that such should be sought for and educated at the common expence of all, than that the happiness of all should be confided to the weak or wicked:

Be it therefore enacted by the General Assembly, that in every county within this commonwealth, there shall be chosen annually, by the electors qualified to vote for Delegates, three of the most honest and able men of their county, to be called the Aldermen of the county; and that the election of the said Aldermen shall be held at the same time and place, before the same persons, and notified and conducted in the same manner as by law is directed for the annual election of Delegates for the county. . . .

The said Aldermen on the first Monday in October, if it be fair, and if not, then on the next fair day, excluding Sunday, shall meet at the court-house of their county, and proceed to divide their said county into hundreds . . . regulating the size of the said hundreds, according to the best of their discretion, so as that they may contain a convenient number of children to make up a school, and be of such convenient size that all the children within each hundred may daily attend the school to be established therein, distinguishing each hundred by a particular name. . . .

The electors aforesaid residing within every hundred shall meet on the third Monday in October after the first election of Aldermen. . . . The electors . . . shall choose the most convenient place within their hundred for building a school-house. . . . The said Aldermen shall forthwith proceed to have a school-house built at the said place, and shall see that the same be kept in repair, and, when necessary, that it be rebuilt; but whenever they shall think necessary that it be rebuilt, they shall give notice as before directed, to the electors of the hundred to meet at the said school-house, on such day as they shall appoint, to determine by vote . . . whether it shall be rebuilt at the same, or what other place in the hundred.

At every of these schools shall be taught reading, writing, and common arithmetick, and the books which shall be used therein for instructing the children to read shall be such as will at the same time make them acquainted with Græcian, Roman, English, and American history. At these schools all the free children, male and female, resident within the respective hundred, shall be entitled to receive tuition gratis, for the term of three years, and as much longer, at their private expence, as their parents, guardians or friends, shall think proper.

Over every ten of these schools . . . an overseer shall be appointed annually by the Aldermen at their first meeting, eminent for his learning, integrity, and fidelity to the commonwealth, whose business and duty it shall be, from time to time, to appoint a teacher to each school, who shall give assurance of fidelity to the commonwealth, and to remove him as he shall see cause; to visit every school once in every half year at the least; to examine the scholars; see that any general plan of reading and instruction recommended by the visiters of William and Mary College shall be observed; and to superintend the conduct of the teacher in every thing relative to his school.

Every teacher shall receive a salary of   by the year, which, with the expences of building and repairing the schoolhouses, shall be provided in such manner as other county expences are by law directed to be provided and shall also have his diet, lodging, and washing found him, to be levied in like manner, save only that such levy shall be on the inhabitants of each hundred for the board of their own teacher only.

And in order that grammar schools may be rendered convenient to the youth in every part of the commonwealth, Be it farther enacted, that on the first Monday in November, after the first appointment of overseers for the hundred schools, if fair, and if not, then on the next fair day, excluding Sunday, after the hour of one in the afternoon, the said overseers appointed for the schools in the [various] counties . . . shall fix on such place in some one of the counties in their district as shall be most proper for situating a grammar school-house, endeavouring that the situation be as central as may be to the inhabitants of the said counties, that it be furnished with good water, convenient to plentiful supplies of provision and fuel, and more than all things that it be healthy. And if a majority of the overseers present should not concur in their choice of any one place proposed, the method of determining shall be as follows: If two places only were proposed, and the votes be divided, they shall decide between them by fair and equal lot; if more than two places were proposed, the question shall be put on those two which on the first division had the greater number of votes; or if no two places had a greater number of votes than the others, as where the votes shall have been equal between one or both of them and some other or others, then it shall be decided by fair and equal lot (unless it can be agreed by a majority of votes) which of the places having equal numbers shall be thrown out of the competition, so that the question shall be put on the remaining two, and if on this ultimate question the votes shall be equally divided, it shall then be decided finally by lot.

The said overseers having determined the place at which the

grammar school for their district shall be built, shall forthwith (unless they can otherwise agree with the proprietors of
the circumjacent lands as to the location and price) make application to the clerk of the county in which the said house is
to be situated, who shall thereupon issue a writ, in the nature
of a writ of ad quod damnum, directed to the sheriff of the
said county commanding him to summon and impannel twelve
fit persons to meet at the place, so destined for the grammar
school house, on a certain day, to be named in the said writ,
not less than five, nor more than ten, days from the date
thereof; and also to give notice of the same to the proprietors
and tenants of the lands to be reviewed; if they be found
within the county, and if not, then to their agents therein if
any they have. Which freeholders shall be charged by the said
sheriff impartially, and to the best of their skill and judgment
to view the lands round about the said place, and to locate
and circumscribe, by certain metes and bounds, one hundred
acres thereof, having regard therein principally to the benefit
and convenience of the said school, but respecting in some measure also the convenience of the said proprietors, and to value
and appraise the same in so many several and distinct parcels
as shall be owned or held by several and distinct owners or
tenants, and according to their respective interests and estates
therein. And after such location and appraisement so made,
the said sheriff shall forthwith return the same under the hands
and seals of the said jurors, together with the writ, to the
clerk's office of the said county and the right and property of
the said proprietors and tenants in the said lands so circumscribed shall be immediately devested and be transferred to the
commonwealth for the use of the said grammar school, in full
and absolute dominion, any want of consent or disability to
consent in the said owners or tenants notwithstanding. But it
shall not be lawful for the said overseers so to situate the said
grammar school-house, nor to the said jurors so to locate the
said lands, as to include the mansion-house of the proprietor of
the lands, nor the offices, curtilage, or garden, thereunto immediately belonging.

The said overseers shall forthwith proceed to have a house of brick or stone, for the said grammar school, with necessary offices, built on the said lands, which grammar school-house shall contain a room for the school, a hall to dine in, four rooms for a master and usher, and ten or twelve lodging rooms for the scholars.

To each of the said grammar schools shall be allowed out of the public treasury, the sum of   pounds. . . .

In these grammar schools shall be taught the Latin and Greek languages, English grammar, geography, and the higher part of numerical arithmetick, to wit, vulgar and decimal fractions, and the extraction of the square and cube roots.

A visiter from each county constituting the district shall be appointed; by the overseers, for the county, in the month of October annually, either from their own body or from their county at large, which visiters or the greater part of them . . . shall have power to choose their own Rector, who shall call and preside at future meetings, to employ from time to time a master, and if necessary, an usher, for the said school, to re-move them at their will, and to settle the price of tuition to be paid by the scholars. They shall also visit the school twice in every year at the least, either together or separately at their discretion, examine the scholars, and see that any general plan of instruction recommended by the visiters of William and Mary College shall be observed. The said masters and ushers, before they enter on the execution of their office, shall give assurance of fidelity to the commonwealth.

A steward shall be employed, and removed at will by the master, on such wages as the visiters shall direct; which stew-ard shall see to the procuring provisions, fuel, servants for cooking, waiting, house cleaning, washing, mending, and gar-dening on the most reasonable terms; the expence of which, together with the steward's wages, shall be divided equally among all the scholars boarding either on the public or private expence. And the part of those who are on private expence, and also the price of their tuitions due to the master or usher, shall be paid quarterly by the respective scholars, the parents, or guardians, and shall be recoverable, if withheld, together with costs, on motion in any Court of Record. . . . The said steward shall also, under the direction of the visiters, see that the houses be kept in repair, and necessary enclosures be made and repaired, the accounts for which, shall, from time to time, be submitted to the Auditors, and on their warrant paid by the Treasurer.

Every overseer of the hundred schools shall, in the month of September annually, after the most diligent and impartial examination and enquiry, appoint from among the boys who shall have been two years at the least at some one of the schools under his superintendance, and whose parents are too poor to give them farther education, some one of the best and most promising genius and disposition, to proceed to the grammar school of his district. . . . the said overseer being previously sworn by them to make such appointment, without favor or affection, according to the best of his skill and judgment, and being interrogated by the said Aldermen, either on their own motion, or on suggestions from the parents, guardians, friends, or teachers of the children, competitors for such appointment; which teachers shall attend for the information of the Aldermen. On which interregatories the said Aldermen, if they be not satisfied with the appointment proposed, shall have right to negative it; whereupon the said visiter may proceed to make a new appointment, and the said Aldermen again to interrogate and negative, and so toties quoties until an appointment be approved.

Every boy so appointed shall be authorised to proceed to the grammar school of his district, there to be educated and boarded during such time as is hereafter limited; and his quota of the expences of the house together with a compensation to the master or usher for his tuition, at the rate of twenty dollars by the year, shall be paid by the Treasurer quarterly on warrant from the Auditors.

A visitation shall be held, for the purpose of probation, annually at the said grammar school, . . . at which one third of the boys sent thither by appointment of the said overseers, and who shall have been there one year only, shall be discontinued as public foundationers, being those who, on the most diligent examination and enquiry, shall be thought to be of the least promising genius and disposition; and of those who shall have been there two years, all shall be discontinued, save one only the best in genius and disposition, who shall be at liberty to continue there four years longer on the public foundation, and shall thence forward be deemed a senior.

The visiters for the districts, . . . at the probation meetings held in the years, distinguished in the Christian computation by odd numbers, and the visiters for all the other districts at their said meetings to be held in those years, distinguished by even numbers, after diligent examination and enquiry as before directed, shall chuse one among the said seniors, of the best learning and most hopeful genius and disposition, who shall be authorised by them to proceed to William and Mary College, there to be educated, boarded, and clothed, three years; the expence of which annually shall be paid by the Treasurer on warrant from the Auditors.

16

Benjamin Rush on
Republican Education

Benjamin Rush (1745–1813) was a steady though not brilliant writer on various social causes. Not least among his interests was improved education. His *Plan for the Establishment of Public Schools and the Diffusion of Knowledge in Pennsylvania* (1786) proposed statewide schooling similar to Thomas Jefferson's *Bill for the More General Diffusion of Knowledge* in 1778 (see Selection 15). In the essay of 1786 reprinted here, Rush put forward the earliest comprehensive plan for an ideal system of national education. This tract and Selection 17 on female education were published in the midst of a busy life that had already seen him, after his studies at Princeton and abroad, surgeon-general in the Revolutionary army, signer of the Declaration of Independence, and professor of medicine in Philadelphia. He was becoming America's best known physician. Though at times self-contradictory and tactlessly critical of others, Rush was one of the eminent members of the American Philosophical Society. (See Selection 19.)

Rush's *Thoughts upon the Mode of Education Proper in a Republic* raises at least one problem in defining "republican" education which was faced by all statesmen who attempted broad surveys of education in the early nation. This problem carried over into the Jacksonian period and indeed into modern times. It begins with Rush's image of the citizen being educated to become a "republican machine." Some historians hold that the image creates a "paradox" (as Rush himself knew his critics would call it) of public education in freedom of dissent simultaneously fostered with education in a "necessary concensus" of patriotic and moral values. The problem, however, appears more convincing a "paradox" for modern democratic logic than for the historical circumstances of Rush's day. For

Rush was advocating education that escaped the restraints of monarchy and aristocracy. At a time when local or regional parochialism rooted in colonial custom was hard to overcome, the cultural *uniformity* that Rush wanted from national schooling was not intellectual *conformity*. He was championing schooling for a self-reliant, free, and informed people whose common strength would be their love of country and their widely shared moral standards. All this does not mean that he was resolving the ancient tension between individual freedom and social order. It does mean that within the context of his age, a time of post-Revolutionary political adjustment, he envisioned both freedom and order compatibly upheld by educated republicans.

The nub of the historical problem here is not Rush's article of political faith. It is the specific device by which he sought to maintain a national standard of moral instruction. For him, that device was the Bible. This places him to the ideological right of Noah Webster and Thomas Jefferson. Webster was closer to center on this score, asserting that he would see the Bible used in the schools as a respected "system of religion and morality." Jefferson and those in his circle stood to the left. They were opposed to theological or Biblical instruction at the elementary and secondary levels, preferring that students read the Bible and moral philosophy on their own. While Rush's position was closer to colonial school traditions, he was not advocating sectarian indoctrination. He wanted a sense of spiritual community, not sectarian dogma, given young people. American public schools eventually reached the Jeffersonian (and the First Amendment) point of view, but not until they first had taken the direction pointed by Rush through much of the nineteenth century.

Despite Rush's separation from the Jeffersonians in his advocacy of Bible instruction, his views on the creation of a state and a national university were shared by most leading statesmen, Federalists and Republicans alike. Actively engaged in the first planning and trusteeship of Presbyterian Dickinson College in 1783, Rush also proposed a public university as the capstone of his *Plan for the Establishment of Public Schools . . . in Pennsylvania*. In this *Plan* of 1786, to which was appended his essay on *The Mode of Education*, four public "colleges" (really academies) would be established throughout the state, including Dickinson College, to feed their best students into the university. In this respect his statewide ladder of instruction was almost identical to Jefferson's plan for Virginia in 1778 (see Selection 15). Rush also became one of the earliest advocates of a secular federal university in a pseudonymous essay for the *Federal Gazette* of Philadelphia in 1788. Although other proponents of this idea did not share his desire to make only graduates of the federal university eligible for federal service, the general idea of a great national institution of higher learning was supported by each of the first six presidents of the United States. John Adams and Monroe favored it in principle; Washington, Jefferson, Madison, and John Quincy Adams all urged Congress to pass bills to implement the idea. But nothing came of these proposals, even though Washington left a bequest to Congress for this purpose, which was never used.

Aside from noting that the idea has never completely died and that congressional misgivings in those early years over the constitutionality of sponsoring a federal university proved to be the major obstacle to the passage of the presidential proposals, it is more important to point to the republican concept of national leadership embodied in the plan for a federal institution of higher learning. Rush asserted that the habits of American citizens could not be changed and that their ignorance and prejudice could not be removed " 'till we inspire them with federal principles, which can be only effected by our young men meeting and spending two or three years together in a national University, and afterwards disseminating their knowledge and principles through every county, township, and village of the United States.' "

Rush's ideal of a centrally and highly educated leadership, shared by most proponents of republican education, was from its outset challenged variously by doctrines of state rights, sectarianism, and democracy applied to education. Insofar as it was interpreted to mean that national university graduates would perform a "filtering down" or elitist function for higher learning, it became unsuited to subsequent democratic developments. But at the time it well expressed the vision, elaborated by Jefferson (see Selections 15, 20, 22), of a benign agrarian republic in which all free citizens were educated to make sensible judgments about public issues to the best of their abilities and to trust further their well-educated representatives to act wisely. A national university would be the top rung on an educational ladder which all white males initially had the opportunity to ascend but whose pinnacle only the most intellectually gifted, not the richest or the well-born, could reach. (See also Selection 17.)

Subsequent editions of this essay, printed in 1789 and 1806, were shortened. The omitted paragraphs indicate that Rush tempered some of his opinions over the years. He softened but did not eliminate his argument for exposing young people to sectarian teaching. He deleted the paragraphs on school discipline and on the comportment of teachers and professors. He removed a sentence advocating instruction in the art of war. These deletions probably made his essay acceptable to a wider readership during the political tensions of John Adams's and Thomas Jefferson's administrations. The only addition Rush made to these later editions was a suggestion that French and German be added to college curricula.

The business of education has acquired a new complexion by the independence of our country. The form of government we have assumed, has created a new class of duties to every American. It becomes us, therefore, to examine our former habits upon this subject, and in laying the foundations for nurseries of wise and good men, to adapt our modes of teaching to the peculiar form of our government.

The first remark that I shall make upon this subject is, that an education in our own, is to be preferred to an education in a foreign country. The principle of patriotism stands in need of the reinforcement of *prejudice*, and it is well known that our strongest prejudices in favour of our country are formed in the first one and twenty years of our lives. The policy of the Lacedamonians is well worthy of our imitation. When Antipater demanded fifty of their children as hostages for the fulfilment of a distant engagement, those wise republicans refused to comply with his demand, but readily offered him double the number of their adult citizens, whose habits and prejudices could not be shaken by residing in a foreign country. Passing by, in this place, the advantages to the community from the early attachment of youth to the laws and constitution of their country, I shall only remark, that young men who have trodden the paths of science together, or have joined in the same sports, whether of swimming, scating, fishing, or hunting, generally feel, thro' life, such ties to each other, as add greatly to the obligations of mutual benevolence.

I conceive the education of our youth in this country to be peculiarly necessary in Pennsylvania, while our citizens are composed of the natives of so many different kingdoms in

---

Benjamin Rush, *A Plan for the Establishment of Public Schools and the Diffusion of Knowledge in Pennsylvania; to which are added Thoughts upon the Mode of Education, Proper in a Republic. Addressed to the Legislature and Citizens of the State* (Philadelphia, 1786), pp. 13–36.

Europe. Our Schools of learning, by producing one general, and uniform system of education, will render the mass of the people more homogeneous, and thereby fit them more easily for uniform and peaceable government.

I proceed, in the next place, to enquire, what mode of education we shall adopt so as to secure to the state all the advantages that are to be derived from the proper instruction of youth; and here I beg leave to remark that the only foundation for a useful education in a republic is to be laid in RELIGION. Without this, there can be no virtue, and without virtue there can be no liberty, and liberty is the object and life of all republican governments.

Such is my veneration for every religion that reveals the attributes of the Deity, or a future state of rewards and punishments, that I had rather see the opinions of Confucius or Mohamed inculcated upon our youth, than see them grow up wholly devoid of a system of religious principles. But the religion I mean to recommend in this place, is the religion of JESUS CHRIST.

It is foreign to my purpose to hint at the arguments which establish the truth of the Christian revelation. My only business is to declare, that all its doctrines and precepts are calculated to promote the happiness of society, and the safety and well being of civil government. A Christian cannot fail of being a republican. The history of the creation of man, and of the relation of our species to each other by birth, which is recorded in the Old Testament, is the best refutation that can be given to the divine right of kings, and the strongest argument that can be used in favour of the original and natural equality of all mankind. A Christian, I say again, cannot fail of being a republican, for every precept of the Gospel inculcates those degrees of humility, self-denial, and brotherly kindness, which are directly opposed to the pride of monarchy and the pageantry of a court. A Christian cannot fail of being useful to the republic, for his religion teacheth him that no man "liveth to himself." And lastly, a Christian cannot fail of being wholly inoffensive, for his religion teacheth him, in all things to do to others what he would wish, in like circumstances, they should do to him.

I am aware that I dissent from one of those paradoxical opinions with which modern times abound; that it is improper to fill the minds of youth with religious prejudices of any kind and that they should be left to choose their own principles, after they have arrived at an age in which they are capable of judging for themselves. Could we preserve the mind in childhood and youth a perfect blank, this plan of education would have more to recommend it; but this we know to be impossible. The human mind runs as naturally into principles as it does after facts. It submits with difficulty to those restraints or partial discoveries which are imposed upon it in the infancy of reason. Hence the impatience of children to be informed upon all subjects that relate to the invisible world. But I beg leave to ask. Why should we pursue a different plan of education with respect to religion from that which we pursue in teaching the arts and sciences? Do we leave our youth to acquire systems of geography, philosophy, or politics, till they have arrived at an age in which they are capable of judgeing for themselves? We do not. I claim no more then for religion, than for the other sciences, and I add further, that if our youth are disposed after they are of age to think for themselves, a knowledge of *one* system will be the best means of conducting them in a free enquiry into other systems of religion, just as an acquaintance with one system of philosophy is the best introduction to the study of all the other systems in the world.

I must beg leave upon this subject to go one step further. In order more effectually to secure to our youth the advantages of a religious education, it is necessary to impose upon them the doctrines and discipline of a particular church. Man is naturally an ungovernable animal, and observations on particular societies and countries will teach us, that when we add the restraints of eclesiastical, to those of domestic and civil government, we produce, in him, the highest degrees of order and virtue. That fashionable liberality which refuses to associate with any one sect of Christians is seldom useful to itself, or to society, and may fitly be compared to the unprofitable bravery of a soldier, who wastes his valour in solitary enterprizes, without the aid or effect of military associations. Far be it from me to recommend the doctrines or modes of worship of any one denomination of Christians. I only recommend to the persons entrusted with the education of youth, to inculcate upon them a strict conformity to that mode of worship which is most agreeable to their consciences, or the inclinations of their parents.

Under this head, I must be excused in not agreeing with those modern writers who have opposed the use of the Bible as a school book. The only objection I know to it is, its division into chapters and verses, and its improper punctuation, which render it a more difficult book to read *well,* than many others; but these defects may easily be corrected; and the disadvantages of them are not to be mentioned with the immense advantages of making children early, and intimately acquainted with the means of acquiring happiness both here and hereafter. How great is the difference between making young people acquainted with the interesting and entertaining truths contained in the Bible, and the fables of Moore and Croxall, or the doubtful histories of antiquity! I maintain that there is no book of its size in the whole world, that contains half so much useful knowledge for the government of states, or the direction of the affairs of individuals as the bible. To object to the practice of having it read in schools, because it tends to destroy our veneration for it, is an argument that applies with equal force, against the frequency of public worship, and all other religious exercises. The first impressions upon the mind are the most durable. They survive the wreck of the memory, and exist in old age after the ideas acquired in middle life have been obliterated. Of how much consequence then must it be to the human mind in the evening of life, to be able to recal those ideas which are most essential to its happiness; and these are to be found chiefly in the Bible. The great delight which old people take in reading the Bible, I am persuaded is derived chiefly from its histories and precepts being *associated* with the events of childhood and youth, the recollection of which forms a material part of their pleasures.

I do not mean to exclude books of history, poetry or even fables from our schools. They may, and should be read frequently by our young people, but if the Bible is made to give way to them altogether, I foresee that it will be read, in a short time, only in churches, and in a few years will probably be found only in the offices of magistrates, and in courts of justice.[1]

NEXT to the duty which young men owe to their Creator, I wish to see a SUPREME REGARD TO THEIR COUNTRY, inculcated upon them. When the Duke of Sully became prime minister to Henry the IVth of France, the first thing he did, he tells us, "Was to subdue and forget his own heart." The same duty is incumbent upon every citizen of a republic. Our country includes family, friends and property, and should be preferred to them all. Let our pupil be taught that he does not belong to himself, but that he is public property. Let him be taught to love his family, but let him be taught, at the same time, that he must forsake and even forget them, when the welfare of his country requires it. He must watch for the state as if its liberties depended upon his vigilance alone, but he must do this in such a manner as not to defraud his creditors, or neglect his family. He must love private life, but he must decline no station, however public or responsable [sic] it may be, when called to it by the suffrages of his fellow-citizens. He must love popularity, but he must despise it when set in competition with the dictates of his judgment, or the real interest of his country. He must love character, and have a due sense of injuries, but he must be taught to appeal only to the laws of the state, to defend the one, and punish the other. He must love family honour, but he must be taught that neither the rank nor antiquity of his ancestors can command respect, without personal merit. He must avoid neutrality in all questions that divide the state, but he must shun the rage, and acrimony of party spirit. He must be taught to love his fellow creatures in every part of the world, but he must cherish with a more intense and peculiar

[1] In a republic where all votes for public officers are given by *ballot,* should not a knowledge of reading and writing be considered as essential qualifications for an elector? and when a man, who is of a doubtful character, offers his vote, would it not be more consistent with sound policy and wise government to oblige him to read a few verses in the Bible to prove his qualifications, than simply to compel him to kiss the *outside* of it?

affection, the citizens of Pennsylvania and of the United States. I do not wish to see our youth educated with a single prejudice against any nation or country; but we impose a task upon human nature, repugnant alike to reason, revelation and the ordinary dimensions of the human heart, when we require him to embrace, with equal affection, the whole family of mankind. He must be taught to amass wealth, but it must be only to encrease his power of contributing to the wants and demands of the state. He must be indulged occasionally in amusement, but he must be taught that study and business should be his principal pursuits in life. Above all he must love life, and endeavour to acquire as many of its conveniences as possible by industry and œconomy, but he must be taught that this life "Is not his own," when the safety of his country requires it. These are practicable lessons, and the history of the commonwealths of Greece and Rome show, that human nature, without the aids of Christianity, has attained these degrees of perfection.

While we inculcate these republican duties upon our pupil, we must not neglect, at the same time, to inspire him with republican principles. He must be taught that there can be no durable liberty but in a republic, and that government, like all other sciences, is of a progressive nature. The chains which have bound this science in Europe are happily unloosed in America. *Here* it is open to investigation and improvement. While philosophy has protected us by its discoveries from a thousand natural evils, government has unhappily followed with an unequal pace. It would be to dishonour human genius only to name the many defects which still exist in the best systems of legislation. We daily see matter of a perishable nature rendered durable by certain chemical operations. In like manner, I conceive, that it is possible to analyze and combine power in such a manner as not only to encrease the happiness, but to promote the duration of republican forms of government far beyond the terms limited for them by history, or the common opinions of mankind.

To assist in rendering religious, moral and political instruction more effectual upon the minds of our youth, it will be necessary to subject their bodies to physical discipline. To obviate the inconveniences of their studious and sedantary mode of life, they should live upon a temperate diet, consisting chiefly of broths, milk and vegetables. The black broth of Sparta, and the barley broth of Scotland, have been alike celebrated for their beneficial effects upon the minds of young people. They should avoid tasting spirituous liquors. They should also be accustomed occasionally to work with their hands, in the intervals of study, and in the busy seasons of the year in the country. Moderate sleep, silence, occasional solitude, and cleanliness, should be inculcated upon them, and the utmost advantage should be taken of a proper direction of those great principles in human conduct,—sensibility, habit, imitation, and association.

The influence [of] these physical causes will be powerful upon the intellects, as well as upon the principles and morals of young people.

To those who have studied human nature, it will not appear paradoxical to recommend, in this essay, a particular attention to vocal music. Its mechanical effects in civilizing the mind, and thereby preparing it for the influence of religion and government, have been so often felt and recorded, that it will be unnecessary to mention facts in favour of its usefulness in order to excite a proper attention to it.

In the education of youth, let the authority of our masters be as *absolute* as possible. The government of schools like the government of private families, should be *arbitrary*, that it may not be *severe*. By this mode of education, we prepare our youth for the subordination of laws, and thereby qualify them for becoming good citizens of the republic. I am satisfied that the most useful citizens have been formed from those youth who have never known or felt their own wills till they were one and twenty years of age, and I have often thought that society owes a great deal of its order and happiness to the deficiencies of parental government, being supplied by those habits of obedience and subordination which are contracted at schools.

I cannot help bearing a testimony, in this place, against the custom, which prevails in some parts of America, (but which is daily falling into disuse in Europe) of crouding boys together under one roof for the purpose of education. The practice is the gloomy remains of monkish ignorance, and is as unfavourable to the improvements of the mind in useful learning, as monasteries are to the spirit of religion. I grant this mode of secluding boys from the intercourse of private families, has a tendency to make them scholars, but our business is to make them men, citizens and christians. The vices of young people are generally learned from each other. The vices of adults seldom infect them. By separating them from each other, therefore, in their hours of relaxation from study, we secure their morals from a principal source of corruption, while we improve their manners, by subjecting them to those restraints, which the difference of age and sex, naturally produce in private families.

I have hitherto said nothing of the AMUSEMENTS that are proper for young people in a republic. Those which promote health and good humour, will have a happy effect upon morals and government. To encrease this influence, let the persons who direct these amusements, be admitted into good company, and subjected, by that means, to restraints in behaviour and moral conduct. Taverns which in most countries are exposed to riot and vice, in Connecticut are places of business and innocent pleasure, because the tavern-keepers in that country are generally men of sober and respectable characters. The theatre will never be perfectly reformed till players are treated with the same respect as persons of other ornamental professions. It is to no purpose to attempt to write or preach down an amusement, which seizes so forcibly upon all the powers of the mind. Let ministers preach *to* players, instead of *against* them; let them open their churches and the ordinances of religion to them and their families, and, I am persuaded, we shall soon see such a reformation in the theatre as can never be effected by all the means that have hitherto been employed for that purpose. It is possible to render the stage, by these means, subservient to the purposes of virtue and even religion. Why should the minister of the gospel exclude the player from his visits, or from his public or private instructions? The

Author of Christianity knew no difference in the occupations of men. He ate and drank daily with publicans and sinners.

From the observations that have been made it is plain, that I consider it as possble to convert men into republican machines. This must be done, if we expect them to perform their parts properly, in the great machine of the government of the state. That republic is sophisticated with monarchy or aristocracy that does not revolve upon the wills of the people, and these must be fitted to each other by means of education before they can be made to produce regularity and unison in government.

Having pointed out those general principles, which should be inculcated alike in all the schools of the state, I proceed now to make a few remarks upon the method of conducting, what is commonly called, a liberal or learned education in a republic.

I shall begin this part of my subject by bearing a testimony against the common practice of attempting to teach boys the learned language, and the arts and sciences too early in life. The first twelve years of life are barely sufficient to instruct a boy in reading, writing and arithmetic. With these, he may be taught those modern languages which are necessary for him to *speak*. The state of the memory, in early life, is favourable to the acquistion of languages, especially when they are conveyed to the mind through the ear. It is, moreover, in early life only, that the organs of speech yield in such a manner as to favour the just pronunciation of foreign languages.

I do not wish the LEARNED OR DEAD LANGUAGES, as they are commonly called, to be reduced below their present just rank in the universities of Europe, especially as I consider an acquaintance with them as the best foundation for a correct and extensive knowledge of the language of our country. Too much pains cannot be taken to teach our youth to read and write our American language with propriety and elegance. The study of the Greek language constituted a material part of the literature of the Athenians, hence the sublimity, purity and immortality of so many of their writings. The advantages of a perfect knowledge of our language, to young men intended for the professions of law, physic or divinity are too obvious to be mentioned, but in a state which boasts of the first commercial city in America, I wish to see it cultivated by young men, who are intended for the compting house, for many such, I hope, will be educated in our colleges. The time is past when an academical education was thought to be unnecessary to qualify a young man for merchandize. I conceive no profession is capable of receiving more embellishments from it.

Connected with the study of our own language is the study of ELOQUENCE. It is well known how great a part it constituted of the Roman education. It is the first accomplishment in a republic, and often sets the whole machine of government in motion. Let our youth, therefore, be instructed in this art. We do not extol it too highly when we attribute as much to the power of eloquence as to the sword in bringing about the American revolution.

With the usual arts and sciences that are taught in our American colleges, I wish to see a regular course of lectures given upon HISTORY and CHRONOLOGY. The science of government, whether it relates to constitutions or laws, can only be advanced by a careful selection of facts, and these are to be found chiefly in history. Above all, let our youth be instructed in the history of the ancient republics, and the progress of liberty and tyranny in the different states of Europe. I wish likewise to see the numerous facts that relate to the origin and present state of COMMERCE, together with the nature and principles of MONEY, reduced to such a system as to be intelligible and agreeable to a young man. If we consider the commerce of our metropolis only as the avenue of the wealth of the state, the study of it merits a place in a young man's education; but, I consider commerce in a much higher light when I recommend the study of it in republican seminaries. I view it as the best security against the influence of hereditary monopolies of land, and, therefore, the surest protection against aristocracy. I consider its effects as next to those of religion in humanizing mankind, and lastly, I view it as the means of uniting the different nations of the world together by the ties of mutual wants and obligations.

CHEMISTRY by unfolding to us the effects of heat and mixture, enlarges our acquaintance with the wonders of nature, and the mysteries of art, hence it has become, in most of the universities of Europe, a necessary branch of a gentleman's education. In a young country, where improvements in agriculture and manufactures are so much to be desired, the cultivation of this science, which explains the principles of both of them, should be considered as an object of the utmost importance.

In a state where every citizen is liable to be a soldier and a legislator, it will be necessary to have some regular instruction given upon the ART OF WAR and upon PRACTICAL LEGISLATION. These branches of knowledge are of too much importance in a republic to be trusted to solitary study, or to a fortuitous acquaintance with books. Let mathematical learning, therefore, be carefully applied, in our colleges, to gunnery and fortification, and let philosophy be applied to the history of those compositions which have been made use of for the terrible purposes of destroying human life. These branches of knowledge will be indispensably necessary in our republic, if unfortunately war should continue hereafter to be the unchristian mode of arbitrating disputes between Christian nations. Again, let our youth be instructed in all the mains of promoting national prosperity and independence, whether they relate to improvements in agriculture, manufactures, or inland navigation. Let him be instructed further in the general principles of legislation, whether they relate to revenue, or to the preservation of life, liberty or property. Let him be directed frequently to attend the courts of justice, where he will have the best opportunities of acquiring habits of arranging and comparing his ideas by observing the secretion of truth, in the examination of witnesses, and where he will hear the laws of the state explained, with all the advantages of that species of eloquence which belongs to the bar. Of so much importance do I conceive it to be, to a young man, to attend occasionally to the decisions of our courts of law, that I wish to see our colleges and academies established, only in county towns.

But further, considering the nature of our connection with the United States it will be necessary to make our pupil acquainted with all the prerogatives of the federal government. He must be instructed in the nature and variety of treaties. He must know the difference in the powers and duties of the several species of ambassadors. He must be taught wherein the obligations of individuals and of states are the same, and wherein they differ. In short, he must acquire a general knowledge of all those laws and forms, which unite the sovereigns of the earth, or separate them from each other.

I have only to add that it will be to no purpose to adopt this, or any other mode of education, unless we make choice of suitable masters to carry our plans into execution. Let our teachers be distinguished for their abilities and knowledge. Let them be grave in their manners,—gentle in their tempers,—exemplary in their morals, and of sound principles in religion and government. Let us not leave their support to the precarious resources to be derived from their pupils, but let such funds be provided for our schools and colleges as will enable us to allow them liberal salaries. By these means we shall render the chairs, —the professorships and rectorships of our colleges and academies objects of competition among learned men. By conferring upon our masters that independence, which is the companion of competency, we shall, moreover, strengthen their authority over the youth committed to their care. Let us remember that a great part of the divines, lawyers, physicians, legislators, soldiers, generals, delegates, counsellors, and governors of the state will probably hereafter pass through their hands. How great then should be the wisdom!—how honourable the rank! and how generous the reward of those men who are to form these necessary and leading members of the republic!

I beg pardon for having delayed so long, to say any thing of the separate and peculiar mode of education proper for WOMEN in a republic. I am sensible that they must concur in all our plans of education for young men, or no laws will ever render them effectual. To qualify our women for this purpose, they should not only be instructed in the usual branches of female education, but they should be instructed in the principles of liberty and government; and the obligations of patriotism, should be inculcated upon them. The opinions and conduct of men are often regulated by the women in the most arduous enterprizes of life; and their approbation is frequently the principal reward of the hero's dangers, and the patriot's toils. Besides, the *first* impressions upon the minds of children are generally derived from the women. Of how much consequence, therefore, is it in a republic, that they should think justly upon the great subjects of liberty and government!

The complaints that have been made against religion, liberty and learning, have been made against each of them in a *separate* state. Perhaps like certain liquors, they should only be used in a state of mixture. They mutually assist in correcting the abuses, and in improving the good effects of each other. From the combined and reciprocal influence of religion, liberty and learning upon the morals, manners and knowledge of individuals, of these, upon government, and of government, upon individuals, it is impossible to measure the degrees of happiness and perfection to which mankind may be raised. For my part, I can form no ideas of the golden age, so much celebrated by the poets, more delightful, than the contemplation of that happiness which it is now in the power of the legislature of Pennsylvania to confer upon her citizens, by establishing proper modes and places of education in every part of the state.

The *present time* is peculiarly favourable to the establishment of these benevolent and necessary institutions in Pennsylvania. The minds of our people have not as yet lost the yielding texture they acquired by the heat of the late revolution. They will *now* receive more readily, than five or even three years hence, new impressions and habits of all kinds. The spirit of liberty *now* pervades every part of the state. The influence of error and deception are *now* of short duration. Seven years hence, the affairs of our state may assume a new complexion. We may be rivetted to a criminal indifference for the safety and happiness of ourselves and our posterity. An aristocratic or democratic junto may arise, that shall find its despotic views connected with the prevalence of ignorance and vice in the state; or a few artful pedagogues who consider learning as useful only in proportion as it favours their pride or avarice, may prevent all new literary establishments from taking place, by raising a hue and cry against them, as the offspring of improper rivalship, or the nurseries of party spirit.

But in vain shall we lavish pains and expence, in establishing nurseries of virtue and knowledge in every part of the state. In vain shall we attempt to give the minds of our citizens a virtuous and uniform bias in early life, while the arms of our state are opened alike to receive into its bosom, and to confer equal privileges upon, the virtuous emigrant, and the annual refuse of the jails of Britain, Ireland and our sister states. Of the many criminals that have been executed within these seven years, four out of five of them have been foreigners, who have arrived here during the war and since the peace. We are yet, perhaps, to see, and deplore the tracks of the enormous vices and crimes these men have left behind them. Legislators of Pennsylvania! —Stewards of the justice and virtue of heaven!—Fathers of children, who may be corrupted and disgraced by bad examples; say—can nothing be done to preserve our morals, manners, and government, from the infection of European vices?

17

Benjamin Rush
on Women's Education

Benjamin Rush (1745–1813) was more concerned with women's formal education than most other public men of his day. As the following address at the Young Ladies' Academy in Philadelphia makes clear, Rush believed that education cannot afford to overlook women who, as mothers, become the first teachers of the republic. Instruction in morals and manners rests primarily with them. Hence he emphasized teaching them ethics, religion, history, poetry, and patriotism. He wanted "ornamental accomplishments," which had traditionally been the major purpose of girls' education among the middle and upper economic classes abroad, to yield to instruction in "principles and knowledge." So he inserted into his plan an "acquaintance" with the elementary principles of the basic sciences and with bookkeeping. An accomplished lady was to be useful as well as ornamental. In advocating religious study, he urged separate sectarian instruction for girls, not because he was championing any one Protestant sect, but because he thought that brotherly unity would be found in the recognition of sectarian diversity.

Lest the modern student decide too easily that there was nothing new here to advance the cause of American women in the 1790s, he might recall that education for most girls in colonial times had been minimal. Literacy alone, or at most the three R's learned at a dame school plus some of the homekeeping skills, was all that was expected of most girls. Young ladies from middle and upper class homes in towns or on southern plantations were expected to be taught dancing, etiquette, singing, and "the social graces." With his utilitarian view toward education, Rush was counseling the people of Philadelphia and the new nation that girls must now be expected to take their places in the orderly, prosperous, and pious agrarian and urban middle-class structure of the new United States.

Rush's view of all education, moreover, was directed by his "materialism," or a biological concept of man in his environment, no less than by his utilitarian beliefs. Rush the physician sought balance and harmony in the relationship between man and his environment. The human body and the faculties of the mind develop from their action or "collision" with experience. The "best" society for him was of course the American republic, in which a perfect state is achieved as the mind acquires the right collective balance of all that its owner experiences or collides against in active life. Here again, an orderly, schematized, and even static concept defines Rush's view of individual learning, as it did his plan for a system of schooling. If democratic changes eventually dissolved his ideal of the republican "machine" (see Selection 16), his emphasis upon morality, piety, and orderliness continued to be a dominant theme in American educational theory.

GENTLEMEN,

I have yielded with diffidence to the solicitations of the Principal of the Academy, in undertaking to express my regard for the prosperity of this seminary of learning, by submitting to your candor, a few Thoughts upon Female Education.

The first remark that I shall make upon this subject, is, that female education should be accommodated to the state of society, manners, and government of the country, in which it is conducted.

This remark leads me at once to add, that the education of young ladies, in this country, should be conducted upon principles very different from what it is in Great Britain, and in some respects, different from what it was when we were part of a monarchical empire.

There are several circumstances in the situation, employments, and duties of women in America, which require a peculiar mode of education.

Benjamin Rush, "Thoughts Upon Female Education, Accomodated to the Present State of Society, Manners, and Government, In The United States of America. Addressed to the Visitors of The Young Ladies' Academy in Philadelphia, 28th July, 1787, At the Close of the Quarterly Examination, And Afterwards Published at the Request of the Visitors." In Benjamin Rush, *Essays, Literary, Moral and Philosophical.* Second edition, with additions (Philadelphia, 1806), pp. 75–92.

I. The early marriages of our women, by contracting the time allowed for education, renders it necessary to contract its plan, and to confine it chiefly to the more useful branches of literature.

II. The state of property in America, renders it necessary for the greatest part of our citizens to employ themselves, in different occupations, for the advancement of their fortunes. This cannot be done without the assistance of the female members of the community. They must be the stewards, and guardians of their husbands' property. That education, therefore, will be most proper for our women, which teaches them to discharge the duties of those offices with the most success and reputation.

III. From the numerous avocations from their families, to which professional life exposes gentlemen in America, a principal share of the instruction of children naturally devolves upon the women. It becomes us therefore to prepare them by a suitable education, for the discharge of this most important duty of mothers.

IV. The equal share that every citizen has in the liberty, and the possible share he may have in the government of our country, make it necessary that our ladies should be qualified to a certain degree by a peculiar and suitable education, to concur in instructing their sons in the principles of liberty and government.

V. In Great Britain the business of servants is a regular occupation; but in America this humble station is the usual retreat of unexpected indigence; hence the servants in this country possess less knowledge and subordination than are required from them; and hence, our ladies are obliged to attend more to the private affairs of their families, than ladies generally do, of the same rank in Great Britain. . . . This circumstance should have great influence upon the nature and extent of female education in America.

The branches of literature most essential for a young lady in this country, appear to be,

I. A knowledge of the English language. She should not only read, but speak and spell it correctly. And to enable her to do this, she should be taught the English grammar, and be frequently examined in applying its rules in common conversation.

II. Pleasure and interest conspire to make the writing of a fair and legible hand, a necessary branch of a lady's education. For this purpose she should be taught not only to shape every letter properly, but to pay the strictest regard to points and capitals. . . .

III. Some knowledge of figures and book-keeping is absolutely necessary to qualify a young lady for the duties which await her in this country. There are certain occupations in which she may assist her husband with this knowledge; and should she survive him, and agreeably to the custom of our country be the executrix of his will, she cannot fail of deriving immense advantages from it.

IV. An acquaintance with geography and some instruction in chronology will enable a young lady to read history, biography, and travels, with advantage; and thereby qualify her not only for a general intercourse with the world, but to be an agreeable companion for a sensible man. To these branches of knowledge may be added, in some instances, a general acquaintance with the first principles of astronomy, natural philosophy and chemistry, particularly, with such parts of them as are calculated to prevent superstition, by explaining the causes, or obviating the effects of natural evil, and such, as are capable of being applied to domestic, and culinary purposes.

V. Vocal music should never be neglected, in the education of a young lady, in this country. Besides preparing her to join in that part of public worship which consists in psalmody, it will enable her to soothe the cares of domestic life. The distress and vexation of a husband—the noise of a nursery, and, even, the sorrows that will sometimes intrude into her own bosom, may all be relieved by a song, where sound and sentiment unite to act upon the mind. . . .

VI. Dancing is by no means an improper branch of education for an American lady. It promotes health, and renders the figure and motions of the body easy and agreeable. I anticipate the time when the resources of conversation shall be so far multiplied, that the amusement of dancing shall be wholly confined to children. But in our present state of society and knowledge, I conceive it to be an agreeable substitute for the ignoble pleasures of drinking, and gaming, in our assemblies of grown people.

VII. The attention of our young ladies should be directed, as soon as they are prepared for it, to the reading of history—travels—poetry—and moral essays. These studies are accommodated, in a peculiar manner, to the present state of society in America, and when a relish is excited for them, in early life, they subdue that passion for reading novels, which so generally prevails among the fair sex. I cannot dismiss this species of writing and reading without observing, that the subjects of novels are by no means accommodated to our present manners. They hold up *life*, it is true, but it is not as yet *life* in America. . . . Let it not be said that the tales of distress, which fill modern novels, have a tendency to soften the female heart in acts of humanity. The fact is the reverse of this. The abortive sympathy which is excited by the recital of imaginary distress, blunts the heart to that which is real; and, hence, we sometimes see instances of young ladies, who weep away a whole forenoon over the criminal sorrows of a fictitious Charlotte or Werter, turning with disdain at three o'clock from the fight of a beggar, who solicits in feeble accents or signs, a small portion only of the crumbs which fall from their fathers' tables.

VIII. It will be necessary to connect all these branches of education with regular instruction in the christian religion. For this purpose the principles of the different sects of christians should be taught and explained, and our pupils should early be furnished with some of the most simple arguments in favour of the truth of christianity. A portion of the bible (of late improperly banished from our schools) should be read by them every day, and such questions should be asked, after reading it as are calculated to imprint upon their minds the interesting stories contained in it.

Rousseau has asserted that the great secret of education consists in "wasting the time of children profitably." There is some truth in this observation. I believe that we often impair their health, and weaken their capacities, by imposing studies upon them, which are not proportioned to their years. But this objection does not apply to religious instruction. There are certain simple propositions in the christian religion, which are suited in a peculiar manner, to the infant state of reason and moral sensibility. . . . The female breast is the natural soil of christianity; and while our women are taught to believe its doctrines, and obey its precepts, the wit of Voltaire, and the style of Bolingbroke, will never be able to destroy its influence upon our citizens.

I cannot help remarking in this place, that christianity exerts the most friendly influence upon science, as well as upon the morals and manners of mankind. Whether this be occasioned by the unity of truth, and the mutual assistance which truths upon different subjects afford each other, or whether the faculties of the mind be sharpened and corrected by embracing the truths of revelation, and thereby prepared to investigate and perceive truths upon other subjects, I will not determine, but I believe that the greatest discoveries in science have been made by christian philosophers, and that there is the most knowledge in those countries where there is the most christianity. If this remark be well founded, then those philosophers who reject christianity, and those christians, whether parents or schoolmasters, who neglect the religious instruction of their children and pupils, *reject* and *neglect* the most effectual means of promoting knowledge in our country.

IX. If the measures that have been recommended for inspiring our pupils with a sense of religious and moral obligation be adopted, the government of them will be easy and agreeable. I shall only remark under this head, that *strictness* of discipline will always render *severity* unnecessary, and that there will be the most instruction in that school, where there is the most order.

I have said nothing in favor of instrumental music as a branch of female education, because I conceive it is by no means accommodated to the present state of society and manners in America. The price of musical instruments, and the extravagant fees demanded by the teachers of instrumental music, form but a small part of my objections to it.

To perform well, upon a musical instrument, requires much

time and long practice. . . . How many useful ideas might be picked up in these hours from history, philosophy, poetry, and the numerous moral essays with which our language abounds, and how much more would the knowledge acquired upon these subjects add to the consequence of a lady, with her husband and with society, than the best performed pieces of music upon a harpsicord or a guitar! Of the many ladies whom we have known, who have spent the most important years of their lives, in learning to play upon instruments of music, how few of them do we see amuse themselves or their friends with them, after they become mistresses of families! Their harpsichords serve only as side-boards for their parlours, and prove by their silence, that necessity and circumstances, will always prevail over fashion, and false maxims of education. . . .

It is agreeable to observe how differently modern writers, and the inspired author of the Proverbs, describe a fine woman. The former confine their praises chiefly to personal charms, and ornamental accomplishments, while the latter celebrates only the virtues of a valuable mistress of a family, and a useful member of society . . .

It should not surprize us that British customs, with respect to female education, have been transplanted into our American schools and families. We see marks of the same incongruity, of time and place, in many other things. We behold our houses accomodated to the climate of Great Britain, by eastern and western directions. We behold our ladies panting in a heat of ninety degrees, under a hat and cushion, which were calculated for the temperature of a British summer. We behold our citizens condemned and punished by a criminal law, which was copied from a country, where maturity in corruption renders public executions a part of the amusements of the nation. It is high time to awaken from this servility—to study our own character—to examine the age of our country—and to adopt manners in every thing, that shall be accommodated to our state of society, and to the forms of our government. In particular it is incumbent upon us to make ornamental accomplishments yield to principles and knowledge, in the education of our women.

A philosopher once said "let me make all the ballads of a country and I care not who makes its laws." He might with more propriety have said, let the ladies of a country be educated properly, and they will not only make and administer its laws, but form its manners and character. It would require a lively imagination to describe or even to comprehend, the happiness of a country, where knowledge and virtue, were generally diffused among the female sex. Our young men would then be restrained from vice by the terror of being banished from their company. . . . The influence of female education would be still more extensive and useful in domestic life. The obligations of gentlemen to qualify themselves by knowledge and industry to discharge the duties of benevolence, would be encreased by marriage; and the patriot—the hero—and the legislator, would find the sweetest reward of their toils, in the approbation and applause of their wives. Children would discover the marks of maternal prudence and wisdom in every station of life; for it has been remarked that there have been few great or good men who have not been blessed with wise and prudent mothers. . . .

I am not enthusiastical upon the subject of education. In the ordinary course of human affairs, we shall probably too soon follow the footsteps of the nations of Europe in manners and vices. The first marks we shall perceive of our declension, will appear among our women. Their idleness, ignorance, and profligacy will be the harbingers of our ruin. Then will the character and performance of a buffoon on the theatre, be the subject of more conversation and praise, than the patriot or the minister of the gospel;—then will our language and pronunciation be enfeebled and corrupted by a flood of French and Italian words;—then will the history of romantic amours, be preferred to the pure and immortal writings of Addison, Hawkesworth and Johnson;—then will our churches be neglected, and the name of the supreme being never be called upon, but in profane exclamations;—then will our Sundays be appropriated, only to feasts and concerts?—and then will begin all that train of domestic and political calamities——.But, I forbear. The prospect is so painful, that I cannot help, silently, imploring the great arbiter of human, affairs, to interpose his almighty goodness, and to deliver us from these evils, that, at least one spot of the earth may be reserved as a monument of the effects of good education, in order to shew in some degree, what our species was, before the fall, and what it shall be, after its restoration. . . .

By the separation of the sexes in the unformed state of their manners, female delicacy is cherished and preserved. . . . The proficiency which the young ladies have discovered in reading—writing—spelling—arithmetic—grammar—geography—music—and their different catechisms, since the last examination, is a less equivocal mark of the merit of our teachers, than any thing I am able to express in their favour.

But the reputation of the academy must be suspended, till the public are convinced, by the future conduct and character of our pupils, of the advantages of the institution. To you, therefore, Young Ladies, an important problem is committed for solution; and that is, whether our present plan of education be a wise one, and whether it be calculated to prepare you for the duties of social and domestic life. I know that the elevation of the female mind, by means of moral, physical and religious truth, is considered by some men as unfriendly to the domestic character of a woman. But this is the prejudice of little minds, and springs from the same spirit which opposes the general diffusion of knowledge among the citizens of our republics. If men believe that ignorance is favourable to the government of the female sex, they are certainly deceived; for a weak and ignorant woman will always be governed with the greatest difficulty. I have sometimes been led to ascribe the invention of ridiculous and expensive fashions in female dress, entirely to the gentlemen*, in order to divert the ladies from improving their minds, and thereby to secure a more arbitrary and un-limited authority over them. It will be in your power, LADIES, to correct the mistakes and practice of our sex upon these sub-jects, by demonstrating, that the female temper can only be governed by reason, and that the cultivation of reason in women, is alike friendly to the order of nature, and to private as well as public happiness.

* The very expensive prints of female dresses which are published an-nually in France, are invented and executed wholly by GENTLEMEN.

18

Noah Webster's Plea
for an American Language

Though some republican educational tracts were ahead of their day
in breadth of view and democratic aspect, the school textbooks of
Noah Webster (1758–1843) and Jedidiah Morse (1761–1826)
were an immediately practical and successful means for awakening
American school children to their national cultural identity. Webster's famous *Spelling Book* (or *Blue-Backed Speller*) was first published in 1783; it was followed in 1784 by a grammar, and in 1785
by a reader. These volumes together made up Webster's *Grammatical Institute of the English Language*. They began the standardization of American spelling and pronunciation, as distinguished from
older British usages. By 1837, the *Spelling Book* is estimated to
have sold about 15 million copies, and 60 million by 1890. Next to
the Bible, the *Speller* was probably the most widely used book in
America. Morse's *Geography Made Easy* (1784) emphasized the
geography of the United States, not that of Europe or Britain. Like
Webster's books, it contained patriotic themes, middle class morality after the fashion of Benjamin Franklin's "Poor Richard," and
enthusiasm for all things American. These textbooks federalized
American schools. In effect, they made the schools into the "republican machines" of which Benjamin Rush dreamed (see Selection
16). While they brought cultural uniformity and homogeneity to
school instruction, they failed to foster intellectual curiosity or independence of mind in students. Linked to a doctrinaire Puritan educational heritage and to the human penchant for the practical, the
new cultural nationalism set a tradition for American schools. It
became the educational part of the American character.

Men often build ideas from the words they possess. Vocabulary is
a primary tool of learning. Believing this, Noah Webster labored to

equip Americans with a basic tool of education. Published in 1828 in two volumes, *An American Dictionary of the English Language* was his masterwork. It was the capstone to a long career that saw him, after graduation from Yale in 1778, a lawyer, schoolmaster, journalist, and finally lexicographer. Along the way he pamphleteered for the federal Constitution, supported George Washington's Federalist policies, agitated for copyright laws under the federal government to protect his *Speller,* formed a rewarding friendship with Benjamin Franklin, edited John Winthrop's *Journal,* wrote on physical and medical science as well as on politics, taught and lectured in several eastern cities, and helped to found Amherst College. Through it all, Webster put to good use his talents for analyzing and defining words and for acquiring encyclopedic knowledge. After 1803 he devoted himself entirely to lexicography and turned out five dictionaries with their various revisions and abridgments, another *Grammar* (1807), and a revision of the Authorized Version of the Bible (1833).

The clear American aim of Webster's work had been anticipated by two other prominent educational theorists. In 1781 John Witherspoon (see Selection 13) compiled a list of "Americanisms" (a word he coined) for the *Pennsylvania Journal.* Benjamin Franklin (see Selections 11–12) had been devising a plan for a "perfect regularity" of the American language. Webster admired it so much, as this selection shows, that he considered adopting Franklin's simplified spelling with a phonetic alphabet into his *Speller.* But, gradually realizing that no speller would win popular acceptance with this arrangement, he reluctantly abandoned Franklin's scheme. What ultimately won Webster's books their popular success and the respect of educated men everywhere, even though their author did not have the benefit of European training in comparative or historical etymology, was their scholarly, even scientific presentation of the problems of American orthography and etymology. Webster's achievement was to record the changes in language that produced American linguistic and literary independence. For American education, his spellers, grammars, readers, and dictionaries were even more than historical record. They became the necessary tools of national cultural continuity.

More popular as public lectures than as printed essays, Webster's *Dissertations on the English Language,* partly reprinted here, best summarize his cultural nationalism. They were first delivered as lectures at Baltimore in 1785 and subsequently given in about twenty towns along the Atlantic seaboard. Upon their publication in 1789, they were dedicated to Benjamin Franklin, whose reformed mode of spelling and pronunciation Webster explained and defended in an appendix, also excerpted here.

Introduction.

A regular study of language has, in all civilized countries, formed a part of a liberal education. The Greeks, Romans, Italians and French successively improved their native tongues, taught them in Academies at home, and rendered them entertaining and useful to the foreign student.

The English tongue, tho later in its progress towards perfection, has attained to a considerable degree of purity, strength and elegance, and been employed, by an active and scientific nation, to record almost all the events and discoveries of ancient and modern times.

This language is the inheritance which the Americans have received from their British parents. To cultivate and adorn it, is a task reserved for men who shall understand the connection between language and logic, and form an adequate idea of the influence which a uniformity of speech may have on national attachments.

It will be readily admitted that the pleasures of reading and conversing, the advantage of accuracy in business, the necessity of clearness and precision in communicating ideas, require us to be able to speak and write our own tongue with ease and correctness. But there are more important reasons, why the language of this country should be reduced to such fixed principles, as may give its pronunciation and construction all the certainty and uniformity which any living tongue is capable of receiving.

The United States were settled by emigrants from different parts of Europe. But their descendants mostly speak the same tongue; and the intercourse among the learned of the different States, which the revolution has begun, and an American Court will perpetuate, must gradually destroy the differences of dialect which our ancestors brought from their native countries. This approximation of dialects will be certain; but without the operation of other causes than an intercourse at Court, it will be slow and partial. The body of the people, governed by habit, will still retain their respective peculiarities of speaking; and for want of schools and proper books, fall into many inaccuracies, which, incorporating with the language of

Noah Webster, *Dissertations on the English Language: With Notes, Historical and Critical. To Which Is Added, by Way of Appendix, an Essay on a Reformed Mode of Spelling, with Dr. Franklin's Arguments on that Subject* (Boston, 1789), 17–37, 288–290, 391–406.

the state where they live, may imperceptibly corrupt the national language. Nothing but the establishment of schools and some uniformity in the use of books, can annihilate differences in speaking and preserve the purity of the American tongue. A sameness of pronunciation is of considerable consequence in a political view; for provincial accents are disagreeable to strangers and sometimes have an unhappy effect upon the social affections. All men have local attachments, which lead them to believe their own practice to be the least exceptionable. Pride and prejudice incline men to treat the practice of their neighbors with some degree of contempt. Thus small differences in pronunciation at first excite ridicule—a habit of laughing at the singularities of strangers is followed by disrespect—and without respect friendship is a name, and social intercourse a mere ceremony.

These remarks hold equally true, with respect to individuals, to small societies and to large communities. Small causes, such as a nick-name, or a vulgar tone in speaking, have actually created a dissocial spirit between the inhabitants of the different states, which is often discoverable in private business and public deliberations. Our political harmony is therefore concerned in a uniformity of language.

As an independent nation, our honor requires us to have a system of our own, in language as well as government. Great Britain, whose children we are, and whose language we speak, should no longer be *our* standard; for the taste of her writers is already corrupted, and her language on the decline. But if it were not so, she is at too great a distance to be our model, and to instruct us in the principles of our own tongue.

It must be considered further, that the English is the common root or stock from which our national language will be derived. All others will gradually waste away—and within a century and a half, North America will be peopled with a hundred millions of men, *all speaking the same language*. Place this idea in comparison with the present and possible future bounds of the language in Europe—consider the Eastern Continent as inhabited by nations, whose knowledge and intercourse are embarrassed by differences of language; then anticipate the period when the people of one quarter of the world, will be able to associate and converse together like children of the same family.* Compare this prospect, which is not visionary, with the state of the English language in Europe, almost

---

* Even supposing that a number of republics, kingdoms or empires, should within a century arise and divide this vast territory; still the subjects of all will speak the same language, and the consequence of this uniformity will be an intimacy of social intercourse hitherto unknown, and a boundless diffusion of knowledge.

confined to an Island and to a few millions of people; then let reason and reputation decide, how far America should be dependent on a transatlantic nation, for her standard and improvements in language.

Let me add, that whatever predilection the Americans may have for their native European tongues, and particularly the British descendants for the English, yet several circumstances render a future separation of the American tongue from the English, necessary and unavoidable. The vicinity of the European nations, with the uninterrupted communication in peace, and the changes of dominion in war, are gradually assimilating their respective languages. The English with others is suffering continual alterations. America, placed at a distance from those nations, will feel, in a much less degree, the influence of the assimilating causes; at the same time, numerous local causes, such as a new country, new associations of people, new combinations of ideas in arts and science, and some intercourse with tribes wholly unknown in Europe, will introduce new words into the American tongue. These causes will produce, in a course of time, a language in North America, as different from the future language of England, as the modern Dutch, Danish and Swedish are from the German, or from one another: Like remote branches of a tree springing from the same stock; or rays of light, shot from the same center, and diverging from each other, in proportion to their distance from the point of separation.

Whether the inhabitants of America can be brought to a perfect uniformity in the pronunciation of words, it is not easy to predict; but it is certain that no attempt of the kind has been made, and an experiment, begun and pursued on the right principles, is the only way to decide the question. Schools in Great Britain have gone far towards demolishing local dialects—commerce has also had its influence—and in America these causes, operating more generally, must have a proportional effect.

In many parts of America, people at present attempt to copy the English phrases and pronunciation—an attempt that is favored by their habits, their prepossessions and the intercourse between the two countries. This attempt has, within the period of a few years, produced a multitude of changes in these particulars, especially among the leading classes of people. These changes make a difference between the language of the higher and common ranks; and indeed between the *same* ranks in *different* states; as the rage for copying the English, does not prevail equally in every part of North America.

But besides the reasons already assigned to prove this imitation absurd, there is a difficulty attending it, which will defeat the end proposed by its advocates; which is, that the English themselves have no standard of pronunciation, nor can they ever have one on the plan they propose. The Authors, who have attempted to give us a standard, make the practice of the court and stage in London the sole criterion of propriety in speaking. An attempt to establish a standard on this foundation is both *unjust* and *idle*. It is unjust, because it is abridging the nation of its rights: The *general practice* of a nation is the rule of propriety, and this practice should at least be consulted in so important a matter, as that of making laws for speaking. While all men are upon a footing and no singularities are accounted vulgar or ridiculous, every man enjoys perfect liberty. But when a particular set of men, in exalted stations, undertake to say, "we are the standards of propriety and elegance, and if all men do not conform to our practice, they shall be accounted vulgar and ignorant," they take a very great liberty with the rules of the language and the rights of civility.

But an attempt to fix a standard on the practice of any particular class of people is highly absurd: As a friend of mine once observed, it is like fixing a light house on a floating island. It is an attempt to *fix* that which is in itself *variable;* at least it must be variable so long as it is supposed that a local practice has no standard but a *local practice;* that is, no standard but *itself*. While this doctrine is believed, it will be impossible for a nation to follow as fast as the standard changes—for if the gentlemen at court constitute a standard, they are above it themselves, and their practice must shift with their passions and their whims.

But this is not all. If the practice of a few men in the capital is to be the standard, a knowledge of this must be communicated to the whole nation. Who shall do this? An able compiler perhaps attempts to give this practice in a dictionary; but it is probable that the pronunciation, even at court, or on the stage, is not uniform. The compiler therefore must follow his particular friends and patrons; in which case he is sure to be opposed and the authority of his standard called in question; or he must give two pronunciations as the standard, which leaves the student in the same uncertainty as it found him. Both these events have actually taken place in England, with respect to the most approved standards; and of course no one is universally followed.

Besides, if language must vary, like fashions, at the caprice of a court, we must have our standard dictionaries republished, with the fashionable pronunciation, at least once in five years; otherwise a gentleman in the country will become intolerably vulgar, by not being in a situation to adopt the fashion of the day. The *new* editions of them will supersede the *old*, and we shall have our pronunciation to re-learn, with the polite alterations, which are generally corruptions.

Such are the consequences of attempting to make a *local* practice the *standard* of language in a *nation*. The attempt must keep the language in perpetual fluctuation, and the learner in uncertainty.

If a standard therefore cannot be fixed on local and variable custom, on what shall it be fixed? If the most eminent speakers are not to direct our practice, where shall we look for a guide? The answer is extremely easy; the *rules of the language itself*, and the *general practice of the nation*, constitute propriety in speaking. If we examine the structure of any language, we shall find a certain principle of analogy running through the whole. We shall find in English that similar combinations of letters have usually the same pronunciation; and that words, having the same terminating syllable, generally have the accent at the same distance from that termination. These principles of analogy were not the result of design—they must have been the effect of accident, or that tendency which all men feel towards uniformity.* But the principles, when established, are productive of great convenience, and become an authority superior to the arbitrary decisions of any man or class of men. There is one exception only to this remark: When a deviation from analogy has become the universal practice of a nation, it then takes place of all rules and becomes the standard of propriety.

The two points therefore, which I conceive to be the basis of a standard in speaking, are these; *universal undisputed practice*, and the *principle of analogy*. *Universal practice* is generally, perhaps always, a rule of propriety; and in disputed points, where people differ in opinion and practice, *analogy* should always decide the controversy.

These are authorities to which all men will submit—they are superior to the opinions and caprices of the great, and to the negligence and ignorance of the multitude. The authority of individuals is always liable to be called in question—but the unanimous consent of a nation, and a fixed principle interwoven with the very construction of a language, coeval and coextensive with it, are like the common laws of a land, or the immutable rules of morality, the

---

* This disposition is taken notice of by Dr. Blair, Lect. 8. Where he observes, "that tho the formation of abstract or general conceptions is supposed to be a difficult operation of the mind, yet such conceptions must have entered into the first formation of languages"—"this invention of abstract terms requires no great exertion of metaphysical capacity"—"Men are *naturally* inclined to call all those objects which resemble each other by one common name—We may daily observe this practised by children, in their first attempts towards acquiring language."

I cannot, with this great critic, call the process by which *similar* objects acquire the *same* name, an act of *abstraction*, or the name an *abstract term*. Logical distinctions may lead us astray. There is in the mind an *instinctive disposition*, or *principle of association*, which will account for all common names and the analogies in language.

propriety of which every man, however refractory, is forced to acknowledge, and to which most men will readily submit. Fashion is usually the child of caprice and the being of a day; principles of propriety are founded in the very nature of things, and remain unmoved and unchanged, amidst all the fluctuations of human affairs and the revolutions of time.

It must be confessed that languages are changing, from age to age, in proportion to improvements in science. Words, as Horace observes, are like leaves of trees; the old ones are dropping off and new ones growing. These changes are the necessary consequences of changes in customs, the introduction of new arts, and new ideas in the sciences. Still the body of a language and its general rules remain for ages the same, and the new words usually conform to these rules; otherwise they stand as exceptions, which are not to overthrow the principle of analogy already established.

But when a language has arrived at a certain stage of improvement, it must be stationary or become retrograde; for improvements in science either cease, or become slow and too inconsiderable to affect materially the tone of a language. This stage of improvement is the period when a nation abounds with writers of the first class, both for abilities and taste. This period in England commenced with the age of Queen Elizabeth and ended with the reign of George II. It would have been fortunate for the language, had the stile of writing and the pronunciation of words been fixed, as they stood in the reign of Queen Ann and her successor. Few improvements have been made since that time; but innumerable corruptions in pronunciation have been introduced by Garrick, and in stile, by Johnson, Gibbon and their imitators.*

The great Sidney wrote in a pure stile; yet the best models of purity and elegance, are the works of Sir William Temple, Dr. Middleton, Lord Bolingbroke, Mr. Addison and Dean Swift. But a little inferior to these, are the writings of Mr. Pope, Sir Richard Steele, Dr. Arbuthnot, with some of their contemporaries. Sir William Blackstone has given the law stile all the elegance and precision of which it is capable. Dr. Price and Dr. Priestley write with purity, and Sir William Jones seems to have copied the ease, simplicity and elegance of Middleton and Addison.

But how few of the modern writers have pursued the same manner of writing? Johnson's stile is a mixture of Latin and English; an intolerable composition of Latinity, affected smoothness, scholastic accuracy and roundness of periods. The benefits derived from his morality and his erudition, will hardly counterbalance the mischief

---

* The progress of corruption in language is described with precision, and philosophical reasons assigned with great judgment, by that celebrated French writer, Condillac, in his Origin of Human Knowledge. Part 2.

done by his manner of writing. The names of a Robertson, a Hume, a Home and a Blair, almost silence criticism; but I must repeat what a very learned Scotch gentleman once acknowledged to me, "that the Scotch writers are not models of the pure English stile." Their stile is generally stiff, sometimes very awkward, and not always correct.° Robertson labors his stile and sometimes introduces a word merely for the sake of rounding a period. Hume has borrowed French idioms without number; in other respects he has given an excellent model of historical stile. Lord Kaims' manner is stiff; and Dr Blair, whose stile is less exceptionable in these particulars, has however introduced, into his writings, several foreign idioms and ungrammatical phrases. The Scotch writers now stand almost the first for erudition; but perhaps no man can write a foreign language with genuin purity.

Gibbon's harmony of prose is calculated to delight our ears; but it is difficult to comprehend his meaning and the chain of his ideas, as fast as we naturally read; and almost impossible to recollect them, at any subsequent period. Perspicuity, the first requisite in stile, is sometimes sacrificed to melody; the mind of a reader is constantly dazzled by a glare of ornament, or charmed from the subject by the music of the language. As he is one of the first, it is hoped he may be the *last*, to attempt the gratification of our *ears*, at the expense of our *understanding*.

Such however is the taste of the age; simplicity of stile is neglected for ornament; and sense is sacrificed to sound.°

Altho stile, or the choice of words and manner of arranging them, may be necessarily liable to change, yet it does not follow that pronunciation and orthography cannot be rendered in a great measure permanent. An orthography, in which there would be a perfect correspondence between the spelling and pronunciation, would go very far towards effecting this desireable object. The Greek language suffered little or no change in these particulars, for about a thousand years; and the Roman was in a great degree fixed for several centuries.

Rapid changes of language proceed from violent causes; but

° Dr. Witherspoon is an exception. His stile is easy, simple and elegant. I consider Dr. Franklin and Dr. Witherspoon as the two best writers in America. The words they use, and their arrangement, appear to flow spontaneously from their manner of thinking. The vast superiority of their stiles over those of Gibbon and Gillies, is owing to this circumstance, that the two American writers have bestowed their labor upon *ideas*, and the English historians upon words.

° The same taste prevailed in Rome, under the Emperors, when genius was prostituted to the mean purposes of flattery.

these causes cannot be supposed to exist in North America. It is contrary to all rational calculation, that the United States will ever be conquered by any one nation, speaking a different language from that of the country. Removed from the danger of corruption by conquest, our language can change only with the slow operation of the causes before–mentioned and the progress of arts and sciences, unless the folly of imitating our parent country should continue to govern us, and lead us into endless innovation. This folly however will lose its influence gradually, as our particular habits of respect for that country shall wear away, and our *amor patriæ* acquire strength and inspire us with a suitable respect for our own national character.

We have therefore the fairest opportunity of establishing a national language, and of giving it uniformity and perspicuity, in North America, that ever presented itself to mankind. Now is the time to begin the plan. The minds of the Americans are roused by the events of a revolution; the necessity of organizing the political body and of forming constitutions of government that shall secure freedom and property, has called all the faculties of the mind into exertion; and the danger of losing the benefits of independence, has disposed every man to embrace any scheme that shall tend, in its future operation, to reconcile the people of America to each other, and weaken the prejudices which oppose a cordial union.

My design, in these dissertations, is critically to investigate the rules of pronunciation in our language; to examin the past and present practice of the English, both in the pronunciation of words and construction of sentences; to exhibit the principal differences beween the practice in England and America, and the differences in the several parts of America, with a view to reconcile them on the principles of *universal practice* and *analogy.* I have no system of my own to offer; my sole design is to explain what I suppose to be authorities, superior to all private opinions, and to examin local dialects by those authorities.

Most writers upon this subject have split upon one rock: They lay down certain rules, arbitrary perhaps or drawn from the principles of other languages, and then condemn all English phrases which do not coincide with those rules. They seem not to consider that grammar is formed on language, and not language on grammar. Instead of examining to find what the English language *is,* they endeavor to show what it *ought to be* according to their rules. It is for this reason that some of the criticisms of the most celebrated philologers are so far from being just, that they tend to overthrow the rules, and corrupt the true idiom, of the English tongue. . . .

On examining the language, and comparing the practice of speak-

ing among the yeomanry of this country, with the stile of Shake-
spear and Addison, I am constrained to declare that the people of
America, in particular the English descendants, speak the most *pure
English* now known in the world. There is hardly a foreign idiom in
their language; by which I mean, a *phrase* that has not been used
by the best English writers from the time of Chaucer. They retain
a few obsolete *words*, which have been dropt by writers, probably
from mere affectation, as those which are substituted are neither
more melodious nor expressive. In many instances they retain correct phrases, instead of which the pretended refiners of the language
have introduced those which are highly improper and absurd.

Let Englishmen take notice that when I speak of the American
yeomanry, the latter are not to be compared to the illiterate peasan-
try of their own country. The yeomanry of this country consist of
substantial independent freeholders, masters of their own persons
and lords of their own soil. These men have considerable education.
They not only learn to read, write and keep accounts; but a vast
proportion of them read newspapers every week, and besides the
Bible, which is found in all families, they read the best English sermons and treatises upon religion, ethics, geography and history;
such as the works of Watts, Addison, Atterbury, Salmon, &c. In the
eastern states, there are public schools sufficient to instruct every
man's children, and most of the children are actually benefited by
these institutions. The people of distant counties in England can
hardly understand one another, so various are their dialects; but in
the extent of twelve hundred miles in America, there are very few, I
question whether a hundred words, except such as are used in
employments wholly local, which are not universally intelligible.

But unless the rage for imitating foreign changes can be restrained, this agreeble and advantageous uniformity will be gradually destroyed. The standard writers abroad give us local practice,
the momentary whims of the great, or their own arbitrary rules to
direct our pronunciation; and we, the apes of fashion, submit to
imitate any thing we hear and see. Sheridan has introduced or
given sanction to more arbitrary and corrupt changes of pronunciation, within a few years, than had before taken place in a century;
and in Perry's Dictionary, not to mention the errors in what he most
arrogantly calls his *"Only sure Guide to* the English Tongue," there
are whole pages in which there are scarcely two or three words
marked for a just pronunciation. There is no Dictionary yet published in Great Britain, in which so many of the analogies of the
language and the just rules of pronunication are preserved, as in
the common practice of the well informed Americans, who have
never consulted any foreign standard: Nor is there any grammatical
treatise, except Dr. Priestley's, which has explained the real idioms

of the language, as they are found in Addison's works, and which remain to this day in the American practice of speaking.

The result of the whole is, that we should adhere to our own practice and general customs, unless it can be made very obvious that such practice is wrong, and that a change will produce some considerable advantage.

Essay

ON THE NECESSITY, ADVANTAGES AND PRACTICABILITY OF REFORMING THE MODE OF SPELLING, AND OF RENDERING THE ORTHOGRAPHY OF WORDS CORRESPONDENT TO THE PRONUNCIATION.

It has been observed by all writers on the English language, that the orthography or spelling of words is very irregular; the same letters often representing different sounds, and the same sounds often expressed by different letters. For this irregularity, two principal causes may be assigned:

1. The changes to which the pronunciation of a language is liable, from the progress of science and civilization.

2. The mixture of different languages, occasioned by revolutions in England, or by a predilection of the learned, for words of foreign growth and ancient origin.

To the first cause, may be ascribed the difference between the spelling and pronunciation of Saxon words. The northern nations of Europe originally spoke much in gutturals. This is evident from the number of aspirates and guttural letters, which still remain in the orthography of words derived from those nations; and from the modern pronunciation of the collateral branches of the Teutonic, the Dutch, Scotch and German. Thus *k* before *n* was once pronounced; as in *knave, know;* the *gh* in *might, though, daughter,* and other similar words; the *g* in *reign, feign,* &c.

But as savages proceed in forming languages, they lose the

guttural sounds, in some measure, and adopt the use of labials, and the more open vowels. The ease of speaking facilitates this progress, and the pronunciation of words is softened, in proportion to a national refinement of manners. This will account for the difference between the ancient and modern languages of France, Spain and Italy; and for the difference between the soft pronunciation of the present languages of those countries, and the more harsh and guttural pronunciation of the northern inhabitants of Europe.

In this progress, the English have lost the sounds of most of the guttural letters. The *k* before *n* in *know*, the *g* in *reign*, and in many other words, are become mute in practice; and the *gh* is softened into the sound of *f*, as in *laugh*, or is silent, as in *brought*.

To this practice of softening the sounds of letters, or wholly suppressing those which are harsh and disagreeable, may be added a popular tendency to abbreviate words of common use. Thus *Southwark*, by a habit of quick pronunciation, is become *Suthark; Worcester* and *Leicester*, are become *Wooster* and *Lester; business, bizness; colonel, curnel; cannot, will not, cant, wont.* In this manner the final *e* is not heard in many modern words, in which it formerly made a syllable. The words *clothes, cares,* and most others of the same kind, were formerly pronounced in two syllables.

Of the other cause of irregularity in the spelling of our language, I have treated sufficiently in the first Dissertation. It is here necessary only to remark, that when words have been introduced from a foreign language into the English, they have generally retained the orthography of the original, however ill adapted to express the English pronunciation. Thus *fatigue, marine, chaise,* retain their French dress, while, to represent the true pronunciation in English, they should be spelt *fateeg, mareen, shaze.* Thus thro an ambition to exhibit the etymology of words, the English, in *Philip, physic, character, chorus,* and other Greek derivatives, preserve the representatives of the

---

* Wont is strictly a contraction of *woll not,* as the word was anciently pronounced.

original Φ and X; yet these words are pronounced, and ought ever to have been spelt, *Fillip, fyzzie* or *fizzic, karacter, korus.*

But such is the state of our language. The pronunciation of the words which are strictly *English,* has been gradually changing for ages, and since the revival of science in Europe, the language has received a vast accession of words from other languages, many of which retain an orthography very ill suited to exhibit the true pronunciation.

The question now occurs; ought the Americans to retain these faults which produce innumerable inconveniences in the acquisition and use of the language, or ought they at once to reform these abuses, and introduce order and regularity into the orthography of the AMERICAN TONGUE?

Let us consider this subject with some attention.

Several attempts were formerly made in England to rectify the orthography of the language.* But I apprehend their schemes failed of success, rather on account of their intrinsic difficulties, than on account of any necessary impracticability of a reform. It was proposed, in most of these schemes, not merely to throw out superfluous and silent letters, but to introduce a number of new characters. Any attempt on such a plan must undoubtedly prove unsuccessful. It is not to be expected that an orthography, perfectly regular and simple, such as would be formed by a "Synod of Grammarians on principles of science," will ever be substituted for that confused mode of spelling which is now established. But it is apprehended that great im-

---

* The words *number, chamber,* and many others in English are from the French *nombre, chambre,* &c. Why was the spelling changed? or rather why is the spelling of *lustre, metre, theatre, not* changed? The cases are precisely similar. The Englishman who first wrote *number* for *nombre,* had no greater authority to make the change, than *any* modern writer has to spell *lustre, metre* in a similar manner, *luster, meter.* The change in the first instance was a valuable one; it conformed the spelling to the pronunciation, and I have taken the liberty, in all my writings, to pursue the principle in *luster, meter, miser, theater, sepulcher,* &c.

* The first by Sir Thomas Smith, secretary of state to Queen Elizabeth: Another by Dr. Gill, a celebrated master of St. Paul's school in London: Another by Mr. Charles Butler, who went so far as to print his book in his proposed orthography: Several in the time of Charles the first; and in the present age, Mr. Elphinstone has published a treatise in a very ridiculous orthography.

provements may be made, and an orthography almost regular, or such as shall obviate most of the present difficulties which occur in learning our language, may be introduced and established with little trouble and opposition.

The principal alterations, necessary to render our orthography sufficiently regular and easy, are these:

1. The omission of all superfluous or silent letters; as *a* in *bread*. Thus *bread, head, give, breast, built, meant, realm, friend,* would be spelt, *bred, hed, giv, brest, bilt, ment, relm, frend*. Would this alteration produce any inconvenience, any embarrassment or expense? By no means. On the other hand, it would lessen the trouble of writing, and much more, of learning the language; it would reduce the true pronunciation to a certainty, and while it would assist foreigners and our own children in acquiring the language, it would render the pronunciation uniform, in different parts of the country, and almost prevent the possibility of changes.

2. A substitution of a character that has a certain definite sound, for one that is more vague and indeterminate. Thus by putting *ee* instead of *ea* or *ie*, the words *mean, near, speak, grieve, zeal,* would become *meen, neer, speek, greev, zeel*. This alteration could not occasion a moments trouble; at the same time it would prevent a doubt respecting the pronunciation; whereas the *ea* and *ie* having different sounds, may give a learner much difficulty. Thus *greef* should be substituted for *grief; kee* for *key; beleev* for *believe; laf* for *laugh; dawter* for *daughter; plow* for *plough; tuf* for *tough; proov* for *prove; blud* for *blood;* and *draft* for *draught*. In this manner *ch* in Greek derivatives, should be changed into *k*; for the English *ch* has a soft sound, as in *cherish;* but *k* always a hard sound. Therefore *character, chorus, cholic, architecture,* should be written *karacter, korus, kolic, arkitecture;* and were they thus written, no person could mistake their true pronunciation.

Thus *ch* in French derivatives should be changed into *sh; machine, chaise, chavalier,* should be written *masheen, shaze, shevaleer;* and *pique, tour, oblique,* should be written peek, *toor, obleek.*

3. A trifling alteration in a character, or the addition of a point would distinguish different sounds, without the substitution of a new character. Thus a very small stroke across *th* would distinguish its two sounds. A point over a vowel, in this manner, *à*, or *ò*, or *ī*, might answer all the purposes of different letters. And for the dipthong *ow*, let the two letters be united by a small stroke, or both engraven on the same piece of metal, with the left hand line of the *w* united to the *o*.

These, with a few other inconsiderable alterations, would answer every purpose, and render the orthography sufficiently correct and regular.

The advantages to be derived from these alterations are numerous, great and permanent.

1. The simplicity of the orthography would facilitate the learning of the language. It is now the work of years for children to learn to spell; and after all, the business is rarely accomplished. A few men, who are bred to some business that requires constant exercise in writing, finally learn to spell most words without hesitation; but most people remain, all their lives, imperfect masters of spelling, and liable to make mistakes, whenever they take up a pen to write a short note. Nay, many people, even of education and fashion, never attempt to write a letter, without frequently consulting a dictionary.

But with the proposed orthography, a child would learn to spell, without trouble, in a very short time, and the orthography being very regular, he would ever afterwards find it difficult to make a mistake. It would, in that case, be as difficult to spell *wrong*, as it is now to spell *right*.

Besides this advantage, foreigners would be able to acquire the pronunciation of English, which is now so difficult and embarrassing, that they are either wholly discouraged on the first attempt, or obliged, after many years labor, to rest contented with an imperfect knowledge of the subject.

2. A correct orthography would render the pronunciation of the language, as uniform as the spelling in books. A general uniformity thro the United States, would be the event of such a reformation as I am here recommending. All persons, of every

rank, would speak with some degree of precision and uniformity.* Such a uniformity in these states is very desireable; it would remove prejudice, and conciliate mutual affection and respect.

3. Such a reform would diminish the number of letters about one sixteenth or eighteenth. This would save a page in eighteen; and a saving of an eighteenth in the expense of books, is an advantage that should not be overlooked.

4. But a capital advantage of this reform in these states would be, that it would make a difference between the English orthography and the American. This will startle those who have not attended to the subject; but I am confident that such an event is an object of vast political consequence. For,

The alteration, however small, would encourage the publication of books in our own country. It would render it, in some measure, necessary that all books should be printed in America. The English would never copy our orthography for their own use; and consequently the same impressions of books would not answer for both countries. The inhabitants of the present generation would read the English impressions; but posterity, being taught a different spelling, would prefer the American orthography.

Besides this, *a national language* is a band of *national union*. Every engine should be employed to render the people of this country *national;* to call their attachments home to their own country; and to inspire them with the pride of national character. However they may boast of Independence, and the freedom of their government, yet their *opinions* are not sufficiently independent; an astonishing respect for the arts and literature of their parent country, and a blind imitation of its manners, are still prevalent among the Americans. Thus an habitual respect for another country, deserved indeed and once laudable, turns their attention from their own interests, and prevents their respecting themselves.

* I once heard Dr. Franklin remark, "that those people spell best, who do not know how to spell;" that is, they spell as their ears dictate, without being guided by rules, and thus fall into regular orthography.

Objections.

1. "This reform of the Alphabet would oblige people to re-learn the language, or it could not be introduced."

But the alterations proposed are so few and so simple, that an hour's attention would enable any person to read the new orthography with facility; and a week's practice would render it so familiar, that a person would write it without hesitation or mistake. Would this small inconvenience prevent its adoption? Would not the numerous national and literary advantages, resulting from the change, induce Americans to make so inconsiderable a sacrifice of time and attention? I am persuaded they would.

But it would not be necessary that men advanced beyond the middle stage of life, should be at the pains to learn the proposed orthography. They would, without inconvenience, continue to use the present. They would read the *new* orthography, without difficulty; but they would write in the *old*. To men thus advanced, and even to the present generation in general, if they should not wish to trouble themselves with a change, the reformation would be almost a matter of indifference. It would be sufficient that children should be taught the new orthography, and that as fast as they come upon the stage, they should be furnished with books in the American spelling. The progress of printing would be proportioned to the demand for books among the rising generation. This progressive introduction of the scheme would be extremely easy; children would learn the proposed orthography more easily than they would the old; and the present generation would not be troubled with the change; so that none but the obstinate and capricious could raise objections or make any opposition. The change would be so inconsiderable, and made on such simple principles, that a column in each newspaper, printed in the new spelling, would in six months, familiarize most people to the change, show the advantages of it, and imperceptibly remove their objections. The only steps necessary to ensure success in the attempts to introduce this reform, would be, a resolution of Congress, ordering all their acts to be engrossed in the new orthography, and recommending the plan to the several universities in America; and also a resolution of the universities to encourage and support it. The printers would begin the reformation by publishing short paragraphs and small tracts in the new orthography; school books would first be published in the same; curiosity would excite attention to it, and men would be gradually reconciled to the plan.

2. "This change would render our present books useless."

This objection is, in some measure, answered under the foregoing head. The truth is, it would not have this effect. The difference of orthography would not render books printed in one, illegible to persons acquainted only with the other. The difference would not be so great as between the orthography of Chaucer, and of the present age; yet Chaucer's works are still read with ease.

3. "This reformation would injure the language by obscuring etymology."

This objection is unfounded. In general, it is not true that the change would obscure etymology; in a few instances, it might; but it would rather restore the etymology of many words; and if it were true that the change would obscure it, this would be no objection to the reformation.

It will perhaps surprize my readers to be told that, in many particular words, the modern spelling is less correct than the ancient. Yet this is a truth that reflects dishonor on our modern refiners of the language. Chaucer, four hundred years ago, wrote *bilder* for *builder; dedly* for *deadly; ernest* for *earnest; erly* for *early; brest* for *breast; hed* for *head;* and certainly his spelling was the most agreeable to the pronunciation.* Sidney wrote *bin, examin, sutable,* with perfect propriety. Dr. Middleton wrote *explane, genuin, revele,* which is the most easy and correct orthography of such words; and also *luster, theater,* for *lustre, theatre.* In these and many other instances, the modern spelling is a corruption; so that allowing many improvements to have been made in orthography, within a century or two, we

---

* In Chaucer's life, prefixed to the edition of his works 1602, I find *move* and *prove* spelt almost correctly, *moove* and *proove.*

must acknowledge also that many corruptions have been introduced.

In answer to the objection, that a change of orthography would obscure etymology, I would remark, that the etymology of most words is already lost, even to the learned; and to the unlearned, etymology is never known. Where is the man that can trace back our English words to the elementary radicals? In a few instances, the student has been able to reach the primitive roots of words; but I presume the radicals of one tenth of the words in our language, have never yet been discovered, even by Junius, Skinner, or any other etymologist. Any man may look into Johnson or Ash, and find that *flesh* is derived from the Saxon *floce; child* from *cild; flood* from *flod; lad* from *leode;* and *loaf* from *laf* or *blaf*. But this discovery will answer no other purpose, than to show, that within a few hundred years, the spelling of some words has been a little changed: We should still be at a vast distance from the primitive roots.

In many instances indeed etymology will assist the learned in understanding the composition and true sense of a word; and it throws much light upon the progress of language. But the true sense of a complex term is not always, nor generally, to be learnt from the sense of the primitives or elementary words. The current meaning of a word depends on its use in a nation. This true sense is to be obtained by attending to good authors, to dictionaries and to practice, rather than to derivation. The former *must* be *right;* the latter *may* lead us into *error.*

But to prove of how little consequence a knowledge of etymology is to most people, let me mention a few words. The word *sincere* is derived from the Latin, *sin cera,* without wax; and thus it came to denote *purity of mind.* I am confident that not a man in a thousand ever suspected this to be the origin of the word; yet all men, that have any knowledge of our language, use the word in its true sense, and understand its customary meaning, as well as Junius did, or any other etymologist.

Yea or *yes* is derived from the imperative of a verb, *avoir* to have, as the word is now spelt. It signifies therefore *have,* or *possess,* or *take* what you ask. But does this explication assist us in using the word? And does not every countryman who labors in the field, understand and use the word with as much precision as the profoundest philosophers?

The word *temper* is derived from an old root, *tem,* which signified *water.* It was borrowed from the act of *cooling,* or moderating heat. Hence the meaning of *temperate, temperance,* and all the ramifications of the original stock. But does this help us to the modern current sense of these words? By no means. It leads us to understand the formation of languages, and in what manner an idea of a visible action gives rise to a correspondent abstract idea; or rather, how a word, from a literal and direct sense, may be applied to express a variety of figurative and collateral ideas. Yet the customary sense of the word is known by practice, and as well understood by an illiterate man of tolerable capacity, as by men of science.

The word *always* is compounded of *all* and *ways;* it had originally no reference to time; and the etymology or composition of the word would only lead us into error. The true meaning of words is that which a nation in general annex to them. Etymology therefore is of no use but to the learned; and for them it will still be preserved, so far as it is now understood, in dictionaries and other books that treat of this particular subject.

4. "The distinction between words of different meanings and similar sound would be destroyed."

"That distinction," to answer in the words of the great Franklin, "is already destroyed in pronunciation." Does not every man pronounce *all* and *awl* precisely alike? And does the sameness of sound ever lead a hearer into a mistake? Does not the construction render the distinction easy and intelligible, the moment the words of the sentence are heard? Is the word *knew* ever mistaken for *new,* even in the rapidity of pronouncing an animated oration? Was *peace* ever mistaken for *piece; pray* for *prey; flour* for *flower?* Never, I presume, is this similarity of sound the occasion of mistakes.

If therefore an identity of *sound,* even in rapid speaking, produces no inconvenience, how much less would an identity of *spelling,* when the eye would have leisure to survey the construction? But experience, the criterion of truth, which has removed the objection in the first case, will also assist us in forming our opinion in the last.

There are many words in our language which, with the *same orthography,* have *two* or more *distinct meanings.* The word *wind,* whether it signifies *to move round,* or *air in motion,* has the *same spelling;* it exhibits no distinction to the *eye* of a silent reader; and yet its meaning is never mistaken. The construction shows at sight in which sense the word is to be understood. *Hail* is used as expression of joy, or to signify frozen drops of water, falling from the clouds. *Rear* is to raise up, or it signifies the hinder part of an army. *Lot* signifies fortune or destiny; a plot of ground; or a certain proportion or share; and yet does this diversity, this contrariety of meanings ever occasion the least difficulty in the ordinary language of books? It cannot be maintained. This diversity is found in all languages;* and altho it may be considered as a defect, and occasion some trouble for foreign learners, yet to natives it produces no sensible inconvenience.

5. "It is idle to conform the orthography of words to the pronounciation, because the latter is continually changing."

This is one of Dr. Johnson's objections, and it is very unworthy of his judgement. So far is this circumstance from being a real objection, that it is alone a sufficient reason for the change of spelling. On his principle of *fixing the orthography,* while the *pronunciation is changing,* any *spoken language* must, in time, lose all relation to the *written language;* that is, the sounds of words would have no affinity with the letters that compose them. In some instances, this is now the case; and no mortal would suspect from the spelling, that *neighbour, wrought,* are pronounced *nabur, rawt.* On this principle, Dr. Johnson ought to have gone back some centuries, and given us, in his dictionary, the primitive Saxon orthography, *wol* for *will;*

---

* In the Roman language *liber* had four or five different meanings; it signified *free, the inward bark of a tree, a book,* sometimes *an epistle,* and also *generous.*

ydilnesse for *idleness; eyen* for *eyes; eche* for *each,* &c. Nay, he should have gone as far as possible into antiquity, and, regardless of the changes of pronounciation, given us the primitive radical language in it's purity. Happily for the language, that doctrine did not prevail till his time; the spelling of words changed with the pronunciation; to these changes we are indebted for numberless improvements; and it is hoped that the progress of them, in conformity with the national practice of speaking, will not be obstructed by the erroneous opinion, even of Dr. Johnson. How much more rational is the opinion of Dr. Franklin, who says, "the orthography of our language began to be fixed too soon." If the pronunciation must vary, from age to age, (and some trifling changes of language will always be taking place) common sense would dictate a correspondent change of spelling. Admit Johnson's principles; take his pedantic orthography for the standard; let it be closely adhered to in future; and the slow changes in the pronunciation of our national tongue, will in time make as great a difference between our *written* and *spoken* language, as there is between the pronunciation of the present English and German. The *spelling* will be no more a guide to the pronunciation, than the orthography of the German or Greek. This event is actually taking place, in consequence of the stupid opinion, advanced by Johnson and other writers, and generally embraced by the nation.

All these objections appear to me of very inconsiderable weight, when opposed to the great, substantial and permanent advantages to be derived from the regular national orthography.

Sensible I am how much easier it is to *propose* improvements, than to *introduce* them. Every thing *new* starts the idea of difficulty; and yet it is often mere novelty that excites the appearance; for on a slight examination of the proposal, the difficulty vanishes. When we firmly *believe* a scheme to be practicable, the work is *half* accomplished. We are more frequently deterred by fear from making an attack, then repulsed in the encounter.

Habit also is opposed to changes; for it renders even our

errors dear to us. Having surmounted all difficulties in childhood, we forget the labor, the fatigue, and the perplexity we
suffered in the attempt, and imagin the progress of our studies
to have been smooth and easy.* What seems intrinsically right,
is so merely thro habit.

Indolence is another obstacle to improvements. The most
arduous task a reformer has to execute, is to make people
think; to rouse them from that lethargy, which, like the mantle
of sleep, covers them in repose and contentment.

But America is in a situation the most favorable for great
reformations; and the present time is, in a singular degree,
auspicious. The minds of the men in this country have been
awakened. New scenes have been, for many years, presenting
new occasions for exertion; unexpected distresses have called
forth the powers of invention; and the application of new
expedients has demanded every possible exercise of wisdom
and talents. Attention is roused; the mind expanded; and the
intellectual faculties invigorated. Here men are prepared to
receive improvements, which would be rejected by nations,
whose habits have not been shaken by similar events.

NOW is the time, and *this* the country, in which we may expect success, in attempting changes favorable to language,
science and government. Delay, in the plan here proposed, may
be fatal; under a tranquil general government, the minds of
men may again sink into indolence; a national acquiescence in
error will follow; and posterity be doomed to struggle with
difficulties, which time and accident will perpetually multiply.

Let us then seize the present moment, and establish a *national language,* as well as a national government. Let us re-

---

* Thus most people suppose the present mode of spelling to be really the
easiest and *best*. This opinion is derived from habit; the new mode of
spelling proposed would save three fourths of the labor now bestowed in
learning to write our language. A child would learn to spell as well in
one year, as he can now in four. This is not a supposition—it is an assertion capable of proof; and yet people, never knowing, or having forgot
the labor of learning, suppose the present mode to be the easiest. No
person, but one who has taught children, has any idea of the difficulty of
learning to spell and pronounce our language in its present form.

member that there is a certain respect due to the opinions of other nations. As an independent people, our reputation abroad demands that, in all things, we should be federal; be *national;* for if we do not respect *ourselves,* we may be assured that *other nations* will not respect us. In short, let it be impressed upon the mind of every American, that to neglect the means of commanding respect abroad, is treason against the character and dignity of a brave independent people.

19

Samuel Harrison Smith's Prize Essay

From the 1770s, under the successive presidencies of Benjamin Franklin, David Rittenhouse, and Thomas Jefferson, the American Philosophical Society at Philadelphia became the country's leading intellectual establishment. Since many of its members were deeply concerned for the educational growth of the country, the Society in 1796 sponsored an essay contest on the theme of liberal education "adapted to the genius" of the new republic. The two winning essays by Samuel Harrison Smith, reprinted in part here, and by the Reverend Samuel Knox, expressed sentiments shared by most far-sighted public men. They both held that there should be a national system of education, supported by taxes, from the primary level to the university. Education, they claimed, is the guarantor of free men in a free republic; it is the best device for revealing to all citizens the laws of nature and the wonders of science and for turning them to man's account. By 1796, these ideas were hardly new—a circumstance acknowledged by the Society's judges when they split the prize between Knox and Smith and stated that none of the essays submitted was "so well adapted to the present state of Society in this Country as could be wished." Innovative educational theory at this time, however, was being put forward by Robert Coram (1761–1796), a librarian and teacher in Wilmington, Delaware. His *Plan for the General Establishment of Schools* (1791) contained ideas similar to Smith's, but Coram was more interested in free compulsory elementary education for all, emphasizing the training of apprentices.

Smith *Remarks* are reprinted here simply because they clearly display the rationale for education shared by republican gentlemen in America. Virtue, wisdom, and the utility of science are all at the heart of any free system of education. To understand and to practice their interrelatedness gives republican life its meaning. That the thinking of these men was generally closer to educational themes of the Lockian and British Enlightenment than to those of the French Enlightenment is suggested by Smith's brief criticisms of Rousseau. The point where Smith went beyond Knox and most other American essayists was in his insistence that the state, not the family or the church, is the supreme arbiter and director of educational matters. His reasoning was not based upon a Platonic design for the state's control of its future leaders. It was founded upon his fear that plurality and diversity in American cultural life would defeat the purposes of political union and of the Revolution.

A graduate of the University of Pennsylvania and only twenty-four when his essay was written, Smith (1772–1845) became a confirmed Jeffersonian and editor of the official Jeffersonian newspaper, the *National Intelligencer and Washington Advertiser* from 1800 until 1810. Throughout a life that saw the rise of Jacksonian democracy in the nation's capital, Smith adhered to what would become the socially and politically conservative view of formal education as the chief republican safeguard against the dangerous political power of ignorant masses. The school reforms of the 1830s and later gradually made this view outdated as educational rhetoric. But Smith's belief that intelligence would be applied to reduce hard physical labor in nineteenth-century America makes his essay, in this respect, a correct forecast of things to come.

The two great objects of a correct education are to make men virtuous and wise. . . .

Without attempting precise definition, it may be sufficiently correct, so far as it regards the objects of this essay, to style VIRTUE that active exertion of our faculties, which, in the highest degree promotes our own happiness and that of our fellow-men; and WISDOM, that intelligent principle, which improves our faculties, affords them the means of useful exertion, and determines the objects on which they are exercised. . . .

Samuel Harrison Smith, *Remarks on Education: Illustrating the Close Connection Between Virtue and Wisdom. To Which Is Annexed, a System of Liberal Education. Which, Having Received the Premium Awarded by the American Philosophical Society, December 15th, 1797, Is Now Published by Their Order* (Philadelphia, 1798), pp. 10–11, 13–20, 22–28, 30, 32, 35–42, 44–47, 49–51, 82–86.

It has been the opinion of some distinguished philosophers that virtue and instinct are the same; and that a wise providence has not left the direction of the moral principle under the capricious and feeble influence of reason. While others have contended, that although man be by nature ignorant and entirely desitute of moral principle, yet that he possesses faculties capable of high improvement, if not of perfection itself. Both these systems, notwithstanding their numerous votaries, are probably founded in error. . . .

To affirm that because education does much, it can therefore accomplish everything, is to pronounce a maxim refuted by universal experience. Every circumstance in this life partakes of a finite nature; and the power of education, however great, has doubtless its limits.

However difficult, if not impossible, it might be to gain the assent of some philosophers to the system of natural inequality in reference to virtue or capacity; they will, without hesitation, agree, that the physical part of man is infinitely modified by nature; they will also grant, that an infinite variety seems to be delighted in by the author of nature; and that this variety is most displayed in those works, which abound, in the highest degree, with qualities that excite our admiration or regard. Both these instances, borrowed from the material objects, furnish striking analogies, illustrative of the existence of variety of morality and intellect in different minds uninfluenced by education. Is it to be believed that an object so important, as variety appears to be in the estimation of the author of nature, should be left to the controul of causes, operating so unequally, and in so contracted a sphere, as reason and civilization? Were it to depend entirely on these accidental circumstance, might it not be highly endangered? Might it not be lost?

There are some things, which, however controverted by the refinements of philosophy, will always continue to be held in secure belief by the good sense of mankind. Such is the conviction of natural biass; of one person possessing genius; another, fancy; a third, memory; etc.

The deductions from this concise and necessarily superficial view of a subject, in some respects intricate, are, that nature is neither so liberal, nor education so omnipotent, as . . . rival systems affirm; that man is indebted to both; that certain passions are born with him, which he cannot exterminate, but may control; that a varied capacity is imparted to him, which, by education he can weaken or improve. But, that still the traces of nature are visible in his thoughts and actions; and that her voice never ceases to be heard amidst all the refinements of art. . . .

It should never be forgotten in discussions similar to this that man is already in a great degree civilized; and that though it may be possible for the savage to resist the force of improvement and remain unshaken in his attachment to his original state, yet that man, once civilized, has it not in his power to return to his natural condition. . . .

We cannot, therefore, err in assuming it as a fact that virtue and wisdom are in some degree necessarily connected; that the crude wisdom which nature bestows is unequal to the production and government of virtue, such as man in his pursuit of happiness discovers it to be his interest to practice; and that to insure this desirable object, it is necessary that the original facilties of the mind should be vigorously exercised, extended, and strengthened. . . .

From a review of history, it will appear, that just in proportion to the cultivation of science and the arts has the happiness of man advanced in the nation which cultivated them. And this arose in a great measure from this consideration. The wants of nature are few in its unimproved state. Man of course is exempt from the necessity of making any great efforts for his support. He is therefore indolent. Not dependent on another, for anything which his heart holds dear, he is reserved, distant, unaccommodating in his deportment. He scarcely merits the epithet of a social being. Of course, if his vices are not numerous, his virtues are still less so.

The very reverse of this takes place as society improves. The dearest part of man's happiness, in this stage of his existence, is connected with a supply of articles, which depend on the industry of one, who is alike dependent on him. Hence a reciprocity of wants! Hence the origin of new and permanent regards, the parents of a thousand new virtues! From what source do these proceed, but from the development of reason, suggesting to man the improvement of his situation? This improvement seems susceptible of endless extension. Hence the conclusion, that reason in alliance with virtue admits of progression without termination, and that the purity of the last is best secured by the strength of the first. . . .

The virtues, which are the exclusive and appropriate offspring of an enlightened understanding, are those which are disconnected with any particular time, person, or place. Existing without reference to these, a spirit of universal philanthropy is inspired, that views the whole world as a single family, and transfers to it the feelings of regard which are indulged towards the most amiable of our acquaintance. This sentiment, free from the alloy of personal consideration, or national attachment, lifts the mind to an elevation infinitely superior to the sensation of individual regard, superior to the ardent feelings of patriotism, and rivals, in a measure, the enjoyment of the sublime ideas we connect with the apprehension of the divine mind. This tone of mind must acknowledge congeniality with the noblest virtues. The mind is full and yet tranquil. The turbulence of passion is subdued into a reverence of reason. Man feels himself too ennobled to do a base or a mean thing. He yields to an irresistible enthusiasm to atchieve [sic] whatever unites the highest portion of greatness with the largest portion of goodness. Language is inadequate to the description of the feelings of a man thus inspired; it hastens to his actions, which can receive only a feeble delineation.

It will be found still more unequivocally, that a diffusion of knowledge strengthens and extends all such virtues as have in a limited degree an existance, independent of uncommon attainments. This class of virtues comprehends those which are created by the relation in which one man stands to another, and which are the basis of what may be denominated common duty.

The discretion with which man is vested implies the necessity of some knowledge. Were it not for this possession, he would be the sport of casualty and accident. He would nominally be his own master, but really a slave to some unknown power.

Nature appears to have been liberal in its endowments to most of her offspring, as far as respects the preservation of each species; but to have been least liberal in this respect to man; doubtless because she has lavished her bounty in imparting to him alone the capacity of gradual and large improvement. . . .

The duties of men are precisely co-extensive with their knowledge. If that be granted, which cannot be denied, that every man is bound to do all the good he can, then follows clearly the obligation of everyone to enlarge the powers of his mind, as the only means of extending the sphere of his usefulness.

It has been observed, . . . that half the knowledge of which philosophy boasts withdraws the mind from the useful employment by occupying it with considerations of idle curiosity and unproductive speculation. But if it be inquired by whom this observation has been made, it will appear that literature and science disclaim it; that it has generally arisen from the indolence and envy of ignorance, or sprung from the malice of blasted pretensions. It is true that he whose years revolve in acquiring, without using, learning, is even more selfish and criminal than the miser, as he hoards from society a greater good. . . .

But has that science been ever named, the prosecution of which is entirely unconnected with the general good? Has not astronomy, now acknowledged to be the most sublime of studies, which unites whatever is great and astonishing both on the moral and physical scale, been the theme of unconscious ignorance and folly? Has not chemistry been assailed by the too successful satire of illiterate wit? That satire which now fastens on the departments of Natural History and Botany? Has not superstition attempted to identify astronomy and profanity; and for a time succeeded? And yet astronomy now holds, by an undissenting voice, an elevated rank among the sciences; and chemistry, notwithstanding the philosopher's stone, unfolds everyday, its high practical importance; and discoveries, which, at first, promised only cold speculative truth, have produced the greatest practical good.

It is worthy of remark, that all kinds of knowledge are intimately allied, and that the perfection of one department of science depends as much on the advancement of other departments, as it does on the accurate development of its own peculiar principles. An exclusive devotedness of the mind to one branch of knowledge, instead of enlarging, will impair it. Instead of furnishing it with truth, it will burden it with error. Of this tendency Locke relates several whimsical instances. . . .

Were a specification to be made of those circumstances most closely connected with the happiness of man, it would appear in how eminent a degree they are promoted by a cultivated understanding.

Under the head of morals, it would appear, that the virtues appropriate to a family would be secured as well as rendered more captivating; secured by the enlightened conviction of the intimate convection [*sic*] between duty and interest; rendered more captivating by their borrowing a new character from the liberal spirit inspired by reason. To the natural tie of parental regard would be added the grateful sensation excited in the mind of a child from the communication of new ideas, and the production, of course, of new pleasures. To the magic of instinct would be superadded the charm of reflection.

The sense of justice and honesty would be confirmed by the folly of injustice and dishonestly. . . .

Patriotism, a virtue which has fertilized the barren rock and given the greatest expansion to the mind and the heart, would become a steady and a rational principle. Founded on on unprejudiced attachment to country, we should cease to glory in error, solely because it proceeded from our ancestors. Love of country would impel us to transfuse into our own system of economy every improvement offered by other countries. In this case, we should not be attached so much to the soil, as to the institutions and manners, of our country.

In physics, it would appear, that in proportion to the extension of philosophical research, new connections and relations are discovered between natural objects, which result in discoveries of high practical use; promoting whatever tends to the convenience and comfort of social life, enlarging the sphere of harmless gratification, and giving birth to new, and frequently ingenious occupations. . . .

Whether reason itself would be fertile in the production of virtue need not be decided. It is probable that reason is only that power which directs the passions to their fit objects, and determines the force with which they ought to be applied. Rousseau says, "It is by the activity of our passions, that our reason improves; we covet knowledge merely because we court enjoyment, and it is impossible to conceive, why a man exempt from fears and desires should take the trouble to reason. The passions, in their turn, owe their origin to our wants."*

The passions, as imparted by nature, are few, but impetuous. The whole energy of the soul here speaks in every word and action. . . .

In proportion to the advancement of the arts and sciences, the passions are increased in number, and abridged in force, by the diversity of objects which solicit their exercise. . . .

That man seems, on the whole, to be the most happy, who, possessed of a large stock of ideas, is in the constant habit of increasing them, and whom every hour of his existence renders more informed. The energy of such a mind is almost without limits; it admits of constant activity; for when fatigued with one train of ideas, it finds repose in another. A rich variety of enjoyment is ever before it, the bare consciousness of possessing which is sufficient of itself to make it happy. . . .

The mind of Rousseau was, without doubt, a great one; it emitted, as copiously as genius or fancy could desire, the sparks of a noble intellect, which dared to disdain the shackles of prejudice, and break the chains of ignorance. But it must be allowed, that in those cases which admitted of personal application, he grossly erred, and generally suffered his strong sense to be overruled by his inexplicable feelings. . . .

Let us, then, consider a moderate increase of the hours of

---

* Rousseau on Inequality of Mankind, 8 vo. Edit. p. 40.

reflection, and a small decrease of those of labour, as a leading feature in a system of republican education. He, who thinks frequently, imbibes a habit of independence, and of self-esteem, which are perhaps the great and the only preservatives of virtue. Let us consider this feature as new, and as one which would be happily distinctive. Let us consider it as the prerogative of political virtue to ennoble man, as much as it is the assumption of political vice to degrade him.

A review of what I have written convinces me that I have entered a field which seems to acknowledge no limits. Points of morality and expedience occur in profusion, whose elucidation still demands the highest talents, after having employed, for ages, the deepest powers of research. . . .

The diffusion of knowledge, co-extensive with that of virtue, would seem to apply with close precision to a republican system of education because;

1. An enlightened nation is always most tenacious of its rights.

2. It is not the interest of such a society to perpetuate error; as it undoubtedly is the interest of many societies differently organized.

3. In a republic, the sources of happiness are open to all without injuring any.

4. If happiness be made at all to depend on the improvement of the mind, and the collision of mind with mind, the happiness of an individual will greatly depend upon the general diffusion of knowledge and a capacity to think and speak correctly.

5. Under a Republic, duly constructed, man feels as strong a biass to improvement, as under a despotism he feels an impulse to ignorance and depression.

We have now reached the goal of the preceding speculations. The necessary limits to an essay of this nature have prohibited minute illustration; but it has, we hope, been made to appear, with sufficient perspicuity, that human happiness depends upon the possession of virtue and wisdom; that virtue cannot be too highly cultivated; that it is only secure when allied with knowledge; and of consequence that knowledge itself cannot possibly be too extensively diffused. It follows that the great object of a liberal plan of education should be the almost universal diffusion of knowledge.

But as knowledge is infinite, and as its complete attainment requires more time than man has at his command, it becomes interesting to assign;

I. The time fit to be devoted to education.

II. The objects proper to be accomplished. . . .

I. THE TIME FIT TO BE DEVOTED TO EDUCATION. . . .

We have seen that in a nation, in which the hours of labour should be abridged, and those of reflection increased, no injury would be sustained by individuals, and little if any, by the nation itself.

It were a vain attempt, however, instantaneously to inspire with a love of science men from whose minds reflection has long been alienated. The improvement proposed must be the effect of a system of education gradually and cautiously developed.

Previously to any prospect of success, one principle must prevail. Society must establish the right to educate, and acknowledge the duty of having educated, all children. A circumstance, so momentously important, must not be left to the negligence of individuals. It is believed that this principle is recognised in almost all our state constitutions. If so, the exercise of it would not be contested. . . .

Without aiming at rigid precision, in considering the claims of labour and study, we shall not, perhaps, materially err in assigning four hours each day to education.

II. THE OBJECTS PROPER TO BE ACCOMPLISHED. . . .

Let us . . . with mental inflexibility, believe that though all men will never be philosophers, yet that all men may be enlightened; and that folly, unless arising from physical origin, may be banished from the society of men. . . .

The first great object of a liberal system of education should be, the admission into the young mind of such ideas only as are either absolutely true, or in the highest degree probable; and the cautious exclusion of all error. . . .

The elements of education, viz. reading and writing, are so obviously necessary that it is useless to do more than enumerate them.

Of nearly equal importance are the first principles of mathematics, as at present almost universally taught.

A tolerably correct idea of Geography would seem, in a Republic especially, to involve great advantages. The interest of the mercantile part of the community is closely connected with correct geographical knowledge. Many important departments of science include an accurate knowledge of it. But the most important consideration is that which contemplates the United States as either allied in friendship, or arrayed in hostility, with the other nations of the earth. In both which cases, it becomes the duty of the citizen to have just ideas of the position, size, and strength, of nations, that he may as much as possible, confide in his own judgment, in forming an opinion of our foreign relations, instead of yielding his mind to a dangerous credulity. A most interesting part of Geography relates to a knowledge of our own country. Correct information on this subject will always conduce to strengthen the bands of friendship, and to dissipate the misrepresentations of party prejudice.

The cultivation of natural philosophy, particularly so far as it relates to agriculture and manufactures, has been heretofore almost entirely neglected. . . . Many of the labours of the farmer and the mechanic, so far from forbidding reflection, invite it. . . .

If we reverse the scene, and behold the farmer enlightened by the knowledge of chemistry, how wide a field of reflection and pleasure, as well as profit, would acknowledge his empire? . . .

The circumscribed advantages, attending Geographical knowledge, will be greatly enlarged by a liberal acquaintance with History. In proportion as this branch of education shall be cultivated, men will see the mighty influence of moral principle, as well on the private individuals of a community, as on those who are called to preside over its public concerns. It will be distinctly seen, that ambition has generally risen on a destruction of every sentiment of virtue, and that it much oftener merits execration than applause. Power, long enjoyed, will appear to be hostile to the happiness, and subversive of the integrity, of the individual in whom it centers. Fanaticism and superstition will appear surrounded with blood and torture. War will stand forth with the boldest prominence of vice and folly, and make it, for a while, doubtful, whether man is most a villain or a fool. In short the mirror which history presents will manifest to man what, it is probable, he will become, should he surrender himself up to those selfish pursuits, which centering in his own fame alone, have ennabled him without horror to wade through the blood and the tears of millions. . . .

The second leading object of education, should be to inspire the mind with a strong disposition to improvement.

It is acknowledged that science is still in its infancy. The combination of ideas is infinite. As this combination advances the circle of knowledge is enlarged, and of course, the sphere of happiness extended. At present science is only cultivated by a few recluse students, too apt to mingle the illusions of imagination with the results of indistinct observation. Hence the reproach that theory and practice oppose each other. But no sooner shall a whole nation be tributary to science, than it will dawn with new lustre. . . .

All science ought to derive its rank from its utility. The real good which it actually does, or is capable of doing, is the only genuine criterion of its value. Man may indulge himself in sublime reveries, but the world will forever remain uninterested in them. It is only when he applies the powers of his mind to objects of general use, that he becomes their benefactor; until he does this he is neither entitled to their gratitude or applause.

He is the best friend of man, who makes discoveries involving effects which benefit mankind the most extensively. Moral truths are therefore of importance but little short of infinite. For they apply to numbers which almost evade enumeration, and to time which loses itself in eternity. These truths, all agree, are not to be fought in the cloister. They are only acquired by uniting the calm and patient reflection of retirement, with the bold and penetrating observation of active life.

In physics, the happiness of mankind is in the highest degree increased by discoveries and improvements connected with agriculture and manufactures. These two occupations employ nine-tenths of most communities, and a much larger proportion of others. Does it not then become an interesting enquiry, whether it be not expedient in infancy and youth to communicate to the mind the leading principles of nature and art in these departments of labour, not only by a theoretic exposition of them, but also by their practical developement.

If almost the whole community be destined to pursue one or other of these avocations from necessity, and if it be the duty of an individual to support himself, whenever he can, by an exertion of his own powers; and if these can only yield a sure support from an ability to be acquired in youth to prosecute a particular branch of agriculture or mechanics, does it not seem to be the duty of society to control education in such a way as to secure to every individual this ability? If this ability existed, how much misery would be annihilated, how much crime would be destroyed? Even under a government,* in which the happiness of men does not appear to have been the leading object, the nobility were obliged to be instructed fully in the principles, and partially in the practice, of a particular trade.

Should, however, the justice of abridging natural right in these cases be doubted, and its expedience denied, the propriety of a union of practical with theoretic instruction will not be contested in reference to those who are designed for agriculture or mechanics. . . .

Let us contemplate the effects of a just system,

    I. On the individual citizen.

    II. On the United States.

    III. On the World.

* In France.

I. The citizen, enlightened, will be a freeman in its truest sense. He will know his rights, and he will understand the rights of others; discerning the connection of his interest with the preservation of these rights, he will as firmly support those of his fellow men as his own. Too well informed to be misled, too virtuous to be corrupted, we shall behold man consistent and inflexible. Not at one moment the child of patriotism, and at another the slave of despotism, we shall see him in principle forever the same. Immutable in his character, inflexible in his honesty, he will feel the dignity of his nature and chearfully obey the claims of duty. . . .

II. Viewing the effects of such a system on the United States, the first result would be the giving perpetuity to those political principles so closely connected with our present happiness. In addition to these might be expected numerous improvements in our political economy.

By these means government without oppression, and protection without danger, will exist in their necessary strength.

Politics are acknowledged to be still in their infancy. No circumstance could so rapidly promote the growth of this science as an universal illumination of mind. . . .

III. The consideration of the effects of such a system on the world.

Nation is influenced as powerfully by nation, as one individual is influenced by another. Hence no sooner shall any one nation demonstrate by practical illustration the goodness of her political institutions, than other nations will imperceptibly introduce corresponding features into their systems. No truth is more certain, than that man will be happy if he can. He only wants a complete conviction of the means, to pursue them with energy and success. This conviction the United States may be destined to flash on the world.

Independent of this necessary effect, other effects will be produced. Many of the most enlightened of our citizens will traverse the globe with the spirit of philosophical research. They will carry with them valuable information and an ardent enthusiasm to diffuse it. Its diffusion will be the era of reform wherever it goes.

But more important, still, will be the example of the most powerful nation on earth, if that example exhibit dignity, humility and intelligence. Scarcely a century can elapse, before the population of America will be equal, and her power superior, to that of Europe. Should the principles be then established, which have been contemplated, and the connection be demonstrated between human happiness and the peaceable enjoyment of industry and the indulgence of reflection, we may expect to see America too enlightened and virtuous to spread the horrors of war over the face of any country, and too magnanimous and powerful to suffer its existence where she can prevent it. Let us, then, with rapture anticipate the era, when the triumph of peace and the prevalence of virtue shall be rendered secure by the diffusion of useful knowledge.

20

Thomas Jefferson's Republican Philosophy of Education

In this famous letter from the more famous correspondence between two senior statesmen, Thomas Jefferson explains to John Adams the point of view that motivated his drafting of the *Bill for the More General Diffusion of Knowledge* in 1778 (see Selection 15), and he also makes clear many of the social ideas and the regional biases that directed his political outlook. Crucial to our understanding of his republican definition of education is Jefferson's emphasis upon a "natural aristocracy" of talent and virtue leading public life and his preference for the political decisions of an uncrowded agrarian people over those of an urban populace. Essential, moreover, to our perception of his membership in the Atlantic intellectual community of the Enlightenment is his conviction that "science is progressive." (See Selection 22.)

The heritage of nineteenth-century American education from the Jeffersonian Enlightenment was the widespread belief that, as Jefferson puts it here, "talents and enterprize" are "ever on the alert." Belief in progress was a nineteenth-century credo that, mixed with optimistic American cultural nationalism (see Selection 14), accelerated the desire for informal personal education and delayed the inauguration of formal school systems. Men thought they could readily learn on their own all the necessary lessons for practical success in a nation of abundance. Individual initiative, not organized formal schooling, was thought to be the major key to American "know-how." Neither Jefferson nor Franklin, nor for that matter any of the founding fathers of the republic, would have predicted or have entirely designed this course of affairs. But it is an irony of our early history that the model of their lives served to encourage later generations toward self-education and intellectual self-reliance sometimes at the expense of strong public schooling.

Monticello Oct. 28. [18]13.

DEAR SIR

According to the reservation between us, of taking up one of the subjects of our correspondence at a time, I turn to your letters of Aug. 16. and Sep. 2. . . .

For I agree with you that there is a natural aristocracy among men. The grounds of this are virtue and talents. Formerly bodily powers gave place among the aristoi. But since the invention of gunpowder has armed the weak as well as the strong with missile death, bodily strength, like beauty, good humor, politeness and other accomplishments, has become but an auxiliary ground of distinction. There is also an artificial aristocracy founded on wealth and birth, without either virtue or talents; for with these it would belong to the first class. The natural aristocracy I consider as the most precious gift of nature for the instruction, the trusts, and government of society. And indeed it would have been inconsistent in creation to have formed man for the social state, and not to have provided virtue and wisdom enough to manage the concerns of the society. May we not even say that that form of government is the best which provides the most effectually for a pure selection of these natural aristoi into the offices of government? The artificial aristocracy is a mischievous ingredient in government, and provision should be made to prevent it's ascendancy. On the question, What is the best provision, you and I differ; but we differ as rational friends, using the free exercise of our own reason, and mutually indulging it's errors. *You* think it best to put the Pseudo-aristoi into a separate chamber of legislation where they may be hindered from doing mischief by their co-ordinate branches, and where also they may be a protection to wealth against the Agrarian and plundering enterprises of the Majority of the people. I think that to give them power in

---

Thomas Jefferson to John Adams, Monticello, October 28, 1813, in Lester J. Cappon, ed., *The Adams-Jefferson Letters* (2 vols.; Chapel Hill: University of North Carolina Press, 1959), II, 387–392. Reprinted by permission of the University of North Carolina Press and the Institute of Early American History and Culture.

order to prevent them from doing mischief, is arming them for
it, and increasing instead of remedying the evil. For if the
coordinate branches can arrest their action, so may they that of
the coordinates. Mischief may be done negatively as well as
positively. Of this a cabal in the Senate of the U. S. has furnished many proofs. Nor do I believe them necessary to protect
the wealthy; because enough of these will find their way into
every branch of the legislation to protect themselves. From 15.
to 20. legislatures of our own, in action for 30. years past, have
proved that no fears of an equalisation of property are to be
apprehended from them.

I think the best remedy is exactly that provided by all our
constitutions, to leave to the citizens the free election and
separation of the aristoi from the pseudo-aristoi, of the wheat
from the chaff. In general they will elect the real good and
wise. In some instances, wealth may corrupt, and birth blind
them; but not in sufficient degree to endanger the society.

It is probable that our difference of opinion may in some
measure be produced by a difference of character in those
among whom we live. From what I have seen of Massachusets
and Connecticut myself, and still more from what I have heard,
and the character given of the former by yourself, . . . who
know them so much better, there seems to be in those two
states a traditionary reverence for certain families, which has
rendered the offices of the government nearly hereditary in
those families. I presume that from an early period of your
history, members of these families happening to possess virtue
and talents, have honestly exercised them for the good of the
people, and by their services have endeared their names to
them.

In coupling Connecticut with you, I mean it politically only,
not morally. For having made the Bible the Common law of
their land they seem to have modelled their morality on the
story of Jacob and Laban. But altho' this hereditary succession
to office with you may in some degree be founded in real
family merit, yet in a much higher degree it has proceeded
from your strict alliance of church and state. These families are
canonised in the eyes of the people on the common principle

'you tickle me, and I will tickle you.' In Virginia we have
nothing of this. Our clergy, before the revolution, having been
secured against rivalship by fixed salaries, did not give themselves the trouble of acquiring influence over the people. Of
wealth, there were great accumulations in particular families,
handed down from generation to generation under the English
law of entails. But the only object of ambition for the wealthy
was a seat in the king's council. All their court then was paid
to the crown and it's creatures; and they Philipised in all colli-
sions between the king and people. Hence they were un-
popular; and that unpopularity continues attached to their
names. A Randolph, a Carter, or a Burwell must have great
personal superiority over a common competitor to be elected
by the people, even at this day.

At the first session of our legislature after the Declaration of
Independence, we passed a law abolishing entails. And this
was followed by one abolishing the privilege of Primogeniture,
and dividing the lands of intestates equally among all their
children, or other representatives. These laws, drawn by myself, laid the axe to the root of Pseudo-aristocracy. And had
another which I prepared been adopted by the legislature, our
work would have been compleat. It was a Bill for the more
general diffusion of learning. This proposed to divide every
county into wards of 5. or 6. miles square, like your townships;
to establish in each ward a free school for reading, writing and
common arithmetic; to provide for the annual selection of the
best subjects from these schools who might receive at the
public expence a higher degree of education at a district school;
and from these district schools to select a certain number of the
most promising subjects to be compleated at an University,
where all the useful sciences should be taught. Worth and
genius would thus have been sought out from every condition
of life, and compleatly prepared by education for defeating
the competition of wealth and birth for public trusts.

My proposition had for a further object to impart to these
wards those portions of self-government for which they are
best qualified, by confiding to them the care of their poor, their
roads, police, elections, the nomination of jurors, administration

of justice in small cases, elementary exercises of militia, in short, to have made them little republics, with a Warden at the head of each, for all those concerns which, being under their eye, they would better manage than the larger republics of the county or state. A general call of ward-meetings by their Wardens on the same day thro' the state would at any time produce the genuine sense of the people on any required point, and would enable the state to act in mass, as your people have so often done, and with so much effect, by their town meetings. The law for religious freedom, which made a part of this system, having put down the aristocracy of the clergy, and restored to the citizen the freedom of the mind, and those of entails and descents nurturing an equality of condition among them, this on Education would have raised the mass of the people to the high ground of moral respectability necessary to their own safety, and to orderly government; and would have compleated the great object of qualifying them to select the veritable aristoi, for the trusts of government, to the exclusion of the Pseudalists: . . . Altho' this law has not yet been acted on but in a small and inefficient degree, it is still considered as before the legislature, with other bills of the revised code, not yet taken up, and I have great hope that some patriotic spirit will, at a favorable moment, call it up, and make it the keystone of the arch of our government.

With respect to Aristocracy, we should further consider that, before the establishment of the American states, nothing was known to History but the Man of the old world, crouded within limits either small or overcharged, and steeped in the vices which that situation generates. A government adapted to such men would be one thing; but a very different one that for the Man of these states. Here every one may have land to labor for himself if he chuses; or, preferring the exercise of any other industry, may exact for it such compensation as not only to afford a comfortable subsistence, but wherewith to provide for a cessation from labor in old age. Every one, by his property, or by his satisfactory situation, is interested in the support of law and order. And such men may safely and advantageously reserve to themselves a wholsome controul over their public affairs, and a degree of freedom, which in the hands of the Canaille of the cities of Europe, would be instantly perverted to the demolition and destruction of every thing public and private. The history of the last 25. years of France, and of the last 40. years in America, nay of it's last 200. years, proves the truth of both parts of this observation.

But even in Europe a change has sensibly taken place in the mind of Man. Science had liberated the ideas of those who read and reflect, and the American example had kindled feelings of right in the people. An insurrection has consequently begun, of science, talents and courage against rank and birth, which have fallen into contempt. It has failed in it's first effort, because the mobs of the cities, the instrument used for it's accomplishment, debased by ignorance, poverty and vice, could not be restrained to rational action. But the world will recover from the panic of this first catastrophe. Science is progressive, and talents and enterprize on the alert. Resort may be had to the people of the country, a more governable power from their principles and subordination; and rank, and birth, and tinsel-aristocracy will finally shrink into insignificance, even there. This however we have no right to meddle with. It suffices for us, if the moral and physical condition of our own citizens qualifies them to select the able and good for the direction of their government, with a recurrence of elections at such short periods as will enable them to displace an unfaithful servant before the mischief he meditates may be irremediable.

I have thus stated my opinion on a point on which we differ, not with a view to controversy, for we are both too old to change opinions which are the result of a long life of inquiry and reflection; but on the suggestion of a former letter of yours, that we ought not to die before we have explained ourselves to each other. We acted in perfect harmony thro' a long and perilous contest for our liberty and independance. A constitution has been acquired which, tho neither of us think perfect, yet both consider as competent to render our fellow-citizens the happiest and the securest on whom the sun has ever shone. If we do not think exactly alike as to it's imperfections, it mat-

ters little to our country which, after devoting to it long lives
of disinterested labor, we have delivered over to our successors
in life, who will be able to take care of it, and of themselves.

I hope . . . that you may continue in tranquility to live and
to rejoice in the prosperity of our country until it shall be your
own wish to take your seat among the Aristoi who have gone
before you. Ever and affectionately yours.

Th: Jefferson

21

Thomas Jefferson on the
Moral Instinct of Man

Thomas Jefferson's social philosophy of education was built upon
his theory of human nature. This letter explains his concept of man's
moral sense or instinct, which is central to his whole social theory
of improving republican man in each successive generation through
education. Thomas Law, recipient of the letter, was a former
British civil servant in India who preferred to settle in the United
States where he wrote on moral philosophy and financial theory.
Jefferson, pursuing his theme, discusses successively man's aesthetic
faculty, human egoism, and lastly utility, which is to him the key
test of virtue. He views utility not in the Benthamic or axiomatic
sense of calculating the greatest good of the greatest number.
Rather he finds that utility or useful actions are motivated by man's
moral "instinct" to do what is useful for the harmony of his society.
His concluding reference to Lord Kames (see Selection 8) emphasizes that the "impulsive feelings" of the virtuous man are sanc-
tioned by "the standard of general feeling" in his society. Here he
is defending his own idea of utilitarian virtue against the perennial
charge then that utility is based upon mere selfishness. Here too
Jefferson's idea of the moral sense was not put on the religious
ground of John Witherspoon's claim for human conscience (see
Selection 13). But both carried with them the weight of public
approval in the young nation. Still, it was Jefferson's pragmatic explanation of virtue, long before the Jamesian definition of pragma-
tism, that, like Benjamin Franklin's, endured longer in the American
character and into twentieth-century educational thought.
  Jefferson the natural scientist sought his most forceful reasoning
through the image of man the biological creature. Men must be
educated to nurture their moral instincts just as they exercise to

develop their bodies. He wrote to his nephew, Peter Carr, in 1787: "The moral sense, or conscience, is as much a part of man as his leg or arm. It is given to all human beings in a stronger or weaker degree, as force of members is given them in a greater or less degree. It may be strengthened by exercise, as may any particular limb of the body." At this earlier time Jefferson believed that the development of the moral sense is not a matter of formal education and that "a moral case" stated to a ploughman and a professor would be decided "as well, and often better" by the former "because he has not been led astray by artificial rules." Over the next quarter of a century, however, Jefferson's hope for the power of formal education to guide and strengthen the moral sense became firm belief.

This whole line of thought was closely bound to his ideas of civil equality. Men are equal in the sense that the majority of them are born with the common moral instinct that makes them prone to do good, and they are subject to improvement. Thus the "natural" or first condition of republican man is civil equality. Indeed Jefferson's whole public career may be interpreted as one statesman's attempt to erase "unnatural" social distinctions among white men through various social improvements, chief among which was education.

Poplar Forest, June 13, 1814.

DEAR SIR,

The copy of your Second Thoughts on Instinctive Impulses, with the letter accompanying it, was received just as I was setting out on a journey to this place, two or three days distant from Monticello. I brought it with me and read it with great satisfaction, and with the more as it contained exactly my own creed on the foundation of morality in man. It is really curious that on a question so fundamental, such a variety of opinions should have prevailed among men, and those, too, of the most exemplary virtue and first order of understanding. It shows how necessary was the care of the Creator in making the moral principle so much a part of our constitution as that no errors

Thomas Jefferson to Thomas Law, Poplar Forest, Virginia, June 13, 1814, in Albert Ellery Bergh, ed., *The Writings of Thomas Jefferson* (20 vols. in 10; Washington, D. C., 1907), XIV, 138–144.

of reasoning or of speculation might lead us astray from its observance in practice. Of all the theories on this question, the most whimsical seems to have been that of Wollaston, who considers *truth* as the foundation of morality. The thief who steals your guinea does wrong only inasmuch as he acts a lie in using your guinea as if it were his own. Truth is certainly a branch of morality, and a very important one to society. But presented as its foundation, it is as if a tree taken up by the roots, had its stem reversed in the air, and one of its branches planted in the ground. Some have made the *love of God* the foundation of morality. This, too, is but a branch of our moral duties, which are generally divided into duties to God and duties to man. If we did a good act merely from the love of God and a belief that it is pleasing to Him, whence arises the morality of the Atheist? It is idle to say, as some do, that no such being exists. We have the same evidence of the fact as of must of those we act on, to wit: their own affirmations, and their reasonings in support of them. I have observed, indeed, generally, that while in Protestant countries the defections from the Platonic Christianity of the priests is to Deism, in Catholic countries they are to Atheism. Diderot, D'Alembert, D'Holbach, Condorcet, are known to have been among the most virtuous of men. Their virtue, then, must have had some other foundation than the love of God.

The Το κυλον [beautiful] of others is founded in a different faculty, that of taste, which is not even a branch of morality. We have indeed an innate sense of what we call beautiful, but that is exercised chiefly on subjects addressed to the fancy, whether through the eye in visible forms, as landscape, animal figure, dress, drapery, architecture, the composition of colors, etc., or to the imagination directly, as imagery, style, or measure in prose or poetry, or whatever else constitutes the domain of criticism or taste, a faculty entirely distinct from the moral one. Self-interest, or rather self-love, or *egoism,* has been more plausibly substituted as the basis of morality. But I consider our relations with others as constituting the boundaries of morality. With ourselves we stand on the ground of identity, not of relation, which last, requiring two subjects, excludes self-love confined to a single one. To ourselves, in strict language, we can owe no duties, obligation requiring also two parties. Self-love, therefore, is no part of morality. Indeed it is exactly its counterpart. It is the sole antagonist of virtue, leading us constantly by our propensities to self-gratification in violation of our moral duties to others. Accordingly, it is against this enemy that are erected the batteries of moralists and religionists, as the only obstacle to the practice of morality. Take from man his selfish propensities, and he can have nothing to seduce him from the practice of virtue. Or subdue those propensities by education, instruction or restraint, and virtue remains without a competitor. Egoism, in a broader sense, has been thus presented as the source of moral action. It has been said that we feed the hungry, clothe the naked, bind up the wounds of the man beaten by thieves, pour oil and wine into them, set him on our own beast and bring him to the inn, because we receive ourselves pleasure from these acts. So Helvetius, one of the best men on earth, and the most ingenious advocate of this principle, after defining "interest" to mean not merely that which is pecuniary, but whatever may procure us pleasure or withdraw us from pain, [*de l'esprit* 2, I,] says, [ib. 2, 2,] "the humane man is he to whom the sight of misfortune is insupportable, and who to rescue himself from this spectacle, is forced to succor the unfortunate object." This indeed is true. But it is one step short of the ultimate question. These good acts give us pleasure, but how happens it that they give us pleasure? Because nature hath implanted in our breasts a love of others, a sense of duty to them, a moral instinct, in short, which prompts us irresistably to feel and to succor their distresses, and protests against the language of Helvetius, [ib. 2, 5,] "what other motive than self-interest could determine a man to generous actions? It is as impossible for him to love what is good for the sake of good, as to love evil for the sake of evil." The Creator would indeed have been a bungling artist, had he intended man for a social animal, without planting in him social dispositions. It is true they are not planted in every man, because there is no rule without exceptions; but it is false reasoning which converts exceptions into the general rule.

Some men are born without the organs of sight, or of hearing, or without hands. Yet it would be wrong to say that man is born without these facilities, and sight, hearing, and hands may with truth enter into the general definition of man.

The want or imperfection of the moral sense in some men, like the want or imperfection of the senses of sight and hearing in others, is no proof that it is a general characteristic of the species. When it is wanting, we endeavor to supply the defect by education, by appeals to reason and calculation, by presenting to the being so unhappily conformed, other motives to do good and to eschew evil, such as the love, or the hatred, or rejection of those among whom he lives, and whose society is necessary to his happiness and even existence; demonstrations by sound calculation that honesty promotes interest in the long run; the rewards and penalties established by the laws; and ultimately the prospects of a future state of retribution for the evil as well as the good done while here. These are the correctives which are supplied by education, and which exercise the functions of the moralist, the preacher, and legislator; and they lead into a course of correct action all those whose disparity is not too profound to be eradicated. Some have argued against the existence of a moral sense, by saying that if nature had given us such a sense, impelling us to virtuous action, and warning us against those which are vicious, then nature would also have designated, by some particular ear-marks, the two sets of actions which are, in themselves, the one virtuous and the other vicious. Whereas, we find, in fact, that the same actions are deemed virtuous in one country and vicious in another. The answer is, that nature has constituted *utility* to man, the standard and test of virtue. Men living in different countries, under different circumstances, different habits and regimens, may have different utilities; the same act, therefore, may be useful, and consequently virtuous in one country which is injurious and vicious in another differently circumstanced. I sincerely, then, believe with you in the general existence of a moral instinct. I think it the brightest gem with which the human character is studded, and the want of it as more degrading than the most hideous of the bodily deformities. I am happy in reviewing the roll of associates in this principle which you present in your second letter, some of which I had not before met with. To these might be added Lord Kaims [*sic*], one of the ablest of our advocates, who goes so far as to say, in his Principles of Natural Religion, that a man owes no duty to which he is not urged by some impulsive feeling. This is correct, if referred to the standard of general feeling in the given case, and not to the feeling of a single individual. Perhaps I may misquote him, it being fifty years since I read his book.

The leisure and solitude of my situation here has led me to the indiscretion of taxing you with a long letter on a subject whereon nothing new can be offered you. I will indulge myself no farther than to repeat the assurances of my continued esteem and respect.

22

Thomas Jefferson's Design for His State University— The Rockfish Gap Report

Few documents of American higher education reflect so well the brightest academic and intellectual climate of their day as does this *Report of the Commissioners Appointed to Fix the Site of the University of Virginia*. The *Report* is generally called "The Rockfish Gap Report" after the place where Thomas Jefferson and several outstanding Virginia statesmen of the late republican age met to draft it in the summer of 1818. Appointed by the Governor to agree upon a suitable location and plan for a new state university, the Commissioners did much more. With Jefferson as their guide and author of the *Report*, they set forth the broad aims of republican education; they produced an exemplary state university curriculum for their day; and they announced standards for university admission, thereby reminding the balky state legislature once again to inaugurate a statewide school system, first proposed four decades earlier by Jefferson (see Selection 15), which would provide able university scholars.

Planning, building, and staffing the University of Virginia was the crowning achievement of Jefferson's retiring years. It was won over the repeated opposition of Federalist and sectarian interests in the Virginia legislature. These interests had hampered Jefferson's educational hopes so long and effectively that the story of public school development in Virginia at this time, as in other states, is a complicated one of patchwork measures passed by a legislature that, beyond political enmity to the Jeffersonian cause, reflected the chronic unwillingness of American citizens to be taxed for decent public schools. It is remarkable indeed that the Jeffersonian side was finally able even to win support for a university. That it did so was mainly due to the untiring efforts of Jefferson's loyal friend and

320	*Theories of Education in Early America*

legislative lieutenant in this cause, Joseph C. Cabell (1778–1856). Two other young men who helped Jefferson in bringing this great scheme toward completion were George Ticknor (1791–1871) and Francis Walker Gilmer (1790–1826). As one of the first American college graduates to study at a German university, Ticknor wrote Jefferson of his exciting intellectual experiences at Göttingen from 1815 to 1817 and of his deep concerns for improving academic affairs at Harvard, where he was installed as a young professor of French, Spanish, and belles-lettres in 1819. Gilmer, a promising young Virginia lawyer and Jefferson's close friend, crossed the Atlantic in 1824 to recruit five reputable foreign scholars for the new faculty, as well as to secure books and equipment. As for Jefferson, the realization of his long dream was a source of such great pride to him that he wished to have posterity remember him best as author of the Declaration of Independence and the Virginia Statute for Religious Freedom and as "Father of the University of Virginia."

The earlier and subsequent history of American higher education justified Jefferson's sense of achievement. Although six other state universities had been chartered before the University of Virginia, only the University of North Carolina began instruction before 1800. And those institutions were not truly public in their early years because of sectarian influences over their control and the largely private sources of their funds. Nor were they free of charge to their students. In contrast to them, the University of Virginia was nonsectarian and secular. It was publicly supported from a state Literary Fund, though not tuition free. After the model of European universities, it offered a program of advanced studies with professors competent to teach them. It even introduced the elective principle into its undergraduate curriculum. And its course of studies, while neither a clear break from the classical curriculum nor a cafeteria offering of "practical" courses, was the broadest incorporation of modern languages, mathematics, and the physical and natural sciences thus far seen in America. When it opened in 1825, the University of Virginia was the first truly "public" institution of higher learning as well as by academic design the first university in the United States.

Modern historians have noted that ideal did not become reality in every respect at Jefferson's university. Because of his increasingly regional or sectional outlook after the Missouri controversy, and because of his conviction that any state institution should keep alive the "vestal flame" of Revolutionary era Whigism or republicanism, Jefferson emphasized, in a last letter to James Madison who succeeded him as Rector of the University, that the Law Professor should be a man of sound republican principles. Since it was to be partly a school of government, Jefferson had already persuaded the visitors to prescribe some textbooks for the law school. Only here did he feel that preemption of the professors' right to select their own class readings was justified. In most colleges, textbooks were then generally chosen by the president and the board of control.

If Jefferson's lapse from his long-cherished attitude toward freedom of inquiry was unfortunate, it has long since been overshadowed by what he achieved through the periodic reawakening of Jeffersonian liberal ideals in American higher learning. "This institution," Jefferson wrote of his university, "will be based on the illimitable freedom of the human mind. For here we are not afraid to follow truth wherever it may lead, nor to tolerate any error so long as reason is left free to combat it." Not only is this an older, Miltonian sentiment; it is also, as one modern example, the sentiment enduringly proclaimed by the Regents of the University of Wisconsin in 1894 when they announced that their institution "should ever encourage that continual and fearless sifting and winnowing by which alone the truth can be found." Behind this Jeffersonian theme lies practical conviction, well expressed in the Rockfish Gap *Report.* Public higher education has ultimately a social, not a private purpose. It is carried on for society's improvement and ultimate progress. Although public higher education has not always resulted in enlightening the general citizenry, as Jefferson and other republican founding fathers thought it should, the ideal stands. Twentieth-century developments in public colleges and universities have reiterated the Jeffersonian faith of this *Report* that the condition of man is not "fixed" and that hope for his improvement is not "delusive."

The Commissioners for the University of Virginia, having met, as by law required, at the tavern, in Rockfish Gap, on the Blue Ridge, on the first day of August, of this present year, 1818; and having formed a board, proceeded on that day to the discharge of the duties assigned to them by the act of the Legislature,

---

"Executive Communication laid before the House of Delegates, December 8, 1818. [Enclosing] The Rockfish Gap Commission Report, August 1818. (In a clerk's handwriting but with manuscript corrections by Thomas Jefferson and containing the autograph signatures of the Commissioners.)" Printed with the permission of the Virginia State Archives. Paragraphing has been added to the text to follow that found in Nathaniel Francis Cabell, ed., *Early History of the University of Virginia as contained in the letters of Thomas Jefferson and Joseph C. Cabell* (Richmond, 1856), pp. 432 ff.

entitled "An act, appropriating part of the revenue of the literary fund, and for other purposes;" and having continued their proceedings by adjournment, from day to day, to Tuesday, the 4th day of August, have agreed to a report on the several matters with which they were charged, which report they now respectfully address and submit to the Legislature of the State.

The first duty enjoined on them, was to enquire and report a site, in some convenient and proper part of the State, for an university, to be called the "University of Virginia." In this enquiry, they supposed that the governing considerations should be the healthiness of the site, the fertility of the neighboring country, and its centrality to the white population of the whole State. For, although the act authorized and required them to receive any voluntary contributions, whether conditional or absolute, which might be offered through them to the President and Directors of the Literary Fund, for the benefit of the University, yet they did not consider this as establishing an auction, or as pledging the location to the highest bidder.

Three places were proposed, to wit: Lexington, in the county of Rockbridge, Staunton, in the county of Augusta, and the Central College, in the county of Albemarle. Each of these was unexceptionable as to healthiness and fertility. It was the degree of centrality to the white population of the State which alone then constituted the important point of comparison between these places; and the Board, after full inquiry, and impartial and mature consideration, are of opinion, that the central point of the white population of the State is nearer to the Central College than to either Lexington or Staunton, by great and important differences; and all other circumstances of the place in general being favorable to it, as a position for an university, they do report the Central College, in Albemarle, to be a convenient and proper part of the State for the University of Virginia.

2. The Board, having thus agreed on a proper site for the University, to be reported to the Legislature, proceeded to the second of the duties assigned to them—that of proposing a plan for its buildings—and they are of opinion that it should consist

of distinct houses or pavilions, arranged at proper distances on each side of a lawn of a proper breadth, and of indefinite extent, in one direction, at least; in each of which should be a lecturing room, with from two to four apartments, for the accommodation of a professor and his family; that these pavilions should be united by a range of dormitories, sufficient each for the accommodation of two students only, this provision being deemed advantageous to morals, to order, and to uninterrupted study; and that a passage of some kind, under cover from the weather, should gave a communication along the whole range. It is supposed that such pavilions, on an average of the larger and smaller, will cost each about $5,000; each dormitory about $350, and hotels of a single room, for a refectory, and two rooms for the tenant, necessary for dieting the students, will cost about $3500 each. The number of these pavilions will depend on the number of professors, and that of the dormitories and hotels on the number of students to be lodged and dieted. The advantages of this plan are: greater security against fire and infection; tranquillity and comfort to the professors and their families thus insulated; retirement to the students; and the admission of enlargement to any degree to which the institution may extend in future times. It is supposed probable, that a building of somewhat more size in the middle of the grounds may be called for in time, in which may be rooms for religious worship, under such impartial regulations as the Visitors shall prescribe, for public examinations, for a library, for the schools of music, drawing, and other associated purposes.

3, 4. In proceeding to the third and fourth duties prescribed by the Legislature, of reporting "the branches of learning, which shall be taught in the University, and the number and description of the professorships they will require," the Commissioners were first to consider at what point it was understood that university education should commence? Certainly not with the alphabet, for reasons of expediency and impracticability, as well from the obvious sense of the Legislature, who, in the same act, make other provision for the primary instruction of the poor children, expecting, doubtless, that in other cases it would be provided by the parent, or become, perhaps, subject of future and further addition for the Legislature. The objects of this primary education determine its character and limits. These objects would be,

To give to every citizen the information he needs for the transaction of his own business;

To enable him to calculate for himself, and to express and preserve his ideas, his contracts and accounts, in writing;

To improve, by reading, his morals and faculties;

To understand his duties to his neighbors and country, and to discharge with competence the functions confided to him by either;

To know his rights; to exercise with order and justice those he retains; to choose with discretion the fiduciaries of those he delegates; and to notice their conduct with diligence, with candor, and judgment;

And, in general, to observe with intelligence and faithfulness all the social relations under which he shall be placed.

To instruct the mass of our citizens in these, their rights, interests and duties, as men and citizens, being then the objects of education in the primary schools, whether private or public, in them should be taught reading, writing and numerical arithmetic, the elements of mensuration (useful in so many callings), and the outlines of geography and history. And this brings us to the point at which are to commence the higher branches of education, of which the Legislature require the development; those, for example, which are,

To form the statesmen, legislators and judges, on whom public prosperity and individual happiness are so much to depend;

To expound the principles and structure of government, the laws which regulate the intercourse of nations, those formed municipally for our own government, and a sound spirit of legislation, which, banishing all arbitrary and unnecessary restraint on individual action, shall leave us free to do whatever does not violate the equal rights of another;

To harmonize and promote the interests of agriculture, manufactures and commerce, and by well informed views of political economy to give a free scope to the public industry;

To develop the reasoning faculties of our youth, enlarge their minds, cultivate their morals, and instill into them the precepts of virtue and order;

To enlighten them with mathematical and physical sciences, which advance the arts, and administer to the health, the subsistence, and comforts of human life;

And, generally, to form them to habits of reflection and correct action, rendering them examples of virtue to others, and of happiness within themselves.

These are the objects of that higher grade of education, the benefits and blessings of which the Legislature now propose to provide for the good and ornament of their country, the gratification and happiness of their fellow-citizens, of the parent especially, and his progeny, on which all his affections are concentrated.

In entering on this field, the Commissioners are aware that they have to encounter much difference of opinion as to the extent which it is expedient that this institution should occupy. Some good men, and even of respectable information, consider the learned sciences as useless acquirements; some think that they do not better the condition of man; and others that education, like private and individual concerns, should be left to private and individual effort; not reflecting that an establishment embracing all the sciences which may be useful and even necessary in the various vocations of life, with the buildings and apparatus belonging to each, are far beyond the reach of individual means, and must either derive existence from public patronage, or not exist at all. This would leave us, then, without those callings which depend on education, or send us to other countries to seek the instruction they require. But the Commissioners are happy in considering the statute under which they are assembled as proof that the Legislature is far from the abandonment of objects so interesting. They are sensible that the advantages of well-directed education, moral, political and economical, are truly above all estimate. Education generates habits of application, of order, and the love of virtue; and controuls, by the force of habit, any innate obliquities in our moral organization. We should be far, too, from the discouraging persuasion that man is fixed, by the law of his nature, at a given point; that his improvement is a chimera, and the hope delusive of rendering ourselves wiser, happier or better than our forefathers were. As well might it be urged that the wild and uncultivated tree, hitherto yielding sour and bitter fruit only, can never be made to yield better; yet we know that the grafting art implants a new tree on the savage stock, producing what is most estimable both in kind and degree. Education, in like manner, engrafts a new man on the native stock, and improves what in his nature was vicious and perverse into qualities of virtue and social worth. And it cannot be but that each generation succeeding to the knowledge acquired by all those who preceded it, adding to it their own acquisitions and discoveries, and handing the mass down for successive and contant accumulation, must advance the knowledge and well-being of mankind, not *infinitely*, as some have said, but *indefinitely*, and to a term which no one can fix and foresee. Indeed, we need look back only half a century, to times which many now living remember well, and see the wonderful advances in the sciences and arts which have been made within that period. Some of these have rendered the elements themselves subservient to the purposes of man, have harnessed them to the yoke of his labors, and effected the great blessings of moderating his own, of accomplishing what was beyond his feeble force, and of extending the comforts of life to a much enlarged circle, to those who had before known its necessaries only. That these are not the vain dreams of sanguine hope, we have before our eyes real and living examples. What, but education, has advanced us beyond the condition of our indigenous neighbors? And what chains them to their present state of barbarism and wretchedness, but a bigotted veneration for the supposed superlative wisdom of their fathers, and the preposterous idea that they are to look backward for better things, and not forward, longing, as it should seem, to return to the days of eating acorns and roots, rather than indulge in the degeneracies of civilization? And how much more encouraging to the achievements of science and improvement is this, than the desponding view that the condition of man cannot be ameliorated, that what has been must ever be, and that to secure ourselves where we are, we must tread with awful reverence in the footsteps of our fathers. This doctrine is the genuine fruit of the alliance between Church and State; the tenants of which, finding themselves but too well in their present condition, oppose all advances which unmask their usurpations, and monopolies of honors, wealth, and power, and fear every change, as endangering the comforts they now hold. Nor must we omit to mention, among the benefits of education, the incalculable advantage of training up able counsellors to administer the affairs of our country in all its departments, legislative, executive and judiciary, and to bear their proper share in the councils of our national government; nothing more than education advancing the prosperity, the power, and the happiness of a nation.

Encouraged, therefore, by the sentiments of the Legislature, manifested in this statute, we present the following tabular statements of the branches of learning which we think should be taught in the University, forming them into groups, each of which are within the powers of a single professor:

    I. Languages, ancient:
        Latin,
        Greek,
        Hebrew.
   II. Languages, modern:
        French,
        Spanish,
        Italian,
        German,
        Anglo-Saxon.
  III. Mathematics, pure:
        Algebra,
        Fluxions,
        Geometry, Elementary,
                Transcendental.
        Architecture, Military,
                Naval.

IV. Physico-Mathematics:
 Mechanics,
 Statics,
 Dynamics,
 Pneumatics,
 Acoustics,
 Optics,
 Astronomy,
 Geography.
V. Physics, or Natural Philosophy:
 Chemistry,
 Mineralogy.
VI. Botany,
 Zoölogy.
VII. Anatomy,
 Medicine.
VIII. Government,
 Political Economy,
 Law of Nature and Nations,
 History, being interwoven with Politics and Law.
IX. Law, municipal.
X. Ideology,
 General Grammar,
 Ethics,
 Rhetoric,
 Belles Lettres, and the fine arts.

Some of the terms used in this table being subject to a difference of acceptation, it is proper to define the meaning and comprehension intended to be given them here:

Geometry, Elementary, is that of straight lines and of the circle.
 Transcendental, is that of all other curves; it includes, of course, Projectiles, a leading branch of the military art.
Military Architecture includes Fortification, another branch of that art.

Statics respect matter generally, in a state of rest, and include
        Hydrostatics, or the laws of fluids particularly, at
        rest or in equilibrio.

Dynamics, used as a general term, include Dynamics proper, or
        the laws of solids in motion; and Hydrodynamics,
        or Hydraulics, those of fluids in motion.

Pneumatics teach the theory of air, its weight, motion, conden-
        sation, rarefaction, &c.

Acoustics, or Phonics, the theory of sound.

Optics, the laws of light and vision.

Physics, or Physiology, in a general sense, mean the doctrine of
        the physical objects of our senses.

Chemistry is meant, with its other usual branches, to compre-
        hend the theory of agriculture.

Mineralogy, in addition to its peculiar subjects, is here under-
        stood to embrace what is real in geology.

Ideology is the doctrine of thought.

General Grammar explains the construction of language.

Some articles in this distribution of sciences will need observation. A professor is proposed for ancient languages, the
Latin, Greek, and Hebrew, particularly; but these languages
being the foundation common to all the sciences, it is difficult
to foresee what may be the extent of this school. At the same
time, no greater obstruction to industrious study could be proposed than the presence, the intrusions, and the noisy turbulence of a multitude of small boys; and if they are to be placed
here for the rudiments of the languages, they may be so numerous that its character and value as an University will be merged
in those of a Grammar school. It is, therefore, greatly to be
wished, that preliminary schools, either on private or public
establishment, could be distributed in districts through the
State, as preparatory to the entrance of students into the University. The tender age at which this part of education com-
mences, generally about the tenth year, would weigh heavily
with parents in sending their sons to a school so distant as the
central establishment would be from most of them. Districts of
such extent as that every parent should be within a day's jour-

ney of his son at school, would be desirable in cases of sickness, and convenient for supplying their ordinary wants, and might be made to lessen sensibly the expense of this part of their education. And where a sparse population would not, within such a compass, furnish subjects sufficient to maintain a school, a competent enlargement of district must, of necessity, there be submitted to. At these district schools or colleges, boys should be rendered able to read the easier authors, Latin and Greek. This would be useful and sufficient for many not intended for an University education. At these, too, might be taught English grammar, the higher branches of numerical arithmetic, the geometry of straight lines and of the circle, the elements of navigation, and geography to a sufficient degree, and thus afford to greater numbers the means of being qualified for the various vocations of life, needing more instruction than merely menial or praedial labor, and the same advantages to youths whose education may have been neglected until too late to lay a foundation in the learned languages. These institutions, intermediate between the primary schools and University, might then be the passage of entrance for youths into the University, where their classical learning might be critically completed, by a study of the authors of highest degree; and it is at this stage only that they should be received at the University. Giving then a portion of their time to a finished knowledge of the Latin and Greek, the rest might be appropriated to the modern languages, or to the commencement of the course of science for which they should be destined. This would generally be about the fifteenth year of their age, when they might go with more safety and contentment to that distance from their parents. Until this preparatory provision shall be made, either the University will be overwhelmed with the grammar school, or a separate establishment, under one or more ushers, for its lower classes, will be advisable, at a mile or two distance from the general one; where, too, may be exercised the stricter government necessary for young boys, but unsuitable for youths arrived at years of discretion.

The considerations which have governed the specification of languages to be taught by the professor of modern languages were, that the French is the language of general intercourse among nations, and, as a depository of human science, is unsurpassed by any other language, living or dead; that the Spanish is highly interesting to us, as the language spoken by so great a portion of the inhabitants of our continents, with whom we shall probably have great intercourse ere long, and is that also in which is written the greater part of the early history of America.

The Italian abounds with works of very superior order, valuable for their matter, and still more distinguished as models of the finest taste in style and composition. And the German now stands in a line with that of the most learned nations in richness of erudition and advance in the sciences. It is too of common descent with the language of our own country, a branch of the same original Gothic stock, and furnishes valuable illustrations for us. But in this point of view, the Anglo-Saxon is of peculiar value. We have placed it among the modern languages, because it is in fact that which we speak, in the earliest form in which we have knowledge of it. It has been undergoing, with time, those gradual changes which all languages, ancient and modern, have experienced; and even now needs only to be printed in the modern character and orthography to be intelligible, in a considerable degree, to an English reader. It has this value, too, above the Greek and Latin, that while it gives the radix of the mass of our language, they explain its innovations only. Obvious proofs of this have been presented to the modern reader in the disquisitions of Horn Tooke; and Fortescue Aland has well explained the great instruction which may be derived from it towards a full understanding of our ancient common law, on which, as a stock, our whole system of law is engrafted. It will form the first link in the chain of an historical review of our language through all its successive changes to the present day, will constitute the foundation of that critical instruction in it which ought to be found in a seminary of general learning, and thus reward amply the few weeks of attention which would alone be requisite for its attainment; a language already fraught with all the eminent science of our parent country, the future vehicle of whatever we may ourselves achieve, and destined to occupy so much space on the globe, claims distinguished attention in American education.

Medicine, where fully taught, is usually subdivided into several professorships, but this cannot well be without the accessory of an hospital, where the student can have the benefit of attending clinical lectures, and of assisting at operations of surgery. With this accessory, the seat of our University is not yet prepared, either by its population or by the numbers of poor who would leave their own houses, and accept of the charities of an hospital. For the present, therefore, we propose but a single professor for both medicine and anatomy. By him the medical science may be taught, with a history and explanations of all its successive theories from Hippocrates to the present day; and anatomy may be fully treated. Vegetable pharmacy will make a part of the botanical course, and mineral and chemical pharmacy of those of mineralogy and chemistry. This degree of medical information is such as the mass of scientific students would wish to possess, as enabling them in their course through life, to estimate with satisfaction the extent and limits of the aid to human life and health, which they may understandingly expect from that art; and it constitutes such a foundation for those intended for the profession, that the finishing course of practice at the bedsides of the sick, and at the operations of surgery in a hospital, can neither be long nor expensive. To seek this finishing elsewhere, must therefore be submitted to for a while.

In conformity with the principles of our Constitution, which places all sects of religion on an equal footing, with the jealousies of the different sects in guarding that equality from encroachment and surprise, and with the sentiments of the Legislature in favor of freedom of religion, manifested on former occasions, we have proposed no professor of divinity; and the rather as the proofs of the being of a God, the creator, preserver, and supreme ruler of the universe, the author of all the relations of morality, and of the laws and obligations these infer, will be within the province of the professor of ethics; to which adding the developments of these moral obligations, of those in which all sects agree, with a knowledge of the languages, Hebrew, Greek, and Latin, a basis will be formed common to   all sects. Proceeding thus far without offence to the Constitution, we have thought it proper at this point to leave every sect to provide, as they think fittest, the means of further instruction in their own peculiar tenets.

We are further of opinion, that after declaring by law that certain sciences shall be taught in the University, fixing the number of professors they require, which we think should, at present, be ten, limiting (except as to the professors who shall be first engaged in each branch,) a maximum for their salaries, (which should be a certain but moderate subsistence, to be made up by liberal tuition fees, as an excitement to assiduity), it will be best to leave to the discretion of the visitors, the grouping of these sciences together, according to the accidental qualifications of the professors; and the introduction also of other branches of science, when enabled by private donations, or by public provision, and called for by the increase of population, or other change of circumstances; to establish beginnings, in short, to be developed by time, as those who come after us shall find expedient. They will be more advanced than we are in science and in useful arts, and will know best what will suit the circumstances of their day.

We have proposed no formal provision for the gymnastics of the school, although a proper object of attention for every institution of youth. These exercises with ancient nations, constituted the principal part of the education of their youth. Their arms and mode of warfare rendered them severe in the extreme; ours, on the same correct principle, should be adapted to our arms and warfare; and the manual exercise, military maneuvres, and tactics generally, should be the frequent exercises of the students, in their hours of recreation. It is at that age of aptness, docility, and emulation of the practices of manhood, that such things are soonest learnt and longest remembered. The use of tools too in the manual arts is worthy of encouragement, by facilitating to such as choose it, an admission into the neighboring workshops. To these should be added the arts which embellish life, dancing, music, and drawing; the last more especially, as an important part of military education. These innocent arts furnish amusement and happiness to those who, having time on their hands, might less inoffensively employ it. Needing, at the same time, no regular incorporation with the institution, they may be left to accessory teachers, who will be paid by the individuals employing them, the University only providing proper apartments for their exercise.

The fifth duty prescribed to the Commissioners, is to propose such general provisions as may be properly enacted by the Legislature, for the better organizing and governing the University.

In the education of youth, provision is to be made for, 1, tuition; 2, diet; 3, lodging; 4, government; and 5, honorary excitements. The first of these constitutes the proper functions of the professors. 2, the dieting of the students should be left to private boarding houses of their own choice, and at their own expense; to be regulated by the Visitors from time to time, the house only being provided by the University within its own precincts, and thereby of course subjected to the general regimen, moral or sumptuary, which they shall prescribe. 3. They should be lodged in dormitories, making a part of the general system of buildings. 4. The best mode of government for youth, in large collections, is certainly a desideratum not yet attained with us. It may be well questioned whether fear after a certain age, is a motive to which we should have ordinary recourse. The human character is susceptible of other incitements to correct conduct, more worthy of employ, and of better effect. Pride of character, laudable ambition, and moral dispositions are innate correctives of the indiscretions of that lively age; and, when strengthened by habitual appeal and exercise, have a happier effect on future character than the degrading motive of <u>fear.</u> Hardening them to disgrace, to corporal punishments, and servile humiliations cannot be the best process for producing erect character. The affectionate deportment between father and son, offers in truth the best example for that of tutor and pupil; and the experience and practice of* other countries, in this respect, may be worthy of enquiry and consideration with us. It will then be for the wisdom and discretion of the Visitors

* A police exercised by the students themselves, under proper direction, has been tried with success in some countries, and the rather as forming them for initiation into the duties and practices of civil life.

to devise and perfect a proper system of government, which, if it be founded in reason and comity, will be more likely to nourish in the minds of our youth the combined spirit of order and self-respect, so congenial with our political institutions, and so important to be woven into the American character. 5. What qualifications shall be required to entitle to entrance into the University, the arrangement of the days and hours of lecturing for the different schools, so as to facilitate to the students the circle of attendence on them; the establishment of periodical and public examinations, the premiums to be given for distinguished merit; whether honorary degrees shall be conferred, and by what appellations; whether the title to these shall depend on the time the candidate has been at the University, or, where nature has given a greater share of understanding, attention, and application; whether he shall not be allowed the advantages resulting from these endowments, with other minor items of government, we are of opinion should be entrusted to the Visitors; and the statute under which we act having provided for the appointment of these, we think they should moreover be charged with

The erection, preservation, and repair of the buildings, the care of the grounds and appurtenances, and of the interest of the University generally.

That they should have power to appoint a bursar, employ a proctor, and all other necessary agents.

To appoint and remove professors, two-thirds of the whole number of Visitors voting for the removal.

To prescribe their duties and the course of education, in conformity with the law.

To establish rules for the government and discipline of the students, not contrary to the laws of the land.

To regulate the tuition fees, and the rent of the dormitories they occupy.

To prescribe and control the duties and proceedings of all officers, servants, and others, with respect to the buildings, lands, appurtenances, and other property and interests of the University.

To draw from the literary fund such moneys as are by law charged on it for this institution; and, in general,

To direct and do all matters and things which, not being inconsistent with the laws of the land, to them shall seem most expedient for promoting the purposes of the said institution; which several functions they should be free to exercise in the form of by-laws, rules, resolutions, orders, instructions, or otherwise, as they should deem proper.

That they should have two stated meetings in the year, and occasional meetings at such times as they should appoint, or on a special call with such notice as themselves shall prescribe by a general rule; which meetings should be at the University, a majority of them constituting a quorum for business; and that on the death or resignation of a member, or on his removal by the President and Directors of the Literary Fund, or the Executive, or such other authority as the Legislature shall think best, such President and Directors, or the Executive, or other authority, should appoint a successor.

That the said Visitors should appoint one of their own body to be Rector, and with him be a body corporate, under the style and title of the Rector and Visitors of the University of Virginia, with the right, as such, to use a common seal; that they should have capacity to plead and be impleaded in all courts of justice, and in all cases interesting to the University, which may be the subjects of legal cognizance and jurisdiction; which pleas should not abate by the determination of their office, but should stand revived in the name of their successors, and they should be capable in law and in trust for the University, of receiving subscriptions and donations, real and personal, as well from bodies corporate, or persons associated, as from private individuals.

And that the said Rector and Visitors should, at all times, conform to such laws as the Legislature may, from time to time, think proper to enact for their government; and the said University should, in all things, and at all times, be subject to the control of the Legislature.

And lastly, the Commissioners report to the Legislature the following conditional offers to the President and Directors of the Literary Fund, for the benefit of the University:

On the condition that Lexington, or its vicinity, shall be selected as the site of the University, and that the same be permanently established there within two years from the date, John Robinson, of Rockbridge county, has executed a deed to the President and Directors of the Literary Fund, to take effect at his death, for the following tracts of land, to wit:

400 acres on the North fork of James river, known by the name of Hart's bottom, purchased of the late Gen. Bowyer.

171 acres adjoining the same, purchased of James Griggsby.

203 acres joining the last mentioned tract, purchased of William Paxton.

112 acres lying on the North river, above the lands of Arthur Glasgow, conveyed to him by William Paxton's heirs.

500 acres adjoining the lands of Arthur Glasgow, Benjamin Camden and David Edmonson.

545 acres lying in Pryor's gap, conveyed to him by the heirs of William Paxton, deceased.

260 acres lying in Childer's gap, purchased of Wm. Mitchell.

300 acres lying, also, in Childer's gap, purchased of Nicholas Jones.

500 acres lying on Buffalo, joining the lands of Jas. Johnston.

340 acres on the Cowpasture river, conveyed to him by General James Breckenridge—reserving the right of selling the two last mentioned tracts, and converting them into other lands contiguous to Hart's bottom, for the benefit of the University; also, the whole of his slaves, amounting to 57 in number; one lot of 22 acres, joining the town of Lexington, to pass immediately on the establishment of the University, together with all the personal estate of every kind, subject only to the payment of his debts and fulfillment of his contracts.

It has not escaped the attention of the Commissioners, that the deed referred to is insufficient to pass the estate in the lands intended to be conveyed, and may be otherwise defective; but, if necessary, this defect may be remedied before the meeting of the Legislature, which the Commissioners are advised will be done.

The Board of Trustees of Washington College have also proposed to transfer the whole of their funds, viz: 100 shares in the funds of the James River Company, 31 acres of land upon which their buildings stand, their philosophical apparatus, their expected interest in the funds of the Cincinnati Society, the libraries of the Graham and Washington Societies, and $3,000 in cash, on condition that a reasonable provision be made for the present professors. A subscription has also been offered by the people of Lexington and its vicinity, amounting to $17,878, all which will appear from the deed and other documents, reference thereto being had.

In this case, also, it has not escaped the attention of the Commissioners, that questions may arise as to the power of the trustees to make the above transfers.

On the condition that the Central College shall be made the site of the University, its whole property, real and personal, in possession or in action, is offered. This consists of a parcel of land of 47 acres, whereon the buildings of the college are begun, one pavilion and its appendix of dormitories being already far advanced, and with one other pavilion, and equal annexation of dormitories, being expected to be completed during the present season—of another parcel of 153 acres, near the former, and including a considerable eminence very favorable for the erection of a future observatory; of the proceeds of the sales of two glebes, amounting to $3,280 86 cents; and of a subscription of $41,248, on papers in hand, besides what is on outstanding papers of unknown amount, not yet returned—out of these sums are to be taken, however, the cost of the lands, of the buildings, and other works done, and for existing contracts. For the conditional transfer of these to the President and Directors of the Literary Fund, a regular power, signed by the subscribers and founders of the Central College generally, has been given to its Visitors and Proctor, and a deed conveying the said property accordingly to the President and Directors of the Literary Fund, has been duly executed by the said Proctor, and acknowledged for record in the office of the clerk of the county court of Albemarle.

Signed and certified by the members present, each in his proper handwriting, this 4th day of August, 1818.

Th: Jefferson
Creed Taylor
Peter Randolph

Phil. C. Pendleton
Spencer Roane
John M. C. Taylor

Wm: Brockenbrough

Arch^d: Rutherford

Arch: Stuart

James Breckenridge

Henry E. Watkins

James Madison

Armistead T. Mason

H^h: Holmes

J. G. Jackson

Thos Wilson

Phil. Slaughter

Wm H. Cabell

Nathl Claiborne

Wm A. C. Dade

Wm Jones

23

De Witt Clinton on Educating New York City's Poor Children

American educational theory loses its liberal dimensions after the last great statements of the eighteenth-century leaders until the rise of the generation of thinkers and reformers in the 1830s and 1840s. This is not to say that there were no new educational ideas generated or tried during the first quarter of the nineteenth century. But the few ideas that did emerge were peculiarly one-dimensional —and for this reason peculiarly American. They were chiefly aimed at the organization and administration of schools and at the function of teaching more children effectively at slight or at no public expense. The new age was one of building upon the principles and pronouncements of the American Enlightenment, using whenever possible the even older religious themes of the colonial past. Where theory was sought, broad ideas about finding the virtuous society through education slowly gave way to specific designs for the institutional growth of schooling. Much that was republican and sectarian in theory yielded to new institutional measures that became democratic and secular in practice. Yet these changes were gradual, and some aspects of the old were never supplanted by the new.

This age witnessed what is sometimes called "The Protestant Counter-Reformation" in American religious life. It was a time of recurring revivals and of purposive denominational growth. Religious impulses guided many of the activities we today think of as secular. Christian behavior as the main theme of social betterment was more emphasized than the humane or enlightened conduct of the Jeffersonian period, though this is not to suggest that Americans necessarily thought the two were mutually exclusive. The central source of social improvement was charitable Christian impulse. The Christian who could, should give of his money, time, and self to those less fortunate. The man who was poor or distressed should demonstrate his faith, if not his gratitude, by improving his Christian life. The individual was always the source and goal of charity. Vast, impersonal social forces of ignorance, poverty, or deprivation were believed to be surmountable by converting or improving individuals. Social agencies could bring change to man's condition as long as they were guided or controlled by a church. And a church in American social terms meant not so much the authority of spiritual dogma as it meant an organization of active believers.

In this climate of belief, a small-town attitude toward large urban complexities characterized the early reformer's mind. To say this is not to be facetious through hindsight. America was rural; most towns were small. But to say this is to probe at the reason why the first significant social reforms to come out of the early 1800s were in the areas of education and temperance. They could be achieved, so it was held, through individual conversion. Reforms that would change political institutions and social systems—prison reform or womens' rights or slavery—would have to wait upon a modified view of the role of the individual within and against the institutions around him.

De Witt Clinton (1769–1828) was President of the "Society for Establishing a Free School in the City of New York, for the Education of such Poor Children as do not Belong to, or are not Provided for by any Religious Society." (The name soon was changed simply to the Free School Society.) In this address to the public, signed by his fellow trustees of the Society, Clinton echoed British educators who were seeking some system of instruction to accommodate poor city youth then going uneducated. He realized that this problem was becoming as real in New York and the few eastern seaboard cities after 1800, though not so large or so pressing, as it was in the cities of England. He paraphrased the Lockian theme that the enforcement of laws is impossible where the habit of discipline has not been developed in early youth. And in a city of intense sectarian rivalries he sought to avoid controversy at the outset by emphasizing the moral but nondenominational character of the Free School. (See also Selection 24.)

When Clinton wrote this appeal, he was Mayor of New York City, an office he held, with the exception of two annual terms, from 1803 to 1815. He held the post longer, and probably did more for the city, than any other mayor. All forms of civic improvement were his concern. He simultaneously served as a state senator (1806–1811) and as lieutenant-governor of New York (1811–1813). He ran unsuccessfully for the presidency against Madison in 1812 and later served three terms as governor of his state. His greatest achievement for his state and commercially for his city was the construction of the Erie Canal. As a New York City man, he was always at the heart of the city's cultural life and growth. Competent in his administration, liberal in his ideas, Clinton had refined tastes but for his day democratic principles, as the opening paragraphs of Selection 24 make clear.

While the various religious and benevolent societies in this city, with a spirit of charity and zeal which the precepts and example of the Divine Author of our religion could alone inspire, amply provide for the education of such poor children as belong to their respective associations, there still remains a large number, living in total neglect of the religious and moral instruction, and unacquainted with the common rudiments of learning, essentially requisite for the due management of the ordinary business of life. This neglect may be imputed either to the extreme indigence of the parents of such children, their intemperance and vice, or to a blind indifference to the best interests of their offspring. The consequences must be obvious to the most careless observer. Children thus brought up in ignorance, and amidst the contagion of bad example, are in imminent danger of ruin; and too many of them, it is to be feared, instead of being useful members of the community, will become the burden and pests of Society. Early instruction and fixed habits of industry, decency, and order, are the surest safeguards of virtuous conduct; and when parents are either unable or unwilling to bestow the necessary attention on the education of their children, it becomes the duty of the public, and of individuals, who have the power, to assist them in the discharge of this important obligation. It is in vain that laws are made for the punishment of crimes, or that good men attempt to stem the torrent of irreligion and vice, if the evil is not checked at its source; and the means of prevention, by the salutary discipline of early education, seasonably applied. It is, certainly, in the power of the opulent and charitable, by a

---

De Witt Clinton, "To the Public. Address of the Trustees of the Society for Establishing a Free School in the City of New York, for the Education of such Poor Children as do not Belong to, or are not Provided by any Religious Society," *New-York Evening Post*, May 21, 1805, p. 3.

timely and judicious interposition of their influence and aid, if not wholly to prevent, at least, to diminish the pernicious effects resulting from the neglected education of the children of the poor.

Influenced by these considerations, and from a sense of the necessity of providing some remedy for an increasing and alarming evil, several individuals, actuated by similar motives, agree to form an association for the purpose of extending the means of education to such poor children as do not belong to, or are not provided for, by any religious society. After meetings, numerously attended, a plan of association was framed, and a Memorial prepared and addressed to the Legislature, soliciting an Act of Incorporation, the better to enable them to carry into effect their benevolent design. Such a law, the Legislature, at their last session, was pleased to pass; and at a meeting of the Society, under the Act of Incorporation, on the sixth instant, *thirteen* Trustees were elected for the ensuing year.

The particular plan of the school, and the rules for its discipline and management, will be made known previous to its commencement. Care will be exercised in the selection of teachers, and, besides the elements of learning usually taught in schools, strict attention will be bestowed on the morals of the Children, and all suitable means be used to counteract the disadvantages resulting from the situation of their parents. It is proposed, also, to establish, on the first day of the week, a school, called a Sunday-School, more particularly for such children as, from peculiar circumstances, are unable to attend on the other days of the week. In this, as in the Common School, it will be a primary object, without observing the peculiar forms of any religious Society, to inculcate the sublime truths of religion and morality, contained in the Holy Scriptures.

This Society, as will appear from its name, interferes with no existing institution, since children already provided with the means of education, or attached to any other Society, will not come under its care. Humble gleaners in the wide field of benevolence, the members of this Association seek such objects only, as are left by those who have gone before, or are fellow-laborers with them, in the great work of charity. They, therefore, look with confidence for the encouragement and support of the affluent and charitable of every denomination of Christians; and when they consider that in no community is to be found a greater spirit of liberal and active benevolence, than among the citizens of New-York, they feel assured that adequate means for the prosecution of their plan will be easily obtained. In addition to the respectable list of original subscriptions, considerable funds will be requisite for the purchase or hire of a piece of ground, and the erection of a suitable building for the school, to pay the teachers, and to defray other charges incident to the establishment. To accomplish this design, and to place the Institution on a solid and respectable foundation, the Society depend on the voluntary bounty of those who may be charitably disposed to contribute their aid in the promotion of an object of great and universal concern.

De Witt Clinton, *President.*
John Murray, Jun., *Vice President.*
Leonard Blee[c]ker, *Treasurer.*
Benj. Douglass Perkins, *Secretary.*
Willian Johnson,
Samuel Miller, D. D.,
Benj. G. Minturn,
Henry Ten Brook.

Gilbert Aspinwall,
Thomas Eddy
Thomas Franklin,
Matthew Franklin,
Adrian Hegeman,

New York, May, (5th month) [18,] 1805.

24

De Witt Clinton Champions the Lancasterian Plan

An effective mixture of Enlightenment equalitarian ideas with Protestant faith was blended into the educational statements of American public men after 1800, as is well illustrated by De Witt Clinton's preceding address and by this address of 1809. Beyond principles, Clinton offered prescription. His opening paragraphs pointed to a new direction for American education, one that would increasingly consider the entire younger school age urban population, one that would seek workable methods of teaching more school children. As President of the Free School Society in New York City (see Selection 23), he was championing a program for poor children not then enrolled in any of the religious charity schools of the city. With some generous financial support from the city and state, in addition to large private gifts, the Free School Society rapidly brought education to poor white children. Neither "public" in the modern sense of being fully tax supported nor truly democratic in the sense of offering education to all young people, the Free School nevertheless anticipated and led to later public school developments. Clinton even criticized "the celebrated Locke" for his undemocratic concern with educating only the sons of gentlemen. This reproach was to be repeated frequently by educators down to the present day. It is about as wide of the mark as that of a modern student of philosophy who would see Plato only as undemocratic. Locke's ideas about learning and teaching were much too clear and innovative to be lost to this unhistorical complaint. But his critics in this matter, like Clinton, have generally only underscored their own democratic, if unhistorical leanings.

De Witt Clinton (1769–1828) was the most influential early advocate of the Lancasterian or monitorial system of school instruction in the United States. The following description is the best contemporary account we have by an American of that simple method by which older and more advanced pupils, or monitors, teach groups of younger children, all supervised by a master. So full is his account that only a few comments are required to guide the modern reader. For one, Andrew Bell (1753–1832), mentioned by Clinton, sponsored a rival monitorial system of instruction in England. His supporters were generally Anglicans. They engaged in a long, profitless, and complicated feud with the dissenting supporters of Joseph Lancaster (1778–1838) over who should receive principal credit for the monitorial innovation in teaching. This rivalry was not so much the reason for Lancaster's abandoning England for the United States as was his own financial and personal instability. Arriving in America in 1818, Lancaster made his base in Baltimore, lectured throughout the country on his system of teaching, and lived to see his method adopted in most of the large eastern and in a few western cities. Ironically, Lancaster was fatally injured on the streets of New York, the same city where his system was most successful. There Clinton's Free School Society used the Lancasterian method from 1806 until 1853, in which time it virtually monopolized school instruction and became educational dogma.

The Lancasterian scheme was surely no philosophy of education in the abstract sense. Yet it was an ideology. And it was very effective in American terms. It was economical, expedient, self-perpetuating, orderly, and easily emulated. To point out its faults is to indicate much that has betrayed the anti-intellectual side of American education: it was mechanical, unimaginative, regimented if not militaristic, and a forecast of school bureaucratization and curricular standardization. One cannot deny, however, that it answered the urgent needs of urban schooling, as Clinton and others saw them in the early nineteenth century.

To his credit, Clinton a man of considerable intellectual gifts, saw more than mere system in the monitorial plan. Earlier than most men, he thought that America soon would enter a benign machine age. His analogy between the system of Lancaster and labor-saving machinery was not only apt and predictive; it also characterized the premium that the American mind placed upon "mechanical arts" through the remaining century. Clinton, moreover, was Franklin-esque in his work for practical and efficient ways of schooling poor children in "useful" knowledge. He was Jeffersonian too in urging that "children of extraordinary genius" be advanced at public expense through *all* levels of knowledge to be prepared for the professions and for civic leadership. But more than this, Clinton went beyond the Jeffersonians who were seeing education as the inculcation of virtue in the young people of an agrarian republic. He looked to the widening of educational opportunities, if not indeed to the democratization of education, as the answer to social disorganization and urban unrest. His espousal of the Lancasterian system tied in with his larger interests in juvenile delinquency and penal reform and with his deep concern for the elimination of crime through the elimination of ignorance.

On an occasion so interesting to this institution [the Free School Society], when it is about to assume a more reputable shape, and to acquire a spacious and permanent habitation, it is no more than a becoming mark of attention to its patrons, benefactors, and friends, assembled for the first time in this place, to delineate its origin, its progress, and its present situation. The station which I occupy in this association, and the request of my much-respected colleagues, have devolved this task upon me— a task which I should perform with unmingled pleasure, if my avocations had afforded me time to execute it with fidelity; and I trust that the humble objects of your bounty, presented this day to your view, will not detract from the solemnity of the occasion—"that ambition will not mock our useful toil, nor grandeur hear with a disdainful smile the simple annals of the poor."

In casting a view over the civilized world, we find an universal accordance in opinion on the benefits of education, but the practical exposition of this opinion exhibits a deplorable contrast. While magnificent colleges and universities are erected and endowed and dedicated to literature, we behold few liberal appropriations for diffusing the blessings of knowledge among all descriptions of people. The fundamental error of Europe has been, to confine the light of knowledge to the wealthy and the great, while the humble and the depressed have been as sedulously excluded from its participation, as the wretched criminal, immured in a dungeon, is from the light of heaven. This cardinal mistake is not only to be found in the institutions of the Old World, and in the condition of its in-

William W. Campbell, *The Life and Writings of De Witt Clinton* (N. Y., 1849), pp. 309–327.

habitants, but it is to be seen in most of the books which have been written on the subject of education. The celebrated Locke, whose treatises on government and the human understanding have crowned him with immortal glory, devoted the powers of his mighty intellect to the elucidation of education; but in the very threshold of his book we discover this radical error: his treatise is professedly intended for the children of gentlemen. "If those of that rank (says he) are, by their education, once set right, they will quickly bring all the rest in order;" and he appears to consider the education of other children as of little importance. The consequence of this monstrous heresy has been, that ignorance, the prolific parent of every crime and vice, has predominated over the great body of people, and a correspondent moral debasement has prevailed. "Man differs more from man than man from beast," says a writer,* once celebrated. This remark, however generally false, will certainly apply with great force to a man in a state of high mental cultivation, and man in a state of extreme ignorance.

This view of human nature is indeed calculated to excite the most painful feelings, and it entirely originates from a consideration of the predominating error which I have expressed. To this source must the crimes and the calamities of the Old World be principally imputed. Ignorance is the cause as well as the effect of bad governments, and without the cultivation of our rational powers, we can entertain no just ideas of the obligations of morality or the excellences of religion. Although England is justly renowned for its cultivation of the arts and sciences, and although the poor-rates of that country exceed five millions sterling per annum, yet (I adopt the words of an eminent British writer) "there is no Protestant country where the education of the poor has been so grossly and infamously neglected as in England."* If one tenth part of that sum had been applied to the education of the poor, the blessings of order, knowledge, and innocence would have been diffused among them, the evil would have been attacked at the fountain-head, and a total revolution would have taken place in

* Montaigne's Essays.
* Edinburgh Review.

the habits and lives of the people, favorable to the cause of industry, good morals, good order, and rational religion.

More just and rational views have been entertained on this subject in the United States. Here, no privileged orders, no factitious distinctions in society, no hereditary nobility, no established religion, no royal prerogatives, exist to interpose barriers between the people, and to create distinct classifications in society. All men being considered as enjoying an equality of rights, the propriety and necessity of dispensing, without distinction, the blessings of education, followed of course. In New England, the greatest attention has been invariably given to this important object. In Connecticut, particularly, the schools are supported, at least three fourths of the year, by the interest of a very large fund created for that purpose, and a small tax on the people; the whole amounting to seventy-eight thousand dollars per annum. The result of this beneficial arrangement is obvious and striking. Our Eastern brethren are a well-informed and moral people. In those States it is as uncommon to find a poor man who cannot read and write, as it is rare to see one in Europe who can.

Pennsylvania has followed the noble example of New England. On the 4th of April last, a law was passed in that State, entitled "An Act to provide for the education of the poor, gratis." The expense of educating them is made a county charge, and the county commissioners are directed to carry the law into execution.

New York has proceeded in the same course, but on a different, and, perhaps, more eligible plan. For a few years back a fund has been accumulating with great celerity, solemnly appropriated to the support of Common Schools. This fund consists, at present, of nearly four hundred thousand dollars in bank-stock, mortgages, and bonds, and produces an annual interest of upwards of twenty-four thousand dollars. The capital will be augmented by the accumulating interest, and the sale of three hundred and thirty-six thousand acres of land. When the interest on the whole amounts to fifty thousand dollars, it will be in a state of distribution. It is highly probable that the whole fund will, in a few years, amount to twelve hundred and fifty thousand dollars, yielding a yearly income of seventy-five thousand dollars. If population is taken as the ratio of distribution, the quota of this city will amount to seven thousand five hundred dollars—a sum amply sufficient on the plan of our establishment, if judiciously applied, to accommodate all our poor with a gratuitous education.

On a comparison of the plan of this State with that of Pennsylvania, it will probably be found that we are entitled to the palm of superior excellence. Our capital is already created, and nothing more is requisite than a judicious distribution; whereas the expense of school establishments in that State is to be satisfied by annual burdens. The people of Pennsylvania are therefore interested against a faithful execution of the plan, because the less that is applied to education, the less they will have to pay in taxation. Abuses and perversions will of course arise and multiply in the administration of the public bounty. And the laws of that State being liable to alteration or repeal, her system has not that permanency and stability to which ours can lay claim. It is true that our Legislature may divert this fund; but it would justly be considered a violation of public faith, and a measure of a very violent character. As long as the public sentiment is correct in this respect, we have no reason to apprehend that any Legislature will be hardy enough to encounter the odium of their constituents and the indignation of posterity. And we have every reason to believe that this great fund, established for sinking vice and ignorance, will never be diverted or destroyed, but that it will remain unimpaired and in full force and vigor to the latest posterity, as an illustrious establishment, erected by the benevolence of the State, for the propagation of knowledge and the diffusion of virtue among the people.

A number of benevolent persons had seen, with concern, the increasing vices of the city, arising, in a great degree, from the neglected education of the poor. Great cities are, at all times, the nurseries and hot-beds of crimes. Bad men from all quarters repair to them, in order to obtain the benefit of concealment, and to enjoy in a superior degree the advantages of rapine and fraud. And the dreadful examples of vice which are presented to youth, and the alluring forms in which it is arrayed, connected with a spirit of extravagance and luxury, the never-failing attendent of great wealth and extensive business, cannot fail of augmenting the mass of moral depravity. "In London," says a distinguished writer on its police, "above twenty thousand individuals rise every morning without knowing how, or by what means, they are to be supported through the passing day, and, in many instances, even where they are to lodge on the ensuing night."* There can be no doubt that hundreds are in the same situation in this city, prowling about our streets for prey, the victims of intemperance, the slaves of idleness, and ready to fall into any vice, rather than to cultivate industry and good order. How can it be expected that persons so careless of themselves, will pay any attention to their children? The mendicant parent bequeaths his squalid poverty to his offspring, and the hardened thief transmits a legacy of infamy to his unfortunate and depraved descendants. Instances have occurred of little children, arraigned at the bar of our criminal courts, who have been derelict and abandoned, without a hand to protect, or a voice to guide them, through life. When interrogated as to their connections, they have replied that they were without home and without friends. In this state of turpitude and idleness, leading lives of roving mendicancy and petty depredation, they existed, a burden and a disgrace to the community.

True it is that charity schools, entitled to eminent praise, were established in this city; but they were attached to particular sects, and did not embrace children of different persuasions. Add to this that some denominations were not provided with these establishments, and that children the most in want of instruction were necessarily excluded, by the irreligion of their parents, from the benefit of education.

After a full view of the case, those persons of whom I have spoken agreed that the evil must be corrected at its source, and that education was the sovereign prescription. Under this impression they petitioned the Legislature, who, agreeably to their application, passed a law, on the 9th of April, 1805, entitled "An Act to incorporate the Society instituted in the city of New York, for the establishment of a free school for the edu-

---

* Colquhoun on Police of London.

cation of poor children who do not belong to, or are not provided for by, any religious society." Thirteen trustees were elected under this act, on the first Monday of the ensuing May, with power to manage the affairs of the corporation. On convening together, they found that they had undertaken a great task and encountered an important responsibility; without funds, without teachers, without a house in which to instruct, and without a system of instruction; and that their only reliance must be on their own industry, on the liberality of the public, on the bounty of the constituted authorities, and the smiles of the Almighty Dispenser of all good.

In the year 1798, an obscure man of the name of Joseph Lancaster, possessed of an original genius and a sagacious mind, and animated by a sublime benevolence, devoted himself to the education of the poor of Great Britain. Wherever he turned his eyes he saw the deplorable state to which they were reduced by the prevalence of ignorance and vice. He first planted his standard of charity in the city of London, where it was calculated that forty thousand children were left as destitute of instruction as the savages of the desert. And he proceeded, by degrees, to form and perfect a system which is, in education, what the neat finished machines for abridging labor and expense are in the mechanic arts.

It comprehends reading, writing, arithmetic, and the knowledge of the Holy Scriptures. It arrives at its object with the least possible trouble and at the least possible expense. Its distinguishing characters are economy, facility, and expedition, and its peculiar improvements are cheapness, activity, order, and emulation. It is impossible on this occasion to give a detailed view of the system. For this I refer you to a publication entitled "Improvements in Education, &c., by Joseph Lancaster;" and for its practical exposition I beg you to look at the operations of this seminary. Reading, in all its processes, from the alphabet upwards, is taught at the same time with writing, commencing with sand, proceeding to the slate, and from thence to the copy-book. And, to borrow a most just and striking remark, "the beauty of the system is, that nothing is trusted to the boy himself; he does not only *repeat* the lesson before a superior, but he *learns* before a superior."* Solitary study does not exist in the establishment. The children are taught in companies. Constant habits of attention and vigilance are formed, and an ardent spirit of emulation kept continually alive. Instruction is performed through the instrumentality of the scholars. The school is divided into classes of ten, and a chief, denominated a monitor, is appointed over each class, who exercises a didactic and supervisional authority. The discipline of the school is enforced by shame, rather than by the infliction of pain. The punishments are varied with circumstances; and a judicious distribution of rewards, calculated to engage the infant mind in the discharge of its duty, forms the key-stone which binds together the whole edifice."

Upon this system Lancaster superintended in person a school of one thousand scholars, at an annual expense of three hundred pounds sterling. In 1806, he proposed, by establishing twenty or thirty schools in different parts of the kingdom, to educate ten thousand poor children, at four shillings per annum each. This proposition has been carried into effect, and he has succeeded in establishing twenty schools in different parts of the kingdom, all of which are under the care of teachers educated by him, few of whom are more than eighteen years old. Several of the schools have each about 300 scholars; that at Manchester has 400. His great school in Borough Road, London, flourishes very much; it has sometimes 1,100 children —seldom less than 1,000.

When I perceive that many boys in our school have been taught to read and write in two months, who did not before know the alphabet, and that even one has accomplished it in three weeks—when I view all the bearings and tendencies of this system—when I contemplate the habits of order which it forms, the spirit of emulation which it excites, the rapid improvement which it produces, the purity of morals which it inculcates—when I behold the extraordinary union of celerity in instruction and economy of expense—and when I perceive one great assembly of a thousand children, under the eye of a

* Edinburgh Review.

single teacher, marching, with unexampled rapidity and with perfect discipline, to the goal of knowledge, I confess that I recognize in Lancaster the benefactor of the human race. I consider his system as creating a new era in education, as a blessing sent down from heaven to redeem the poor and distressed of this world from the power and dominion of ignorance.

Although the merits of this apostle of benevolence have been generally acknowledged in his own country, and he has received the countenance and protection of the first men of Great Britain, yet calumny has lifted up her voice against him, and attempts have been made to rob him of his laurels. Danger to the Established Church and to Government has been apprehended from his endeavors to pour light upon mankind. This insinuation has been abundantly repelled by the tenor of his life—his carefully steering clear, in his instructions, of any peculiar creed, and his confining himself to the general truths of Christianity. "I have," says Lancaster, "been eight years engaged in the benevolent work of superintending the education of the poor. I have had three thousand children, who owe their education to me, some of whom have left school, are apprenticed or in place, and are going on well. I have had great influence with both parents and children, among whom there is, nevertheless, no one instance of a convert to my religious profession." That knowledge is the parent of sedition and insurrection, and that in proportion as the public mind is illuminated, the principles of anarchy are disseminated, is a proposition that can never admit of debate, at least in this country.

But Lancaster has also been accused of arrogating to himself surreptitious honors, and attempts have been made to transfer the entire merit of his great discovery to Dr. Bell. Whatever he borrowed from that gentleman he has candidly acknowledged. The use of sand, in teaching, undoubtedly came to him through that channel; but it has been practised for ages by the Brahmins. He may also be indebted to Bell for some other improvements, but the vital leading principles of his system are emphatically an original discovery.

The trustees of this institution, after due deliberation, did not hesitate to adopt the system of Lancaster; and, in carrying it into effect, they derived essential aid from one of their body who had seen it practised in England, and who had had personal communications with its author. A teacher was also selected who has fully answered every reasonable expectation. He has generally followed the prescribed plan. Wherever he has deviated, he has improved. A more numerous, a better governed school, affording equal facilities to improvement, is not to be found in the United States.

Provided thus with an excellent system and an able teacher, the school was opened on the 6th of May, 1806, in a small apartment in Bancker street. This was the first scion of the Lancaster stock in the United States; and from this humble beginning, in the course of little more than three years, you all observe the rapidity with which we have ascended.

One great desideratum still remained to be supplied. Without sufficient funds, nothing could be efficiently done. Animated appeals were made to the bounty of our citizens, and five thousand six hundred and forty-eight dollars were collected by subscription. Application was also made to the Legislature of this State for assistance, and on the 27th of February, 1807, a law was passed appropriating four thousand dollars, "for the purpose of erecting a suitable building, or buildings, for the instruction of poor children; and every year thereafter, the sum of one thousand dollars, for the purpose of promoting the benevolent objects of the Society." The preamble of this liberal act contains a legislative declaration of the excellence of the Lancaster system, in the following words: "*Whereas,* the Trustees of the Society for establishing a Free School in the City of New York for the education of such poor children as do not belong to, or are not provided for by, any religious society, have, by their memorial, solicited the aid of the Legislature; and whereas their plan of extending the benefits of education to poor children, and the excellent mode of instruction adopted by them, are highly deserving of the encouragement of Government."

Application was also made to the Corporation of the city for assistance; and the tenement in Bancker street being in all respects inadequate to the accommodation of the increasing establishment, that body appropriated a building adjacent to the Almshouse, for the temporary accommodation of the school, and the sum of five hundred dollars towards putting it in repair; the Society agreeing to receive and educate fifty children from the Almshouse. To this place the school was removed on the 1st of May, 1807, where it has continued until to-day.

The Corporation also presented the ground of this edifice, on which was an arsenal, to the Society, on condition of their educating the children of the Almshouse gratuitously; and also the sum of fifteen hundred dollars to aid in the completion of this building. The value of this lot and the old building, may be fairly estimated at ten thousand dollars; and the Society have expended above thirteen thousand dollars in the erection and completion of this edifice and the adjacent buildings. The income of the school during the last year has been about sixteen hundred dollars, and its expense did not differ much from that sum. This room will contain nearly six hundred scholars, and below there are apartments for the family of the teacher, for the meeting of the trustees, and for a female school, which may contain one hundred scholars, and may be considered as an useful adjunct to this institution. This seminary was established about twelve years ago by a number of young women belonging to, or professing with, the Society of Friends, who have, with meritorious zeal and exemplary industry, devoted much of their personal attention, and all their influence, to the education of poor girls in the elementary parts of education and needlework. The signal success which attended this Free School animated the trustees with a desire to extend its usefulness, and to render it coëxtensive with the wants of the community and commensurate with the objects of public bounty. A statute was accordingly passed, on their application, on the 1st of April, 1808, altering the style of this corporation, denominating it "The Free-School Society of New York," and extending its powers to all children who are the objects of a gratuitous education.

From this elevation of prosperity and this position of philanthropy, the Society had the satisfaction of seeing that the wise and the good of this and the neighboring States had turned their attention to this establishment. A number of ladies of this city, distinguished for their consideration in society, and honored and respected for their undeviating cultivation of the charities of life, established a society for the very humane, charitable, and laudable purposes of protecting, relieving, and instructing orphan children. This institution was incorporated on the 7th of April, 1807, under the style of "The Orphan Asylum Society in the City of New York;" and at a subsequent period the Legislature, under a full conviction of its great merits and claims to public patronage, made a disposition in its favor, which will, in process of time, produce five thousand dollars.

A large building, fifty feet square and three stories high, has been erected for its accommodation, in the suburbs of the city, and it now contains seventy children, who are supported by the zeal and benevolence of its worthy members, and educated on the plan of this institution, at an annual expense of two thousand dollars.

An economical school, whose principal object is the instruction of the children of the refugees from the West Indies, was opened some time since in this city where, in addition to the elementary parts of education, grammar, history, geography, and the French language are taught. It is conducted on the plan of Lancaster, with modifications and extensions, and is patronized and cherished by French and American gentlemen of great worth and respectability, who are entitled to every praise for their benevolence. Children of either sex are admitted, without distinction of nation, religion, or fortune. This seminary is in a flourishing condition, and contains two hundred scholars. There are two masters in this seminary, and two women who teach needle-work; and there is a printing-press, where such as have any talents in that way are taught that important art.

We have also the satisfaction of seeing the benefits of this system extended, either in whole or in part, to the charity schools of the Dutch, Episcopal, and Methodist Churches, and of the Presbyterian Church in Rutgers street; and also to the school founded by the Manumission Society, for the education of the people of color, which has, in consequence of this amelioration, been augmented from seventy to one hundred and thirty children.

In Philadelphia the same laudable spirit has been manifested. Two deputations from that city have visited us for the express purpose of examining our school. One of these made so favorable a report on their return, that a number of the more enterprising and benevolent citizens, composed of members belonging to the Society of Friends, immediately associated under the name of the "Adelphi Society," and raised, by private subscription, a sum sufficient to purchase a suitable lot of ground, to erect a handsome two-story brick building seventy-five feet in length and thirty-five in breadth, in which they formed two spacious rooms. The Adelphi school now contains two hundred children, under the care of one teacher, and is eminently prosperous. The other deputation made also a favorable report, and "The Philadelphia Free-School Society," an old and respectable institution, adopted, in consequence, our system, where it flourishes beyond expectation.

Two female schools, one called the "Aimwell School," in Philadelphia, and another in Burlington, N.J., have also embraced our plan with equal success.

I trust that I shall be pardoned for this detail. The origin and progress of beneficial discoveries cannot be too minutely specified; and when their diffusion can only be exceeded by their excellence, we have peculiar reason to congratulate the friends of humanity. This prompt and general encouragement is honorable to our national character, and shows conclusively that the habits, manners, and opinions of the American people are favorable to the reception of truth and the propagation of knowledge. And no earthly consideration could induce the benevolent man to whom we are indebted for what we see this day, to exchange his feelings, if from the obscure mansions of indigence, in which, in all human probability, he now is instilling comfort into the hearts and infusing knowledge into the minds of the poor, he could hear the voice of a great and enlightened people pronouncing his eulogium, and see this parent seminary, and the establishments which have sprung from its bosom, diffusing light, imparting joy, and dispensing virtue. His tree of knowledge is indeed transplanted to a more fertile soil and a more congenial clime. It has flourished with uncommon vigor and beauty; its luxuriant and wide-spreading branches afford shelter to all who require it; its ambrosial fragrance fills the land, and its head reaches the heavens!

Far be it from my intention to prevent future exertion. For, although much has been done, yet much remains to do, to carry into full effect the system. It would be improper to conceal from you, that, in order to finish this edifice, we have incurred a considerable debt, which our ordinary income cannot extinguish; and that, therefore, we must repose ourselves on the public beneficence. It has been usual to supply the more indigent children with necessaries, to protect them against the inclemencies of winter; for without this provision their attendance would be utterly impracticable. This has hitherto been accomplished by the bounty of individuals, and to no other source can we at present appeal with success.

The law from which we derive our corporate existence does not confine us to one seminary, but contemplates the establishment of schools. A restriction to a single institution would greatly impair our usefulness, and would effectually discourage those exertions which are necessary in order to spread knowledge among all the indigent.

Col. Henry Rutgers, with his characteristic benevolence, has made a donation of two lots in Henry street, worth at least twenty-five hundred dollars, to this corporation. By a condition contained in one of the deeds, it is necessary that we should erect a school-house by June, 1811; and it is highly proper, without any reference to the condition, that this should be accomplished as soon as possible, in order to meet the wants of the indigent in that populous part of the city. If some charitable and public-spirited citizen would follow up this beneficience, and make a similar conveyance on the opposite side of the city, and if the liberality of the public shall dispense the means of erecting the necessary buildings, then the exigencies of all our poor, with respect to education, would be amply supplied for a number of years.

After our youth are instructed in the elements of useful knowledge, it is indispensable to their future usefulness that some calling should be marked out for them. As most of them will undoubtedly be brought up in useful trades, pecuniary means to facilitate their progress to this object would, if properly applied, greatly redound to the benefit of the individual, as well as to the poor of the community.

In such an extensive and comprehensive establishment we are to expect, according to the course of human events, that children of extraordinary genius and merit will rise up, entitled to extraordinary patronage. To select such from the common mass—to watch over their future destiny—to advance them through all the stages of education and through all the grades of knowledge, and to settle them in useful and honorable professions, are duties of primary importance, and indispensable obligations. This, however, will require considerable funds; but of what estimation are pecuniary sacrifices, when put in the scale against the important benefits that may result? And if we could draw aside the veil of futurity, perhaps we might see in the offspring of this establishment, so patronized and so encouraged, characters that will do honor to human nature—that will have it in their power

> The applause of listening senates to command,
>   The threats of pain and ruin to despise;
> To scatter plenty o'er a smiling land,
>   And read their history in a nation's eyes.

25

Archibald De Bow Murphey's Comprehensive Plan for North Carolina

Archibald De Bow Murphey (1777?–1832) wrote to Thomas Ruffin: "I bequeath this Report to the State as the richest Legacy that I shall ever be able to give it." And it was. Murphey, who contributed so much to North Carolina as state senator from Orange County from 1812 to 1818, as superior court judge, and as tireless worker for cultural and economic improvements, did not live to see his plan adopted. Sectional rivalries within the state together with general apathy among the people toward tax-supported projects of any kind stifled his proposals in the legislature. Not until 1839 was the first state school law passed, and not until Calvin H. Wiley's famous tenure as first superintendent of common schools in North Carolina did public schools there become popular.

Yet later generations of North Carolinians came to regard Murphey as father of the state's common school movement. This *Report on Education,* submitted to the legislature in November, 1817, may be compared revealingly with Thomas Jefferson's Bill of 1778 (see Selection 15). Public funds were mainly to support the primary schools, in which, unlike Jefferson's plan for free tuition to all white boys and girls in the first three years, tuition would be charged to all white children, except those too poor to pay it. Unlike Jefferson's rather strict formula for determining the number of students to be supported at public expense at each level of instruction, Murphey would leave the number of publicly supported students to the discretion of the directing Board of Public Instruction. Secondary schools for Jefferson were "grammar schools"; for Murphey they were "academies," the commonly accepted term; both were to be supported by combined public funds and private subscriptions. Thus Murphey's plan essentially followed Jefferson's earlier design.

The broader educational theory behind Murphey's blueprint, however, shows the changes in educational circumstances that had occurred during the forty years since Jefferson's Bill of 1778, and it clearly places this *Report* at the source of the nineteenth-century educational mainstream. The inexpensive Lancasterian system of instruction (see Selection 24) appealed to Murphey because his was a poor state and teachers were scarce. The regimentation in Lancaster's method served to calm Murphey's anxiety over disorder in the schools, as also did his Lockian ideas of early child discipline and his advocacy of military training in the schools. He was drafting his *Report* in an earlier age of college riots and rebellions. But he clearly did not appreciate the fact that Lancaster's plan was designed for the basic education of large numbers of students, which meant then an urban situation, the very point raised by Joseph C. Cabell in his letter to Lancaster (Selection 26).

Most significant is his overall theory of education under state control. He proposed state-sponsored schooling of deaf and dumb children, thus extending the idea of the state's responsibility to handicapped as well as to poor children. Secondary schooling for white girls and public schooling for any black children were outside his ken. He was aware of what was being done to centralize schooling in Prussia, and his ideas today do have some taint of authoritarianism. But to Murphey a poor state in a free larger society could never lift itself out of its predicament without some central means and authority for improving the lot of its citizens. Democracy must purchase some degree of control. This was the increasing nineteenth-century problem, not so much the Jeffersonian republican problem. The idea of the least government as the best government was beginning to wane. So the seeds of the modern bureaucratic state school system were planted by Murphey with only the benign idea of civic improvement. Conditions in North Carolina would permit no other means of cultural advance. The mind of a people was surely no less a premium than an urgent program of state internal improvements. Both should have government support. Following their initial enthusiasm for his plan, Murphey's fellow citizens did not see things his way. The Panic of 1819 and the ensuing depression throttled any chance of their interest being soon re-awakened.

The Committee to whom were referred the so much of the Message of his Excellency the Governor, as relates to public instruction, Report In Part:

Archibald De Bow Murphey, *Report on Education Submitted to the Legislature of North Carolina, 1817* (Raleigh, North Carolina, [1818?]). Reprinted in William Henry Hoyt, ed., *The Papers of Archibald D. Murphey.* Publications of the North Carolina Historical Commission. 2 vols. (Raleigh, 1914), vol. II, pp. 63–83.

That we have much reason to thank Providence for the arrival of a period, when our country enjoying peace with foreign nations, and free from domestic inquietude, turns her attention to improving her physical resources, and the moral and intellectual condition of her citizens. The war of party spirit which for twenty years has disturbed her tranquility and perverted her ambition, has terminated; and political strife has yielded its place to an honorable zeal for the public welfare. Enlightened statesmen will avail themselves of this auspicious period to place the fortunes of the state upon a basis not to be shaken: to found and cherish institutions which shall guarantee to the people the permanence of their government, and enable them to appreciate its excellence. The legislature of North Carolina, giving to their ambition an honorable direction, have resolved to improve this period for the best interests of the State; to adopt and carry into effect liberal plans of internal improvements; to give encouragement to literature, and to diffuse the lights of knowledge among all classes of the community. Let us foster the spirit which has gone abroad: it will lead to the happiest results. If we ourselves should not live to witness them, we shall at least have the satisfaction of having contributed to produce them, and of seeing our children receive from our hands a country growing rich in physical resources, and advancing in moral and intellectual excellence. This is the true way of giving strength and permanence to the government; of giving to it root in the hearts of the people, and nurturing it with their affections. What people will not love a government whose constant solicitude is for their happiness, and whose ambition is to elevate their character in the scale of intelligent beings. Having commenced this great work of Humanity, let us persevere in it with a patience that shall not tire, and with a zeal that shall not abate; praying to the Father of all good, that he will enlighten and direct our course and finally crown our labors with success.

Your committee have entered upon the duties assigned to them with a full conviction of their importance, and of the difficulties which attend their discharge. But believing that let the subject be taken up when it may, those difficulties will exist, and availing themselves of the light thrown upon the subject by the wisdom of others, they have prepared a system of public instruction for North Carolina, which with much deference they beg leave to submit to the consideration of the General Assembly. In digesting this system, they have adhered to the general principles of the report on this subject, submitted by a committee to the last Legislature, and have embraced a provision for the poor as well as rich, and a gradation of schools from the lowest to the highest.

To give effect to any general plan of public education, it is essentially necessary that ample funds be provided, and that these funds, and also the execution of the general plan, be committed to the care and direction of a board composed of intelligent and efficient men. Your committee reserve for a more special report their views with respect to the creation of a fund for public instruction. This subject requires a minuteness of detail, which would only embarrass the general views which it is their object now to present to the consideration of the General Assembly.

Your committee have considered the subject referred to them under the following divisions:

1st. The creation of a fund for Public Instruction.

2d. The constitution of a board to manage the fund and to carry into execution the plan of public instruction.

3d. The organization of schools.

4th. The course of studies to be prescribed for each.

5th. The modes of instruction.

6th. The discipline and government of the schools.

7th. The education of poor children at the public expense.

8th. An Assylum for the deaf and dumb.

Having reserved for a more special report the creation of a fund for public instruction, your committee will first submit their views with respect to the constitution of a board for the management of this fund, and the execution and superintendence of the general plan of education which they recommend.

The Board of Public Instruction.

As the whole community will be interested in the plan of education, the members of the board should be selected from different parts of the State. They have charge of all our literary institutions; and to give more weight and respectability to their deliberations and resolves, the governor of the State should be placed at their head. It will be their province to manage and apply the fund committed to their care, to carry into execution from time to time as it shall be found practicable, the different parts of the plan of public education; to superintend the same when in full operation; to prescribe general rules and regulations for the discipline and government of the schools; to make annual reports to the legislature of their proceedings and of the state of the schools under their charge. Your committee do therefore recommend.

1st. That there shall be elected by joint ballot of the two houses of the General Assembly, six directors, who shall be styled 'The board of public instruction;' that three of the directors shall reside at or to the eastward of the city of Raleigh, and three shall reside at or to the westward thereof.

2d. That the governor for the time being, shall be 'ex officio' president of the board; but the board may appoint a vice president who shall preside in the absence of the governor.

3d. The board shall appoint a secretary and such other officers as may be necessary for conducting their business, who shall receive a reasonable compensation for their services.

4th. Until otherwise ordered, the members of the board shall receive the same compensation for their traveling to and from the place of their meeting; and the same 'per diem' during their attendance on the board, as is now allowed by law to members of the General Assembly. They shall hold an annual meeting in the city of Raleigh at or near the time of the meeting of the General Assembly. The president of the board may at his own pleasure, or shall at the request of any two directors thereof, convene extra meetings of the board for the transaction of any extraordinary business. A majority of the whole number of directors shall be necessary to constitute a board for the transaction of business, but the president or any single director may adjourn from day to day until a board be formed.

5th. The board may at any time enact, alter or amend such rules as to them may seem proper for the purpose of regulating the order of their proceedings; they may adjourn for any period or meet at any place, where they may think the public interest shall require. They shall have power, subject to the limitations to be provided by law, to establish and locate the several academies directed by law, to be established; to determine the number and titles of the professorships therein; to examine, appoint and regulate the compensation of the several professors and teachers; to appoint in the first instance the trustees of the several academies; to prescribe the course of instruction and discipline of the several academies and primary schools, according to such general rules as shall be established by law; to provide some just and particular mode of advancing from the primary schools to the academies, and from academies to the university, as many of the most meritorious children educated at the public expense, as the proceeds of the fund for public instruction may suffice to educate and maintain, after the whole system of public instruction hereby recommended, shall have been put in operation; to manage the fund for public instruction, and apply its proceeds in carrying into execution and supporting the plan of education committed to their care; and in giving effect to this plan, the board shall regard the primary schools at its foundation, and care shall be taken that the proceeds of the fund for public instruction, shall not be applied to the establishment of any academy, so long it is probable that such an application may leave any primary schools unprovided for. And the board shall have power to enact, alter or amend such bye-laws rules and regulations relative to the various subjects committed to their trust, as to them may seem expedient: Provided the same be not inconsistent with the laws of the State; and they shall recommend to the General Assembly from time to time, such general laws in relation to public instruction, as may in their opinion, be calculated to promote the intellectual and moral improvement of the State.

6th. The directors of the board of public instruction for the time being shall, *ex officio*, be trustees of the university of this State.

7th. The treasurer of the State shall have charge of the fund for public instruction, and the proceeds thereof shall be paid upon warrants drawn by the president of the board; and all expenses incurred in carrying into effect the system of public instruction and supporting the same, shall be charged upon this fund and paid out of the proceeds thereof.

8th. The board of public instruction shall annually submit to the General Assembly at or near the commencement of their session, a view of the state of public education within the State, embracing a history of the progress or declension of the University in the year next preceding, and illustrating its actual condition and future prospects; and also setting forth the condition of the fund committed to their trust for public instruction.

9th. The board of public instruction shall be a body politic in law; shall have a common seal and perpetual succession; shall by the name and style of "The Board of Public Instruction," be capable of suing and being sued, pleading and being impleaded; and shall have and enjoy all the rights and privileges of a corporation.

The Organization of Schools.

In arranging the system of schools, your committee have endeavored to make the progress of education natural and regular; beginning with primary schools, in which the first rudiments of learning are taught, and proceeding to Academies, in which youth are to be instructed in languages, ancient and modern history, mathematics and other branches of science, preparatory to entering into the University, in which instruction is to be given in all the higher branches of the sciences and the principles of the useful arts.

In making this arrangement the greatest difficulties have occurred in organizing the primary schools. These difficulties arise from the condition of the country and the State of its population; it being found impossible to divide the State into small sections of territory, each containing an adequate population for the support of a school. Any attempt to divide the territory of the State into such small sections, with a view of locating a school in each, would prove unavailing; and however desirable it may be, that a school should be established convenient to every family, the time has not arrived when it can be done. But so far as it is practicable to extend the convenience it should be done. The primary schools are of the first importance in any general plan of public education; every citizen has an interest in them, as the learning indispensable to all, of reading, writing and arithmetic, is here to be taught. By judicious management and a proper selection of books for children while they are learning to read, much instruction in their moral and religious duties may be given to them in these schools. Your committee have diligently examined the different plans of public instruction which have been submitted to the general assembly of our sister State, Virginia, and also those which have been carried into effect in some of the New England States; they have also examined the plan which was drawn up and adopted by the national convention of France, and which now forms the basis of public instruction in all the communes of that empire; and deriving much aid from this examination upon every part of the subject referred to them, they have suggested a system which they hope may be found to suit the conditions of North Carolina. In designating the schools of different grades, they have adopted the names in common use.—Your committee do therefore recommend that as to

The Primary Schools.

1. Each county in this State be divided into two or more townships; and that one or more primary schools be established in each township, provided a lot of ground not less than four acres and a sufficient house erected thereon, be provided and vested in the board of public instruction. And that every incorporated town in the State containing more than one hundred families, shall be divided into wards. Such town containing less than one hundred families shall be considered as forming only one ward. Each ward upon conveying to the board of public instruction a lot of ground of the value of two hundred dollars

or upwards, and erecting thereon a house of the value of two hundred and fifty dollars, shall be entitled to the privileges and benefits of a primary school.

2. The court of Pleas and Quarter sessions shall annually elect for each township in their respective counties, five persons as trustees of the primary schools to be established in such township, who shall have power to fix the scites of the primary schools to be established thereon, superintend and manage the same, make rules for their government, appoint trustees, appoint teachers, and remove them at pleasure. They shall select such children residing within their township, whose parents are unable to pay for their schooling, who shall be taught at the said schools for three years, without charge. They shall report to the board of public instruction, the rules which they may adopt for the government of said schools, and shall annually report to the said board the state of the schools, the number and conduct of the pupils, and their progress in learning; the conduct of the teacher, and also every thing connected with the schools of any importance.

3. In addition to the pupils who are to be taught free from charge, the teacher of any primary school may receive as many other scholars, and at the rates, which the trustees of the school may establish; and the trustees may purchase for the use of the pupils educated at the public expense, such books, stationery and other implements for learning, as may be necessary.

4th. The teacher of each primary school shall receive a salary of one hundred dollars, to be paid out of the fund for public instruction.

This plan for establishing primary schools is simple, and can easily be carried into execution. It divides the expenses of these schools between the public and those individuals for whose immediate benefit they are established; it secures a regular stipend to the teachers, and yet holds out inducements to them to be active and faithful in their calling; and it enables every neighborhood, whether the number of its inhabitants be few or many, to have a primary school, at the cheap price of a small lot of ground, and a house erected thereon, sufficient for the purposes of the school—Were these schools in full operation in every section of the State, even in the present state of our population, more than fifteen thousand children would be annually taught in them. These schools would be to the rich a convenience, and to the poor, a blessing.

Academies.

After children shall have gone through the course of studies prescribed for the primary schools, those of them who are to be further advanced in education, will be placed in the Academies, where they will be instructed in languages, ancient and modern history, mathematics and other branches of science preparatory to their entering into the University. The Academies shall be located in different districts of the State for the convenience of the people, and the expenses of purchasing suitable sites and erecting thereon the necessary buildings, shall be divided between the public at large and the several districts. Private liberality has of late erected many small Academies in the State, which deserve the consideration and patronage of the Legislature. From the benefits which have accrued to the public from these small Academies, we may form an opinion of the good which would flow from larger institutions of the same sort, if regularly located throughout the State, and aided with suitable funds. The state of learning among us will never become respectable until we have such regular Academical institutions—Your committee do therefore recommend,

1st. That the board of public instruction shall divide the State into ten Academical districts, containing each, one or more counties, and as near as practicable, an equal number of white population, and number the districts from one upwards.

2d. When in any of the districts there is an Academy already established, the trustees thereof may submit to the board of public instruction, a report on the actual condition of their institution, its relative position to the boundaries of the district, the number and dimensions of the buildings, their value and state of repair, the extent of ground on which they are erected;

the number and denomination of the professors and teachers employed therein, and of the pupils educated thereat. If the board should think the Academy properly situated for the benefit of the district, and that its buildings and grounds will answer their intended purposes, notice thereof shall be given to the trustees; and upon conveyance being made of the said ground and houses to the board of public instruction, the academy shall be entitled to the same benefits which may be extended to any academy that may be erected, and shall be subject to the same rules and regulations in relation to the government thereof, which the board of public instruction or the general assembly may provide for the general government of the academies of the State. But the trustees of such academies may continue to hold their offices and to supply vacancies occurring in their body.

3d. In case the buildings of any academy already established and so accepted by the board of public instruction, require repair or any enlargement or alteration, the board shall appropriate a sum sufficient to repair, alter or enlarge the said buildings, provided the sum so appropriated shall not exceed one-third part of the entire value of such buildings, when so altered, repaired or enlarged. The alterations or enlargement of the buildings shall be planned by the board of public instruction and executed according to their order.

4th. In any academical district where there is no academy now established, or none which the board of public instruction shall think will answer their intended purpose, the board may accept a lot of ground, of sufficient extent in their estimation, and conveniently situated for the erection of an academy for the district; provided that two-third parts of the sum required for the erection of suitable buildings for the said academy be previously subscribed by one or more persons, and the payment thereof assured to the board of public instruction.

5th. When any conveyance of the lot of ground on which the buildings are erected, shall be accepted of by the board, they shall appoint eleven persons residing within the district, trustees of the academy, who shall be deemed a body corporate by such title as the board of public instruction shall prescribe;

shall have and enjoy all the rights and privileges of a corporation; shall have power to elect a president from their own body, and to fill all vacancies which shall occur therein. They may make, alter or amend, such bye-laws, rules and regulations, as they shall deem necessary or expedient, for the government of their own body, and of the professors, teachers and pupils of the academy of which they have charge: provided they be not inconsistent with such general regulations as the board of public instruction may provide for the general government of the academies of the State.

6th. The trustees shall provide by contract for the erection of the necessary buildings for their academy, and appoint a treasurer who shall have authority to collect the several sums subscribed thereto, and shall be entitled to receive in virtue of their order upon the board of public instruction, signed by their president, such sums of money as the board may, from time to time, appropriate for the erection of the buildings, their repairs or alterations, salaries of professors and teachers, and other purposes of the academy.

7th. As soon as any academy is ready for the admission of pupils, the trustees may recommend to the board of public instruction, any person to be a professor or teacher therein, who, if approved after examination in some mode to be prescribed by the board, shall be regarded as a professor or teacher of such academy, but subject to removal at the pleasure of the trustees or of the board. Where vacancies shall occur among the professors or teachers during the recess of the board, the trustees may make temporary appointments, to be confirmed or disapproved by the board at their next session.

8th. The trustees of any academy may fix the salaries of their respective teachers, subject to the control of the board of public instruction. One-third part of the salaries shall be paid by the board at such times and in such way as they shall prescribe.

9th. The professors and teachers in any academy shall be bound to instruct, free of charge for tuition, the pupils whom the board of public instruction may designate to be taught in said academy at the public expense.

Your committee have perhaps gone into unnecessary details

respecting the academies. Their plan simply is, to divide the State into ten academical districts, and that one academy be erected in each; that the State shall advance one-third of the sum required for the erection of necessary buildings, and one-third of the sum to be paid in salaries to professors and teachers—making it their duty to teach poor children free of charge.

The University.

This institution has been in operation for twenty years, and has been eminently useful to the State. It has contributed, perhaps, more than any other cause, to diffuse a taste for reading among the people, and excite a spirit of liberal improvement; it has contributed to change our manners and elevate our character; it has given to society many useful members, not only in the liberal professions, but in the walks of private life; and the number of its pupils who are honored with seats in this legislature is a proof of the estimation in which they are held by their fellow-citizens. When this institution was first founded, it was fondly hoped that it would be cherished with pride by the legislature. But unfortunately the nature of the funds with which it was endowed, in a short time rendered it odious to some, and cooled the ardor of others. The torrent of prejudice could not be stemmed; the fostering protection of the legislature was withheld, and the institution left dependent upon private munificence.

Individuals contributed not only to relieve its necessities, but to rear up its edifices and establish a permanent fund for its support. At the head of these individuals, stood the late Governor Smith, Charles Gerard and Gen. Thomas Person. The first two made valuable donations in lands, and the last, in a sum of money with which one of the halls of the university has been erected. To enable them to complete the main edifice, the trustees have been compelled to sell most of the lands devised to them by Mr. Gerard, and as the lands conveyed to them by Governor Smith lie within the Indian boundary, the trustees have not been able as yet to turn them to a productive account.

With the aid thus derived from individuals, together with occasional funds derived from escheats, the institution has progressed thus far. The Legislature, after exhausting its patience in endeavoring to collect the arrearages of debts due to the State, transferred to the trustees of the University those arrearages, with the hope that they would be able to enforce payment. But no better fortune has attended their efforts than those of the State, and this transfer has proved of no avail to the institution. The surplus remaining in the hands of administrators where the next of kin have made no claim within seven years, have also been transferred to the trustees; but this has as yet yielded a very small fund, and probably never will yield much. The legislature have enlarged the rights of inheritance, and in this way have nearly deprived the institution of the revenue from escheats. Amidst all these embarrassments, the trustees have never lost sight of the necessity of accumulating a fund in bank stock, the annual proceeds of which would enable them to continue the operations of the institution; and they have succeeded so far as to be able to support two professorships, and employ two or three tutors. But there is little prospect of adding to this fund, until the lands given by Governor Smith can be sold; and if that period be waited for, the institution must necessarily languish and sink in respectability. It is at this moment almost destitute of a Library, and entirely destitute of the Apparatus necessary for instructing youth in the mathematical and physical sciences. Add to this, that one half of the necessary buildings have not been erected.

In this state of things, and at a moment when former prejudices have died away, when liberal ideas begin to prevail, when the pride of this State is awakening and an honorable ambition is cherished for her glory, an appeal is made to the patriotism and the generous feelings of the legislature in favor of an institution, which in all civilized nations, has been regarded as the nursery of moral greatness, and the palladium of civil liberty. That people who cultivate the sciences and the arts with most success, acquire a most enviable superiority over others. Learned men by their discoveries and works give a lasting splendor to national character; and such is the enthusiasm of man, that there is not an individual, however humble in life his lot may be, who does not feel proud to belong to a country honored with great men and magnificent institutions. It is due to North Carolina, it is due to the great man,[1] who first proposed the foundation of the University, to foster it with the parental fondness and to give to it an importance commensurate with the high destinies of the State. Your committee deem this subject of so much interest, that they beg leave in a future report to submit to the two houses a plan for increasing the funds of the University.

This institution has uniformly labored under the double disadvantages of a want of funds, and the want of subsidiary institutions, in which youth could be instructed preparatory to their entering upon a course of the higher branches of science in the University. This latter disadvantage has been so great, that the trustees have been compelled to convert the University, in part into a grammar school. This disadvantage has been of late removed in part, by the establishment of academies in different parts of the State; but it will continue to be much felt, until regular academical institutions shall be made and the course of instruction prescribed for them.

Another serious disadvantage and a consequence of the one last mentioned, is the necessity, which the peculiar state of academical learning has imposed upon the trustees, of conferring the honorary degrees of an University upon young men who have not made that progress in the sciences, of which their diploma purports to be a testimonial. This is an evil that is found in almost all the Universities of the Union. A young man enters into an University with only slight acquirements in classical education, and after remaining four years, during which time he is instructed in only the outlines of the general principles of science, he receives a degree: the consequence is that he leaves the University with his mind trained only to general and loose habits of thinking: and if he enters into professional life,

[1] Gen. William R. Davie.

he has to begin his education anew. The great object of education is to discipline the mind, to give to it habits of activity, of close investigation: in fine, to teach men *to think*. And it is a reproach upon almost all the literary institutions of our country, that the course of studies pursued in them teach most young men only how to become literary triflers. Their multifarious occupations dissipate their time and attention: They acquire much superficial knowledge: but they remain ignorant of the profounder and more abstract truths of philosophy. Indeed the road to the profound sciences is of late so infested with pleasant elementary books, compilations, abridgments, summaries and encyclopedias, that few, very few, in our country ever travel it.

To remove this reproach upon the state of learning among us, a new plan of instruction in our university must be organized; a plan which shall give to the different classes in the institution, an arrangement founded upon a philosophical division of the present improved state of knowledge; and which in its execution shall train the mind both to liberal views and minute investigation.

Your committee have been thus particular in submitting to the two houses an exposition of the actual condition of the university, with a view of recalling their consideration to the solemn injunction of the constitution as to every part of the subject referred to them; "that a school or schools shall be established by the legislature for the convenient instruction of youth, with such salaries to the masters, paid by the public, as may enable them to instruct at low prices; and all useful learning shall be duly encouraged and promoted in one or more universities." Our university is the only institution which the legislature has yet founded and endowed in compliance with this injunction; but even as to this institution the spirit of the constitution is far from being complied with. We have not buildings for the accommodation of youth, nor books, nor apparatus for their instruction—your committee do therefore recommend,

1st. That three additional buildings be erected at the university; two for the accommodation of students, and one for the library and apparatus. This last building to contain suitable rooms for the delivery of lectures by the different professors.

2nd. That a library and suitable apparatus for instructing youth in the mathematical and physical sciences, be procured for the use of the said institution.

3rd. That funds be assigned for endowing to [two] professorships, and supporting six additional teachers.

These are the present wants of the university; as our population encreases, the number of buildings must be encreased, and more funds be provided for supporting teachers. In a subsequent part of this report your committee have recommended that there be four classes in the university with a professor at the head of each, who shall be assisted with such adjunct professors or teachers, as the state of the institution may require.

The Course of Studies.

1st. In the primary schools should be taught reading, writing and arithmetic. A judicious selection of books should from time to time be made by the board of public instruction for the use of small children: Books which will excite their curiosity and improve their moral dispositions. And the board should be empowered to compile and have printed for the use of primary schools, such books as they may think will best subserve the purposes of intellectual and moral instruction. In these books should be contained many of the historical parts of the old and new testament, that children may early be made acquainted with the book which contains the word of truth, and the doctrines of eternal life.

2nd. In the academies should be taught the Latin, Greek, French and English languages, the higher rules of arithmetic, the six first books of Euclid's elements, Algebra, Geography, the elements of Astronomy, taught with the use of the Globes, ancient and modern history. The basis of a good education is classical and mathematical knowledge; and no young man ought to be admitted into the university without such knowledge.

3d. In the university the course of education should occupy four years; and there should be four classes, to be designated.

1st. The class of languages—In this class should be studied, 1st. the more difficult Latin, Greek and French classes: 2nd Ancient and modern history: 3d. Belles letters: 4th. Rhetoric.

2d. The class of mathematics—In this class should be studied, 1st. Pure mathematics: 2d. Their application to the purposes of physical science.

3d. The class of physical sciences.—In this class should be taught, 1st. Physics: 2d. Chemistry: 3d. The philosophy of natural history: 4th. Mineralogy: 5th. Botany: 6th. Zoology.

4th. The class of moral and political science.—In this class should be taught. 1st. The philosophy of the human mind: 2d. morals: 3d. The law of nature and of nations: 4th. Government and legislation: 5th. Political economy.

The Modes of Instruction.

The great object of education is intellectual and moral improvement; and that the mode of instruction is to be preferred which best serves to effect this object. That mode is to be found only in a correct knowledge of the human mind, its habits, passions, and manner of operation. The philosophy of the mind, which in ages preceding had been cultivated only in its detached branches, has of late years received form and system in the schools of Scotland. This new science promises the happiest results. It has sapped the foundation of scepticism by establishing the authority of those primitive truths and intuitive principles, which form the basis of all demonstration; it has taught to man the extent of his intellectual powers, and marking the line which separates truth from hypothetical conjecture, has pointed out to his view the boundaries which Providence has prescribed to his enquiries. It has determined the laws of the various faculties of the mind, and furnished a system of philosophic logic for conducting our enquiries in every branch of knowledge.

This new science has given birth to new methods of instruction; methods, which being founded upon a correct knowledge of the faculties of the mind, have eminently facilitated their development. Pestalozzi in Switzerland and Joseph Lancaster in England, seem to have been most successful in the application of new methods to the instruction of children. Their methods are different, but each is founded upon a profound knowledge of the human mind. The basis of each method is, *the excitement of the curiosity of children;* thereby awakening their minds and preparing them to receive instruction. The success which has attended the application of their methods, particularly that of Lancaster, has been astonishing. Although but few years have elapsed since Lancastrian schools were first established, they have spread over the British empire, extended into the continent of Europe, the Island of St. Domingo, and the United States. Various improvements in the details of his plan have been suggested by experience and adopted; and it is probable that in time, his will become the universal mode of instruction for children. The Lancastrian plan is equally distinguished by its simplicity, its facility of application, the rapid intellectual improvement which it gives, and the exact discipline which it enforces. The moral effects of the plan are also astonishing; exact and correct habits are the surest safeguards of morals; and it has been often remarked, that out of the immense number of children and grown persons instructed in Lancaster's schools, few, very few, have ever been prosecuted in a court of justice for any offence. Your committee do therefore recommend that whenever it be practicable, the Lancastrian mode of instruction be introduced into the primary schools. The general principles of this method may be successfully introduced into the academies and university: And your committee indulge the hope, that the board of public instruction, and the professors and teachers in these respective institutions, will use their best endeavors to adopt and enforce the best methods of instruction which the present state of knowledge will enable them to devise.

The Discipline and Government of the Schools.

In a republic, the first duty of a citizen is obedience to the law. We acknowledge no sovereign but the law, and from infancy to manhood our children should be taught to bow with reverence to its majesty. In childhood, parental authority enforces the first lessons of obedience; in youth, this authority is aided by the municipal law which in manhood wields the entire supremacy. As the political power and the social happiness of a state depend upon the obedience of its citizens, it becomes an object of the first importance to teach youth to reverence the law, and cherish habits of implicit obedience to its authority. Such obedience not only contributes to the strength and tranquility of the state, but also constitutes the basis of good manners, of deference and respect in social intercourse. But in our country, youth generally become acquainted with the freedom of our political institutions, much sooner than with the principles upon which that freedom is bottomed, and by which it is to be preserved; and few learn, until experience teaches them in the school of practical life, that true liberty consists not in doing what they please, but in doing that which the law permits. The consequence has been, that riot and disorder have dishonored almost all the colleges and Universities of the Union.

The temples of science have been converted into theatres for acting disgraceful scenes of licentiousness and rebellion. How often has the generous patriot shed tears of regret for such criminal follies of youth? Follies which cast reproach upon learning, and bring scandal upon the state. This evil can only be corrected by the moral effects of early education; by instilling into children upon the first dawnings of reason, the principles of duty, and by nurturing those principles as reason advances, until obedience to authority shall become a habit of their nature. When this course shall be found ineffectual the arm of the civil power must be stretched forth to its aid.

The discipline of a University may be much aided by the arrangement of the buildings, and the location of the different classes. Each class should live together in separate buildings, and each be under the special care of its own professors and teachers. A regular system of subordination may in this way be established; each class would have its own character to maintain, and the *Esprit de Corps* of the classes would influence all their actions. Similar arrangements may, in part, be made in the several academies, and the like good effect expected from them.

The amusements of youth may also be made auxiliary to the exactness of discipline. The late president of the United States, Mr. Jefferson, has recommended upon this part of the subject, that through the whole course of instruction at a college or university, at the hours of recreation on certain days, all the students should be taught the manual exercise, military evolutions and manoeuvers, should be under a standing organization as a military corps, and with proper officers to train and command them. There can be no doubt that much may be done in this way towards enforcing habits of subordination and strict discipline—it will be the province of the board of public instruction, who have the general superintending care of all the literary institutions of the state, to devise for them systems of discipline and government; and your committee hope they will discharge their duty with fidelity.

The Education of Poor Children at the Public Expense.

One of the strongest reasons which we can have for establishing a general plan of public instruction, is the condition of the poor children of our country. Such always has been, and probably always will be the allotments of human life, that the poor will form a large portion of every community: and it is the duty of those who manage the affairs of a State, to extend relief to this unfortunate part of our species in every way in their power.

Providence, in the impartial distribution of its favors, whilst it has denied to the poor many of the comforts of life, has generally bestowed upon them the blessing of intelligent children. Poverty is the school of genius; it is a school in which the active powers of man are developed and disciplined, and in which that moral courage is acquired, which enables him to toil with difficulties, privations and want. From this school generally come forth those men who act the principle parts upon the theatre of life; men who impress a character upon the age in which they live. But it is a school which if left to itself runs wild; vice in all its depraved forms grows up in it. The State should take this school under her special care, and nurturing the genius which there grows in rich luxuriance, give to it an honorable and profitable direction. Poor children are the peculiar property of the State, and by proper cultivation they will constitute a fund of intellectual and moral worth, which will greatly subserve the public interest. Your committee have therefore endeavored to provide for the education of all poor children in the primary schools; they have also provided for the advancement into the academies and university, of such of those children as are most distinguished for genius and give the best assurance of future usefulness. For three years they are to be educated in the primary schools free of charge; the portion of them who shall be selected for further advancement, shall, during the whole course of their future education, be clothed, fed and taught at the public expense. The number of children who are to be thus advanced, will depend upon the state of the fund set apart for public instruction, and your committee think it will be most advisable to leave the number to the discretion of the board, who shall have charge of the fund; and also to leave to them the providing of some just and particular mode of advancing this number from the primary schools to the academies, and from the academies to the university.

An Asylum for the Deaf and Dumb.

If there be any of our species who are entitled to the public consideration of the government, it is surely the deaf and dumb. Since the method of instructing them in language and science has been discovered, numerous asylums in different countries have been established for their instruction. While we are engaged in making provision for others, humanity demands that we should make a suitable provision for them. Your committee do therefore recommend that as soon as the state of the fund for public instruction will admit, the board who have charge of that fund, be directed to establish at some suitable place in the State, an Asylum for the Instruction of the Deaf and Dumb.

Your committee have now submitted to the two houses their general views upon the subject referred to them. They have proposed the creation of a fund for public instruction, the appointment of a board to manage this fund, and to carry into effect the plan of education which they have recommended. This plan embraces a gradation of schools from the lowest to the highest, and contains a provision for the education of poor children— and of the deaf and dumb.

When this or some other more judicious plan of public education, when light and knowledge shall be shed upon all, may we not indulge the hope, that men will be convinced that wisdom's ways are ways of pleasantness and all her paths are paths of peace; and be induced by such conviction to regulate their conduct by the rule of christian morality, of doing unto others as they wish they would do unto them; and that they will learn to do justly, to love mercy and to walk humbly before their God.

Your committee will forthwith report bills to carry into effect the several measures recommended in this report.

Respectfully submitted,

A. D. Murphey, *Chairman.*

November 29, 1817

26

Joseph C. Cabell Questions the Lancasterian System

Joseph Carrington Cabell (1778–1856), loyal friend and co-worker with Thomas Jefferson is legislating for the University of Virginia (see Selection 22), here puts a key question about the Lancasterian method of instruction to its author. (See Selection 24.) How effective will it be in schools with small numbers of pupils? Or how effective can it really be in an agrarian country? The success of the system in England and in New York City at relatively large urban schools must have made the answer self-evident to Cabell even before he wrote. Yet he was hoping that Lancaster could somehow reassure him of the method's probable effectiveness in rural areas. For Cabell, as a state legislator for twenty-three years and mainstay of the University of Virginia after Jefferson, constantly sought improved methods of instruction for the schools of his state. Like Archibald De Bow Murphey in North Carolina (see Selection 25), whose career his own paralleled, Cabell also worked for state internal improvements, conceiving of them and education both as common areas for constructive actions by state government. Cabell even became known as "the De Witt Clinton of Virginia."

While Murphey took for granted the utility of the Lancasterian method on a statewide scale, Cabell questioned it in a way that pointed not only directly to its potential weakness then in Virginia but also to its impracticality for most of the United States. Though largely successful in New York City, the Lancasterian system proved to be a fad, chiefly due to the reasons that Cabell here suggests.

Warminister, Virginia, 1st July. 1819.

SIR.

There was scarcely any one in this country more gratified by
the intelligence of your arrival in America than the stranger
who now has the honor to address you. The perusal of various
articles in the Edinburgh Review, & some of your own writings
had inspired me with a high respect for the Author of a system
of elementary instruction by which one man is competent to
teach a thousand pupils more rapidly than the smallest number
can be advanced in the ordinary method. As I understand your
object in coming to the United States is to be useful thro the
means of the diffusion of your new plan of education I hope I
shall not trespass too far on your valuable time in addressing
you a letter of enquiry in respect to it. That your system is immensely valuable in large towns where great numbers can be
brought together into one school, no doubt can be entertained.
But as we have but few of these in the United States, and as the
greater part of the population, especially in the Southern section is thinly scattered over a vast extent of territory, the value
of the system to this nation, will depend essentially upon its
applicability to small Country Schools. Upon this point it is
that I am particularly desirous of information. The Edinburgh
Review states that "the Essence of the new method consists in
economizing the expence of education by teaching very large
numbers at once. Beautiful & useful as it is, when applied to
schools of a certain size, it is wholly inapplicable to small seminaries; at least it loses all its advantages. One teacher now super-
intends a school of 1000 or 1200 children. Yet in pa: 137 of your
work entitled improvements in education you say "The System
of tuition & rewards which are described in the former part of
this work, will be found well adapted to initiatory schools," and
in pa: 135 you observe that "the number of children that attend
a school of this class is very fluctuating, and seldom exceeds

---

Joseph C. Cabell to Joseph Lancaster, Warminster, Virginia, July 1, 1819,
A. L. S., Joseph Lancaster Papers, American Antiquarian Society. Printed
with the kind permission of the American Antiquarian Society.

thirty." I have no recollection of anything in the context either of the Edinburgh Review or of your works, which would put this subject in a different point of view. There seems to me to be a plain difference of opinion between yourself and the Editor of the Review: and I hope you will be found to be correct, because upon this question depends almost the whole value of your system to the American people. Of this you will be satisfied when I inform you that of the Rural initiatory schools in Virginia hardly one in a hundred consists of more than thirty scholars. I am of the opinion they would not average more than twenty: yet I believe that schools of thirty children, male & female, could be made up generally over the country if the introduction of an improved method depended on the presence of that number. Altho' in such small seminaries the economy of the system would in a great degree be lost, yet I hope the rapidity might be retained. If your present vocations allow you time to answer this enquiry, I should be exceedingly happy to hear from you: & should you give me the information I expect & desire, you may enable me to be of service to my country.

I am, Sir, with great respect, your obt. servt.

Joseph C. Cabell

27

Daniel Webster's Argument for Dartmouth College

The background of this case need not be lengthily described because much of it is included here in Daniel Webster's argument. The central issue was whether the state legislature of New Hampshire could retroactively alter the charter of Dartmouth College. Such a change had been made by the legislature in 1816 when it elevated the college to a "university" and made other alterations in the board of control. The trustees of the original college contested the action of the legislature by retaining Daniel Webster (1782–1852) of the class of 1801 to argue their case before the United States Supreme Court on appeal from the Supreme Court of New Hampshire. This was Webster's first appearance before the federal Supreme Court. His emotional peroration, which constitutes the last four paragraphs of this document, is legendary in American college lore. It expressed the affection and nostalgia of the American small college alumnus for his *alma mater*. But Webster's words are not a part of the official Court report of the case. They were written from memory by Chauncey A. Goodrich, who heard Webster's argument and over three decades later reported the closing remarks to a gathering of Dartmouth College alumni.

The relevance of Webster's argument for educational theory lies not in his plea for the sanctity of a corporate charter *per se*. It lies rather in the ideal integrity of a college community or in the integrity of any community of learning which must have the protection of the law to preserve its corporate identity. The property of the trustees of Dartmouth College under the original charter is the proximate but not the underlying issue here for educational thought. At bottom lie the safeguards in law that must be furnished a group of academic people if they are to carry forward their seeking and teaching independent of outside public opinion. That such inquiry under private auspices may be as blind to the truth and as easily perverted and debased as inquiry under public auspices is not really the primary intellectual issue here in the long history of the struggle for freedom of the mind. To say this is not to gloss over the fact that it was precisely to create a freer and non-sectarian atmosphere for learning at Dartmouth College that the New Hampshire legislature altered the College's original charter. Nor is it really of first importance here that Daniel Webster went on to become the leading spokesman for northern political conservatism and for American nationalism throughout the Jacksonian age. The opposing Jeffersonian attitude, it will be remembered, insisted that the better chance for sustained free inquiry comes through representative public control of institutions of higher learning. Both sides, in any case, agreed upon the fundamental legal need to protect the independence and integrity of any scholarly community. (See also Selection 28.)

The Trustees of Dartmouth
College v. Woodward.

The charter granted by the British crown to the trustees of Dartmouth College, in New-Hampshire, in the year 1769, is a contract within the meaning of that clause of the constitution of the United States, (art. 1. s. 10.) which declares that no State shall make any law impairing the obligation of contracts. The charter was not dissolved by the revolution.

An act of the State legislature of New-Hampshire, altering the charter, without the consent of the corporation, in a material respect, is an act impairing the obligation of the charter, and is unconstitutional and void.

"The Trustees of Dartmouth College v. Woodward," in Henry Wheaton, *Reports of Cases Argued and Adjudged in The Supreme Court of the United States. February Term, 1819.* (New York, 1819), IV, 518, 551–557, 560–569, 574–575, 582–584, 587–591, 594–600. The last four paragraphs are taken from Rufus Choate, *A Discourse Delivered before the Faculty, Students, and Alumni of Dartmouth College . . . July 27, 1853, Commemorative of Daniel Webster* (Boston and Cambridge, 1853), pp. 34–40.

Under its charter, Dartmouth College was a private and not a public corporation. That a corporation is established for purposes of general charity, or for education generally, does not, *per se*, make it a public corporation, liable to the control of the legislature. . . .

March 10th, and 11th, 1818

Mr. *Webster*, for the plaintiffs in error. The general question is, whether the acts of the 27th of June, and of the 18th and 26th of December, 1816, are valid and binding on the rights of the plaintiffs, *without their acceptance or assent*.

The substance of the facts recited in the preamble to the charter is, that Dr. Wheelock had founded a CHARITY, on funds owned and procured by himself; that he was, at that time, the sole dispenser and sole administrator, as well as the legal owner of these funds; that he had made his will, devising this property in trust to continue the existence and uses of the school, and appointed trustees; that, in this state of things, he had been invited to fix his school permanently in New-Hampshire, and to extend the design of it to the education of the youth of that province; that, before he removed his school, or accepted this invitation, which his friends in England had advised him to accept, he applied for a charter, to be granted, not to whomsoever the king or government of the province should please, but to such persons as he named and appointed, viz. the persons whom he had already appointed to be the future trustees of his charity by his will. The Charter, or letters patent, then proceed to create such a corporation, and to appoint twelve persons to constitute it, by the name of the "Trustees of Dartmouth College;" to have perpetual existence, as such corporation, and with power to hold and dispose of lands and goods, for the use of the College, with all the ordinary powers of corporations. They are in their discretion to apply the funds and property of the College to the support of the president, tutors, ministers, and other officers of the College, and such missionaries and schoolmasters as they may see fit to employ among the Indians. There are to be twelve trustees forever, *and no more;* and they are to have the right of filling vacancies occuring in their own body. The Rev. Mr. Wheelock is declared to be the FOUNDER of the College, and is, by the charter, appointed first president, with power to appoint a successor, by his last will. All proper powers of government, superintendence, and visitation, are vested in the trustees. They are to appoint and remove all officers at their discretion; to fix their salaries, and assign their duties; and to make all ordinances, orders, and laws, for the government of the students. And to the end that the persons who had acted as depositaries of the contributions in England, and who had also been contributors themselves, might be satisfied of the good use of their contributions, the president was annually, or when required, to transmit to them an account of the progress of the institution, and the disbursements of its funds, so long as they should continue to act in that trust. These letters patent are to be good and effectual in law, *against the king, his heirs and successors forever,* without further grant or confirmation; and the trustees are to hold all and singular these privileges, advantages, liberties, and immunities, to them and to their successors forever. No funds are given to the college by this charter. A corporate existence and capacity are given to the trustees, with the privileges and immunities which have been mentioned, to enable the founder and his associates the better to manage the funds which they themselves had contributed, and such others as they might afterwards obtain.

After the institution, thus created and constituted, had existed, uninterruptedly and usefully, nearly fifty years, the legislature of New-Hampshire passed the acts in question. The first act makes the twelve trustees under the charter, and nine other individuals to be appointed by the governor and council, a corporation, by a new name; and to this new corporation transfers all the *property, rights, powers, liberties, and privileges* of the old corporation; with further power to establish NEW COLLEGES AND AN INSTITUTE, and to apply all or any part of the funds to these purposes, subject to the power and control of a board of twenty-five overseers, to be appointed by the governor and council. The second act makes further provisions for executing the objects of the first, and the last act authorizes the defendant, the treasurer of the plaintiffs, to retain and hold their property, against their will.

If these acts are valid, the old corporation is abolished, and a new one created. The first act does, in fact, if it can have effect, *create a new corporation,* and transfer to it all the property and franchises of the old. The two corporations are not the same, in any thing which essentially belongs to the existence of a corporation. They have different names, and different powers, rights and duties. Their organization is wholly different. The powers of the corporation are not vested in the same, or similar hands. In one, the trustees are twelve, and no more. In the other, they are twenty-one. In one, the power is a single board. In the other, it is divided between two boards. Although the act professes to include the old trustees in the new corporation, yet that was without their assent, and against their remonstrance; and no person can be compelled to be a member of such a corporation against his will. It was neither expected nor intended, that they should be members of the new corporation. The act itself treats the old corporation as at an end, and going on the ground that all its functions have ceased, it provides *for the first meeting and organization of the new corporation.* It expressly provides, also, that the new corporation shall have and hold all the property of the old; a provision which would be quite unnecessary upon any other ground, than that the old corporation was dissolved. But if it could be contended, that the effect of these acts was not entirely to abolish the old corporation, yet it is manifest that they impair and invade the rights, property, and powers of the trustees under the charter, *as a corporation,* and the legal rights, privileges, and immunities which belong to them, *as individual members* of the corporation. The twelve trustees were the *sole* legal owners of all the property acquired under the charter. By the acts others are admitted, against *their* will, to be joint owners. The twelve individuals, who are trustees, were possessed of all the franchises and immunities conferred by the charter. By the acts, *nine* other trustees, and *twenty-five* overseers, are admitted against their will, to divide these franchises and immunities with them. If, either as a corporation, or as individuals, they have any *legal rights,* this forcible intrusion of others violates those rights, as manifestly as an entire and complete ouster and dispossession. These acts alter the whole constitution of the corporation. They affect the rights of the whole body, as a corporation, and the rights of the individuals who compose it. They revoke corporate powers and franchises. They alienate and transfer the property of the College to others. By the charter, the trustees had a right to fill vacancies in their own number. This is now taken away. They were to consist of twelve, and by express provision, of no more. This is altered. They and their successors, appointed by themselves, were forever to hold the property. The legislature has found successors for them, before their seats are vacant. The powers and privileges, which the twelve were to exercise *exclusively,* are now to be exercised by others. By one of the acts, they are subjected to heavy penalties, if they exercise their offices, or any of those powers and privileges granted them by charter, and which they had exercised for fifty years. They are to be *punished* for not accepting the new grant, and taking its benefits. This, it must be confessed, is rather a summary mode of settling a question of constitutional right. Not only are new trustees forced into the corporation, but new trusts and uses are created. The College is turned into a University. Power is given to create new colleges, and to authorize any diversion of the funds, which may be agreeable to the new boards, sufficient latitude is given by the undefined power of establishing an *Institute.* To these new Colleges, and this *Institute,* the funds contributed by the founder, Dr. Wheelock, and by the original donors, the Earl of Dartmouth and others, are to be applied, in plain and manifest disregard of the uses to which they were given. The president, one of the old trustees, had a right to his office, salary, and emoluments, subject to the twelve trustees alone. His title to these is now changed, and he is made accountable to new masters. So also all the professors and tutors. If the legislature can at pleasure make these alterations and changes, in the rights and privileges of the plaintiffs, it may, with equal propriety, abolish these rights and privileges altogether. The same power which can do any part of this work, can accomplish the whole. And, indeed, the argument, on which these acts have been hitherto defended, goes altogether on the ground, that this is such a corporation as the legislature may abolish at pleasure; and that its members have no *rights, liberties, franchises, property or privileges,* which the legislature may not revoke, annul, alienate or transfer to others whenever it sees fit.

It will be contended by the plaintiffs, *that these acts are not valid and binding on them without their assent.* 1. Because they are against common right, and the constitution of New-Hampshire. 2. Because they are repugnant to the constitution of the United States. I am aware of the limits which bound the jurisdiction of the Court in this case; and that on this record nothing can be decided, but the single question, whether these acts are repugnant to the constitution of the United States. . . . It cannot be pretended that the legislature, as successor to the king in this part of his prerogative, has any power to revoke, vacate, or alter this charter. If, therefore, the legislature has not this power by any specific grant contained in the constitution; nor as included in its ordinary legislative powers; nor by reason of its succession to the prerogatives of the crown in this particular; on what ground would the authority to pass these acts rest, even if there were no special prohibitory clauses in the constitution, and the bill of rights?

But there are prohibitions in the constitution and bill of rights of New-Hampshire, introduced for the purpose of limiting the legislative power, and of protecting the rights and property of the citizens. One prohibition is, "that no person shall be deprived of his property, immunities or privileges, put out of the protection of the law, or deprived of his life, liberty, or estate, but by judgment of his peers, or the law of the land." In the opinion, however, which was given in the Court below, it is denied that the trustees, under the charter, had any property, immunity, liberty or privilege, in this corporation, within the meaning of this prohibition in the bill of rights. It is said, that it is a *public corporation,* and *public property.* That the trustees have no greater interest in it than any other individuals. That it is not private property, which they can sell, or

transmit to their heirs; and that, *therefore*, they have no interest
in it. That their office is a public trust like that of the governor,
or a judge; and that they have no more concern in the property
of the college, than the governor in the property of the State,
or than the judges in the fines which they impose on the
culprits at their bar. That it is nothing to them whether their
powers shall be extended or lessened, any more than it is to
the Courts, whether their jurisdiction shall be enlarged or
diminished. It is necessary, therefore, to inquire into the true
nature and character of the corporation, which was created by
the charter of 1769.

There are divers sorts of corporations; and it may be safely
admitted, that the legislature has more power over some, than
over others.[a] Some corporations are for government and political arrangement; such for example as cities, counties, and the
towns in New England. These may be changed and modified
as public convenience may require, due regard being always
had to the rights of property. Of such corporations, all who
live within the limits are of course obliged to be members, and
to submit to the duties which the law imposes on them as such.
Other civil corporations are for the advancement of trade and
business, such as banks, insurance companies, and the like.
These are created, not by general law, but usually by grant.
Their constitution is special. It is such as the legislature sees fit
to give, and the grantees to accept.

The corporation in question is not a *civil*, although it is a
lay corporation. It is an *eleemosynary* corporation. It is a
private charity, originally founded and endowed by an individual, with a charter obtained for it at *his* request, for the better
administration of *his charity*. "The eleemosynary sort of corporations are such as are constituted for the perpetual distribu-
tions of the free alms or bounty of the founder of them, to such
persons as he has directed. Of this are all hospitals for the
maintenance of the poor, sick, and impotent; and all colleges
both in our universities and out of them."[a] Eleemosynary corpo-

[a] 1 *Wooddes.* 474. 1 *Bl. Com.* 467.
[a] 1 *Bl. Com.* 471.

rations are for the management of private property, according
to the will of the donors. They are private corporations. A college is as much a private corporation as a hospital; especially a
college founded as this was, by private bounty. A college is a
charity. "The establishment of learning," says Lord Hardwicke,
"is a charity, and so considered in the statute of Elizabeth. A
devise to a college, for their benefit, is a laudable *charity*, and
deserves encouragement."[b] The legal signification of *a charity*
is derived chiefly from the statute 43 Eliz. c. 4. "Those purposes," says Sir W. Grant, "are considered *charitable* which that
statute enumerates."[c] *Colleges* are enumerated as *charities* in
that statute. The government, in these cases, lends its aid to
perpetuate the beneficent intention of the donor, by granting
a charter, under which his private charity shall continue to be
dispensed, after his death. This is done either by incorporating
the *objects* of the charity, as, for instance, the scholars in a
college, or the poor in a hospital; or by incorporating those who
are to be governors, or trustees, of the charity.[d] In cases of the
first sort, the *founder* is, by the common law, *visitor*. In early
times it became a maxim, that he who gave the property might
regulate it in future. *Cujus est dare, ejus est disponere.* This
right of *visitation* descended from the founder to his heir, as
a right of property, and precisely as his other property went to
his heir; and in default of heirs, it went to the King, as all other
property goes to the King, for the want of heirs. The right of
visitation arises from the property. It grows out of the endowment. The founder may, if he please, part with it, at the time
when he establishes the charity, and may vest it in others.
Therefore, if he chooses that governors, trustees, or overseers,
should be appointed in the charter, he may cause it to be
done, *and his power of visitation will be transferred to them*,
instead of descending to his heirs. The persons thus assigned
or appointed by the founder will be visitors, with all the powers
of the founder, in exclusion of his heir.[a] The right of visitation

[b] I *Ves.* 537.
[c] 9 *Ves.* 405.
[d] 1 *Wooddes.* 474.
[a] 1 *Bl. Com.* 471.

then accrues to them as a matter of property, by the gift, transfer, or appointment of the founder. This is a private right which
they can assert in all legal modes, and in which they have the
same protection of the law as in all other rights. As visitors,
they may make rules, ordinances, and statutes, and alter and
repeal them, as far as permitted so to do by the charter.[b]
Although the charter proceeds from the crown, or the government, it is considered as the will of the donor. It is obtained at
his request. He imposes it as the rule which is to prevail in the
dispensation of his bounty in all future times. The king, or
government, which grants the charter, is not thereby the
founder, but he who furnishes the funds. The gift of the
revenues is the foundation.[c] The leading case on this subject
is Phillips v. Bury.[a] This was an ejectment brought to recover
the rectory house, &c. of Exeter College, in Oxford. The question was, whether the plaintiff or defendant was legal rector.
Exeter College was founded by an individual, and incorporated
by a charter granted by Queen Elizabeth. The controversy
turned upon the power of the visitor, and, in the discussion
of the cause, the nature of College charters and corporations
was very fully considered; and it was determined that the
college was a *private* corporation, and that the founder had a
right to appoint a visitor, and give him such power as he
thought fit.[b] The learned Bishop Stillingfleet's argument in the
same cause, as a member of the House of Lords, when it was
there heard, exhibits very clearly the nature of colleges and
similar corporations.[c] These opinions received the sanction of
the House of Lords, and they seem to be settled and undoubted
law. Where there is a charter, vesting proper powers of government in *trustees*, or *governors*, they are *visitors;* and there is no
control in any body else; except only that the Courts of Equity

[b] *2 T. R.* 350, 351.
[c] 1 *Bl. Com.* 480.
[a] Reported in 1 *Lord Raymond*, 5. *Comb.* 265. *Holt*, 715. 1 *Show.* 360.
4 *Mod.* 106. *Skinn.* 447.
[b] Lord Holt's judgment, copied from his own manuscript, is in 2 *T. R.*
346.
[c] 1 *Burns' Eccles. Law*, 443.

or of law will interfere so far as to preserve the revenues and prevent the perversion of the funds, and to keep the visitors within their prescribed bounds.[d] "The foundations of colleges," says Lord Mansfield, "are to be considered in two views, viz. as they are *corporations,* and as they are *eleemosynary.* As eleemosynary, they are the creatures of the founder; he may delegate his power, either generally or specially; he may prescribe particular modes and manners, as to the exercise of part of it. If he makes a general visitor, (as by the general words *visitator sit*) the person so constituted has all incidental power; but he may be restrained as to particular instances. The founder may appoint a special visitor for a particular purpose and no further. The founder may make a general visitor; and yet appoint an inferior particular power, to be executed without going to the visitor in the first instance."[a] And even if the king be founder, if he grant a charter incorporating trustees and governors, *they are visitors,* and the king cannot visit.[b] A subsequent donation, or engrafted fellowship, falls under the same general visitatorial power, if not otherwise specially provided.[c] In New-England, and perhaps throughout the United States, eleemosynary corporations have been generally established in the latter mode, that is, by incorporating *governors* or *trustees,* and vesting in them the right of visitation. Small variations may have been in some instances adopted; as in the case of Harvard College, where some power of inspection is given to the overseers, but not, strictly speaking, a visitatorial power, which still belongs, it is apprehended, to the fellows, or members of the corporation. In general, there are many donors. A charter is obtained, comprising them all, or some of them, and such others as they choose to include, with the right of appointing their successors. They are thus the visitors of their own charity, and appoint others, such as they may see fit, to exercise the

---

[d] Green v. Rutherforth, 1 *Ves.* 472. Attorney General v. Foundling Hospital, 2 *Ves. jr.* 47. *Kyd on Corp.* 195. *Coop. Eq. Pl.* 292.
[a] St. John's College, Cambridge v. Todington, 1 *Burr.* 200.
[b] Attorney General v. Middleton, 2 *Ves.* 328.
[c] Green v. Rutherforth, *ubi supra.* St. John's College v. Todington, *ubi supra.*

same office in time to come. All such corporations are private. The case before the Court is clearly that of an eleemosynary corporation. It is, in the strictest legal sense, a private charity. In King v. St. Catherine's Hall,[a] that college is called *a private eleemosynary lay corporation.* It was endowed by a private f under, and incorporated by letters patent. And in the same manner was Dartmouth College founded and incorporated. Dr. Wheelock is declared by the charter to be its founder. It was established by him, on funds contributed and collected by himself. As such founder, he had a right of visitation, which he assigned to the trustees, and they received it by his consent and appointment, and held it under the charter.[b] He appointed these trustees visitors, and in that respect to take place of his heir; as he might have appointed devisees to take his estate, instead of his heir. Little, probably, did he think, at that time, that the legislature would ever take away this property and these privileges, and give them to others. Little did he suppose, that this charter secured to him and his successors no legal rights. Little did the other donors think so. If they had, the college would have been, what the university is now, a thing upon paper, existing only in name. The numerous academies in New-England have been established substantially in the same manner. They hold their property by the same tenure, and no other. Nor has Harvard College any surer title than Dartmouth College. It may, to-day, have more friends; but to-morrow it may have more enemies. Its legal rights are the same. So also of Yale College; and indeed of all the others. When the legislature gives to these institutions, it may, and does, accompany its grants with such conditions as it pleases. The grant of lands by the legislature of New-Hampshire to Dartmouth College, in 1789, was accompanied with various conditions. When donations are made, by the legislature, or others, to a charity already existing, without any condition, or the specification of any new use, the donation follows the nature of the charity. Hence the doctrine, that all eleemosynary corporations are

[a] 4 *Term Rep.* 233.
[b] *Bl. Com. up. supr.*

private bodies. They are founded by private persons, and on private property. The public cannot be charitable in these institutions. It is not the money of the public, but of private persons, which is dispensed. It may be public, that is general, in its uses and advantages; and the State may very laudably add contributions of its own to the funds; but it is still private in the tenure of the property; and in the right of administering the funds. If the doctrine laid down by Lord Holt, and the House of Lords, in Phillips v. Bury, and recognized and established in all the other cases, be correct, the property of this college was private property; it was vested in the trustees by the charter, and to be administered by them, according to the will of the founder and donors, as expressed in the charter. They were also *visitors* of the charity, in the most ample sense. *They* had, therefore, as they contend, *privileges, property,* and *immunities,* within the true meaning of the bill of rights. They had rights, and still have them, which they can assert against the legislature, as well as against other wrongdoers. It makes no difference, that the estate is holden for certain trusts. The legal estate is still theirs. They have a right in the property, and they have a right of visiting and superintending the trust; and this is an object of legal protection, as much as any other right. The charter declares, that the powers conferred on the trustees, are "privileges, advantages, liberties, and immunities;" and that they shall be forever holden by them and their successors. The New-Hampshire bill of rights declares, that no one shall be deprived of his "property, privileges, or immunities," but by judgment of his peers, or the law of the land . . . The granting of the corporation is but making the trust perpetual, and does not alter the nature of the charity. The very object sought in obtaining such charter, and in giving property to such a corporation, is to make and keep it private property, and to clothe it with all the security and inviolability of private property. The intent is, that there shall be a legal private ownership, and that the legal owners shall maintain and protect the property, for the benefit of those for whose use it was designed. Who ever endowed the public? Who ever appointed a legislature to administer his charity? Or who ever heard, before, that a gift to a *College,* or *Hospital,* or an *Asylum,* was, in reality, nothing but a gift to the State? The State of Vermont is a principal donor to Dartmouth College. The lands given lie in that State. This appears in the special verdict. Is Vermont to be considered as having intended a gift to the State of New-Hampshire in this case; as it has been said is to be the reasonable construction of all donations to the College? The legislature of New-Hampshire affects to represent the *public,* and therefore claims a right to control all property destined to public use. What hinders Vermont from considering herself equally the representative of the *public,* and from resuming her grants, at her own pleasure? Her right to do so is less doubtful than the power of New-Hampshire to pass the laws in question. In University v. Foy,[a] the Supreme Court of North-Carolina pronounced unconstitutional and void, a law repealing a grant to the University of North-Carolina; although that University was originally erected and endowed by a statute of the State. That case was a grant of *lands,* and the Court decided that it could not be resumed. This is the grant of a power and capacity *to hold lands.* Where is the difference of the cases, upon principle? . . . That the power of electing and appointing the officers of this college is not only a right of the trustees as a corporation generally, and in the aggregate, but *that each individual trustee has also his own individual franchise in such right of election and appointment,* is according to the language of all the authorities. Lord Holt says, "it is agreeable to reason and the rules of law, that a franchise should be vested in the corporation aggregate, and yet the benefit of it to redound to the particular members, and to be enjoyed by them in their private capacity. Where the privilege of election is used by particular persons, *it is a particular right, vested in every particular man.*"[a]

It is also to be considered, that the president and professors of this college have rights to be affected by these acts. Their interest is similar to that of *fellows* in the English colleges; because they derive their living wholly, or in part, from the

[a] 2 *Heywood's R.*
[a] 2 *Lord Raym.* 952.

founder's bounty. The president is one of the trustees, or corporators. The professors are not necessarily members of the
corporation; but they are appointed by the trustees, are remov-
able only by them, and have fixed salaries, payable out of the
general funds of the college. Both president and professors
have *freeholds* in their offices; subject only to be removed, by
the trustees, as their legal visitors, for good cause. All the
authorities speak of fellowships in colleges as *freeholds*, notwithstanding the fellows may be liable to be suspended or removed, for misbehaviour, by their constituted visitors. Nothing
could have been less expected, in this age, than that there
should have been an attempt, by acts of the legislature, to take
away these college livings, the inadequate, but the only support of literary men, who have devoted their lives to the
instruction of youth. The president and professors were appointed by the twelve trustees. They were accountable to nobody else, and could be removed by nobody else. They
accepted their offices on this tenure. Yet the legislature has
appointed other persons, with power to remove these officers,
and to deprive them of their livings; and those other persons
have exercised that power. No description of private property
has been regarded as more sacred than college livings. They
are the estates and freeholds of a most deserving class of men;
of scholars who have consented to forego the advantages of
professional and public employments, and to devote themselves to science and literature, and the instruction of youth,
in the quiet retreats of academic life. Whether, to dispossess
and oust them; to deprive them of their office, and turn them
out of their livings; to do this, not by the power of their legal
visitors, or governors, but by acts of the legislature; and to do
it without forfeiture, and without fault; whether all this be not
in the highest degree an indefensible and arbitrary proceeding,
is a question, of which there would seem to be but one side
fit for a lawyer or a scholar to espouse. . . .

If it could be made to appear, that the trustees and the
president and professors held their offices and franchises during the pleasure of the legislature, and that the property
holden belonged to the State, then indeed the legislature have

done no more than they had a right to do. But this is not so.
The charter is a charter of *privileges* and *immunities*; and
these are holden by the trustees expressly *against* the State
forever. It is admitted, that the State, by its Courts of law, can
enforce the will of the donor, and compel a faithful execution
of the trust. The plaintiffs claim no exemption from legal responsibility. They hold themselves at all times answerable to
the law of the land, for their conduct in the trust committed
to them. They ask only to hold the property of which they are
owners, and the franchises which belong to them, until they
shall be found by due course and process of law to have for-
feited them. It can make no difference, whether the legislature
exercise the power it has assumed, by removing the trustees
and the president and professors, directly, and by name, or by
appointing others to expel them. The principle is the same,
and, in point of fact, the result has been the same. If the entire
franchise cannot be taken away, neither can it be essentially
impaired. If the trustees are legal owners of the property, they
are *sole* owners. If they are visitors, they are *sole* visitors. No
one will be found to say, that if the legislature may do what it
has done, it may not do any thing and every thing which it
may choose to do, relative to the property of the corporation,
and the privileges of its members and officers.

If the view which has been taken of this question be at all
correct, this was an eleemosynary corporation; a private charity.
The property was private property. The trustees were visitors,
and their right to hold the charter, administer the funds, and
visit and govern the college, was a *franchise* and *privilege*,
solemnly granted to them. The use being public, in no way
diminishes their legal estate in the property, or their title to
the franchise. There is no principle, nor any case, which declares that a gift to such a corporation is a gift to the public.
The acts in question violate property. They take away privileges, immunities, and franchises. They deny to the trustees the
protection of the law; and they are retrospective in their operation. In all which respects, they are against the constitution of
New-Hampshire.

2. The plaintiffs contend, in the second place, that the acts

in question are repugnant to the 10th section of the 1st article of the constitution of the United States. The material words of that section are: "no State shall pass any bill of attainder, *ex post facto* law, or law impairing the obligation of contracts."

The object of these most important provisions in the national constitution has often been discussed, both here and elsewhere. It is exhibited with great clearness and force by one of the distinguished persons who framed that instrument. "Bills of attainder, *ex post facto* laws, and laws impairing the obligation of contracts, are contrary to the first principles of the social compact, and to every principle of sound legislation. The two former are expressly prohibited by the declarations prefixed to some of the State constitutions, and all of them are prohibited by the spirit and scope of these fundamental charters. Our own experience has taught us, nevertheless, that additional fences against these dangers ought not to be omitted. Very properly, therefore, have the Convention added this constitutional bulwark in favour of personal security and private rights; and I am much deceived if they have not, in so doing, as faithfully consulted the genuine sentiments as the undoubted interests of their constituents. The sober people of America are weary of the fluctuating policy which has directed the public councils. They have seen with regret, and with indignation, that sudden changes, and legislative interferences, in cases affecting personal rights, became jobs in the hands of enterprising and influential speculators; and snares to the more industrious and less informed part of the community. They have seen, too, that one legislative interference is but the link of a long chain of repetitions; every subsequent interference being naturally produced by the effects of the preceding."[a] It has already been decided in this Court, that a *grant* is a contract, within the meaning of this provision; and that a grant by a State is also a contract as much as the grant of an individual.[b] It has also been

[a] *Letters of Publius, or The Federalist,* (No. 44., by Mr. MADISON.)
[b] In Fletcher v. Peck, 6 *Cranch* 87, this Court says, "a contract is a compact between two or more parties, and is either executory or executed. An executory contract is one in which a party binds himself to do, or not to do, a particular thing; such was the law under which the conveyance was

decided, that a grant by a State before the revolution, is as much to be protected as a grant since.[a] . . .

It was in consequence of the "privileges bestowed," that Dr. Wheelock and his associates, undertook to exert themselves for the instruction and education of youth in this college; and it was on the same consideration that the founder endowed it with his property. And because charters of incorporation are of the nature of contracts, they cannot be altered or varied, but by consent of the original *parties*. If a charter be granted by the king, it may be altered by a new charter granted by the king, and accepted by the corporators. But if the first charter be granted by parliament, the consent of parliament must be obtained to any alteration. In King v. Miller,[a] Lord Kenyon says, "Where a corporation takes its rise from the king's charter, the king by granting, and the corporation by accepting, an-

---

made by the government. A contract executed is one in which the object of contract is performed; and this, says Blackstone, differs in nothing from a grant. The contract between Georgia and the purchasers was executed by the grant. A contract executed, as well as one which is executory, contains obligations binding on the parties. A grant, in its own nature, amounts to an extinguishment of the right of the grantor, and implies a contract not to reassert that right. If under a fair construction of the constitution, grants are comprehended under the term contracts, is a grant from the State excluded from the operation of the provision? Is the clause to be considered as inhibiting the State from impairing the obligation of contracts between two individuals, but as excluding from that inhibition contracts made with itself? The words themselves contain no such distinction. They are general, and are applicable to contracts of every description. If contracts made with the State are to be exempted from their operation, the exception must arise from the character of the contracting party, not from the words which are employed. Whatever respect might have been felt for the State sovereignties, it is not to be disguised, that the framers of the constitution viewed, with some apprehension, the violent acts which might grow out of the feelings of the moment; and that the people of the United States, in adopting that instrument, have manifested a determination to shield themselves, and their property, from the effects of those sudden and strong passions to which men are exposed. The restrictions on the legislative power of the States, are obviously founded in this sentiment; and the constitution of the United States contains what may be deemed a bill of rights, for the people of each State."
[a] New-Jersey v. Wilson, 7 *Cranch,* 164.
[a] 6 *T. R.* 277.

other charter, may alter it, because it is done with the consent of all the parties who are competent to consent to the alteration."[b] There are, in this case, all the essential constituent parts of a contract. There is something to be contracted about; there are parties, and there are plain terms in which the agreement of the parties, on the subject of the contract, is expressed. There are mutual considerations and inducements. The charter recites, that the founder, on his part, has agreed to establish his seminary in New-Hampshire, and to enlarge it, beyond its original design, among other things, for the benefit of that province; and thereupon a charter is given to him and his associates, designated by himself, promising and assuring to them, under the plighted faith of the State, the right of governing the college, and administering its concerns, in the manner provided in the charter. There is a complete and perfect grant to them of all the power of superintendence, visitation, and government. Is not this a contract? If lands or money had been granted to him and his associates, for the same purposes, such grant could not be rescinded. And is there any difference, in legal contemplation, between a grant of corporate franchises, and a grant of tangible property? No such difference is recognized in any decided case, nor does it exist in the common apprehension of mankind.

It is therefore contended, that this case falls within the true meaning of this provision of the constitution, as expounded in the decisions of this Court; that the charter of 1769, is a contract, a stipulation, or agreement; mutual in its considerations, express and formal in its terms, and of a most binding and solemn nature. That the acts in question *impair* this contract, has already been sufficiently shown. They repeal and abrogate its most essential parts.

Much has heretofore been said on the *necessity* of admitting such a power in the legislature as has been assumed in this case. Many cases of possible evil have been imagined, which might otherwise be without remedy. Abuses, it is contended, might arise in the management of such institutions, which the

[b] *Vide also*, 2 *Bro. Ch. R.* 662. *Ex parte* Bolton School.

ordinary courts of law would be unable to correct. But this is only another instance of that habit of supposing extreme cases, and then of reasoning from them, which is the constant refuge of those who are obliged to defend a cause which, upon its merits, is indefensible. It would be sufficient to say, in answer, that it is not pretended, that there was here any such case of necessity. But a still more satisfactory answer is, that the apprehension of danger is groundless, and, therefore, the whole argument fails. Experience has not taught us that there is danger of great evils or of great inconvenience from this source. Hitherto, neither in our own country nor elsewhere, have such cases of necessity occurred. The judicial establishments of the State are presumed to be competent to prevent abuses and violations of trust, in cases of this kind, as well as in all others. If they be not, they are imperfect, and their amendment would be a most proper subject for legislative wisdom. Under the government and protection of the general laws of the land, those institutions have always been found safe, as well as useful. They go on with the progress of society, accomodating themselves easily, without sudden change or violence, to the alterations which take place in its condition; and in the knowledge, the habits, and pursuits of men. The English colleges were founded in Catholic ages. Their religion was reformed with the general reformation of the nation; and they are suited perfectly well to the purpose of educating the protestant youth of modern times. Dartmouth College was established under a charter granted by the provincial government; but a better constitution for a college, or one more adapted to the condition of things under the present government, in all material respects, could not now be framed. Nothing in it was found to need alteration at the revolution. The wise men of that day saw in it one of the best hopes of future times, and commended it, as it was, with parental care, to the protection and guardianship of the government of the State. A charter of more liberal sentiments, of wiser provisions, drawn with more care, or in a better spirit, could not be expected at any time, or from any source. The college needed no change in its organization or government. That which it did need was the kindness, the patronage, the bounty of the legislature; not a mock elevation to the character of a university, without the solid benefit of a shilling's donation to sustain the character; not the swelling and empty authority of establishing *institutes* and *other colleges*. This unsubstantial pageantry would seem to have been in derision of the scanty endowment and limited means of an unobtrusive, but useful and growing seminary. Least of all was there a necessity, or pretence of necessity, to infringe its legal rights, violate its franchises and privileges, and pour upon it these overwhelming streams of litigation. But this argument, from *necessity*, would equally apply in all other cases. If it be well founded, it would prove, that whenever any inconvenience or evil should be experienced from the restrictions imposed on the legislature by the constitution, these restrictions ought to be disregarded. It is enough to say, that the people have thought otherwise. They have, most wisely, chosen to take the risk of occasional inconvenience from the want of power, in order that there might be a settled limit to its exercise, and a permanent security against its abuse. They have imposed prohibitions and restraints; and they have not rendered these altogether vain and nugatory by conferring the power of dispensation. If inconvenience should arise, which the legislature cannot remedy under the power conferred upon it, it is not answerable for such inconvenience. That which it cannot do within the limits prescribed to it, it cannot do at all. No legislature in this country is able, and may the time never come when it shall be able, to apply to itself the memorable expression of a Roman pontiff; "*Licet hoc* DE JURE *non possumus, volumus tamen* DE PLENITUDINE POTESTATIS."

The case before the Court is not of ordinary importance, nor of every day occurrence. It affects not this college only, but every college, and all the literary institutions of the country. They have flourished, hitherto, and have become in a high degree respectable and useful to the community. They have all a common principle of existence, the inviolability of their charters. It will be a dangerous, a most dangerous experiment, to hold these institutions subject to the rise and fall of popular parties, and the fluctuations of political opinions. If the franchise may be at any time taken away, or impaired, the property also may be taken away, or its use perverted. Benefactors will have no certainty of effecting the object of their bounty; and learned men will be deterred from devoting themselves to the service of such institutions, from the precarious title of their offices. Colleges and halls will be deserted by all better spirits, and become a theatre for the contention of politics. Party and faction will be cherished in the places consecrated to piety and learning. These consequences are neither remote nor possible only. They are certain and immediate.

When the Court in North-Carolina declared the law of the State, which repealed a grant to its university, unconstitutional and void, the legislature had the candour and the wisdom to repeal the law. This example, so honourable to the State which exhibited it, is most fit to be followed on this occasion. And there is good reason to hope, that a State which has hitherto been so much distinguished for temperate councils, cautious legislation, and regard to law, will not fail to adopt a course which will accord with her highest and best interest, and, in no small degree, elevate her reputation. It was for many obvious reasons most anxiously desired, that the question of the power of the legislature over this charter should have been finally decided in the State Court. An earnest hope was entertained that the judges of that Court might have viewed the case in a light favourable to the rights of the trustees. That hope has failed. It is here that those rights are now to be maintained, or they are prostrated forever *Omnia alia perfugia bonorum, subsidia, consilia, auxilia, jura ceciderunt. Quem enim alium appellem? quem obtestor? quem implorem? Nisi hoc loco, nisi apud vos, nisi per vos, judices, salutem nostram, quae spe exigua extremaque pendet, temerimus; nihil est præterea quo confugere possimus.*

This, Sir, is my case! It is the case, not merely of that humble institution, it is the case of every College in the land. It is more. It is the case of every Eleemosynary Institution throughout our country—of all those great charities founded by the piety of our ancestors to alleviate human misery, and scatter blessings along the pathway of life. It is more! It is, in some sense, the case of every man among us who has property of which he may be stripped, for the question is simply this: Shall our State Legislatures be allowed to take *that* which is not their own, to turn it from its original use, and apply it to such ends or purposes as they, in their discretion, shall see fit!

Sir, you may destroy this little Institution; it is weak; it is in your hands! I know it is one of the lesser lights in the literary horizon of our country. You may put it out. But, if you do so, you must carry through your work! You must extinguish, one after another, all those greater lights of science which, for more than a century, have thrown their radiance over our land!

It is, Sir, as I have said, a small College. And yet, *there are those who love it—*.

Sir, I know not how others may feel (glancing at the opponents of the College before him), but, for myself, when I see my alma mater surrounded, like Caesar in the senate house, by those who are reiterating stab after stab, I would not, for this right hand, have her turn to me, and say, *Et tu quoque mi fili!* *And thou too, my son!*

28

John Marshall's Opinion in the Dartmouth College Case

The United States Supreme Court in this case made the first and most far-reaching of its few decisions in the realm of education down at least to the time of *Plessy* v. *Ferguson* (1896). Responding favorably to the arguments of Daniel Webster (see Selection 27), Chief Justice John Marshall (1755–1835) decided that Dartmouth College's colonial charter could not be retroactively altered by an act of the state legislature. Marshall reasoned that since state legislatures were forbidden by the federal Constitution "to pass any law impairing the obligation of contracts" respecting property, and that since the charter of this private eleemosynary institution was "a contract for the security and disposition of property," the act of the state legislature was therefore unconstitutional. The legislature, by amending the College's charter and enlarging the number of corporation trustees, Marshall concluded, was substituting "the will of the state for the will of the donors, in every essential operation of the college." The college, he claimed, would be converted "into a machine entirely subservient to the will of the government." He therefore reversed the judgment of the lower state court as "repugnant" to the Constitution of the United States. (The defendant Woodward of this case was William H. Woodward, secretary-treasurer of the state-created corporation, "The Trustees of Dartmouth University.")

Marshall's decision not only underscored the sanctity of contracts in private property, a sound article of republicanism that brought lasting protection and benefits to American business life, but it also safeguarded the founding and proliferation of nineteenth-century, privately controlled, denominational colleges. Thereafter, promoters of private colleges knew that once they had obtained a state charter, they were secure in the future control of the institution. By this decision, state university development was slowed or weakened.

Lest his decision be too easily read as a partisan Federalist or "conservative" declaration made by Thomas Jefferson's ideological rival from Virginia, Marshall's concession to the state's case should be noted. The act of the New Hampshire state legislature, he granted, "may" have been "for the advantage of this college . . . and . . . for the advantage of literature in general." He was admitting that there was possible wisdom in effective state actions for higher learning in the same year that Jefferson and other distinguished Virginians drew a comprehensive plan for their state university (see Selection 22). Jefferson, too, agreed with Marshall on the constitutional sanctity of private contract. But if historical speculation is at all sensible here, a jurist with Jefferson's social views in Marshall's place probably would not have followed Webster in building his decision primarily upon the contractual obligation to the original charter of the college. A Jeffersonian would have emphasized the dependence of the college's future welfare upon liberal public representation on its board of control. Here lay the difference between the two great Virginians. This difference was at the core of later arguments between supporters of private colleges and advocates of state supported institutions.

Although attempts were made throughout the Jeffersonian period by the executive branch of the federal government and the Congress to influence the course of republican education, chiefly in pursuit of a national university (see Selection 16), none of these efforts was to give the license and lasting impetus to American education for many years that was supplied by this one decision from John Marshall.

Feb. 2d, 1819.

The opinion of the Court was delivered by Mr. Chief Justice MARSHALL.

This is an action of trover, brought by the Trustees of Dartmouth College against William H. Woodward, in the State Court of New–Hampshire, for the book of records, corporate

---

"The Trustees of Dartmouth College v. Woodword," in Henry Wheaton, *Reports of Cases Argued and Adjudged in The Supreme Court of the United States. February Term, 1819* (New York, 1819), IV, 624–654.

seal, and other corporate property, to which the plaintiffs allege themselves to be entitled.

A special verdict, after setting out the rights of the parties, finds for the defendant, if certain acts of the legislature of New–Hampshire, passed on the 27th of June, and on the 18th of December, 1816, be valid, and binding on the trustees without their assent, and not repugnant to the constitution of the United States; otherwise, it finds for the plaintiffs.

The Superior Court of Judicature of New–Hampshire rendered a judgment upon this verdict for the defendant, which judgment has been brought before this Court by writ of error. The single question now to be considered is, do the acts to which the verdict refers violate the constitution of the United States?

This Court can be insensible neither to the magnitude nor delicacy of this question. The validity of a legislative act is to be examined; and the opinion of the highest law tribunal of a State is to be revised: an opinion which carries with it intrinsic evidence of the diligence, of the ability, and the integrity, with which it was formed. On more than one occasion, this Court has expressed the cautious circumspection with which it approaches the consideration of such questions; and has declared, that, in no doubtful case, would it pronounce a legislative act to be contrary to the constitution. But the American people have said, in the constitution of the United States, that "no State shall pass any bill of attainder, *ex post facto* law, or law impairing the obligation of contracts." In the same instrument they have also said, "that the judicial power shall extend to all cases in law and equity arising under the constitution." On the judges of this Court, then, is imposed the high and solemn duty of protecting, from even legislative violation, those contracts which the constitution of our country has placed beyond legislative control; and, however irksome the task may be, this is a duty from which we dare not shrink.

The title of the plantiffs originates in a charter dated the 13th day of December, in the year 1769, incorporating twelve persons therein mentioned, by the name of "The Trustees of Dartmouth College," granting to them and their successors the usual corporate privileges and powers, and authorizing the trustees, who are to govern the college, to fill up all vacancies which may be created in their own body.

The defendant claims under three acts of the legislature of New–Hampshire, the most material of which was passed on the 27th of June, 1816, and is entitled, "an act to amend the charter, and enlarge and improve the corporation of Dartmouth College." Among other alterations in the charter, this act increases the number of trustees to twenty-one, gives the appointment of the additional members to the executive of the State, and creates a board of overseers, with power to inspect and control the most important acts of the trustees. This board consists of twenty-five persons. The president of the senate, the speaker of the house of representatives, of New–Hampshire, and the governor and lieutenant governor of Vermont, for the time being, are to be members *ex officio*. The board is to be completed by the governor and council of New–Hampshire, who are also empowered to fill all vacancies which may occur. The acts of the 18th and 26th of December are supplemental to that of the 27th of June, and are principally intended to carry that act into effect.

The majority of the trustees of the college have refused to accept this amended charter, and have brought this suit for the corporate property, which is in possession of a person holding by virtue of the acts which have been stated.

It can require no argument to prove, that the circumstances of this case constitute a contract. An application is made to the crown for a charter to incorporate a religious and literary institution. In the application, it is stated that large contributions have been made for the object, which will be conferred on the corporation, as soon as it shall be created. The charter is granted, and on its faith the property is conveyed. Surely in this transaction every ingredient of a complete and legitimate contract is to be found.

The points for consideration are,

1. Is this contract protected by the constitution of the United States?

2. Is it impaired by the acts under which the defendant holds?

1. On the first point it has been argued, that the word "contract," in its broadest sense, would comprehend the political relations between the government and its citizens, would extend to offices held within a State for State purposes, and to many of those laws concerning civil institutions, which must change with circumstances, and be modified by ordinary legislation; which deeply concern the public, and which, to preserve good government, the public judgment must control. That even marriage is a contract, and its obligations are affected by the laws respecting divorces. That the clause in the constitution, if construed in its greatest latitude, would prohibit these laws. Taken in its broad unlimited sense, the clause would be an unprofitable and vexatious interference with the internal concerns of a State, would unnecessarily and unwisely embarrass its legislation, and render immutable those civil institutions, which are established for purposes of internal government, and which, to subserve those purposes, ought to vary with varying circumstances. That as the framers of the constitution could never have intended to insert in that instrument a provision so unnecessary, so mischievous, and so repugnant to its general spirit, the term *"contract"* must be understood in a more limited sense. That it must be understood as intended to guard against a power of at least doubtful utility, the abuse of which had been extensively felt; and to restrain the legislature in future from violating the right to property. That anterior to the formation of the constitution, a course of legislation had prevailed in many, if not in all, of the States, which weakened the confidence of man in man, and embarrassed all transactions between individuals, by dispensing with a faithful performance of engagements. To be correct this mischief, by restraining the power which produced it, the State legislatures were forbidden "to pass any law impairing the obligation of contracts," that is, of contracts respecting property, under which some individual could claim a right to something beneficial to himself; and that since the clause in the constitution must in construction receive some limitation, it may be confined, and ought to be confined, to cases of this description; to cases within the mischief it was intended to remedy.

The general correctness of these observations cannot be controverted. That the framers of the constitution did not intend to restrain the States in the regulation of their civil institutions, adopted for internal government, and that the instrument they have given us, is not to be so construed, may be admitted. The provision of the constitution never has been understood to embrace other contracts, than those which respect property, or some object of value, and confer rights which may be asserted in a court of justice. It never has been understood to restrict the general right of the legislature to legislate on the subject of divorces. Those acts enable some tribunal, not to impair a marriage contract, but to liberate one of the parties because it has been broken by the other. When any State legislature shall pass an act annulling all marriage contracts, or allowing either party to annul it without the consent of the other, it will be time enough to inquire, whether such an act be constitutional.

The parties in this case differ less on general principles, less on the true construction of the constitution in the abstract, than on the application of those principles to this case, and on the true construction of the charter of 1769. This is the point on which the cause essentially depends. If the act of incorporation be a grant of political power, if it create a civil institution to be employed in the administration of the government, or if the funds of the college be public property, or if the State of New–Hampshire, as a government, be alone interested in its transactions, the subject is one in which the legislature of the State may act according to its own judgment, unrestrained by any limitation of its power imposed by the constitution of the United States.

But if this be a private eleemosynary institution, endowed with a capacity to take property for objects unconnected with government, whose funds are bestowed by individuals on the faith of the charter; if the donors have stipulated for the future disposition and management of those funds in the manner prescribed by themselves; there may be more difficulty in the case, although neither the persons who have made these stipulations, nor those for whose benefit they were made, should be parties to the cause. Those who are no longer interested in the property, may yet retain such an interest in the preservation of their own arrangements, as to have a right to insist, that those arrangements shall be held sacred. Or, if they have themselves disappeared, it becomes a subject of serious and anxious inquiry, whether those whom they have legally empowered to represent them forever, may not assert all the rights which they possessed, while in being; whether, if they be without personal representatives who may feel injured by a violation of the compact, the trustees be not so completely their representatives in the eye of the law, as to stand in their place, not only as respects the government of the college, but also as respects the maintenance of the college charter.

It becomes then the duty of the Court most seriously to examine this charter, and to ascertain its true character.

From the instrument itself, it appears, that about the year 1754, the Rev. Eleazer Wheelock established at his own expense, and on his own estate, a charity school for the instruction of Indians in the christian religion. The success of this institution inspired him with the design of soliciting contributions in England for carrying on, and extending, his undertaking. In this pious work he employed the Rev. Nathaniel Whitaker, who, by virtue of a power of attorney from Dr. Wheelock, appointed the Earl of Dartmouth and others, trustees of the money, which had been, and should be, contributed; which appointment Dr. Wheelock confirmed by a deed of trust authorizing the trustees to fix on a site for the college. They determined to establish the school on Connecticut river, in the western part of New–Hampshire; that situation being supposed favourable for carrying on the original design among the Indians, and also for promoting learning among the English; and the proprietors in the neighbourhood having made large offers of land, on condition, that the college should there be placed. Dr. Wheelock then applied to the crown for an act of incorporation; and represented the expediency of appointing those whom he had, by his last will, named as trustees in America, to be members of the proposed corporation. "In consideration of the premises," "for the education and instruction of the youth of the Indian tribes," &c. "and also of English youth, and any others," the charter was granted, and the trustees of Dartmouth College were by that name created a body corporate, with power, *for the use of the said college*, to acquire real and personal property, and to pay the president, tutors, and other officers of the college, such salaries as they shall allow.

The charter proceeds to appoint Eleazer Wheelock, "the founder of said college," president thereof, with power by his last will to appoint a successor, who is to continue in office until disapproved by the trustees. In case of vacancy, the trustees may appoint a president, and in case of the ceasing of a president, the senior professor or tutor, *being one of the trustees,* shall exercise the office, until an appointment shall be made. The trustees have power to appoint and displace professors, tutors, and other officers, and to supply any vacancies which may be created in their own body, by death, resignation, removal, or disability; and also to make orders, ordinances, and laws, for the government of the college, the same not being repugnant to the laws of Great Britain, or of New–Hampshire, and not excluding any person on account of his speculative sentiments in religion, or his being of a religious profession different from that of the trustees.

This charter was accepted, and the property both real and personal, which had been contributed for the benefit of the college, was conveyed to, and vested in, the corporate body.

From this brief review of the most essential parts of the charter, it is apparent, that the funds of the college consisted entirely of private donations. It is, perhaps, not very important, who were the donors. The probability is, that the Earl of Dartmouth, and the other trustees in England, were, in fact, the largest contributors. Yet the legal conclusion, from the facts recited in the charter, would probably be, that Dr. Wheelock was the founder of the college.

The origin of the institution was, undoubtedly, the Indian charity school, established by Dr. Wheelock, at his own expense. It was at his instance, and to enlarge this school, that contributions were solicited in England. The person soliciting these contributions was his agent; and the trustees, who received the money, were appointed by, and act under, his authority. It is not too much to say, that the funds were obtained by him, in trust, to be applied by him to the purposes of his enlarged school. The charter of incorporation was granted at his instance. The persons named by him in his last will, as the trustees of his charity school, compose a part of the corporation, and he is declared to be the founder of the college, and its president for life. Were the inquiry material, we should feel some hesitation in saying, that Dr. Wheelock was not, in law, to be considered as the founder[a] of this institution, and as possessing all the rights appertaining to that character. But be this as it may, Dartmouth College is really endowed by private individuals, who have bestowed their funds for the propagation of the christian religion among the Indians, and for the promotion of piety and learning generally. From these funds the salaries of the tutors are drawn; and these salaries lessen the expense of education to the students. It is then an eleemosynary,[a] and, as far as respects its funds, a private corporation.

Do its objects stamp on it a different character? Are the trustees and professors public officers, invested with any portion of political power, partaking in any degree in the administration of civil government, and performing duties which flow from the sovereign authority?

That education is an object of national concern, and a proper subject of legislation, all admit. That there may be an institution founded by government, and placed entirely under its immediate control, the officers of which would be public officers, amenable exclusively to government, none will deny. But is Dartmouth College such an institution? Is education altogether in the hands of government? Does every teacher of youth become a public officer, and do donations for the purpose of education necessarily become public property, so far that the will of the legislature, not the will of the donor, becomes the law of the donation? These questions are of serious moment to society, and deserve to be well considered.

[a] 1 *Bl. Com.* 481.

[a] 1 *Bl. Com.* 471.

Doctor Wheelock, as the keeper of his charity school, instructing the Indians in the art of reading, and in our holy religion; sustaining them at his own expense, and on the voluntary contributions of the charitable, could scarcely be considered as a public officer, exercising any portion of those duties which belong to government; nor could the legislature have supposed, that his private funds, or those given by others, were subject to legislative management, because they were applied to the purposes of education. When, afterwards, his school was enlarged, and the liberal contributions made in England, and in America, enabled him to extend his cares to the education of the youth of his own country, no change was wrought in his own character, or in the nature of his duties. Had he employed assistant tutors with the funds contributed by others, or had the trustees in England established a school with Dr. Wheelock at its head, and paid salaries to him and his assistants, they would still have been private tutors; and the fact, that they were employed in the education of youth, could not have converted them into public officers, concerned in the administration of public duties, or have given the legislature a right to interfere in the management of the fund. The trustees, in whose care that fund was placed by the contributors, would have been permitted to execute their trust uncontrolled by legislative authority.

Whence, then, can be derived the idea, that Dartmouth College has become a public institution, and its trustees public officers, exercising powers conferred by the public for public objects? Not from the source whence its funds were drawn; for its foundation is purely private and eleemosynary—Not from the application of those funds; for money may be given for education, and the persons receiving it do not, by being employed in the education of youth, become members of the civil government. Is it from the act of incorporation? Let this subject be considered.

A corporation is an artificial being, invisible, intangible, and existing only in contemplation of law. Being the mere creature of law, it possesses only those properties which the charter of its creation confers upon it, either expressly, or as incidental to its very existence. These are such as are supposed best calculated to effect the object for which it was created. Among the most important are immortality, and, if the expression may be allowed, individuality; properties, by which a perpetual succession of many persons are considered as the same, and may act as a single individual. They enable a corporation to manage its own affairs, and to hold property without the perplexing intricacies, the hazardous and endless necessity, of perpetual conveyances for the purpose of transmitting it from hand to hand. It is chiefly for the purpose of clothing bodies of men, in succession, with these qualities and capacities, that corporations were invented, and are in use. By these means, a perpetual succession of individuals are capable of acting for the promotion of the particular object, like one immortal being. But this being does not share in the civil government of the country, unless that be the purpose for which it was created. Its immortality no more confers on it political power, or a political character, than immortality would confer such power or character on a natural person. It is no more a State instrument, than a natural person exercising the same powers would be. If, then, a natural person, employed by individuals in the education of youth, or for the government of a seminary in which youth is educated, would not become a public officer, or be considered as a member of the civil government, how is it, that this artificial being, created by law, for the purpose of being employed by the same individuals for the same purposes, should become a part of the civil government of the country? Is it because its existence, its capacities, its powers, are given by law? Because the government has given it the power to take and to hold property in a particular form, and for particular purposes, has the government a consequent right substantially to change that form, or to vary the purposes to which the property is to be applied? This principle has never been asserted or recognized, and is supported by no authority. Can it derive aid from reason?

The objects for which a corporation is created are universally such as the government wishes to promote. They are deemed beneficial to the country; and this benefit constitutes the consideration, and, in most cases, the sole consideration of the grant. In most eleemosynary institutions, the object would be difficult, perhaps unattainable, without the aid of a charter of incorporation. Charitable, or public spirited individuals, desirous of making permanent appropriations for charitable or other useful purposes, find it impossible to effect their design securely, and certainly, without an incorporating act. They apply to the government, state their beneficent object, and offer to advance the money necessary for its accomplishment, provided the government will confer on the instrument which is to execute their designs the capacity to execute them. The proposition is considered and approved. The benefit to the public is considered as an ample compensation for the faculty it confers, and the corporation is created. If the advantages to the public constitute a full compensation for the faculty it gives, there can be no reason for exacting a further compensation, by claiming a right to exercise over this artificial being a power which changes its nature, and touches the fund, for the security and application of which it was created. There can be no reason for implying in a charter, given for a valuable consideration, a power which is not only not expressed, but is in direct contradiction to its express stipulations.

From the fact, then, that a charter of incorporation has been granted, nothing can be inferred which changes the character of the institution, or transfers to the government any new power over it. The character of civil institutions does not grow out of their incorporation, but out of the manner in which they are formed, and the objects for which they are created. The right to change them is not founded on their being incorporated, but on their being the instruments of government, created for its purposes. The same institutions, created for the same objects, though not incorporated, would be public institutions, and, of course, be controllable by the legislature. The incorporating act neither gives nor prevents this control. Neither, in reason, can the incorporating act change the character of a private eleemosynary institution.

We are next led to the inquiry, for whose benefit the property given to Dartmouth College was secured? The counsel for the defendant have insisted, that the beneficial interest is in the people of New–Hampshire. The charter, after reciting the preliminary measures which had been taken, and the application for an act of incorporation, proceeds thus: "Know ye, therefore, that we, considering the premises, and being willing to encourage the laudable and charitable design of spreading christian knowledge among the savages of our American wilderness, and, also, that the best means of education be established, in our province of New–Hampshire, for the benefit of said province, do, of our special grace," &c. Do these expressions bestow on New–Hampshire any exclusive right to the property of the college, any exclusive interest in the labours of the professors? Or do they merely indicate a willingness that New–Hampshire should enjoy those advantages which result to all from the establishment of a seminary of learning in the neighbourhood? On this point we think it impossible to entertain a serious doubt. The words themselves, unexplained by the context, indicate, that the "benefit intended for the province" is that which is derived from "establishing the best means of education therein;" that is, from establishing in the province Dartmouth College, as constituted by the charter. But, if these words, considered alone, could admit of doubt, that doubt is completely removed by an inspection of the entire instrument.

The particular interests of New–Hampshire never entered into the mind of the donors, never constituted a motive for their donation. The propagation of the christian religion among the savages, and the dissemination of useful knowledge among the youth of the country, were the avowed and the sole objects of their contributions. In these, New–Hampshire would participate; but nothing particular or exclusive was intended for her. Even the site of the college was selected, not for the sake of New–Hampshire, but because it was "most subservient to the great ends in view," and because liberal donations of land were offered by the proprietors, on condition that the institution should be there established. The real advantages from the location of the college, are, perhaps, not less considerable to those on the west, than to those on the east side of Connecticut river. The clause which constitutes the incorporation, and expresses the objects for which it was made, declares those objects to be the instruction of the Indians, "and also of the English youth, and any others." So that the objects of the contributors, and the incorporating act, were the same; the promotion of christianity, and of education generally, not the interests of New–Hampshire particularly.

From this review of the charter, it appears, that Dartmouth College is an eleemosynary institution, incorporated for the purpose of perpetuating the application of the bounty of the donors, to the specified objects of that bounty; that its trustees or governors were originally named by the founder, and invested with the power of perpetuating themselves; that they are not public officers, nor is it a civil institution, participating in the administration of government; but a charity school, or a seminary of education, incorporated for the preservation of its property, and the perpetual application of that property to the objects of its creation.

Yet a question remains to be considered, of more real difficulty, on which more doubt has been entertained than on all that have been discussed. The founders of the college, at least those whose contributions were in money, have parted with the property bestowed upon it, and their representatives have no interest in that property. The donors of land are equally without interest, so long as the corporation shall exist. Could they be found, they are unaffected by any alteration in its constitution, and probably regardless of its form, or even of its existence. The students are fluctuating, and no individual among our youth has a vested interest in the institution, which can be asserted in a Court of justice. Neither the founders of the college, nor the youth for whose benefit it was founded, complain of the alteration made in its charter, or think themselves injured by it. The trustees alone complain, and the trustees have no beneficial interest to be protected. Can this be such a contract, as the constitution intended to withdraw from the power of State legislation? Contracts, the parties to which have a vested beneficial interest, and those only, it has been said, are the objects about which the constitution is solicitous, and to which its protection is extended.

The Court has bestowed on this argument the most deliberate consideration, and the result will be stated. Dr. Wheelock, acting for himself, and for those who, at his solicitation, had made contributions to his school, applied for this charter, as the instrument which should enable him, and them, to perpetuate their beneficent intention. It was granted. An artificial, immortal being, was created by the crown, capable of receiving and distributing forever, according to the will of the donors, the donations which should be made to it. On this being, the contributions which had been collected were immediately bestowed. These gifts were made, not indeed to make a profit for the donors, or their posterity, but for something in their opinion of inestimable value; for something which they deemed a full equivalent for the money with which it was purchased. The consideration for which they stipulated, is the perpetual application of the fund to its object, in the mode prescribed by themselves. Their descendants may take no interest in the preservation of this consideration. But in this respect their descendants are not their representatives. They are represented by the corporation. The corporation is the assignee of their rights, stands in their place, and distributes their bounty, as they would themselves have distributed it, had they been immortal. So with respect to the students who are to derive learning from this source. The corporation is a trustee for them also. Their potential rights, which, taken distributively, are imperceptible, amount collectively to a most important interest. These are, in the aggregate, to be exercised, asserted and protected, by the corporation. They were as completely out of the donors, at the instant of their being vested in the corporation, and as incapable of being asserted by the students, as at present.

According to the theory of the British constitution, their parliament is omnipotent. To annul corporate rights might give a shock to public opinion, which that government has chosen to avoid; but its power is not questioned. Had parliament, immediately after the emanation of this charter, and the execution of those conveyances which followed it, annulled the instrument, so that the living donors would have witnessed the disappointment of their hopes, the perfidy of the transaction would have been universally acknowledged. Yet then, as now, the donors would have had no interest in the property; then, as now, those who might be students would have had no rights to be violated; then, as now, it might be said, that the trustees, in whom the rights of all were combined, possessed no private, individual, beneficial interest in the property confided to their protection. Yet the contract would at that time have been deemed sacred by all. What has since occurred to strip it of its inviolability? Circumstances have not changed it. In reason, in justice, and in law, it is now what it was in 1769.

This is plainly a contract to which the donors, the trustees, and the crown, (to whose rights and obligations New–Hampshire succeeds,) were the original parties. It is a contract made on a valuable consideration. It is a contract for the security and disposition of property. It is a contract, on the faith of which, real and personal estate has been conveyed to the corporation. It is then a contract within the letter of the constitution, and within its spirit also, unless the fact, that the property is invested by the donors in trustees for the promotion of religion and education, for the benefit of persons who are perpetually changing, though the objects remain the same, shall create a particular exception, taking this case out of the prohibition contained in the constitution.

It is more than possible, that the preservation of rights of this description was not particularly in the view of the framers of the constitution, when the clause under consideration was introduced into that instrument. It is probable, that interferences of more frequent recurrence, to which the temptation was stronger, and of which the mischief was more extensive, constituted the great motive for imposing this restriction on the State legislatures. But although a particular and a rare case may not, in itself, be of sufficient magnitude to induce a rule, yet it must be governed by the rule, when established, unless some plain and strong reason for excluding it can be given. It is not enough to say, that this particular case was not in the mind of the Convention, when the article was framed, nor of the American people, when it was adopted. It is necessary to go farther, and to say that, had this particular case been suggested, the language would have been so varied, as to exclude it, or it would have been made a special exception. The case being within the words of the rule, must be within its operation likewise, unless there be something in the literal construction so obviously absurd, or mischievous, or repugnant to the general spirit of the instrument, as to justify those who expound the constitution in making it an exception.

On what safe and intelligible ground can this exception stand. There is no expression in the constitution, no sentiment delivered by its contemporaneous expounders, which would justify us in making it. In the absence of all authority of this kind, is there, in the nature and reason of the case itself, that which would sustain a construction of the constitution, not warranted by its words? Are contracts of this description of a character to excite so little interest, that we must exclude them from the provisions of the constitution, as being unworthy of the attention of those who framed the instrument? Or does public policy so imperiously demand their remaining exposed to legislative alteration, as to compel us, or rather permit us to say, that these words, which were introduced to give stability to contracts, and which in their plain import comprehend this contract, must yet be so construed, as to exclude it?

Almost all eleemosynary corporations, those which are created for the promotion of religion, of charity, or of education, are of the same character. The law of this case is the law of all. In every literary or charitable institution, unless the objects of the bounty be themselves incorporated, the whole legal interest is in trustees, and can be asserted only by them. The donors, or claimants of the bounty, if they can appear in Court at all, can appear only to complain of the trustees. In all other situations, they are identified with, and personated by, the trustees; and their rights are to be defended and maintained by them. Religion, Charity, and Education, are, in the law of England, legatees or donees, capable of receiving bequests or donations in this form. They appear in Court, and claim or defend by the corporation. Are they of so little estimation in the United States, that contracts for their benefit must be excluded from the protection of words, which in their natural import include them? Or do such contracts so necessarily require new modelling by the authority of the legislature, that the ordinary rules of contruction must be disregarded in order to leave them exposed to legislative alteration?

All feel, that these objects are not deemed unimportant in the United States. The interest which this case has excited, proves that they are not. The framers of the constitution did not deem them unworthy of its care and protection. They have, though in a different mode, manifested their respect for science, by reserving to the government of the Union the power "to promote the progress of science and useful arts, by securing for limited times, to authors and inventors, the exclusive right to their respective writings and discoveries." They have so far withdrawn science, and the useful arts, from the action of the State governments. Why then should they be supposed so regardless of contracts made for the advancement of literature, as to intend to exclude them from provisions, made for the security of ordinary contracts between man and man? No reason for making this supposition is perceived.

If the insignificance of the object does not require that we should exclude contracts respecting it from the protection of the constitution; neither, as we conceive, is the policy of leaving them subject to legislative alteration so apparent, as to require a forced construction of that instrument in order to effect it. These eleemosynary institutions do not fill the place, which would otherwise be occupied by government, but that which would otherwise remain vacant. They are complete acquisitions to literature. They are donations to education; donations, which any government must be disposed rather to encourage than to discountenance. It requires no very critical examination of the human mind to enable us to determine, that one great inducement to these gifts is the conviction felt by the giver, that the disposition he makes of them is immutable. It is probable, that no man ever was, and that no man ever will be, the founder of a college, believing at the time, that an act of incorporation constitutes no security for the institution; believing, that it is immediately to be deemed a public institution, whose funds are to be governed and applied, not by the will of the donor, but by the will of the legislature. All such gifts are made in the pleasing, perhaps delusive hope, that the charity will flow forever in the channel which the givers have marked out for it. If every man finds in his own bosom strong evidence of the universality of this sentiment, there can be but little reason to imagine, that the framers of our constitution were strangers to it, and that, feeling the necessity and policy of giving permanence and security to contracts, of withdrawing them from the influence of legislative bodies, whose fluctuating policy, and repeated interferences, produced the most perplexing and injurious embarrassments, they still deemed it necessary to leave these contracts subject to those interferences. The motives for such an exception must be very powerful, to justify the construction which makes it.

The motives suggested at the bar grow out of the original appointment of the trustees, which is supposed to have been in a spirit hostile to the genius of our government, and the presumption, that, if allowed to continue themselves, they now are, and must remain forever, what they originally were. Hence is inferred the necessity of applying to this corporation, and to other similar corporations, the correcting and improving hand of the legislature.

It has been urged repeatedly, and certainly with a degree of earnestness which attracted attention, that the trustees deriving their power from a regal source, must, necessarily, partake of the spirit of their origin; and that their first principles, unimproved by that resplendent light which has been shed around them, must continue to govern the college, and to guide the students. Before we inquire into the influence which this argument ought to have on the constitutional question, it may not be amiss to examine the fact on which it rests. The first trustees were undoubtedly named in the charter by the crown; but at whose suggestion were they named? By whom were they selected? The charter informs us. Dr. Wheelock had represented, "that, for many weighty reasons, it would be expedient, that the gentlemen whom he had already nominated, in his last will, to be trustees in America, should be of the corporation now proposed." When, afterwards, the trustees are named in the charter, can it be doubted that the persons mentioned by Dr. Wheelock in his will were appointed? Some were probably added by the crown, with the approbation of Dr. Wheelock. Among these is the Doctor himself. If any others were appointed at the instance of the crown, they are the governor, three members of the council, and the speaker of the house of representatives, of the colony of New–Hampshire. The stations filled by these persons ought to rescue them from any other imputation than too great a dependence on the crown. If in the revolution that followed, they acted under the influence of this sentiment, they must have ceased to be trustees; if they took part with their countrymen, the imputation, which suspicion might excite, would no longer attach to them. The original trustees, then, or most of them, were named by Dr. Wheelock, and those who were added to his nomination, most probably with his approbation, were among the most eminent and respectable individuals in New–Hampshire.

The only evidence which we possess of the character of Dr. Wheelock is furnished by this charter. The judicious means employed for the accomplishment of his object, and the success which attended his endeavours, would lead to the opinion, that he united a sound understanding to that humanity and benevolence which suggested his undertaking. It surely cannot be assumed, that his trustees were selected without judgment. With as little probability can it be assumed, that, while the light of science, and of liberal principles, pervades the whole community, these originally benighted trustees remain in utter darkness, incapable of participating in the general improvement; that, while the human race is rapidly advancing, they are stationary. Reasoning *a priori,* we should believe, that learned and intelligent men, selected by its patrons for the government of a literary institution, would select learned and intelligent men for their successors; men as well fitted for the government of a college as those who might be chosen by other means. Should this reasoning ever prove erroneous in a particular case, public opinion, as has been stated at the bar, would correct the institution. The mere possibility of the contrary would not justify a construction of the constitution, which should exclude these contracts from the protection of a provision whose terms comprehend them.

The opinion of the Court, after mature deliberation, is, that this is a contract, the obligation of which cannot be impaired, without violating the constitution of the United States. This opinion appears to us to be equally supported by reason, and by the former decisions of this Court.

2. We next proceed to the inquiry, whether its obligation has been impaired by those acts of the legislature of New–Hampshire, to which the special verdict refers.

From the review of this charter, which has been taken, it appears, that the whole power of governing the college, of appointing and removing tutors, of fixing their salaries, of directing the course of study to be pursued by the students, and of filling up vacancies created in their own body, was vested in the trustees. On the part of the crown it was expressly stipulated, that this corporation, thus constituted, should continue forever; and that the number of trustees should forever consist of twelve, and no more. By this contract the crown was bound, and could have made no violent alteration in its essential terms, without impairing its obligation.

By the revolution, the duties, as well as the powers, of government devolved on the people of New–Hampshire. It is admitted, that among the latter was comprehended the transcendent power of parliament, as well as that of the executive department. It is too clear to require the support of argument, that all contracts, and rights, respecting property, remained unchanged by the revolution. The obligations then, which were created by the charter to Dartmouth College, were the same in the new, that they had been in the old government. The power of the government was also the same. A repeal of this charter at any time prior to the adoption of the present constitution of the United States, would have been an extraordinary and unprecedented act of power, but one which could have been contested only by the restrictions upon the legislature, to be found in the constitution of the State. But the constitution of the United States has imposed this additional limitation, that the legislature of a State shall pass no act "impairing the obligation of contracts."

It has been already stated, that the act "to amend the charter, and enlarge and improve the corporation of Dartmouth College," increases the number of trustees to twenty-one, gives the appointment of the additional members to the executive of the State, and creates a board of overseers, to consist of twenty-five persons, of whom twenty-one are also appointed by the executive of New–Hampshire, who have power to inspect and control the most important acts of the trustees.

On the effect of this law, two opinions cannot be entertained. Between acting directly, and acting through the agency of trustees and overseers, no essential difference is perceived. The whole power of governing the college is transferred from trustees appointed according to the will of the founder, expressed in the charter, to the executive of New–Hampshire. The management and application of the funds of this eleemosynary institution, which are placed by the donors in the hands of trustees named in the charter, and empowered to perpetuate themselves, are placed by this act under the control of the government of the State. The will of the State is substituted for the will of the donors, in every essential operation of the college. This is not an immaterial change. The founders of the college contracted, not merely for the perpetual application of the funds which they gave, to the objects for which those funds were given; they contracted also, to secure that application by the constitution of the corporation. They contracted for a system, which should, as far as human foresight can provide, retain forever the government of the literary institution they had formed, in the hands of persons approved by themselves. This system is totally changed. The charter of 1769 exists no longer. It is reorganized; and reorganized in such a manner, as to convert a literary institution, moulded according to the will of its founders, and placed under the control of private literary men, into a machine entirely subservient to the will of government. This may be for the advantage of this college in particular, and may be for the advantage of literature in general; but it is not according to the will of the donors, and is subversive of that contract, on the faith of which their property was given.

In the view which has been taken of this interesting case, the Court has confined itself to the rights possessed by the trustees, as the assignees and representatives of the donors and founders, for the benefit of religion and literature. Yet it is not clear, that the trustees ought to be considered as destitute of such beneficial interest in themselves, as the law may respect. In addition to their being the legal owners of the property, and to their having a freehold right in the powers confided to them, the charter itself countenances the idea, that trustees may also be tutors with salaries. The first president was one of the original trustees; and the charter provides, that in case of vacancy in that office, "the senior professor or tutor, *being one of the trustees,* shall exercise the office of president, until the trustees shall make choice of, and appoint a president." According to the tenor of the charter, then, the trustees might, without impropriety, appoint a president and other professors from their own body. This is a power not entirely unconnected with an interest. Even if the proposition of the counsel for the defendant were sustained; if it were admitted, that those contracts only are protected by the constitution, a beneficial interest in which is vested in the party, who appears in Court to assert that interest; yet, it is by no means clear, that the trustees of Dartmouth College have no beneficial interest in themselves.

But the Court has deemed it unnecessary to investigate this particular point, being of opinion, on general principles, that in these private eleemosynary institutions, the body corporate, as possessing the whole legal and equitable interest, and completely representing the donors, for the purpose of executing the trust, has rights which are protected by the constitution.

It results from this opinion, that the acts of the legislature of New-Hampshire, which are stated in the special verdict found in this cause, are repugnant to the constitution of the United States; and that the judgment on this special verdict ought to have been for the plaintiffs. The judgment of the State Court must, therefore, be reversed.

Index